A Practical Guide to Foreign Investment in the United States
Second Edition

BNA International Inc.
A Subsidiary of The Bureau of National Affairs, Inc., Washington, D.C.

A Practical Guide to Foreign Investment in the United States

Second Edition

John I. Forry

BNA International Inc.

A Subsidiary of The Bureau of National Affairs, Inc., Washington, D.C.

A Practical Guide to
Foreign Investment in the United States
Published by
BNA INTERNATIONAL INC.
17 Dartmouth Street, London SW1H 9BL
A Subsidiary of The Bureau of National Affairs, Inc., Washington, D.C.
First edition September 1979
Second edition November 1982

This volume and the supplement are dedicated to my wife, Carol Ann Micken

---

Library of Congress Cataloging in Publication Data:

Forry, John I.
A practical guide to foreign investment in the United States.

Includes index.
1. Investments, Foreign — Law and legislation — United States. 2. Investments, Foreign — Taxation — Law and legislation — United States. I. Title.
KF1575.F685 1982 346.73'07 82-16845
ISBN 0-906524-05-9 347.3067
ISBN 0-906524-06-7 (forms supplement)

Typeset and printed in Great Britain by
Moffat Litho & Design Ltd. London

Preface from the First Edition

Foreign investors — nonresident alien individuals, foreign corporations, and other foreign persons — often have played important roles in the United States by, for example, the provision of foreign capital for the country's Revolutionary War, the purchase of bonds for the construction of major railroads, cities, and other elements of the U.S. industrial revolution, and the establishment of major U.S. investment banking houses with foreign capital in the twentieth century. In recent years, the rate and the variety of such foreign investments in the United States have increased substantially. Accordingly, this publication is intended as a practical guide which will describe the important legal, tax, and related considerations, and outline selected structures, for such investments. In view of this practical orientation, reference citations generally are restricted to selected principal statutory, treaty, administrative, and judicial sources.

* * *

The first two chapters of this volume summarize selected portions of the U.S. legal system with which a foreign investor most likely will be required to contend in organizing a business enterprise or other investment in the United States, and the general U.S. taxation of foreign investors. It should be noted that the guide focuses on investments by private enterprise and generally does not explore detailed legal and tax issues of foreign government investments, agencies, and individual representatives in the United States.

The subsequent chapters deal with specific types of transactions and investments. These include those frequently constituting initial U.S. involvement — real estate or natural resource investments, licensing activities, and import activities — and those often involving more extensive U.S. operations — establishment of a new business enterprise, acquisition of a U.S. corporation, and use of the United States as a base for foreign operations. A separate chapter is devoted to portfolio investments in stock and debt securities. In many of such transactions and investments, awareness of *foreign* as well as U.S. tax and other issues is required; examples of such issues are included in certain of these chapters. Since the guide has been prepared by U.S. individuals, however, descriptions of foreign laws should be reviewed by investors with appropriate advisers abroad. A further two chapters examine U.S. immigration laws and tax planning for individual foreign investors. In this area, coordination between immigration and tax planning is increasingly important.

The glossary lists for convenience many of the principal abbreviations and reference terms for the citations in the footnotes to the volume.

Selected forms relevant to foreign investors are included in a separate supplement to the volume. These should be examined carefully because they contain important details of substantive law and taxation, disclosure requirements, and procedural rules.

Due in part to the variety of transactions and investments and the applicable areas of law and taxation, certain chapters have been the principal responsibility of specially selected authors, whose contributions have been edited to integrate them effectively into the balance of the text. Where this approach has been used, the Table of Contents indicates the author's name. Brief biographies of the individual authors appear in alphabetical order immediately following the preface. I am especially grateful to these individuals for their efforts in connection with the guide and hope their professional reputations will be further substantiated by such efforts.

In addition, I have appreciated the editorial comments of Steven J. Cohen of Touche Ross & Co. in San Francisco, and Stuart R. Singer, Esq., of Los Angeles, as to the chapter on U.S. taxation of foreign investors; of Austin T. Fragomen, Jr., Esq., of New York, and Albert S. Golbert, Esq., of Los Angeles, as to the chapter on immigration laws; of Mr. Golbert also as to the chapter on the United States as a base for foreign operations; of Mark R. Joelson, Esq., of Washington, D.C., as to antitrust aspects discussed at various points; of Susan E. Sola as to the footnotes in all chapters; and of Carol A. Micken, Esq., as to the supplement of selected forms. Ms. Micken has aided me also with her comments, research, and support in the preparation of the final manuscript and galleys for the guide.

I have also appreciated the editorial assistance of Edward J. Crockett and Noel Fox and the interest and support of Leonard L. Silverstein, Esq., of Tax Management Inc. in publishing the guide.

John I. Forry
September 1979

Preface to the Second Edition

The principal revisions in this second edition are intended to be practical for both of the groups to which the original edition of this guide in English and the subsequent adaptation in French primarily were directed: first, for foreign persons; and second — at least as to the U.S. regulatory and tax systems applicable to investments from abroad and the alternative structures for specific types of investments — for U.S. persons dealing with foreign investors.

This edition, first, reflects major changes in U.S. federal income taxation of real estate investments from abroad, particularly in revised Chapter III. Second, it adds a separate Chapter XII on principal U.S. reporting requirements in connection with investments from abroad, because of the proliferation and importance of these requirements. Third, it incorporates in other chapters and in the supplement of forms other significant changes subsequent to preparation of the original edition. The matters set forth in this edition generally include developments through the beginning of 1982; selected major federal tax and other developments through approximately August 1982 were added immediately prior to publication.

As in the original edition, I am especially grateful to the chapter authors, who have been principally responsible for the revisions of and additions to their respective chapters as indicated in the Table of Contents. I have also appreciated the revisions of Allen J. Gross, Esq., of Philadelphia, and Michael L. Wolfram, Esq., of Los Angeles, as to labor law aspects and of Lawrence H. Pretty, Esq., of Los Angeles, as to patent law aspects discussed in the chapter on the structure of the U.S. legal system; of Charles Marshall, Jr., Esq., of Los Angeles as to the chapter on reporting requirements and portions of the supplement of forms; and of Carol A. Micken, Esq., of Los Angeles as to the supplement of forms and preparation of the final manuscript and galleys for the second edition. I have also benefited from the editorial assistance of J. J. Cavanagh and Donald F. Farwell, who has supervised the printing and final review of the text and supplement, and the interest and support of Robert C. Pugh of BNA International Inc. in publishing this edition.

John I. Forry
September 1982

Biographies

Author and Editor

John I. Forry, Los Angeles. Member of the Bars of California, the U.S. Tax Court, and the U.S. Supreme Court. A.B., Amherst College; J.D., Harvard University. Recent publications: "How to Structure Foreign Investments in U.S. Real Estate", Tax Ideas, Prentice-Hall, Inc., 1975, 1977; "Planning Investments from Abroad in U.S. Real Estate", 9 International Lawyer 239, 1975; *Current Legal Aspects of Foreign Investment in the United States,* American Bar Association, 1976 (co-author and co-editor); "Taxing Multinational Enterprises: Basic Issues of International Income Tax Harmonization", 10 International Lawyer 623, 1976 (co-author); "U.S. Tax Laws and Inbound Foreign Investment", International Tax Report, 1976; "Acquiring a U.S. Corporation from Abroad: Corporate Law, Contract Terms and Related Considerations", 1 International Financial Law Review 423, 1980. Recent activities: Chairman, Committee on U.S. Activities of Foreigners and Tax Treaties, American Bar Association Section of Taxation, 1979-1981; Chairman, International Law Section, 1978-1979, and Chairman, Foreign Tax Law Committee, 1974-1976, Los Angeles County Bar Association; Adjunct Professor of Law, Southwestern University, 1973-1979; Instructor in International Taxation, University of Southern California, 1976—. Member: American, International, and Los Angeles County Bar Associations; International Fiscal Association.

Chapter Authors

C. Richard Allen, Los Angeles. Member of the Bar of California. B.A., Dartmouth College; J.D., University of Chicago. Recent publications: "Bank Insider Abuses: When Does the Ax Fall?", 96 Banking Law Journal 804, 1979 (co-author); "Federal Election Law — The Fine Art of Giving", 2 Los Angeles Lawyer (No. 9) 42, 1979. Member: American and Los Angeles County Bar Associations.

Marcus B. Finnegan (1927-1979), Washington, D.C. Member of the Bars of the District of Columbia, New York, Virginia, and the U.S. Supreme Court. B.S., United States Military Academy; J.D., University of Virginia; LL.M., George Washington University. Recent activities: Consultant to the United Nations on Licensing and Antitrust, 1972-1979; President, Licensing Executives Society-USA, 1973-1974; President, Licensing Executives Society-International, 1975; Professorial Lecturer in

Law, George Washington University, 1971-1979. Member: Advisory Board, Patent, Trademark & Copyright Journal.

David W. Hill, Washington, D.C. Member of the Bars of the District of Columbia, the U.S. Court of Customs and Patent Appeals, and the U.S. Supreme Court. B.S., United States Military Academy; J.D., and LL.M. with highest honors in Patent and Trade Regulation Law, George Washington University. Recent publications: "Practical Guidelines for Dealing with Delays in Trademark Prosecution", 70 Trademark Reporter 455, 1980; "Antitrust Violations as a Defense to Trademark Infringement", 71 Trademark Reporter 148, 1981; "The Licensing of Patent Applications: Legal and Competitive Effects", 63 Journal of the Patent Office Society 483, 1981. Recent activities: Technical Adviser, U.S. Court of Customs and Patent Appeals, 1976-1977. Member: American and District of Columbia Bar Associations; American Patent Law Association.

William L. Johnson, Los Angeles. Member of the Bars of California and the U.S. Tax Court. A.B., Amherst College; J.D., Yale University. Recent publications: "Foreign Situs Irrevocable Life Insurance Trusts", CLU Journal, 1975; "How to Operate Under the Section 367 Ruling Procedures", U.S. Taxation of International Operations, Prentice-Hall, Inc., 1977 (co-author); "States and Estates", Tax Haven and Shelter Report, 1978. Member: American, International, and Los Angeles County Bar Associations.

Alex Kozinski, Washington, D.C. Member of the Bars of California and the District of Columbia. B.A. and J.D., University of California at Los Angeles. Recent publication: "A Market Oriented Revision of the Patent System", 21 U.C.L.A. Law Review 1942, 1974, and 6 Patent Law Review 111, 1974. Recent activities: Law Clerk to Judge Anthony M. Kennedy, U.S. Court of Appeals, Ninth Circuit, 1975-1976; Law Clerk to Chief Justice Warren E. Burger, U.S. Supreme Court, 1976-1977; Special Counsel, U.S. Merit Systems Protection Board, 1981-1982; Chief Judge, U.S. Claims Court, 1982—. Member: American and Los Angeles County Bar Associations.

Paul McCarthy, Chicago. Member of the Bar of Illinois. A.B., Cornell University; J.D., University of Michigan; M.C.L., University of Chicago. Recent publications: "Government Regulation of Foreign Investment in the United States", *Current Legal Aspects of Foreign Investment in the United States,* American Bar Association, 1976; "Commerce Department Regulations Governing Participation by United States Persons in Foreign Boycotts", 11 Vanderbilt Journal of Transnational Law 194, 1978; "Advising Foreign Investors in the U.S.: Direct Investment", 61 Chicago Bar Record 286, 1980. Recent activities: Professor of Law, Boston University Law School, 1967-1972; Instructor in Law, Haile Selassie I University, 1966-1968. Member: American Bar Association; American Foreign Law Association.

Eugene T. Rossides, Washington, D.C. Member of the Bars of the District of Columbia, New York, and the U.S. Supreme Court. A.B. and J.D., Columbia University. Recent publications: *U.S. Customs, Tariffs and Trade,* Bureau of National Affairs, 1977; Chief Editor, *U.S. Import Weekly*, Bureau of National Affairs, 1979—; Editor, *Doing Business in Greece,* American Hellenic Institute, 1980. Recent activity: Assistant Secretary of the U.S. Department of the Treasury, 1969-1973. Member: American, Customs, Federal, and New York Bar Associations.

A. Stuard Young, Jr., Philadelphia. Member of the Bars of the District of Columbia and Pennsylvania. B.S. in Econ., University of Pennsylvania; J.D., Georgetown University. Recent publication: ''Investment Companies Discrimination: United States'', 9(v) International Business Lawyer 182, 1981. Recent activities: Chairman, Committee on Regulated Investment Companies, American Bar Association Section of Taxation, 1981—; Chairman, Subcommittee on Investment Companies and Investment Advisers of the Committee on Federal Regulation of Securities, American Bar Association Section on Corporation, Banking and Business Law, 1976—. Member: American, Federal, Inter-American, International, Pennsylvania, and Philadelphia Bar Associations; American Law Institute.

Table of Contents

Chapter II
U.S. Taxation of Foreign Investors 55

Chapter III
Real Estate and Natural Resource Investments 75

Chapter VI
Establishment of a New Business Enterprise 163

Chapter VII
Acquisition of a U.S. Corporation 215

Chapter XII

Reporting of U.S. Investments from Abroad 329

[C. Richard Allen]

Chapter I

Structure of the U.S. Legal System

This chapter is intended to summarize for a foreign investor selected portions of the U.S. legal system with which he will most likely be required to contend in organizing a business enterprise or other investment in the United States. Subsequent chapters will deal with specific types of transactions and investments, and appropriate use will be made there of the terms and concepts summarized in this chapter and in Chapter II dealing with U.S. taxation of foreign investors. Accordingly, even a foreign investor who is generally familiar with the legal and tax climate in the United States should review these first two chapters.

The Federal System

The United States, unlike most areas of similar economic size elsewhere in the industrialized world, is not divided by customs, language, or tariff barriers. However, this apparent uniformity does not reflect the variety of regulations with which the investor must comply in the various states where he will conduct business or make other investments. This is due to the U.S. federal system of government, under which the U.S. Constitution parcels out only specified powers exclusively to the federal government, such as the powers to control imports and exports, to regulate immigration, and to protect patents and copyrights.

All other powers, particularly those pertaining to the regulation and the taxation of local business enterprises, are shared by the federal and state governments, with all residual power ultimately vested at the *state* level. Each state government may — and generally does — delegate certain of its powers to local authorities, consisting principally of city and county governments. Accordingly, the type and manner of regulation and taxation will almost certainly vary according to the place where a business enterprise will operate or another type of investment will be made. For example, as described further below, if an enterprise is to operate in more than one state, obtaining qualification to do business in one state will not automatically entitle the investor to operate that same business in other states.

Once steps have been taken to comply with state and local regulations, it is necessary to consider also federal regulation and taxation. The remainder of this chapter will not describe all basic state, local, and federal regulations, but instead will summarize selected principal areas of such regulation which may be relevant to organizing business and other investments from abroad in the United States.

It should be noted that a detailed explanation of the federal and state judicial systems and procedures for conducting legal actions is not attempted here. However, certain legal remedies and penalties are noted here and in subsequent chapters dealing with specific types of transactions and investments by foreign persons.

Furthermore, it should be noted that — perhaps because of the diversity of legal and tax rules in the United States — U.S. attorneys and accountants often have more responsibility in structuring and negotiating transactions than their counterparts in other countries.

Principal Forms of U.S. Business Enterprises

The principal types of U.S. business enterprises which an investor may choose to employ may conveniently be divided into two categories: (1) those where all participants are personally liable for the obligations of the business; and (2) those where certain or all of the participants can limit the extent of their liability, generally to the respective amounts which they have originally invested or agreed to invest in the enterprise.

Business Forms with Unlimited Liability

The principal forms of business enterprise in this category are the sole proprietorship, the general partnership, and the unincorporated joint venture.

The sole proprietorship. This is the simplest of all forms of enterprises: an individual person is the direct owner of the assets of the business and is wholly responsible for its liabilities. There are no special laws applicable to the establishment of such an enterprise; one need only obtain the business licenses and permits necessary for conducting the particular business activity, such as described further below.

Responsibility for operation of the sole proprietorship lies with the owner, subject to any delegation of responsibility he may choose to make. A sole proprietorship ceases to exist at the will of the owner or upon his death, disability, insolvency, or legal incapacity. No formalities generally are required in selling the business; however, certain state jurisdictions may require that notice be given to creditors, for example, by publication in a newspaper of general circulation.

While there is no limitation on the size of such a business, sole proprietorships tend to be relatively small since their assets are necessarily limited to the resources of individual owners, and unlimited liability may create a serious risk to their economic security.

The general partnership.[1] A partnership is defined broadly as an association of two or more persons — whether individuals, corporations, or other legal entities — to carry on as co-owners a business for profit. Unless the formal requirements of organizing a corporation or limited partnership are complied with, the association usually is considered a general partnership. Where the partnership is a general partnership, all partners have unlimited liability for the debts of the business.

Once two persons agree to join the business, the Uniform Partnership Act, as adopted and/or amended by the state where the business is carried on, automatically becomes applicable. This act regulates the rights and duties among the partners in the absence of a partnership agreement. For example, general partners usually are presumed to share equally in the profits and losses of the business, have equal rights to participate in the management and conduct of the business, have the right to veto the admission of additional partners, and have the power by any one partner acting alone to buy and sell assets and enter into other contracts on behalf of the partnership during the usual course of its business. However, such rights may be modified or totally eliminated as to any partner under the partnership agreement. While the partnership agreement may so limit a partner's ability to contract on behalf of the partnership, such agreement will not be binding on third parties with whom that partner may deal, unless such parties are actually aware of the existence of the limitation.

Certain aspects of the general partnership relationship cannot be altered by agreement. For example, each partner generally has the right to examine partnership books and records and to receive accurate information from the other partners to the best of their knowledge as to matters affecting the partnership. More significantly, it is well established that the relationship among partners is of a fiduciary nature, so that one partner or group of partners may not gain an advantage over co-partners by unfair means. This covenant of fair dealing is implicit in every general or limited partnership relationship and may not be removed by mutual agreement of the partners. Similarly, the partnership agreement may provide for the expulsion of a partner, leaving the business to the remaining partners, if there are provisions for fairly and adequately compensating the expelled partner for his interest.

A general partnership may buy, sell, and own property, and may sue and be sued in its own name. Partnership property may also be held for the partnership in the name of a partner or other person.

A general partnership usually is dissolved by the death, bankruptcy, or express will of any partner, by termination of the term of the partnership as specified in the partnership agreement, or by the expulsion of any partner pursuant to the agreement. The partnership agreement may regulate in advance the time and manner of dissolution. However, each partner has the right to dissolve the partnership at any time and demand an accounting of partnership assets, even in contravention of the agreement. In such a case, however, that partner may be liable to the remaining partners for breach of contract. The remaining partners ordinarily may continue the business in the partnership's name, provided they compensate the withdrawing partner for his interest, less any damages due from him.

When a general partnership is dissolved, ordinarily a notice of dissolution must be published in a newspaper of general circulation in each place where the partnership operated its business, and an affidavit evidencing such publication must then be filed with the appropriate county clerk or other authority. There are no sanctions for failing to comply with these requirements; however, absent such notification, each of the partners may continue to have power on behalf of the partnership to take actions for which the other partners may be liable.

The unincorporated joint venture. This type of business association is quite similar to the general partnership, differing primarily in the duration and scope of the enterprise. Whereas a partnership generally involves the operation of an ongoing business, requiring a substantial sustained effort by one or more of the partners, an unincorporated joint venture involves a single undertaking or a series of related undertakings, not requiring the full-time effort of one or more of the venturers. Like a partnership, such a joint venture is created by the implied or express agreement of the parties, and their mutual rights and duties are similar. However, due to the limited scope of the enterprise, such joint venturers usually are considered to have less power to bind each other with respect to third parties than do the members of a general partnership.

Business Forms Involving Limited Liability

The principal forms of business enterprises in this category are the limited partnership and the general business corporation.

The limited partnership.[2] A limited partnership is a business association with the attributes of a general partnership having, however, one or more limited partners. A limited partner is not bound by the obligations of the partnership beyond the investment he has obligated himself to make in the business; each general partner is, however, personally liable for all partnership obligations. While each limited partnership must have at least one general partner, it is not necessary that this be an individual; a corporation, itself an entity of limited liability, may be the general partner of a limited partnership. A corporation may also be a limited partner.

Unlike the case of a general partnership, under the Uniform Limited Partnership Act as adopted and/or amended by each state, there are strict requirements for forming a limited partnership. Persons desiring to enter into a limited partnership usually must execute a certificate containing the following information: (1) the name of the partnership; (2) the character of the business; (3) the location of the principal place of business; (4) the name and address of each partner, designating specifically the general and limited partners; (5) the duration of the partnership; (6) the amount of cash and value of other property contributed by each limited partner (a limited partner's contribution generally may *not* consist of services); (7) any additional contribution to be made by the limited partners in the future; (8) the time, if agreed upon, when the contribution of each limited partner must be returned; (9) the share of the profits which each limited partner is to receive; (10) the right, if any, of limited partners to name a substituted general partner; (11) any right of the partnership to admit additional limited partners; (12) any priority of one limited partner over the others; (13) the right, if given, of the remaining general partners to continue the business upon the death of any general partner; (14) the right of any limited partner to receive property other than cash upon dissolution; and (15) the right of any limited partner to participate in major partnership decisions.

This certificate generally must be filed with the county recorder or other specified authority where the principal place of the partnership's business is located. If the partnership has places of business or property in other counties or other subdivisions in the same state, copies of the certificate may have to be filed there also. Failure to do so may mean that third parties dealing with the partnership will not be bound by the agreement limiting the liability of the limited partners. Moreover, qualification as a limited partnership under the law of one state will not automatically result in similar qualification in other states where the partnership may be doing business; a business must take steps to establish itself as a limited partnership in every state in which it plans to operate.

The general partners are responsible for the operation of the business of the limited partnership. Limited partners may not participate in management and control of the business; if they do so, they risk becoming liable as general partners. A limited partner may, however, participate in major decisions of the partnership, such as election or removal of partners, termination of the business, or amendment of the partnership certificate. Limited partners may lend money and transact other business with the partnership and, with some restrictions, may claim with other creditors a *pro rata* share of the assets should the business become insolvent.

A limited partnership is dissolved broadly in the same manner and for the same causes as a general partnership. The death, disability, or bankruptcy of a limited partner does not, however, dissolve the partnership. A limited partner's interest is freely assignable to third parties. However, unless the assignee becomes a substituted limited partner by consent of the remaining partners, he is entitled only to a share of the profits of the business commensurate with his interest and may not inspect partnership books and records or participate in any partnership decisions.

The general business corporation.[3] The corporation is the most extensively regulated form of U.S. business enterprise. However, corporations are used primarily to assure limited liability to all participants, continuity of existence regardless of the death or disability of any shareholder, and certain tax advantages.

Corporations are chartered pursuant to specific laws in each state. While the federal government has the power to grant corporate charters, it does so only in special circumstances. A corporate charter need be obtained from one state only; the corporation may thereafter do business in other states, provided it complies with local qualification procedures. While state laws differ in material respects regarding corporations, the general regulation involved may be summarized as follows:

Initially, a name must be selected by the proposed incorporators and approval of the same sought from the Secretary of State or other appropriate authority of the state. Such approval normally is given if the name is not inherently deceptive or so similar to that of another corporation as to cause confusion. Many jurisdictions further require that the proposed name contain the term "incorporated" or "company" or abbreviations thereof, or another word implying limited liability. The name, once approved, should be reserved by payment of a nominal fee for a sufficient period to permit completion of the process of incorporation.

The actual incorporation process may be undertaken by any individual, partnership, association, or corporation. While some states require at least three incorporators, the modern trend — adopted by California, Delaware, and New York, for example — is to require no more than one incorporator. While the persons on whose behalf the corporation is established may themselves act as incorporators, this is not required; in fact there are organizations in every state which will, for a fee, undertake the incorporation process.

The incorporators must file with the Secretary of State or other appropriate state authority a document which may, depending on the state, be called the articles of incorporation, the certificate of incorporation, or a similar title. The articles generally must contain the following: the name of the corporation; a statement of the purposes and powers of the corporation; the name and address of a person who is to serve as agent for service of process; and the classes of stock authorized to be issued, the number of shares authorized in each class, and any preferences or qualifications applicable to such stock. The articles also may contain provisions limiting the sale of stock to certain classes of persons, placing other reasonable restrictions on the sale or hypothecation of stock by the shareholders, or requiring a greater than usual vote of shareholders for certain corporate actions, and any other lawful provisions with respect to the management or conduct of the corporation's business. Filing of the articles must be accompanied by a fee and, often, by the first year's state corporation or franchise tax, an annual levy on the corporation which is payable regardless of whether it conducts any business.

Filing of the articles effects the initial establishment of the corporation. The next step is for the incorporators to hold a meeting to adopt the by-laws of the corporation and elect the first board of directors. The by-laws are not filed or published, but constitute the internal regulations by which the corporation is to operate, and generally may be amended from time to time by the directors. They deal with such matters as the rules for conducting shareholders' and directors' meetings, the number and qualification of the officers and directors and the length of their terms and definition of their powers and responsibilities, issuance and transfer of stock, declaration of dividends, and determination of the fiscal year of the corporation.

The directors are the individuals responsible for making fundamental decisions with respect to the operation of the corporation's business. Many states require that corporations have at least three directors; however, certain states make an exception in the case of closely held corporations having one or two shareholders, in which case the number of directors may be one or two, respectively.

Once the directors are elected, the incorporators resign and the directors then hold (or continue) their meeting, appointing the officers of the corporation, issuing stock to the shareholders, and taking such other administrative steps as seem appropriate. The officers are the individuals responsible for day-to-day operation of the corporation's business; they generally include a president, one or more vice presidents, a secretary, and a treasurer. All of these posts need not necessarily be held by different individuals, although state laws may prohibit certain offices being held by the same individual. The officers serve at the will of the directors and may be discharged by them at any time with or without cause. However, an officer discharged without good cause will remain entitled to compensation or damages under any employment contract which he may have with the corporation.

Corporate stock generally may be issued for cash, property, or services. The board of directors determines the value of the property or services exchanged for the corporation's stock and, absent a showing of fraud, this valuation is binding on the corporation. The issuance, sale, and purchase of stock — as of securities of any enterprise — is closely regulated by both state and federal securities laws, which are discussed further below.

A further requirement in a number of states is the filing of a certificate with the Secretary of State or other appropriate authority setting forth the names and addresses of the directors and officers of the corporation, and designating an agent for receiving service of legal process in case a suit should be brought against it. This agent may be either an individual residing in the state or, often, another corporation which has taken steps to qualify as a proper agent.

Once the corporation has been fully established, it is considered a legal entity separate from its shareholders with the capacities to acquire, own, and use property, to enter into and enforce contracts, and otherwise to carry on business activities. Debts incurred by the corporation are its responsibility alone, and the shareholders, directors, and officers will not normally be personally responsible for these obligations. In order to preserve this limited liability, however, it is necessary that the corporation be treated by the parties as a separate entity rather than as a vehicle for conducting the shareholders' personal affairs. The shareholders, directors, and officers should scrupulously observe formalities in dealing with the corporation's assets. All major decisions concerning the conduct of the business should be taken only pursuant to a written resolution of the directors and/or shareholders. Books and records of the corporation should be kept carefully and assets owned by the corporation should be differentiated clearly from those owned by shareholders. Shareholders may lend money to the corporation or borrow from it, and may enter into employment contracts calling for the payment of adequate salaries by the corporation. However, any such transactions between the corporation and its shareholders must be clearly documented. Similarly, any profits paid to shareholders as dividends should be authorized out of proper reserves by a resolution of the board of directors.

One of the principal advantages of incorporation in Delaware is that many of such corporate formalities are simplified, within certain limits, under Delaware law. In addition, a closely held corporation may be able to employ somewhat simplified procedures under Delaware or other state laws.

Corporate directors owe to the shareholders fiduciary duties of care and of loyalty in making decisions pertaining to corporate business. They must exercise independent judgment in the conduct of the business and generally may not shift this ultimate responsibility to others by executing powers of attorney or by other means. They may not put the interests of one group of shareholders over that of another, nor their own interests before those of the corporation. A director may be personally liable for losses incurred as a result of his failure properly to fulfill these duties.

Shareholders elect and remove directors, amend the articles of incorporation, and vote on any substantial change in the structure of the corporation. While a majority vote of the shareholders normally is sufficient, the interests of minority shareholders may be protected under certain state laws by requiring a two-thirds or other larger vote to take certain steps, such as a change in the number of directors or shares outstanding. In addition, such a greater than majority requirement for a particular decision often will be specified in the articles.

In order to qualify to conduct active business in another state, a corporation generally is required to obtain permission from the state's Secretary of State or other appropriate state authority. This is obtained by the filing of a petition stating the corporate name, the state of incorporation, the location of the principal office of the corporation, the location of its principal office within the new state, and the name of an agent for service of process within the new state. A certificate of good standing from an official in the state of incorporation and possibly a copy of its articles of incorporation must accompany the application, together with a filing fee and, often, the first year's franchise tax. A certificate of qualification may not be issued where the name of the corporation may cause confusion with a business name previously reserved in the new state. The most common significant state penalty for conducting business without the required qualification is denial of the corporation's power to institute judicial actions there to enforce claims.

A corporation ceases to exist by merger into another corporation in accordance with state law or by dissolution. Merger occurs when the assets and liabilities of the corporation are acquired by another corporation and the shareholders of the merged corporation receive the stock of the surviving corporation in exchange for their original stock. A merger must be approved by the board of directors of each corporation and by the shareholders of the merged corporation — and often of the surviving corporation as well. Shareholders of the merged corporation who object to the merger usually are entitled to require the corporation to purchase their stock at fair market value.

A corporation may be dissolved by the vote of its board of directors together with the approval of a certain percentage of its shareholders, usually those holding a majority of the voting power. The corporation also may be dissolved by order of a court upon the petition of a certain number of its directors or a certain portion of its shareholders. The grounds for such involuntary dissolution generally include (1) a deadlock among shareholders or directors preventing the business of the corporation from being carried on or (2) fraud, mismanagement, abuse of authority, or persistent unfairness toward the shareholders by those in control of the corporation or (3) waste of the property of the corporation by the officers or directors. In certain of these situations, the court alternatively may appoint an outside individual to manage corporate affairs for a limited period.

General Business Tax and License System

This section briefly lists the principal elements of the U.S. tax and license system with which any U.S. business enterprise must comply.

Federal Taxes and Regulation

Income taxes.[4] Federal income tax rates on individuals currently are graduated from zero for an unmarried individual with no more than $2,300 of annual taxable income up to a maximum rate of 50% (after 1981) on such an individual's annual taxable income in excess of $81,000 ($41,500 for 1982 and $55,300 for 1983). Rates on estates and trusts are approximately the same. Married individuals filing a joint tax return pay somewhat over twice the tax calculated at the lower graduated rate of one-half of their combined income. Beginning in 1985, individual tax rate brackets currently are intended to be indexed for inflation. In addition, only four-tenths of long-term capital gains from assets held more than one year generally are taxed to such persons. In the case of commodity futures, the long-term holding period is more than six months and, for taxable gains from futures traded on a regulated exchange, the maximum tax rate for individuals generally is 32%.

Income taxes imposed on corporations are less finely graduated, amounting to 15% (16% for 1982) of annual taxable ordinary income up to $25,000, 18% (19% for 1982)-40% of income between $25,000 and $100,000, and 46% of all income over $100,000. Long-term capital gains generally are taxed at a maximum of 28%.

Numerous deductions for business expenses, most interest expenses, individual retirement account contributions of $2,000-$2,250 per year by employed individuals, depreciation under the accelerated cost recovery system for tangible business property placed in service by the taxpayer after 1980 and other depreciation of other business property, natural resource depletion, net operating loss carrybacks for three years and carryforwards for 15 years, and the like generally are permitted in determining taxable income. Investment tax credits of usually up to 10% for investments in certain property used in the United States (but often with a reduction in tax basis for depreciation purposes equal to at least one-half of the credit), a credit of 25% of increases in research and development expenditures before 1986, job tax credits, and other credits may reduce the actual tax payable. State and local income, property, and certain other taxes — but not non-business motor vehicle fuel taxes — also are deductible for federal income tax purposes.

Certain deductions and other items of so called tax preference income are subject to additional minimum taxes of 20% in the case of an individual and 15% in the case of a corporation, as well as up to a 15% reduction in the amount which is allowed as a deduction for income tax purposes by a corporation.

The use of registered rather than bearer debt instruments is required after 1982 for most publicly offered corporate or domestic governmental obligations with a maturity of more than one year in order to permit: (1) deduction of the interest by the issuer; (2) avoidance of an excise tax on the issuer; (3) federal tax exemption of the interest in the case of a state, municipal, or similar governmental obligation; and (4) capital gain treatment, or use of losses, upon the holder's disposition of the obligation. In addition, after June 1983 payments of interest and dividends to most noncorporate recipients are subject to a withholding tax of 10% (except interest payments by an individual); however, this is credited against the recipient's total federal income tax liability.

Since a sole proprietorship is not considered a taxable entity separate from its owner for income tax purposes, it is not required to file an income tax return or pay such taxes. Following each quarter of an individual owner's taxable year — almost without exception, the calendar year — he must file a report with the U.S. Internal Revenue Service estimating his tax liability for that period and enclosing a tax payment in that amount. After the end of his tax year, he must file a detailed statement of his income and computation of his tax liability, and pay any additional sum he may owe. If he has overestimated his tax liability, he is then entitled to a refund of the overpayment.

A partnership, whether general or limited, is not considered a taxable entity separate from its partners. However, the partnership must file an annual return showing its income, which is then apportioned among the partners. Unless the partners have identical fiscal years, the tax year of the partnership generally must be the calendar year. Under certain circumstances, joint owners of certain passive investments, such as an inactive real property investment, may elect out of treatment of the venture as a partnership for income tax purposes. Like the individual owner of a sole proprietorship, each partner must make estimated tax payments during the year on his total income from all sources, including the partnership, and then file a tax return at the end of the year, reconciling the actual tax liability with the estimated payments.

A corporation is considered a taxable entity separate from its shareholders. Thus, a corporation must make quarterly estimated income tax payments and then file a final income tax return at the end of its tax year. This year generally may be determined by the corporation's own election upon its commencement of business. Payments made to employees as reasonable salaries, or to creditors as interest at arm's length rates, generally are deductible by the corporation. However, dividends paid to shareholders out of corporate earnings and profits are not deductible, nor does the shareholder receive any credit for corporate taxes already paid on the distributed income. Under certain circumstances, as discussed in Chapter II regarding U.S. taxation of foreign investors and in other chapters, the U.S. Internal Revenue Service may seek to treat even a limited partnership as an association taxable as a corporation —

particularly where the sole general partner is a corporation without substantial net worth independently of its interest in the partnership.

Certain small so called Subchapter S corporations with no more than 35 shareholders may elect to avoid taxation as separate entities, with profits and losses of the business credited and charged directly to the shareholders for federal income tax purposes. It should be noted, however, that such election may not be made where any of the shareholders is a corporation or is a nonresident alien of the United States for income tax purposes. Limitations on passive income have, however, recently been eased and, for new corporations, eliminated; the limitation on foreign income also has been eliminated.

Gift and estate taxes.[5] The Tax Reform Act of 1976 established a unified system of federal taxation of gifts and estates of individuals. For U.S. citizens and for aliens domiciled in the United States, the rates of tax are graduated from 18% for a cumulative value of gifts and estate of up to $10,000 for an individual, to 50% (53-70% before 1985) of the excess of such value over $2.5 million. Various exclusions, deductions, and credits are provided — for example, an exclusion of $10,000 in gifts each calendar year to each donee, a marital deduction for all gifts to the donor's spouse and all property passing to the decedent's spouse for at least the spouse's lifetime benefit, a lifetime credit against the unified gift and estate tax of $192,800 ($62,800-$155,800 before 1987) which is equivalent to an exemption from tax of $600,000 in property value, a deduction for certain farm and closely held business holdings, and a credit for certain state death taxes. The gift tax is payable by the donor for gifts made in each calendar year, and the estate tax by the decedent's executor. In the case of a gift, the recipient's basis in the property for federal tax purposes generally remains that of the donor. However, upon inheritance the basis is adjusted to the fair market value of the property at the date of death, subject to certain variations.

In addition, a federal tax similar to the estate tax currently is imposed on certain generation-skipping transfers after June 11, 1976 (or after 1982, for certain transfers created prior to that date).

Chapter II deals at greater length with the particular income, gift, and estate taxation of foreign persons.

Employment taxes. Any U.S. business which hires employees is required to comply with provisions of the tax laws applicable specifically to employers. A new business which intends to hire employees must request the assignment of an employer identification number by the U.S. Internal Revenue Service. All payments made by the business with respect to employment taxes are then handled in an account bearing that number. Federal employment taxes are of three kinds: (1) employee withholding, (2) unemployment insurance contributions, and (3) social security contributions.

(1) *Employee withholding.* Each employer is required to deduct from the salaries or wages of his employees the amount which the latter are assumed to owe in federal income taxes, under certain formulae based on compensation levels. The money is then periodically paid to the federal government. Failure to follow these procedures scrupulously, or misuse of the money withheld, may result in civil and criminal penalties.

(2) *Unemployment insurance.* Each employer is required to pay an excise tax amounting to a small percentage of salaries and wages paid during the year, as a contribution to a federal unemployment insurance fund. However, the employer may deduct therefrom any payments made to an approved state unemployment insurance fund. Unlike withholding taxes, which are a contribution by the employee, unemployment insurance is paid totally by the employer, over and above salaries or wages paid to employees.

(3) *Social security contributions.* Federal law requires both employers and employees to contribute to a federally operated old age and disability pension and hospital insurance plan. Each year, a certain tax rate is imposed for such contribution, and one-half of the amount is deducted by the employer from the salary payable to the employee while the other half is paid directly by the employer. As in the case of withholding taxes, these sums must be paid to the federal government on a periodic basis. Similar taxes are imposed on the income of self-employed individuals.

It should be noted that substantial controversy has arisen as to whether individuals treated as independent contractors should be reclassified as employees for which the above taxes are payable, and further developments in this area should be followed by employers.

Excise and oil taxes. Federal taxes are imposed on consumption of certain goods and services and business enterprises involved in the United States in the sale of such goods and services must comply with federal regulations for the collection and remittance of such revenues. Among these are motor vehicles and their component parts, petroleum products, firearms, alcoholic beverages, tobacco, certain telephone and other communications facilities, and commercial transportation of persons by air.

The Crude Oil Windfall Profit Tax Act of 1980 added an excise tax of 30-70% on the excess of the sale price of most crude oil over its base price in 1979, although the tax is temporary by its terms and will be reduced to 15% by 1986 for newly discovered oil. In addition, special taxes on crude oil and certain other chemicals support two trust funds for remedial actions necessitated by releases of hazardous substances.[6]

Customs duties. The federal duties on goods imported into the United

States vary according to a number of factors — such as the country of origin and the type of goods involved — and are subject to a complex system of assessment, levy, and collection. There is no similar levy on the exportation of goods, since this is constitutionally prohibited. Import activities are treated separately in Chapter V, as are certain export activities in Chapter VIII.

Business licenses. Unlike the states, the federal government does not engage in general licensing and similar regulation of businesses. However, federal licenses are required for enterprises engaged in special areas, for example, the operation of radio or television stations, operation or ownership of ships or aircraft, manufacturing and interstate shipping of pharmaceuticals, and importation or exportation of certain commodities. Certain of such matters are discussed in greater detail in Chapter VI dealing with establishment of a new enterprise by a foreign investor, and in Chapters V and VIII on import and export activities.

Environmental and consumer protection regulations. The United States has in recent years become increasingly concerned with possible damage to the natural environment caused by various activities of human society. In 1970 the Environmental Protection Agency was created and charged with promulgating and enforcing environmental quality standards.[7] The Agency has, *inter alia,* established such standards with regard to air pollution — for example, sulphur oxides, carbon monoxide, photochemical oxidants, hydrocarbons, nitrogen dioxide, and particulate matter — as well as water pollution, pesticides, nuclear radiation, and solid waste disposal. For example, such standards set the maximum level of emissions from various manufacturing facilities, and cover the construction and operation of landfills for hazardous wastes. The agency has also mandated adoption of plans in each state to deal with air pollution. Government actions which may have environmental impact — including the issuance of discretionary permits for private activities — may require an environmental impact report in advance. Any release without advance permit, and any site used for disposal, of a hazardous substance must be reported to the Agency. While the extensive details of these and related regulations cannot be described here, the potential investor in the United States — particularly in a manufacturing facility — should investigate the application and cost of such requirements.

Numerous federal laws, regulations, and government authorities also regulate business enterprises which furnish consumer products — goods or services — to the public. The Federal Trade Commission is particularly active in this area. Its enforcement authority applicable generally to such business includes, for example, consumer credit regulations which restrict any business extending credit to consumers, as well as any business which reports on the creditworthiness of consumers; regulations restricting the language and extent of express warranties and waivers of implied warranties; and regulation of false advertising.

As to specific consumer products and industries, for example, the Consumer Products Safety Commission promulgates for various products sold to the public minimum safety standards governing performance, composition, contents, design, construction, finish, and packaging, as well as requiring appropriate warning labels or instructions to ensure safe operation. The Federal Trade Commission also regulates labeling of nonfood and nondrug products. The Food and Drug Administration governs the content and labeling of foods, drugs, cosmetics, and therapeutic devices; and the U.S. Department of Agriculture oversees food quality. The U.S. Department of Transportation administers motor vehicle quality and safety laws.

State Taxes and Regulation

Income taxes. Not every state has an income tax. However, most of the highly industrialized states — such as New York, California, Illinois, and Pennsylvania — do levy taxes on income; Texas is perhaps the only notable exception. While it is difficult to generalize, many states which levy an income tax tend to follow the model of the federal tax law, including taxation of individual residents on worldwide net income at graduated rates. In addition, as mentioned above, corporations usually are subject to a minimum annual franchise or similar tax on state income. Tax rates vary significantly among the states, as does the degree of graduation, *i.e.,* the rate at which the percentage of taxation increases with income, but may often reach 9-11%. Because such taxes are deductible for federal income tax purposes, the effective additional rate usually is reduced substantially.

A different problem arises in determining which portion of corporate income is subject to tax in a specific state. Certain states, such as California, employ a unitary tax method which may require presentation of the worldwide business income of domestic and foreign affiliated corporations and other enterprises which are operated as a unit, of which the state's portion is then calculated based on the portion of worldwide assets, payroll, and sales in the state.

Gift and inheritance taxes. Most states have a gift tax and/or an inheritance or similar tax. While it is difficult to generalize, the rates for both taxes often are similar within a given state. However, these taxes may include not only general exclusions similar to the $10,000 per year per donee exclusion under the federal gift tax, but also numerous specific exclusions and/or rate variations for different recipients depending on their relationship to the donor or decedent. It should be noted that such an inheritance tax usually is payable by each heir, rather than being the liability primarily of the executor or estate.

Chapter II deals with certain aspects of such state income, gift, and inheritance or similar taxation relevant to foreign persons.

Employment taxes. Those states which levy an income tax normally require an employer to withhold such tax from employees' salaries or wages. In addition, the state may require tax payments for the benefit of unemployment or disability insurance funds to be paid by the employer, withheld from the paychecks of employees, or made by a combination of the two. Before commencing business, a new employer should contact the state authority which administers the collection of these taxes for assignment of an account number and instructions on withholding and payment of these taxes.

Sales and use taxes. If a business enterprise sells goods to the public, it will normally be required to collect sales taxes levied by the state. The taxes generally amount to a small percentage of the sale price and are collected from the customer. Before commencing business, the seller must obtain a permit from the state entitling it to collect these taxes. The state may require the posting of a bond to secure proper remittance of the collected taxes as a condition for issuing the permit. The seller is required to maintain records of the taxes collected and to turn the collections over to the state on a quarterly or other periodic basis. The state authorities may audit these books and records from time to time, to ensure that all the collected taxes have been properly remitted.

Use taxes complement sales taxes by being imposed on the local use of goods purchased in another state which, if sold locally, would have been subject to sales tax.

Exceptions to such taxes generally include a bulk sale of all of an enterprise's business and goods to a single purchaser. However, a sale of stock of an incorporated enterprise may be subject to stock transfer tax.

Motor vehicle taxes. Each state licenses the operation of motor vehicles belonging to its residents. Such licenses are renewable on a yearly basis and involve the payment of a license tax, usually graduated according to the value of the vehicle.

Special commodity taxes. Each state may levy taxes on specific commodities such as alcoholic beverages, cigarettes, and motor vehicle fuel. Businesses involved in the sale of these commodities are required to collect such taxes and turn them over to the state.

Special business taxes. Many states impose special taxes on certain types of businesses, such as banks and insurance companies. Severance or production taxes may be imposed on mining or oil, gas, or other natural resources production within the state. Although it is practically impossible to generalize with respect to such taxes, their principal features can be determined relatively expeditiously under any particular state's laws.

Business licenses. Certain types of businesses require licenses from the states where they intend to operate. For example, many states require automobile dealers, retail sellers of petroleum, and sellers of alcoholic beverages to obtain state licenses; the list of such businesses varies from state to state.

Requirements for obtaining such state licenses may be quite stringent, especially where such licensed activities require the collection of revenues on behalf of the state. For example, to obtain an automobile dealer's license, one may have to provide the names, personal histories, and fingerprints of the persons managing the proposed business and information concerning the business bank account and the property on which the proposed dealership will be located, and one may have to post a bond or deposit. An investigation then may be made of the premises before a license may be issued. A similarly cumbersome process usually is required to obtain or transfer a license for the sale of alcoholic beverages.

License requirements for banking, insurance, and certain other highly regulated industries are discussed further in Chapter VI regarding establishment of a new business enterprise.

Professional licenses. Where the business enterprise dispenses professional services to the public, each state will normally require an individual providing the services to obtain a professional license. Accountants, architects, attorneys, medical doctors and other medical practitioners, and real estate brokers are licensed in virtually every state. Many other professions — for example, investment advisers as noted further below — also require licenses in many states.

Professional licenses generally are more difficult to obtain than business licenses because they require a specialized education, the passing of an examination, and/or certain prior experience. Holding such a professional license in one state does not normally entitle the licensee to practice the profession in another state, except in certain occasional transactions.

Environmental and consumer protection regulations. As noted further above, one aspect of federal environmental protection policy requires that each state promulgate and enforce plans for air pollution control. The stringency of such plans in any particular state depends on the level of human and industrial pollutants, natural pollution sources, and meteorological conditions which mitigate or exacerbate pollution effects.

In addition to these plans, many states have their own environmental protection and impact report laws. A state may, for example, require motor vehicles and other air pollution sources to carry filtering equipment not mandated by federal laws, or limit construction in coastal or other areas where rare animal species or other natural resources may be endangered, or regulate the use of waterways for solid wastes, or control noise or population density or permit such controls by local authorities.

Almost all states now have income, sales, and/or property tax incentives for investment in air and water pollution control equipment.

States also generally have extensive usury and other regulations for consumer protection, frequently more stringent than federal regulations. Usury limits on interest rates often will not apply to corporate or other business borrowers, will have higher limits for banks and other institutional lenders, and may be overridden up to federally permitted rates on certain types of loans. Other general regulations apply in the areas of credit reporting, consumer warranties, and product safety. Additional regulations may deal with specific products or industries — for example, construction of swimming pools, contracts for health studio services, or motor vehicle repair shops. The possible application of these regulations should be investigated before an investment is made in an enterprise providing any consumer goods or services.

Local Taxes and Regulation

Sales taxes. A separate sales tax may be imposed by local authorities in addition to the sales tax imposed by the state. The seller of goods will be required to collect this tax also, and turn such collections over to the local government directly or to state authorities who then return the funds to local authorities.

Property taxes. Local authorities normally levy annual taxes on the ownership of property located within the boundaries of their respective jurisdictions as percentages of the values at which they assess the property. Both real property and personal property or inventory normally are subject to tax, although certain nonbusiness and other personal property may be specifically excluded. Where property is situated within a city, the tax rate may reflect levies by both the city and the county within which the city is located. Special purpose assessment districts also may levy annual charges on real property within each district. Property taxes create a lien on the taxed property, and failure to pay such taxes can result in sale of the property in satisfaction of the lien.

Miscellaneous taxes. Local authorities may impose a variety of other taxes. Among these are taxes on the transfer of real property, on use of certain utilities such as gas, telephone, and electricity, on hotel rooms, and on the sale of certain commodities such as cigarettes.

Business licenses and taxes. Before commencing any type of business it is generally necessary to obtain a business license from the local authorities. These are the municipal government, if the business is within the boundaries of a city or town or, in other cases, the county or similar unit of government. Obtaining and maintaining a business license generally involves the payment of a tax. This tax may be imposed at a flat rate, or may vary with the type of business, or its gross receipts or other measure of business volume.

Fictitious name filing. An unincorporated business enterprise — such as a sole proprietorship or partnership — which is to be operated under a name other than that of the owners generally is required to file a fictitious name statement with the clerk of the county or other appropriate authority where the business is to operate. Such statement generally must contain the name of the business and the names and addresses of its principals and is required to be published in a local newspaper of general circulation.

Zoning, subdivision, and building permits. Local authorities generally control the use of real property by zoning various parts of the city or county or other unit for specific uses — perhaps the best known major exception being the city of Houston, Texas. For example, commercial establishments cannot be operated on property zoned for residential development and industrial buildings may not be constructed where the zoning plan calls for recreational facilities. The zoning plan generally also includes restrictions on the occupation density of new buildings and/or their height. If incorrectly zoned property is acquired, it is possible in certain circumstances to obtain a zoning variance or nonconforming use permit. However, this can be expensive and time consuming.

Separate local permits generally are required in order to subdivide property into lots or condominiums. In addition, building permits in compliance with local building and fire codes must be obtained for new construction.

Each of these steps may be complicated by state *and* local environmental quality laws that require environmental impact reports and/or hearings before the relevant permit may be issued.

Health and safety regulations. Local authorities generally enforce various regulations for local health and safety. For example, during new building construction the structure will be inspected by local authorities to ensure compliance with applicable regulations and a certificate of compliance or occupancy must be obtained before the building may be occupied. Changes in regulations also may require improvements in fire safety to existing structures.

Operation of hazardous machine systems and storage and use of flammable or hazardous materials often are regulated. Similarly, health and hygiene regulations and inspections govern the operation of restaurants and other public eating and drinking establishments.

Securities Laws

Both the federal government and the states extensively regulate the issuance and trading of securities. Securities usually are broadly defined to include, for example, shares of stock, notes, bonds, and any other evidence of indebtedness or of a participatory interest in a business enterprise, whether or not evidenced by a written instrument. There are various statutory and other exemptions from such definitions. However, in the case of a purchase or sale of an equity interest or evidence of indebtedness of a business enterprise, securities law issues usually must be considered.

Federal Regulation

The two principal U.S. statutes regulating securities transactions at the federal level are the Securities Act of 1933[8] (the "1933 Act") and the Securities Exchange Act of 1934[9] (the "1934 Act"). The former act principally regulates the conduct of issuers of new securities, while the latter act principally regulates trading of securities which have already been issued. In addition, a number of other federal statutes pertain to various aspects of securities investment, as noted further below.

The Securities Act of 1933. The 1933 Act requires, among other things, that issuers of securities register them prior to issuance with the Securities and Exchange Commission (the "SEC"), the agency charged with administering the federal securities laws. Certain types of securities and types of transactions are exempted from this portion of the 1933 Act. However, similar state regulation still may be applicable.

(1) *Exemptions.* The 1933 Act is inapplicable to transactions which do not involve an issuer, underwriter, or dealer in securities. These transactions constitute normal securities trading and are regulated by the 1934 Act discussed below.

In addition, the 1933 Act is inapplicable to the sale of securities which are part of an issue offered and sold only to residents of a single state. This exemption is applicable only where the issuer of the securities is a resident of and does business within the state; if the issuer is a corporation, it must be incorporated in the state as well as do business there. The SEC has promulgated rules which define more specifically the terms of this exemption, and any proposed issuance should be scrutinized in light of these rules to determine whether the exemption applies.

A further exemption from the registration requirements applies to securities issues not involving a public offering. What constitutes a public offering in contrast to a private offering can be a difficult question. However, the SEC has provided certain standards which define a private offering essentially as one where no advertising or other broadly based sales techniques are used, the purchasers are individuals who are experienced in business and are able to bear the economic risk of the investment, they are given the opportunity to make inquiries of the issuer concerning the securities, no more than 35 persons purchase the securities (excluding those who purchase at least $150,000 worth), and certain restrictions are placed on retransfer of the securities by the purchasers.

Another important exemption from the 1933 Act's registration requirements covers exchanges between the securities issuer and its existing securities holders, if no commission or other remuneration is paid for soliciting such exchanges.

In addition, it is possible under so called Regulation A to issue up to $1.5 million worth of securities to the public by filing with the SEC certain documents which are less extensive than those required generally under the 1933 Act. A similar abbreviated form is available for initial offerings of up to $5 million worth of securities. Such exemptions are available only with respect to certain issuers (including limited partnerships) and types of securities.

There are also several special exemptions from the registration requirements covering (a) securities of governments and banks, (b) commercial paper, (c) securities of charitable organizations, and (d) insurance policies and annuity contracts.

(2) *Registration requirements.* If none of the exemptions discussed above is applicable, an issuer may not sell or offer securities unless they have first been registered with the SEC. The registration statement must contain information pertaining to the registrant's properties and business, a description of the significant provisions of the securities to be offered for sale and their relationship to the registrant's other capital securities, information about the management of the registrant, and financial statements certified by an independent public accountant.

After the registration statement has been filed, the securities may be offered for sale by certain limited means. However, no sales may actually be completed until the effective date of the registration statement; this is usually a minimum of 20 days after the date of filing, but often is a shorter period for a larger issuer. During this period, the statement is examined by the SEC for accuracy and completeness. If a problem is found, the registrant is required to amend the registration. The SEC's concern with respect to the registration process under the 1933 Act is that prospective purchasers be provided information on all matters which may be significant to an investor (other than matters particular to each investor's own situation) in his decision whether to make the investment. The SEC determines only that the registration statement contains the items of information required by its rules, and does *not* verify the accuracy or completeness of the substantive information or make any judgment as to whether the securities are a sound or prudent investment.

After the effective date of the registration statement, the securities may be offered for sale by any means and sales may be consummated so long as each offeree receives before such consummation a prospectus incorporating required information from the registration statement. The registration statement must be further amended to reflect any material changes in financial data or other facts during the offering. The SEC may suspend the registration if it later discovers material misstatements in the registration statement, and individuals making wilful misstatements in the registration statement may be subject to criminal penalties. Moreover, individuals who are responsible for such misstatements may be liable for damages suffered by investors who relied on the erroneous information in purchasing the securities.

The SEC is adopting an integrated disclosure system under which certain of those issuers which are also required to file under the 1934 Act discussed below may substantially shorten their registration statements for new securities issues by referring investors to those filings. In addition, the registration process for new securities issues may be permanently simplified to permit a large corporation or other issuer to file one registration statement announcing its long-term plans for sales of stock and/or debt securities, which can then take place whenever the issuer desires.

It should be noted that certain special current and proposed registration forms and rules for *foreign* issuers under both the 1933 and 1934 Acts are referred to in Chapter VII in connection with a foreign investor's use of stock or other securities to acquire a controlling interest in the assets or shares of an existing U.S. corporation.

(3) *Antifraud provisions.* Notwithstanding any exemption from registration requirements or compliance with such requirements, the 1933 Act separately prohibits use of the channels of interstate commerce or the mails to make fraudulent misstatements or to use any other fraudulent device in the offer or sale of *any* securities. Persons violating this provision are subject to criminal penalties.

The Securities Exchange Act of 1934. The 1934 Act regulates the trading of securities subsequent to their issuance. Its coverage is limited principally to those securities listed and registered for public trading on the national securities exchanges and to unlisted equity securities of corporations and other issuers — so called Section 12(g) issuers — having assets in excess of $3 million and at least 500 shareholders (or 300 shareholders after reaching the 500 point). Securities which do not meet these requirements may be traded without reference to federal regulation, except with respect to the 1933 Act's antifraud provisions noted above and the 1934 Act's rules against deception and misuse of inside information discussed further below.

(1) *Registration requirements.* Securities subject to the 1934 Act must be registered by the issuer with the SEC. The registration statement must include a description of the issuer's business, its management, and its capital structure, and must be accompanied by a financial statement certified by an independent public accountant. Following the original registration, periodic reports — for example, on Forms 8-K and 10-K — must keep current the information in the original report.

(2) *Proxy solicitation requirements.* Proxies are authorizations given by shareholders to third parties instructing those parties to exercise the shareholders' voting rights in a specified manner when such holders are not present at shareholders' meetings. For example, the directors of publicly traded corporations frequently solicit proxies from shareholders prior to a scheduled meeting of shareholders for the purpose of approving or disapproving proposed actions affecting the operating structure of the corporation. With respect to those corporations subject to the 1934 Act, a proxy solicitation must be accompanied by a proxy statement which notifies the shareholder of the matters to be acted on at the proposed meeting, advises him of any rights with respect to such actions, and identifies the persons soliciting the proxy, their connection with the corporation, and their interest, if any, in the outcome of the matter to be decided. If the proxy solicitation is made on behalf of the corporation's management and relates to an annual meeting where directors are to be elected, the solicitation must further be accompanied by an annual report describing the condition of the corporation, together with corporate financial statements for the two previous fiscal years, with the statement for the latest year being certified by an independent public accountant.

False or misleading statements in proxy solicitation materials are prohibited by law. Prior to distribution of the materials, copies must be filed with the SEC to determine whether they comply with its disclosure requirements. However, the SEC does not purport to pass on the merits of the matters to be voted on or to verify the accuracy or adequacy of the substantive statements made.

(3) *Short swing profits by insiders.* With respect to corporations and securities subject to the 1934 Act, each director, officer, and any person owning 10% or more of an outstanding class of such an equity security must file a statement with the SEC detailing his ownership of the corporation. An additional statement must be filed with the SEC for each month where such ownership has changed.

These individuals — commonly termed insiders — also are prohibited from profiting by purchase and sale of their stock, if such a purchase and sale occur within six months of each other. It should be noted that it does not matter, for the purposes of this rule, whether the sale follows the purchase or the purchase follows the sale (for example, where the shares have decreased in market price in the interim). Nor is there any necessity to show use of inside information or intent to defraud by the insider. The rule operates mechanically, without regard to such factors. Any profits which the insider has made in contravention of this rule accrue to the benefit of the corporation, and the corporation itself or any of its shareholders may bring suit to recover such profits.

(4) *Deception and nondisclosure of information.* The 1934 Act also prohibits the use of manipulative or deceptive devices in connection with the purchase or sale of *any* securities. This prohibition is *not* limited to securities listed on a national securities exchange or those of corporations having over $3 million in assets and at least 500 shareholders.

Rules promulgated by the SEC under the 1934 Act — particularly Rule 10b-5 — and court decisions have interpreted the statute's terms to prohibit not only fraud as understood under common law in the purchase and sale of securities, but also the making of material misstatements, or the *failure* to state material facts where such facts are necessary to avoid misleading the other party. This latter prohibition has been further refined to cover the purchase or sale of securities on the basis of secret or inside information not available to the general public. While generally this involves insiders such as officers, directors, and key employees who are in possession of such inside information, the statutory prohibition is not limited to such individuals. In particular, outside individuals who have received such information from insiders, in a manner calculated to keep it from becoming public, have been held to violate this rule where they bought or sold securities on the basis of the information.

Persons violating these rules may be subject to criminal penalties. The SEC also may seek an injunction from a federal court ordering the cessation of such prohibited practices. In addition, a civil action may be brought by purchasers or others to recover profits made by use of a deceptive device or inside information.

(2) *Margin, securities exchange, and other rules.* The 1934 Act also regulates margin requirements, *i.e.,* the use of credit in the purchase of securities, and requires certain internal corporate control systems. In addition, it establishes registration procedures for the various securities exchanges, securities brokers and dealers, and brokers' associations, such as the National Association of Securities Dealers. Such exchanges and associations in turn have adopted extensive regulations governing their listed issuers and members.

Other principal securities and similar acts. Various other principal federal acts regulate certain aspects of securities investments. The Investment Company Act of 1940[10] requires enterprises engaged primarily in the business of investing, reinvesting, and trading securities, whose own securities are held by the public, to register with the SEC, to make public certain financial information, and to comply with certain other restrictions.

Similarly, the Investment Advisers Act of 1940[11] requires, with certain exceptions, that individuals or firms engaged for profit in the business of advising others respecting securities transactions must register with the SEC and conform to certain standards designed to protect investors.

The Trust Indenture Act of 1939[12] prohibits the offer of debt securities to the public pursuant to trust indentures under which more than $1 million of securities may be outstanding, unless certain requirements protecting the investors are met. The Public Utility Holding Company Act of 1935[13] specifically regulates the issuance of securities by public utility companies. Finally, the Securities Investor Protection Act of 1970[14] provides for the orderly liquidation of brokerage firms and protection of their customers.

Trading in commodity futures generally is not subject to the securities acts noted above, but is regulated under the Commodity Exchange Act of 1922.[15]

State Regulation

The purchase and sale of securities also is extensively regulated at the state level. State securities regulations vary so widely, however, that the description here can only summarize the principal types of regulation which may be encountered. It should be noted that federal registration provides no general exemption from state securities laws, nor does compliance with one state's laws provide compliance with the requirements of another state where the securities may be issued or traded.

State securities regulation can be divided into three principal categories: (1) requirements — often referred to as Blue Sky laws — that securities be registered or licensed prior to issuance or trading, (2) antifraud provisions, and (3) registration and licensing requirements for certain persons engaged in the securities business. The great majority of states have a combination of all three of these types.

Registration of securities. The type of action required before securities may be issued or traded will vary with the state and with the securities in question. Generally this will involve an application with the Commissioner of Corporations or other appropriate authority, which must include detailed information concerning the business structure of the issuer and its products, past performance, and management, and must be accompanied by supporting documents such as audited financial statements. In certain states, the filing of the registration statement alone is sufficient to commence trading the securities unless the state authority takes affirmative action to stop such trading. In the great majority of states, however, neither sales nor offers of securities may be commenced until permission is obtained from the appropriate authority.

The standard for granting such permission frequently is stated in terms of whether the sale is in the public interest, or is fair, just, and equitable. Accordingly, unlike the case of federal law where *disclosure* is the primary purpose of registration, under most state securities statutes disclosure is merely the first step enabling the state authority to pass judgment on the fairness of the proposed investment.

Most state securities statutes exempt from the registration requirement government securities, short-term commercial paper, bank and trust company securities and, particularly, securities listed on national securities exchanges. In addition, certain types of transactions are exempted, frequently including private resale by an owner of securities, transactions between nonresidents of the state, and purchase or sale of interests in certain partnerships and joint ventures. However, under certain circumstances an alternative authority — for example, the Commissioner of Banking in the case of bank securities, or the Commissioner of Real Estate in the case of real estate ventures — may enforce registration requirements.

Many states now exempt securities issues not involving a public offering, under standards similar to those for the federal 1933 Act exemption described further above. Also exempt may be the issuance of stock in new closely held corporations owned by only a few shareholders, where no public offering is made in connection with the sale and certain restrictions are placed on retransfer of the stock. Generally, however, the issuer must file a notification of the transaction with the appropriate state securities authority, and the stock may not be retransferred without permission from that authority.

Most states also use abbreviated registration procedures for securities registered under federal law, for which the required application is substantially less extensive than otherwise. In addition, no affirmative permission may then be necessary to issue or trade the securities, compliance being automatically obtained upon compliance with federal securities registration law.

Antifraud provisions. Most states have provisions under which fraud in the purchase or sale of securities is made a criminal offense, and the Attorney General or other appropriate authority of the state is given broad powers to investigate suspected fraudulent practices and seek to have them enjoined by court proceeding. Unjustified refusal to cooperate in such an investigation may itself result in criminal penalties.

Fraud is defined quite broadly under such statutes. It generally includes deceptive practices, the making of false statements in the purchase or sale of securities, and violation of any statute relating to the sale of securities, including any federal statute. In addition, persons who purchase securities as a result of such fraudulent practices may recover damages; in certain states, they may recover against a surety bond which must be filed in connection with the sale of securities in the state.

Registration of persons engaged in the securities business. Almost every state requires registration — often with the Commissioner of Corporations — of persons who are engaged in business as brokers or dealers in securities. Applicants generally are required to provide information on their financial responsibility and reputation, plus information concerning the proposed business. Registration may be denied if the regulatory authority determines that the applicant does not meet requirements or that the proposed plan of business is unfair, unjust, or inequitable to the public. Many states also require such safeguards as bonding or minimum capital.

Registrants usually are required to notify the regulatory authority of any subsequent change in the plan or character of the business from that described in the registration application, and to comply with periodic financial reporting and bookkeeping requirements. Registrations generally must be renewed annually on the basis of fairly elaborate renewal applications. The regulatory agency normally is given the power to suspend or revoke the registration of brokers or dealers whose conduct falls short of the statutory requirements.

Many states now regulate not only securities brokers and dealers but also investment advisers, *i.e.*, individuals in the business of advising investors as to securities purchases and sales. By comparison to federal law, state regulation may contain fewer exemptions from this registration.

Antitrust Laws

In the United States, antitrust laws have been enacted largely with the view that enhanced competition will assure efficiency in the allocation of goods and services. The federal government has been more active than the states in enforcing antitrust laws, although state legislation usually also is applicable and the states are becoming more vigorous in this area. The separate area of unfair competition covers other practices viewed as improper in the operation of a business, and primarily is a matter of state law which must be examined specifically where business is to be conducted.

This section focuses on federal antitrust laws and, following a brief summary of the substantive statutes, discusses in light of U.S. judicial decisions interpreting the statutes certain arrangements which generally involve consideration of antitrust prohibitions.

Federal Antitrust Statutes

The principal federal antitrust statutes are the Sherman Act, the Clayton Act, including the Robinson-Patman Act which amended it, and the Federal Trade Commission Act.[16] Two other statutes, the Antitrust Civil Process Act and the Antitrust Procedures and Penalties Act, deal primarily with procedural matters.[17]

The Sherman Act, enacted in 1890, is the oldest of the federal antitrust statutes, and broadly prohibits (1) all contracts, combinations, or conspiracies in restraint of trade or commerce; and (2) monopolization of or attempts to monopolize any portion of interstate trade or commerce. In addition to substantial criminal penalties, goods which are transported interstate pursuant to a contract declared illegal by the act are subject to forfeiture.

The Clayton Act, enacted in 1914, primarily prohibits any of the following where the effect may be substantially to lessen competition or tend to create a monopoly in any line of commerce in any section of the United States: (a) price or related discrimination by the seller between purchasers of goods of like grade and quality, this portion being the Robinson-Patman Act added in 1936; (b) tying of the sale or lease of one product to the purchase of a second product; (c) entry into certain commercial transactions with the condition or understanding that one of the parties will henceforth refuse to deal with a competitor of the other party; and (d) direct or indirect acquisition of the whole or any part of the share capital or assets of one corporation by another corporation. The act grants limited exemptions from the operation of the federal antitrust laws to labor, agricultural, and horticultural organizations created for the mutual help of their members and not conducted for profit — *i.e.,* principally labor unions and agricultural cooperatives.

The Clayton Act also authorizes government and private actions for any antitrust violation. The act provides for injunctions and damages, including recovery by private parties of triple monetary damages, attorneys' fees, and other legal expenses. The government, however, is limited to recovery of actual damages plus costs. Criminal penalties also are possible in certain limited cases.

The Federal Trade Commission Act, also enacted in 1914, establishes the Federal Trade Commission — referred to further above in connection with consumer protection regulations — with broad powers to prohibit individuals, partnerships, or corporations (with certain exceptions) from using unfair methods of competition and unfair or deceptive acts or practices in or affecting commerce. The Commission may order persons to cease and desist from practices violating these prohibitions and, once such an order becomes final, may institute action to collect up to $10,000 for each violation.

Specific Arrangements

Price fixing. Unlike the anticartel laws of many countries, the British Restrictive Trade Practices Act, and the competition law of the European

Economic Community, U.S. antitrust laws as interpreted by judicial decisions make price fixing and similar cartel arrangements unlawful *per se* — *i.e.,* no economic rationale, no matter how persuasive, will justify such an arrangement. This rule applies to all arrangements among competitors which have the purpose *or* effect of directly or indirectly inhibiting price competition. Maximum as well as minimum price arrangements are invalidated. For example, an arrangement whereby large oil refiners undertook to buy and store gasoline offered by smaller producers to stabilize the market price for gasoline has been held a *per se* violation. Even so called fair trade prices mandated by state laws may be invalid.[18]

However, where the purpose is not to affect prices *and* the effect on prices is not the principal effect, courts will determine under what is referred to as the rule of reason whether the anticompetitive effects are outweighed by procompetitive effects. Here a violation will be determined only where the arrangement is significantly and unreasonably anticompetitive in character or effect.

Horizontal market division. Another activity viewed as a *per se* violation is division of a market among competitors. For example, in the leading judicial decision in this area, the U.S. Supreme Court invalidated an arrangement whereby operators of independent supermarket chains entered into a program which utilized, *inter alia,* market division in order to compete more effectively with larger regional and national supermarket chains.[19]

As in the case of price restraints, where market division is neither the purpose of the arrangement *nor* its principal effect, courts will apply the rule of reason to determine whether to prohibit an arrangement. However, if the parties to the arrangement wield substantial power in the relevant market, a *per se* analysis is likely to be applied.

Boycott or concerted refusal to deal. A third activity held to be *per se* illegal is a boycott or concerted refusal to deal. Such a boycott takes place when two or more business enterprises interfere with the essential relationships of competing businesses to force them out of the market. This may occur, for example, by inducing common suppliers not to provide the competing businesses with goods required in their businesses, or by inducing common customers not to purchase from the competing businesses. It is not necessary to show that an intentional boycott will have an adverse effect on competition.[20] Conversely, arrangements which have the principal effect of interfering with the market relationships of competitors, even if not so intended, are *per se* illegal. For example, where an association of retail lumber dealers circulated among its members a list of those wholesalers who engaged in retail sales, from which a wholesaler could have his name removed only on giving assurances that he would discontinue selling at retail, the arrangement was invalidated even though there was no agreement among the retail dealers to boycott wholesalers who were on the list.[21] Furthermore, it is no justification for a boycott that the objects of the boycott also are engaged in wrongful or tortious conduct.[22]

However, not all concerted activity which may exclude certain competitors from a market is *per se* invalid. For example, the rule of reason analysis, rather than the *per se* rule, was applied where a cement manufacturers' association gathered and circulated credit and other information about contractors who purchased cement, even though this prevented certain contractors from having their orders filled.[23]

Other horizontal market arrangements. Various horizontal arrangements among competitors additional to those discussed above have been determined to violate U.S. antitrust laws. For example, an arrangement by several large producers of corrugated industrial containers for the exchange of price information violated Section 1 of the Sherman Act, because this exchange of price information tended to stabilize prices — albeit at a low level — since the industry was dominated by relatively few large firms.[24]

Efforts by various industries to standardize products or terms of trade have likewise been invalidated from time to time.[25] Such standardization is a complex area requiring particularly careful consideration of antitrust issues.

It should be noted that Section 8 of the Clayton Act prohibits interlocking directorships on the boards of competing corporations.

Resale price maintenance. Not only horizontal arrangements among competitors but vertical arrangements between business enterprises at different points in the production and distribution chain may involve antitrust prohibitions. For example, resale price maintenance where the manufacturer or distributor of the product requires businesses further in the distribution chain — generally at the retail level — to sell the product at a set price has been determined to be *per se* illegal, even where the arrangement involved setting a maximum price to be charged by retailers.[26]

On the other hand, merely suggesting the price at which retailers should sell the product, provided no pressure is brought on retailers who refuse to comply with the suggested price, advertising the availability of the product at the suggested price, and printing the suggested price on packages containing the product, all have been permitted.

Territorial resale restrictions. A territorial resale restriction where a business enterprise — generally the manufacturer — permits resale by a business further in the distribution chain — generally a distributor or retailer — only to customers located within a given territory was held just a few years ago to be *per se* unlawful. This rule came under considerable criticism, and in a recent case the U.S. Supreme Court overruled the earlier decision so that such restraints are not now *per se* violations.[27] Nonetheless, courts still may find such arrangements to be in violation of U.S. antitrust laws under the rule of reason in any particular instance where competition is substantially impaired.

Tying arrangements. Tying takes place where the supplier of the tying product — whether goods or services — conditions its sale or lease to customers on the simultaneous purchase or lease of a second tied product. Such an arrangement generally violates U.S. antitrust laws, although the simple existence of a tie is not illegal. Under current judicial interpretation the supplier usually must have significant market power with respect to the tying product, and the market for the tied product must be substantially affected by the tie.[28] Market power in the tying product generally can be shown where the product is patented, copyrighted, or significantly differentiated by potential purchasers from similar products of other suppliers. Proof that commerce in the tied product is affected substantially can include tied sales which are significant in dollar volume, or which constitute a significant portion of sales in the tied product. However, it may be shown that a package of goods and services constitutes a single product, in which case the supplier can insist on selling it as a unit rather than as two or more products.

Special problems arise where the tying product is patented or copyrighted. For example, it is illegal to condition the license of a copyright on acceptance of a license for an additional copyright. Similarly, with certain exceptions, the licensor of a patent may not insist that the patented product be used only in conjunction with other goods manufactured by him, or that the licensee simultaneously purchase a license for other patents as well.[29] In addition, since a patent or copyright is a monopoly granted by the federal government, an attempt at tying may be viewed as an abuse of that monopoly even where an antitrust violation is not involved, and a court may in such event refuse to enforce the license royalty agreement, effectively denying patent or copyright protection.

Certain antitrust aspects particular to license agreements are noted further in Chapter IV respecting licensing activities.

Price discrimination. One of the few specific prohibitions in the federal antitrust statutes is that under the Robinson-Patman Act against price discrimination, as noted further above. Prohibited differences in price may occur even if the monetary price charged is the same, if related allowances or facilities such as delivery terms, return privileges, credit terms, ancillary services, or other significant terms of the two transactions differ. Likewise included are the payment or receipt of price concessions in the form of brokerage commissions, and the provision of services or advertising allowances between purchaser and supplier other than on proportionally equal terms. The law also prohibits the reverse practice where a large purchaser extracts a more advantageous price from suppliers than do its smaller competitors, and purchasers generally are prohibited from inducing suppliers to engage in any prohibited discriminatory pricing practices. The prohibition applies even where the price advantage simply offsets costs of the purchaser in performing functions advantageous to the supplier.[30]

These price discrimination prohibitions apply only to goods and other tangible personal property — intangible property, services, and other products are not covered. Moreover, the two goods sold at different prices must be of like grade and quality and any differences between them must be trivial in nature. A price difference may be justified to the extent it reflects actual cost differences. The supplier also may show that the change in price was in response to changed market conditions between two sales — for example, in order to meet increased competition.

Even where price discrimination exists, if the favored businesses do not thereby enjoy a competitive advantage, such discrimination is not unlawful.[31] The question whether the effect of a particular price discrimination is substantially to lessen competition or tend to create a monopoly, as required by the statute, is perhaps the most difficult issue in this area. Where an enterprise slashes prices drastically (perhaps below costs) in one of its marketing areas to drive local competitors out of business, the law clearly is violated. Where less predatory discrimination results in attracting business away from competitors, generally a further showing either that a significant reduction in the number of sellers has taken place or that the industry has otherwise become more concentrated is required. However, in at least one situation a violation was established merely on the basis of differences in price between markets which were coupled with a general and lasting decline in local price structure.[32]

Acquisitions and mergers. The acquisition of a controlling interest in the assets or shares of a U.S. corporation, whether effected by merger or otherwise, is treated separately in Chapter VII. Accordingly, considerations under Sections 1 and 2 of the Sherman Act, Section 7 of the Clayton Act, and Section 5 of the Federal Trade Commission Act in connection with such an acquisition are discussed at that point, as are the premerger notification requirements of the federal government.

Export trade. Certain exceptions to the application of U.S. antitrust laws involving exports from the United States are discussed in Chapter VIII covering the United States as a base for foreign operations.

Labor Laws

U.S. laws regulating the relationship between an employer and his employees fall roughly into two categories: (1) those regulating the rights of employees to organize and bargain collectively with the employer; and (2) those regulating the wages, terms, and conditions of employment.

Regulation of Labor Organizations and Bargaining

The federal government generally has pre-empted this area so that state regulation is largely precluded. The principal federal labor policy is provided by the National Labor Relations Act (the "NLRA").[33] The NLRA first assures to employees the rights (1) to form, join, or assist labor organizations; (2) to bargain collectively with the employer; and (3) to engage in concerted activity for the purpose of collective bargaining or mutual aid and protection. These rights are discussed in further detail below. In addition, the obligations of the employer under the NLRA are (a) not to interfere with any of the foregoing rights of his employees, and (b) to bargain in good faith with any union which a bargaining unit of his employees designates as its exclusive bargaining representative.

The NLRA also establishes the National Labor Relations Board (the "NLRB") charged with enforcing these rights and obligations. The application of federal labor laws, and hence the jurisdiction of the NLRB, extends to employers engaged in commerce or activities which affect commerce, and all but the smallest employers probably fall within this reach. However, the NLRB may in its discretion refuse to exercise jurisdiction, and in such cases the matter generally is left to state authorities. Where the NLRB exercises jurisdiction, it has broad powers to impose sanctions if it determines that a violation of applicable law constituting an unfair labor practice has occurred. The sanctioned party may obtain review by the federal circuit court in the judicial circuit where the employer is located, and the ruling of this court is subject to discretionary review by the U.S. Supreme Court.

The right to form, join, or assist labor organizations. Unlike the system in many other countries — including Western European nations — where collective bargaining occurs on an industry-wide basis for a large geographical area or the entire country, in the United States collective bargaining often occurs on an individual facility basis. Accordingly, the bargaining unit organizing process by a labor union generally commences when a union representative contacts a business facility's employees to obtain their signatures on union authorization cards which express support for the union. When at least 30% of a proposed unit have so signed, the union may request the NLRB to conduct a certification election by secret ballot to determine whether a majority of the unit wishes the union to represent all employees in the unit exclusively in bargaining with the employer. If two or more unions are involved, the union which obtains a majority of the votes cast becomes the bargaining unit's representative. It should be noted, however, that unions currently represent less than 25% of all U.S. employees and lose more than half of the certification elections.

The goal of the law here is to assure employees' freedom in deciding whether to join the union without coercion from either the employer or the union. Accordingly, during the union organizing process, the employer may not place pressure on employees either to refuse to sign union authorization cards or to vote against the union in the certification election by, for example, interrogating them to determine whether they favor the union or engaging in surveillance to establish which of them are engaged in union support activity. The employer may not increase employee wages and other benefits in response to the organizing effort, since this is economic coercion to vote against the union. The employer may not punish employees who engage in union organizing activity by discharging them, lowering their pay, making their employment unpleasant, or threatening them with reprisals.

On the other hand, both the employer and the union are permitted to inform employees of the disadvantages and advantages of union membership. Accordingly, the employer is free to express to employees his view of unions — for example, that union membership will not be in their interests. He may also inform employees of his rights in dealing with the union, including the right to replace employees who strike at the behest of the union, and of any negative consequences for the business from the union's election so long as such stated consequences are based on facts. He generally may disseminate such information to employees in work areas during working hours, while excluding the union from doing so.

The union similarly is prohibited from placing pressure on employees by, for example, threatening them with physical or economic reprisals for failure to support it. It may disseminate information to employees on the employer's premises through outside organizers only on the same basis as may other persons, so that the employer may not discriminate against union organizers if he permits access to other persons. The union also may distribute literature outside the employer's premises and may establish pickets there carrying union placards, but may not block ingress and egress to the employer's premises in doing so.

In the event of a possible unfair labor practice, the employer, an employee, or the union may seek relief from the NLRB by filing an unfair labor practice charge. If the NLRB makes a factual determination that such a practice has occurred, it may order the offending party to desist from the wrongful activity. It may impose other sanctions as well — for example, set aside the result of a completed certification election where the wrongful conduct may have exerted a decisive influence on the vote and order a rerun election. In cases in which the employer's unfair labor practices are so flagrant that a fair rerun election seems impossible, the NLRB may order the employer to bargain with the union despite the union's election loss.

If the union is certified, it remains the exclusive bargaining representative of the unit unless it is decertified as a result of a similar election procedure. The union also may be challenged periodically by other unions, in which event the unit may elect to keep its current union representation or switch to one of the new unions.

The right to bargain collectively with the employer. Once the union has been certified as the bargaining representative, the employer is required to bargain in good faith with the union as to wages and employment conditions of all employees in the bargaining unit, and may not bargain with individual employees or groups of employees within the unit. The subjects of such collective bargaining fall into three categories: (1) mandatory, (2) permissive, and (3) prohibited. Mandatory subjects of bargaining are wages, hours, and other terms and conditions of employment such as retirement and pension benefits, holidays, work assignments, safety rules, and procedures for settling disputes under the collective bargaining agreement. Permissive bargaining subjects are those more distantly removed from the terms of employment but in which employees nonetheless may have an interest, such as performance bonds, procedures for employee ratification of the collective bargaining agreement and for employee strike votes, union labels on the employer's products, and the size and composition of the supervisory personnel force. The employer cannot be required under the NRLA to negotiate a permissive subject, and may in its discretion refuse to do so. Prohibited bargaining subjects are those that require a party to agree to a provision that is unlawful or repugnant to the policy of the NLRA, and insistence upon such a provision is a violation of the duty to bargain in good faith. Prohibited subjects include, for example, a so called closed shop whereby an individual must be a member of the union before he can be employed, or contractual provisions that discriminate against employees on the basis of race or sex.

During collective bargaining, neither party is required to concede to all of the other's demands. However, each must deal reasonably with the other, make honest attempts to reach compromises, and not make unrealistic offers or refuse to make any concessions. Similarly, a party may not continue shifting positions when agreement is imminent, or engage in other dilatory tactics. A party's failure so to bargain in good faith is an unfair labor practice, and the other party may seek sanctions from the NLRB against the party failing to bargain.

If an impasse occurs despite such good faith, each side also has various economic weapons. The union may call a strike, picket the premises of the employer, and/or call a boycott of the employer's products as discussed further below. On the other hand, the employer may lock out employees. If the union calls a strike, the employer also may hire temporary or permanent replacements as discussed below. Once a bargaining impasse has been reached, the employer also may unilaterally implement its final offer to the union, including increased wages and benefits, even though an agreement has not been reached.

After the execution of the collective bargaining agreement, both sides must deal with each other in good faith in its interpretation and enforcement. The employer's breach of a collective bargaining agreement with respect to a mandatory bargaining subject constitutes an unfair labor practice subject to sanctions by the NLRB. On the other hand, the employer's breach of a contract with respect to a permissive bargaining subject does not constitute an unfair labor practice, although the employer may be sued in court for breach of contract.

Most collective bargaining agreements designate specific procedures for resolving disputes or grievances. If an employee believes the employer has denied him rights under the agreement by, for example, discharging or failing to promote him, a union representative generally will attempt to resolve the grievance informally with the employer's representatives. If this fails, under the agreement the grievance normally proceeds to arbitration by an impartial third party. The parties generally may not bypass arbitration by suing for breach of contract, because courts will not take jurisdiction of matters which the parties have contractually committed to arbitration. Even where the alleged breach also constitutes an unfair labor practice, the NLRB also may leave the resolution to the arbitrator. The prevailing party may obtain enforcement of the arbitrator's decision by an appropriate state or federal court, if the court is satisfied that the arbitrator acted within the authority granted in the agreement.

The right to engage in concerted activity. Employees may act in concert to place economic pressure on the employer to accede to their demands by striking, picketing, and/or inducing a boycott of the employer's products, subject to certain limitations and rules as described briefly below:

(1) *Strikes.* Generally a strike must be directed strictly against the primary employer, the one with whom employees have a dispute, and it is illegal to undertake secondary activity against another person — for example, a supplier, customer, or competitor of the employer — in the hope that the other person will in turn exert economic pressure on the employer. However, if the other person is economically aligned with the employer, or cooperates with the employer in resisting the union, a strike against that person is not prohibited.

A strike must not be violent, as defined rather pragmatically by determining whether physical injury or property damage is likely to result. A sit-down strike where employees occupy the employer's premises and refuse to work or to leave generally is illegal. In addition, the union may not call a strike without having given 60 days' notice to the employer and 30 days' notice to federal and state mediation agencies of its intention to renegotiate an existing collective bargaining agreement, so that the union must attempt negotiation for that period before resorting to a strike.

Likewise the employer may not initiate a lockout during this 60-day period. Partial or intermittent strikes and work slowdowns are unprotected under the NLRA, so that employees are not permitted to stay on the job and disrupt the employer's operations. Strikes to promote featherbedding by forcing the hiring of additional employees who will not perform substantial services are prohibited.

Striking employees generally are not entitled to be paid current wages and benefits by the employer during their strike. However, they are considered to continue as employees during the strike, and afterwards are entitled to be reinstated to their former positions without loss of job seniority or other perquisites *if* their positions are still available. This right to reinstatement continues as long after the strike has ended as a job vacancy occurs and there remains an unreinstated striker qualified to fill it. In this connection, the employer may hire replacements during the strike and generally need not discharge them to make room for striking employees once the strike is over. However, this is not true if the strike is in protest of an unfair labor practice by the employer rather than to place economic pressure on the employer during bargaining, because in that case striking employees are entitled to return to their jobs as soon as they end their strike. It is also an unfair labor practice to discharge striking employees and *then* to hire replacements, because this is viewed as punishment of the striking employees. Any other discrimination against employees on the basis of their participation in a strike also is an unfair labor practice.

All of these rights of employees apply only if the strike has been properly called and the striking employees have not engaged in prohibited or otherwise unprotected activities. For example, if employees walk off their jobs without the union's having given the required 60-day notice or if employees engage in violence, partial strikes, or work slowdowns, such employees may be discharged by the employer.

(2) *Picketing.* Picketing by individuals standing or walking outside the entrances to the employer's premises, generally carrying signs and placards, is permitted for two principal objectives: first, to inform others that the employer is engaged in a labor dispute and attract support for the employees' cause; and second, to induce others — particularly members of labor unions aligned with the union posting the pickets — not to cross the picket line to enter the employer's premises for purchases, deliveries, or performance of work, with resulting detriment to his business.

However, similarly to strikes, secondary picketing is prohibited except against an ally of the employer. In addition, mass picketing whereby individuals are physically constrained from entering the premises and picketing coupled with violence or threats of violence constitute unfair labor practices and are prohibited.

(3) *Boycotts.* Employees may inform the public that the employer is engaged in a labor dispute and attempt to induce the public not to purchase his goods or services. They may also advertise that such goods are being distributed by another person if this does not induce a work stoppage or interfere with deliveries to that person, and may post pickets outside the premises of the second person to inform the public of the boycotted goods if such picketing is not coercive and specifies precisely which goods are being boycotted.

Regulation of Wages and Employment Conditions

Minimum wages and maximum hours. The federal government establishes the minimum wage rate payable to employees by most employers. This currently is $3.35 per hour. In addition, federal law sets the maximum work week in most industries at 40 hours. If an employer wishes to have employees work in excess of 40 hours per week, he must generally pay them at least one and one-half times the wage rate at which they are normally employed. The various exemptions to these provisions include those employed in executive, administrative, and professional capacities, and many small retail establishments whose business primarily is intrastate.[34]

The federal minimum wage and maximum hour laws are pre-emptive in the sense that no state may pass laws setting a lower wage or longer hours. However, states may pass wage and hour standards which are more stringent than the federal. This generally should be investigated with respect to specific professions and classes of employees, such as minors and handicapped persons.

Health and safety conditions. Both the federal and the state governments extensively regulate health and safety conditions in employment. The principal federal statute is the Occupational Safety and Health Act of 1970,[35] which is applicable to all employees engaged in commerce. Regulations under the act set health and safety standards in various occupations, and the U.S. Secretary of Labor or his representative is directed to inspect and investigate places of employment to assure that the standards are met. However, the U.S. Supreme Court has held that the employer may refuse access to his premises unless the inspector has obtained a warrant from an appropriate court.[36]

If a minor violation of the regulations is found, a citation may be issued informing the employer of the nature of the violation and specifying the time allowed to effect a remedy. For more substantial and willful violations, civil and criminal penalties may be imposed. If a violation involves immediate danger of death or serious physical harm to employees, an injunction may be obtained in federal court against continued violation by the employer.

State regulation in this area frequently is more extensive and detailed than federal regulation. Violations may result in criminal and civil penalties, and it is prudent to obtain information on such regulations from the industrial safety board of each state where the enterprise's employees will work.

Employment discrimination. Under federal law, an employer is specifically prohibited from discriminating on the basis of race, sex, religion, or national origin in hiring, in setting compensation, or in establishing other terms, conditions, or privileges of employment.[37] This applies to both overt and covert discrimination. In this regard, courts have defined two types of discrimination: disparate treatment and disparate impact. Disparate treatment involves intentional discrimination and dissimilar treatment for similarly situated employees. Disparate impact involves an apparently neutral practice which is applied equally to all persons regardless of their race, sex, or national origin and which was not designed to discriminate, but nonetheless excludes a materially higher proportion of minorities from employment than nonminorities and cannot be justified as job related and a business necessity.

With respect to religious discrimination, the employer must take reasonable steps to accommodate the religious preferences of employees and normally may not penalize an employee for actions mandated by his religious beliefs — for example, refusing to work during a religious holiday or sabbath.

As to all of the above criteria except race, a narrowly defined exception permits discrimination necessitated by a *bona fide* requirement of the work to be accomplished. For example, a state prison may refuse to hire women as prison guards in male penitentiaries, since in that environment females would be subject to particular danger not applicable to men. On the other hand, a requirement that prison guards be of a minimum height and weight which discriminates heavily against women applicants may be prohibited because no direct relationship has been shown between the ability to perform the duties of a prison guard and such height and weight requirements. Even if an employer can demonstrate an unusually strong customer preference for a person of a certain sex, gender will not therefore be recognized as a *bona fide* occupational qualification.[38]

It should be noted that the U.S. Supreme Court has held that a Japanese owned *U.S.* corporation which discriminates in favor of Japanese nationals in filling managerial positions is *not* completely exempt from the federal ban on national origin discrimination under the U.S. treaty of friendship, commerce, and navigation with Japan. The court did not decide whether the usually narrow exception under federal law for a *bona fide* occupational qualification should be broadened for foreign owned U.S. companies operating under such a treaty and giving a preference in employment to nationals from the owners' home country. A federal circuit court has indicated that even a company organized in Japan may not be exempt from discrimination limits, but noted that the *bona fide* occupational qualification exception may be broadened for such a foreign owned company.[39] Further developments in this area are expected.

An individual who believes he has been subjected to illegal discrimination may apply for relief to the Equal Employment Opportunity Commission, which will investigate and seek to mediate the controversy. If this proves unsuccessful, the employee or the Commission may sue the employer in federal court. If the employer is found to have engaged in prohibited discrimination, he may be ordered to hire, promote, or reinstate the aggrieved individual *and* to pay such compensation as the individual would have earned had the discrimination not taken place. In addition, the court may require the employer to pay the legal expenses of the employee.

Under federal law, an employer may not because of age discharge, refuse to hire, or otherwise discriminate against individuals over 40 years of age but less than 70.[40] This statute is designed particularly to prevent forced retirement of individuals at any age less than 70.

Finally, most states and many local governments have enacted their own antidiscrimination legislation which is often patterned after the federal scheme. In many instances, however, the state or local law is more stringent than federal law. For example, some states prohibit discrimination on the basis of age for all persons over 40, not just those between the ages of 40 and 70. Other state statutes include handicapped individuals as a protected group. An individual in one of these jurisdictions that has local protective legislation may seek relief from illegal discrimination at both the federal and the state or local levels.

Additional employment regulations. Various additional federal and state laws regulate employment terms. For example, if the employer wishes to establish a pension plan for his employees, he must comply with the provisions of the federal Employee Retirement Income Security Act of 1974 as amended by the Multiemployer Pension Plan Amendments Act of 1980.[41] These provisions, *inter alia,* require purchase of insurance from a federal agency to assure the solvency of the plan and, in the case of a multiemployer plan covering, for example, members of a union, may require payment of unfunded pension liabilities even if the employer withdraws from the plan.

State laws may require payment of employee wages no less frequently than, for example, twice a month. They may also limit the term of a labor contract to, for example, seven years. There is a developing trend in many states to restrict the ability of an employer to terminate an employee working without an individual or collectively bargained employment contract by changing the traditional rule that employment is terminable at will to a requirement that there be just cause for termination.[42]

State laws also may substantially limit restrictions which the employer may place on competition by a former employee, even if the employee agrees to such restrictions in writing.

Accordingly, the prospective employer must investigate in detail to ensure compliance with all such special federal and state employment regulations.

Protection of Intellectual Property

In the United States, four types of intellectual property are protected: (1) patents, (2) trade secrets, (3) copyrights, and (4) trademarks and service marks. Patents and copyrights are regulated almost exclusively by federal law, protection of trade secrets is a matter of state law, and trademarks and service marks are regulated by both federal and state law.

Patenting of Inventions

The most complete protection for an invention is that secured by a patent from the U.S. Patent and Trademark Office (the "Patent Office"). Obtaining such a patent may be a complicated, costly, and time consuming process, particularly in light of the requirements for patentability and the procedures discussed below. However, the successful patentee obtains a monopoly on the invention with certain rights against persons who copy the invention without obtaining a license, as also summarized further below.

Requirements for patentability

(1) *Categories of inventions.* The federal Patent Act of 1952 (the "Patent Act") provides that "[w]hoever invents or discovers any new and useful process, machine, manufacture, or composition of matter, or any new and useful improvement thereof, may obtain a patent therefor. . . ."[43] Patents also are available for ornamental designs for manufactured articles and certain narrowly defined categories of plants.[44] Unless an invention can be classified in one of these categories, a patent will be unavailable regardless how novel or useful it may be. While the precise definition of these categories is complicated and will not be attempted here, items *not* patentable include, for example: discoveries of scientific principles and of natural phenomena, such as the use of sulphuric ether as an anesthetic during surgical operations; novel ways of organizing or operating a business; and most computer programs, because they are considered to involve merely common mental steps to perform calculations. However, a composition of matter now can include a micro-organism of artificially modified genetic structure.[45]

(2) *Application by inventor.* If an invention falls within one of the patentable categories, several other requirements must be met before the patent can be obtained. Application for the patent must be filed in the name of the individual who actually conceives the invention, even if he has given up all or part of his rights in the invention or has been hired by another to create the invention. If more than one individual participates in the conception, construction, or testing of the invention, all with an active role in the inventive process must sign the patent application.

(3) *Novelty.* The Patent Act provides a monopoly only for the *first* inventor; thus, it denies a patent either if the invention has been known publicly or used by others in the United States, or if the invention has been patented or described in a printed publication in the United States *or* a foreign country, *before the invention by the patent applicant.*[46] This is referred to as the requirement of novelty. It is quite narrow, because to fail under this standard the invention must have been anticipated by an identical device, not merely one which is a close approximation.

Where two applications are filed claiming the same invention, the Patent Office will undertake what is referred to as an interference proceeding to determine which party first conceived the invention and reduced it to practice. Approximately one in 120-125 patents is engaged in such a proceeding.[47] The first party to file an application, or senior party, is given a substantial procedural advantage since the burden of proof is placed on the second or junior party. For determining such filing priority, the date of filing for a patent in one of certain foreign countries which afford similar privileges for U.S. applications is used, if the U.S. application has been filed within one year after that foreign application.[48]

(4) *Timely application.* The Patent Act also requires timely application; thus, it provides that no patent may be obtained either if the invention has been in public use or sale in the United States, or if the invention has been patented or described in a printed publication in the United States *or* a foreign country, *more than one year prior to the date of the U.S. patent application.*[49] Unlike the novelty requirement, violation of this timeliness requirement may result from action of other inventors *or* of the applicant himself. For example, it is not permissible to accept firm orders for sales of items embodying the invention more than one year prior to application for the patent. However, the inventor need not seek a patent before he is convinced of the efficacy of the invention, and may test an invention including public participation in such testing, may apprise the public that the invention is in development, and may seek to determine who may be interested in purchasing the invention.[50]

Yet another requirement denies a U.S. patent to any person who has obtained a patent in a foreign country prior to application for a U.S. patent, if the foreign patent application was filed more than one year prior to filing the U.S. application.[51] The sum of these two requirements is as follows: (a) application for a foreign patent should if possible not be made more than one year before the date of the U.S. patent application; and (b) if such a foreign application has been made more than one year previously, all measures should be taken to avoid actual issuance of the foreign patent before filing the U.S. patent application.

Finally, if the invention was created in the United States, it is illegal to file a foreign patent application for it prior to applying for a U.S. patent, or within six months after the U.S. application, unless a special license is obtained from the Patent Office.[52]

(5) *Obviousness.* Perhaps the most stringent and yet most nebulous requirement in the Patent Act is that an invention not be obvious to an individual with ordinary skill in the art to which the the subject matter of the patent application pertains at the time the invention was made, because the monopoly granted by the patent system is not available for small and insignificant changes which any competent technician could have devised.[53] Because many inventions with the benefit of hindsight appear obvious, certain collateral factors may be examined in determining obviousness including, *inter alia,* whether substantial efforts have been expended by others unsuccessfully in seeking to solve the same problem and whether the invention has been a commercial success.[54]

(6) *Utility.* As quoted further above from the Patent Act, an invention also must be useful to be patentable. Generally such utility is clear from the nature of the invention. However, this requirement may be applied to deny patentability, for example, for a chemical compound which has no present use. When a use for such an invention is discovered, a use patent probably can be obtained for that specific purpose. In addition, where the invention may only be used for purposes contrary to public health, safety, or morals, a patent will be denied for lack of utility. For example, a machine for producing heroin might fall within this category.

Patent prosecution procedures. An inventor who believes that his invention meets patentability requirements generally consults a patent attorney registered to practice before the Patent Office to undertake a search to determine the state of prior art and assess the likelihood of success of a patent application, and to prepare the application and arrange for preparation of appropriate drawings. The application is filed with the Patent Office, and thereafter the applicant may inscribe the words "Patent Pending" on each item he markets embodying the invention to warn potential imitators that the invention may become subject to U.S. patent protection.

The Patent Office determines — including through any appropriate interference proceeding as noted further above — whether the invention meets the patentability requirements of the Patent Act, and in such event the patent is issued. The average time period for such proceeding is approximately two years, although rule changes to reduce the time and costs are being considered. During that time the Patent Office may request modifications in the patent application to ensure compliance with the Patent Act. If the Patent Office denies a patent, appeal is available in federal courts.

Once the U.S. patent is granted, the patentee should inscribe the patent number on each item he markets embodying the invention, as notice to any who would copy the invention.[55]

Patent rights and remedies. Once a U.S. patent is obtained, the patentee has the exclusive right to make, use, and sell the patented invention in the United States for a period of 17 years, except that a shorter period of up to 14 years applies to a design patent.[56] He may manufacture and sell products using the patented invention, or assign his rights in the patent to another party. Such an assignment must be in writing, and should be recorded with the Patent Office because an unrecorded conveyance is void against a subsequent purchaser who acquires the same rights without notice of the prior assignment.[57]

The patentee also may license others to make, use, and/or sell the patented invention, either exclusively or on a shared basis, in all or parts of the United States. Such arrangements involving patents and other technology are considered in detail in Chapter IV dealing with licensing activities.

If a person produces, uses, or sells an invention subject to a valid patent and neither is the owner of the patent nor has obtained a license for such use, that person may be subjected to a civil action for infringement of the patent by the patentee, his assignees, and/or his licensees.[58] Infringement occurs even where a patent licensee exceeds the terms of his license by, for example, manufacturing more than permitted or selling in a territory not covered by the license. Anyone using a product acquired from an infringer also is an infringer, whether or not the user is aware of the infringement. Any such action must be brought in federal court, and must consider two separate issues: (1) whether the patent is valid, and (2) whether an infringement has occurred.

Every patent issued by the Patent Office is presumed valid,[59] but this may be rebutted by showing that the Patent Office failed to consider fully the state of the relevant art when issuing the patent. While statistics vary depending on the area within the United States where suit is brought, it is fair to say that, of the patents taken through judicial trial, a number approaching (and in certain areas of the country exceeding) one-half are held invalid, many on the issue of obviousness.[60] However, these figures do not reflect the fact that many strong patents go unchallenged or that litigation on patents often is terminated favorably to the patent owner prior to trial.

As to the second question, infringement clearly is established if the accused item is identical to the patented invention. Where the accused item varies in certain respects from the patented one, the original claims of the patent contained in the patent application define the essential elements of the patented invention and delineate the area of potential infringement. Hence, artful drafting of these claims can be crucial to avoid overclaiming which results in invalidation, and underclaiming which makes the patent ineffective to stop infringements.

Upon a determination that the patent is valid and has been infringed, the court may use various remedies such as an injunction against further infringement, compensation for the patent owner's lost profits, requirement of a reasonable royalty for use made of the invention, and in an exceptional case award to the prevailing party of certain legal expenses. However, monetary damages may not be provided for infringements committed more than six years prior to commencement of the infringement suit.[61]

Protection of Trade Secrets

An alternative and increasingly popular means of protecting an invention is to maintain it as a trade secret under state laws rather than obtaining a federal patent for it, due to several reasons. First, unlike patent law which seeks to encourage complete and speedy disclosure of the invention, trade secret laws protect and encourage the secrecy of the invention. Second, the potential subject matter of a trade secret is not as narrowly limited as is the subject matter of a patent and may include, for example, methods of doing business, customer lists, credit ratings, blueprints, architectural plans, tables of data, information regarding manufacturing techniques, and other nonpatentable matters. Because a trade secret need not meet the stringent standard of nonobviousness applicable to a patentable invention, generally any information not publicly known which gives one business enterprise a competitive advantage over another is the proper subject of such a secret. Third, while a U.S. patent allows the inventor precisely 17 years of exclusivity, trade secrets can and have been maintained for hundreds of years.[62] Fourth, protection under trade secret laws avoids the cost, delay, and uncertainty of patent prosecution — which is particularly important where the value of the invention is marginal or its useful life is likely to be short.

There are, however, several drawbacks to reliance on trade secret laws. First, such laws do not protect against independent discovery of the same invention, whereas a patent gives protection even against independent inventors. Second, once the secret is made public, all protection is lost. Accordingly, maintenance of the secret may require restrictions on employees and methods of doing business in order to safeguard the secret, which may interfere significantly with efficient operation of the business. Third, certain inventions by their nature are difficult to maintain as trade secrets. For example, a mechanical device often is easy to subject to reverse engineering to discover its secret, whereas a chemical compound may be difficult.

State tort laws generally give the owner of the trade secret a legal action against (1) persons who disclose the secret without authorization, and (2) persons who take advantage of the secret learned through improper means. For example, the employer who entrusts an employee with the secret may sue the employee if the latter proceeds to manufacture by use of the secret, or discloses the secret to a competitor. Similarly, suit may be brought against a competitor who uses the secret obtained by stealing it or by inducing an employee to disclose it. If the owner's suit is successful, he may obtain monetary damages as well as an injunction to enforce the other party to secrecy. In such a suit the owner generally must show confidential disclosure of the secret with the understanding that it would not be used for other than specific purposes, the fact that the recipient of the secret was not previously aware of it, and an understanding between the parties that the owner would be compensated if the recipient made use of the secret. Accordingly, it is prudent for the owner to secure a written agreement on these matters signed by both parties before a valuable trade secret is disclosed.

Copyrights

The federal Copyright Act (the "Copyright Act") which became effective January 1, 1978, substantially modernized this area by, *inter alia,* incorporating advances of reproduction technology, and federal regulation of copyrights now almost excludes state regulation. More specifically, the Copyright Act protects against copying by unauthorized persons of all "original works of authorship fixed in any tangible medium of expression."[63] These include literary works; musical works including accompanying words; dramatic works including accompanying music; pantomimes and choreographic works; pictorial, graphic and sculptural works; motion pictures; and sound recordings.

Protection under the Copyright Act is acquired by placing all three of the following on every copy of a protectable work published by authority of the copyright owner in the United States or elsewhere: (1) the symbol © , the word "Copyright", or the abbreviation "Copr.";[64] (2) the year of the first publication of the work; and (3) the name of the owner of the copyright.[65] Failure to place these on a published work bars legal action for copyright infringement against any person misled by the omission.

In addition to compliance with marking requirements, it is prudent for the owner to register the copyright immediately with the U.S. Copyright Office in order to obtain statutory damages and other specific rights under the Copyright Act. This is obtained by application to the Register of Copyright including information on the copyright claimant and the work sought to be copyrighted, accompanied by two copies of the best edition of the work. In order to obtain maximum protection under the act, registration should be effected within three months after publication of the work.[66] It should be noted that works first published in or by persons of certain foreign countries which are parties to a convention with the United States enjoy this same U.S. protection as works of U.S. persons first published in the United States.

The copyright vests initially in the author of the work. However, in the case of a work made for hire, the employer or other person who commissioned the work is considered the author unless a contrary written agreement is executed by the parties. Ownership may be transferred in whole or in part by execution of a written instrument, which should be recorded in the Copyright Office to provide constructive notice against a person who subsequently attempts to obtain similar rights from the original copyright owner, and such a transfer or license may be terminated by a similar instrument.[67]

The exclusivity under the Copyright Act continues for the lifetime of the author and for 50 years after his death.[68] However, a U.S. copyright existing at the January 1, 1978, effective date of the new Copyright Act must be renewed during the last year of its original 28-year term, whereupon a further 47-year term will commence; any prior copyright which was already renewed at January 1, 1978, was extended to provide a total of 75 years of protection. In the event of unauthorized use of the work during this period, the copyright owner may institute suit in federal court to recover either actual monetary damages suffered because of the infringement *or* statutory damages. Statutory damages generally range, subject to the discretion of the court, from $250 to $10,000 for each infringement. However, if the infringement is wilful, these damages may range up to $50,000. In addition, an injunction against further infringement and an order for impounding and destruction of any infringing copies of the work may be obtained. The court also may order the infringer to pay the legal expenses of the copyright owner. Finally, wilful infringement of a copyright for purposes of commercial advantage or private financial gain is a criminal offense punishable by a fine of up to $10,000 and/or imprisonment for up to one year. However, any such civil *or* criminal action must be commenced within three years after the date of infringement.[69]

Trademarks and Service Marks

Both the federal government and the states protect the use of trademarks. In general, a trademark consists of either words or symbols which by repetitive or constant use and/or through advertising have become associated in the minds of the public with the particular business enterprise, so that use of the same mark by other businesses would create confusion as to the source of the goods. Parallel protection is afforded by the federal government and by many states to a business enterprise which does not produce goods but instead dispenses services, for the exclusive use of any service mark readily identified with its services. The protection afforded by these laws varies in large measure with the nature of the mark itself because generally a fanciful, nondescriptive mark is more readily associated with only one business than a descriptive one. For example, "General Foods" must compete for the public's attention in substantially the same market with "General Mills" and "Best Foods."

Once in use within a particular state, a trademark and often a service mark may be registered with the appropriate state authority, generally the Secretary of State. Such registration statutes vary significantly from state to state, as do the protection given marks and the remedies against infringers, and the applicable law in each state where marked goods or services are to be marketed should be examined.

A trademark used on goods in interstate or foreign commerce also may be registered with the Patent Office under the federal Lanham Act of 1946.[70] The application must contain a description of the mark, state the types of goods as to which it is used, specify the date when it was first used in interstate or foreign commerce, and be accompanied by a drawing of the mark and the appropriate application fee. The registration remains in force for 20 years and may be renewed for like periods. Any mark consisting of words, pictures, or a combination of both may be registered unless it contains one or more of the following: (1) matter which is immoral, deceptive, or scandalous, or which disparages or falsely suggests a connection with individuals, living or dead, institutions, beliefs, or national symbols, or brings them into contempt or disrepute; (2) the flag of the United States or of any state or subdivision thereof or of a foreign country, or the coat of arms or insignia of the same; (3) the name, image, or identifying signature of any living individual without his consent, or the portrait of a deceased President of the United States during the life of his widow without her written consent; (4) matter which so resembles a mark previously registered or in use by another person that it is likely to cause confusion or to deceive the public with respect to the origin of the goods of the applicant; (5) matter which is merely descriptive, or is misdescriptive of the goods; (6) matter which is merely geographically descriptive of the origin of the goods; or (7) a word which is primarily merely a surname. However, a mark falling within one or more of the last three of these exclusions may nonetheless be registered, if it is shown to have become distinctive of the applicant's goods in commerce.

Federal trademark registration is desirable for several reasons. First, such registration provides constructive notice throughout the entire United States that the mark is claimed by the applicant. Second, the federal registrant has the option of bringing an infringement suit in either federal or state court, whereas if no federal registration is effected, such a suit must be brought if at all in state court. Similarly, other rights available to a federal registrant differ from those available under many state laws and in certain respects can be broader. Third, a mark registered with the Patent Office may then be registered fairly readily in many foreign countries, while state registration does not confer this benefit. Fourth — as noted further in Chapter V below dealing with import activities — most federally registered trademarks also may be filed with the U.S. Department of the Treasury to cause the Customs Service to prevent importation of goods bearing infringing marks.

A trademark or service mark may be assigned or licensed by its owner. However, care must be taken that actual use in commerce is not discontinued, because the mark then may be considered abandoned and any rights in it to have ceased. Registration of a mark also must be renewed occasionally. For example, in the case of federal trademark registration it is necessary six years after issuance to file with the U.S. Commissioner of Patents and Trademarks an affidavit stating that the mark has continued in use.

If a registered mark is infringed, remedies under state laws may vary. In the case of a federally registered trademark, the court is empowered under federal law to issue an injunction against further infringement, order destruction of any infringing marks still in the infringer's possession, and require the infringer to pay monetary damages to the owner of the mark.

General Regulation of Foreign Investments

Federal Regulation

Unlike most countries, the United States generally does not regulate investments from abroad. However, under the federal Foreign Assets Control Regulations pursuant to the Trading with the Enemy Act, all U.S. investments and other transactions with persons of certain listed countries require licenses from the U.S. Department of the Treasury. The federal Alien Property Custodian Regulations under the same act also provide that, in time of declared war with any country, the U.S. property of persons of that country will vest in a federal official. Alternatively, foreign owned U.S. assets may be blocked or frozen for a period (without changing their ownership) by the President either in time of war under the same act, or in the absence of war under the International Emergency Economic Powers Act of 1977 subject to the provisions of the National Emergencies Act. Accordingly, foreign investors residing or organized in countries which may become hostile to the United States may wish to consider the use of trusts or other methods to ensure the transfer of U.S. assets to neutral or friendly persons.[71]

Major investments by foreign governments or others having substantial implications for U.S. national interests also are reviewed — but cannot be prohibited — by an interagency Committee on Foreign Investment which is chaired by the Department of the Treasury. This committee likewise monitors foreign investment trends in the United States.[72] Restrictions on investments or activities abroad by U.S. enterprises — for example, in Canada and Japan — also occasionally have prompted discussions of possible restrictions on U.S. investments or imports from such countries.

In this connection, it should be noted that a foreign national (but not a lawfully admitted resident alien) is prohibited from making campaign contributions to a candidate for U.S. political office.[73]

Any general federal restriction on foreign investments may be limited by equal protection, due process, and other rights under the U.S. Constitution. However, these are more likely to benefit individual employees and other persons lawfully present within the United States, rather than nonresident alien individuals and foreign legal entities.

Any such federal restriction also may be subject to treaty rights of foreign persons from specific countries under, for example, a treaty of friendship, commerce, and navigation which grants such persons the right to invest or engage in business on the same basis as U.S. persons, or which grants such rights as are afforded the most favored nationals of any other country.[74]

In spite of the absence of broad federal regulation of foreign investments, substantial federal reporting requirements generally apply in connection with such investments. These are discussed in Chapter XII. Furthermore, general federal and state taxation of foreign persons, as described separately in Chapter II, may require annual or more frequent tax returns and related reporting.

State Regulation

The principal general state law restrictions affecting equally al investments from abroad are those on *inheritance* by foreign persons. These not only may limit foreign acquisition of U.S. investments by inheritance, but may discourage U.S. investment by any nonresident alien individual who may wish to bequeath his holdings to other foreign persons. Such state restrictions may be divided into two principal categories: (1) those which prohibit inheritance in case of local judicial determination that the heir's country will deprive him of his inheritance (potentially applicable especially to communist controlled countries) — such as Connecticut, Massachusetts, New Jersey, New York, and Wisconsin; and (2) those that prohibit inheritance in case of a determination that the heir's country would not reciprocally permit a U.S. person to inherit from one of its own domiciliaries — such as Montana, Nebraska, Nevada, North Carolina, Oklahoma, and Wyoming. A few states impose other inheritance restrictions — for example, Kansas requires that an alien heir be eligible for U.S. citizenship. On the other hand, various state statutes provide that, if a general state restriction on foreign ownership of particular property applies, a foreign heir nevertheless will have a substantial period to dispose of the property.[75] The U.S. Supreme Court has invalidated the application of such an Oregon inheritance statute where the state court commented critically on the political system of the foreign country involved. However, generally this has not been interpreted to invalidate the application of existing state foreign deprivation and reciprocity statutes which are limited to a mechanical reading of foreign law.[76]

Additional types of general state restrictions on foreign investments (with the exception primarily of real estate and natural resource restrictions which are discussed specifically in Chapter III) often have been invalidated or subjected to narrow judicial interpretation under the equal protection clause of the Fourteenth Amendment, or the foreign relations and other provisions of the U.S. Constitution. State laws distinguishing between alien individuals (particularly nonresident aliens) and citizens as to local government employment and similar personal service activities — while subject to close judicial scrutiny under the equal protection clause — often are upheld as serving a compelling public purpose. However, state discrimination against foreign investments — particularly such restrictions that are newly put in place — may run afoul of the exclusive federal power to conduct U.S. foreign relations.[77] General state law restrictions on foreign investments also may be specifically invalidated by the federal Civil Rights Act of 1964[78] if based on race or national origin.

As noted above in connection with federal restrictions, any state inheritance or other types of restrictions on foreign investments also may be modified or invalidated by treaty rights of foreign persons from specific countries.

Special Rules

In addition to the general requirements above, special federal and state regulation of foreign investments in U.S. agricultural and other real estate and natural resources is discussed in Chapter III. Special national limitations on imports are covered in Chapter V. Foreign investment limitations in certain industries and other selected aspects of new U.S. business enterprises are discussed in Chapter VI. Special additional reporting in connection with foreign investments in real estate and certain industries is covered in Chapter XII.

Footnotes to Chapter I

1. *See generally* Uniform Partnership Act.
2. *See generally* Uniform Limited Partnership Act.
3. *See generally* Model Business Corporation Act.
4. *See generally* I.R.C. Subtitles A, C, especially §§1, 11, 3451 *et seq.;* Economic Recovery Tax Act of 1981, Pub. L. 97-34, 95 Stat. 172 (Aug. 13, 1981); Tax Equity and Fiscal Responsibility Act of 1982, Pub. L. 97-248 (Sept. 3, 1982).
5. *See generally* I.R.C. Subtitle B, especially §§2001-2057, 2201-2209, 2501-2622; I.R.C. §1023.
6. Pub. L. 96-223 (Apr. 2, 1980), 94 Stat. 229; Pub. L. 96-510 (Dec. 11, 1980), 94 Stat. 2767.
7. 35 Fed. Reg. 15623; *see, e.g.,* National Environmental Policy Act of 1969, 42 U.S.C. §§4321 *et seq.*; Environmental Quality Improvement Act of 1970, 42 U.S.C. §§4371 *et seq.*; Fair Credit Reporting Act of 1970, 15 U.S.C. §§1681 *et seq.*; Truth in Lending Regulations, 12 C.F.R. Part 226; 15 U.S.C. §§2301 *et seq.* The increasingly controversial area of nuclear power and materials is governed substantially by the Nuclear Regulatory Commission. *See, e.g.,* 42 U.S.C. §§5841 *et seq.*
8. 15 U.S.C. §§77a-77aa.
9. 15 U.S.C. §§78a-78hh.
10. 15 U.S.C. §§80a-I through 80a-52.
11. 15 U.S.C. §§80b-1 through 80b-21.
12. 15 U.S.C. §§77aaa-77bbbb.
13. 15 U.S.C. §§79-79b.
14. 15 U.S.C. §§78aaa-78*lll*.
15. 7 U.S.C. §§1 *et seq.*
16. 15 U.S.C. §§1-7, 12-27, 41-58.
17. 15 U.S.C. §§1311-1314; 15 U.S.C. §§1-3, 16, 28, 29; 47 U.S.C. §401; 49 U.S.C. §§43-45.
18. *See* United States v. Socony-Vacuum Oil Co., 310 U.S. 150 (1940); Consumer Goods Pricing Act of 1975, Pub. L. 94-145 (Dec. 12, 1975), 89 Stat. 101.
19. United States v. Topco Assocs., 405 U.S. 596 (1972).
20. *See* Klor's Inc. v. Broadway-Hale Stores, Inc., 359 U.S. 207 (1959).
21. Eastern States Retail Lumber Dealers' Ass'n v. United States, 234 U.S. 600 (1914).
22. *See* Silver v. New York Stock Exch., 373 U.S. 341 (1963); Fashion Originator's Guild of America v. F.T.C., 312 U.S. 457 (1941).
23. Cement Mfrs.' Protective Ass'n v. United States, 268 U.S. 588 (1925).
24. United States v. Container Corp. of America, 393 U.S. 333 (1969).
25. *See, e.g.,* Milk & Ice Cream Can Inst. v. F.T.C., 152 F. 2d 478 (7th Cir. 1946); Bond Crown & Cork Co. v. F.T.C., 176 F. 2d 974 (4th Cir. 1949); National Macaroni Mfrs.' Ass'n v. F.T.C., 345 F. 2d 421 (7th Cir. 1965); Paramount Famous Lasky Corp. v. United States, 282 U.S. 30 (1930); United States v. First Nat'l Pictures, Inc., 282 U.S. 44 (1930).
26. *See, e.g.,* Albrecht v. Herald Co., 390 U.S. 145 (1968); Keifer-Stewart Co. v. Seagram & Sons, Inc., 340 U.S. 211 (1951); Dr. Miles Medical Co. v. John D. Park & Sons Co., 220 U.S. 373 (1911).
27. United States v. Arnold, Schwinn & Co., 388 U.S. 365 (1967), *overruled by* Continental T.V., Inc. v. G.T.E. Sylvania, Inc., 433 U.S. 36(1977).
28. *See* United States v. Loew's, Inc., 371 U.S. 38 (1962); Fortner Enterprises, Inc. v. United States Steel Corp., 394 U.S. 495 (1969).
29. *See, e.g.,* Zenith Radio Corp. v. Hazeltine Research, Inc., 395 U.S. 100 (1969); United States v. Paramount Pictures, Inc., 334 U.S. 131 (1948); Morton Salt Co. v. G. S. Suppiger Co., 314 U.S. 488 (1942). *But see, e.g.,* Dehydrating Process Co. v. A. O. Smith Corp., 292 F. 2d 653 (1st Cir. 1961), *cert. denied,* 368 U.S. 931 (1961).
30. *See* Mueller Co. v. F.T.C., 323 F. 2d 44 (7th Cir. 1963), *cert. denied,* 377 U.S. 923 (1964).
31. *See* Minneapolis-Honeywell Regulator Co. v. F.T.C., 191 F. 2d 786 (7th cir. 1951), *cert. dismissed,* 344 U.S. 206 (1952).
32. *See, e.g.,* Moore v. Mead's Fine Bread Co., 348 U.S. 115 (1954); Utah Pie Co. v. Continental Baking Co., 386 U.S. 685 (1967).
33. 29 U.S.C. §§151 *et seq.*
34. *See generally* 29 U.S.C. §213.
35. 29 U.S.C. §§651-678.
36. Marshall v. Barlow's, Inc., 436 U.S. 307 (1978).
37. 42 U.S.C. §§2000e through 2000e-17; *see also* 29 U.S.C. §206(d) (Equal Pay Act prohibiting

sex discrimination in wages for equal work); 42 U.S.C. §1981 (prohibiting race discrimination). Additionally, certain federal contractors or recipients of federal funds have affirmative obligations to women and minorities, pursuant to Executive Order 11246, 41 C.F.R. §§60-2.1 *et seq.*, and to handicapped persons and Vietnam era veterans pursuant to the Rehabilitation Act of 1973, 29 U.S.C. §§701 *et seq.*, and the Vietnam Era Veterans' Readjustment Assistance Act, 38 U.S.C. §§2011-2014, respectively.

38. *See* Dothard v. Rawlinson, 433 U.S. 321 (1977); Fernandez v. Wynn Oil Co., 653 F. 2d 1273 (9th Cir. 1981).

39. Sumitomo Shoji America, Inc. v. Avagliano, 50 U.S.L.W. 4643 (U.S. Sup. Ct. 1982), *rev'g* 638 F.2d 552 (2d Cir. 1981); *see also* Spiess v. C. Itoh & Co. (America), Inc., 643 F.2d 353 (5th Cir. 1981).

40. 29 U.S.C. §§621-634.

41. 29 U.S.C. §§1001 *et seq.*

42. *Cf.* California, Illinois, New Hampshire.

43. 35 U.S.C. §101.

44. 35 U.S.C. §§161, 171.

45. *See, e.g.,* Morton v. New York Eye Infirmary, 17 Fed. Cases 879 (S.D.N.Y. 1862); Gottschalk v. Benson, 409 U.S. 63 (1972); Diamond v. Chakrabarty, 447 U.S. 303 (1980).

46. 35 U.S.C. §102(a).

47. A. Seidel, *What the General Practitioner Should Know About Patent Law and Practice* 71(3rd Ed. 1975).

48. 35 U.S.C. §119; *see also* Patent Cooperation Treaty, Pub. L. 94-131 (Nov. 14, 1975), 89 Stat. 685 (entered into force January 24, 1978). These countries include, *inter alia,* Algeria, Argentina, Australia, Austria, the Bahamas, Belgium, Benin, Bolivia, Brazil, Bulgaria, Cameroon, Canada, Central African Republic, Chad, Costa Rica, Cuba, Cyprus, Czechoslovakia, Denmark, Dominican Republic, Ecuador, Egypt, Estonia, Finland, France, Gabon, Federal Republic of Germany, German Democratic Republic, Ghana, Greece, Guatemala, Haiti, Honduras, Hungary, Iceland, Indonesia, Iran, Iraq, Ireland, Israel, Italy, Ivory Coast, Japan, Jordan, Kenya, Korea, Latvia, Lebanon, Liechtenstein, Luxembourg, Malagasy, Malawi, Malta, Mauritania, Mauritius, Mexico, Monaco, Morocco, Nauru, the Netherlands, New Zealand, Nicaragua, Niger, Nigeria, Norway, Papua New Guinea, Paraguay, the Philippines, Poland, Portugal, Romania, San Marino, Senegal, South Africa, Spain, Sri Lanka, Sweden, Switzerland, Syrian Arab Republic, Togo, Trinidad and Tobago, Tunisia, Turkey, Uganda, U.S.S.R., United Kingdom, United Republic of Tanzania, Upper Volta, Uruguay, Vatican City, Vietnam, Western Samoa, Yugoslavia, Zaire, Zambia, and Zimbabwe.

49. 35 U.S.C. §102(b).

50. *See, e.g.,* City of Elizabeth v. Nicholson Pavement Co., 97 U.S. 126 (1877).

51. 35 U.S.C. §102(d).

52. 35 U.S.C. §§184-186.

53. 35 U.S.C. §103.

54. *See, e.g.,* Graham v. John Deere Co., 383 U.S. 1 (1966).

55. 35 U.S.C. §287.

56. 35 U.S.C. §§154,173, 271(a). Unlike certain other countries, the United States does not require the payment of a tax to maintain the life of the patent.

57. 35 U.S.C. §261.

58. 35 U.S.C. §281.

59. 35 U.S.C. §282.

60. *See* Comment, "A Market-Oriented Revision of the Patent System," 21 U.C.L.A. L. Rev. 1042, 1061-1063 (1974).

61. *See generally* 35 U.S.C. §§283-286.

62. The formula for Smith's black coughdrops apparently is over 100 years old; the secret metallurgical process used to manufacture the best grade of cymbals has been kept a secret in the same family for centuries. A. Seidel, *supra* note 47, at 134.

63. 17 U.S.C. App. §102(a). This may prohibit videotape copying even for home and other personal use, although legislation may clarify an exemption for such use. *See* Universal City Studios, Inc. v. Sony Corp. of America, 659 F.2d 963 (9th Cir. 1981).

64. If the copyrighted work is a phonorecord, the symbol Ⓟ must be used instead. *See* 17 U.S.C. App. §402(b).

65. 17 U.S.C. App. §401(b). In addition, it is the responsibility of the copyright owner to deposit two copies of the best edition of the work with the U.S. Library of Congress within three months after

publication. However, this deposit requirement is expressly excluded as a condition of copyright protection. 17 U.S.C. §407.

66. *See* 17 U.S.C. App. §§408-409, 411-412; Universal Copyright Convention. Two copies of the best edition of the work must accompany the application only for a work first published in the United States. For an unpublished work, or a work first published outside the United States, only a single such copy need be submitted.

67. *See* 17 U.S.C. App. §§201, 203-205.

68. 17 U.S.C. App. §302(a). This period applies to works created after January 1, 1978, and only to those which are not anonymous or pseudonymous; somewhat different time limits are provided for other works. *See* 17 U.S.C. App. §§302-304.

69. *See* 17 U.S.C. App. §§502-507.

70. 15 U.S.C. §§1051 *et seq.* Several trademark conventions also apply.

71. *See* 50 U.S.C. App. §§1-44; 50 U.S.C. §§1601-1706; 31 C.F.R. Parts 500, 515, 520, 530; 8 C.F.R. Parts 501-510. The countries requiring licenses under the Foreign Assets Control Regulations currently include Cambodia, Cuba, North Korea, North and South Vietnam, and the People's Republic of China. However, the President of the United States announced that effective January 1, 1979, the United States recognized the government of the People's Republic of China as the sole legal government of China, an Agreement on Trade Relations was negotiated betweeen the two countries in July 1979, and the Department of the Treasury has unblocked U.S. assets of that government and its nationals. *Cf.* Memorandum of Dec. 30, 1978, 44 Fed. Reg. 1075; Proclamation 4697, 44 Fed. Reg. 61161 (1979). Unofficial relations are maintained between Taiwan and the United States through the American Institute in Taiwan. Taiwan Relations Act of 1979, Pub. L. 96-8 (Apr. 10, 1979) , 93 Stat. 14. In addition, special restrictions on transactions with Iran and property of the Iranian government were adopted in early 1980. *See* E.O. 12205, 3 C.F.R. 248 (1980); 31 C.F.R. Part 535.

For discussion of certain U.S. asset transfer techniques in light of U.S. blockage or vesting risks, *see* W. Knight, Jr., " 'Failsafe' Legal Structures to Protect U.S. Assets of Foreign Investors," 9 Int'l Bus. Lawyer 109 (1981).

72. E.O. 11858, 3 C.F.R. 990 (1971-1975 compilation).

73. 2 U.S.C. §441e. However, a U.S. subsidiary corporation of a foreign corporation may continue to maintain a political action committee with contributions from U.S. nationals, or may contribute to state and local election campaigns, if no foreign national directs such decisions. Furthermore, a U.S. incorporated trade association apparently may maintain a separate campaign fund out of its general revenues, even if its members include foreign persons. *See* Fed. Elections Comm'n Advisory Opinions 1978-21, 1980-111, 1982-10.

74. *Cf.* United States-Argentina Treaty of Friendship, Commerce and Navigation of 1853, Art. IX; United States-Saudi Arabia Treaty of General Relations of 1933, Art. II. The multilateral Code of Liberalization of Capital Movements adopted by the Organization for Economic Cooperation and Development, of which the United States is a member, does not provide for mandatory rules. *See, e.g.,* G. Baldwin, "Protection of the Property and Person of the Foreign Investor," in *Current Legal Aspects of Foreign Investment in the United States* (Am. Bar Ass'n 1976); W. Grimes & P. Williams, "Limitations Imposed by the Constitution and Treaties of the United States on the Treatment of Foreign Direct Investment," in *Foreign Investment in the United States* (D.C. Bar Ass'n 1980).

75. *See, e.g.,* F. Morrison, "Limitations on Alien Investment in American Real Estate," 60 Minn. L. Rev. 621, 637-638 (1976); N. Sommerfeld, "State Laws Affecting Inheritance by and Distributions to Aliens of U.S. Assets from U.S. Estates," in *International Estate Planning* (Am. Bar Ass'n 1980).

76. *See* Zschernig v. Miller, 389 U.S. 429 (1968); F. Morrison, *supra* note 75, at 646-650; W. Weber, "Foreign Direct Investment in United States Real Estate: Xenophobic or Principled Reaction?" 28 U. Fla. L. Rev. 491, 515-516 (1976).

77. *See, e.g.,* Ambach v. Norwick, 441 U.S. 68(1979) (state law limiting public school teacher certificates to U.S. citizens or those who have applied for U.S. citizenship upheld under exception of greater latitude for state in the case of certain governmental positions); Sugarman v. Dougall, 413 U.S. 634(1973) (flat ban on aliens holding permanent positions in state civil service violates equal protection clause); G. Baldwin, *supra* note 74; W. Grimes & P. Williams, *supra* note 74; J. Meschke, "U.S. Constitutional and Federal Laws and Regulations Affecting Alien Ownership of U.S. Property," in *International Estate Planning* (Am. Bar Ass'n 1980).

78. Pub. L. 88-352 (July 2, 1964), 78 Stat. 255. However, with respect to discrimination based generally on alienage, *see, e.g.,* 42 U.S.C. §2000e-1.

Chapter II

U.S. Taxation of Foreign Investors

This chapter describes principally the special U.S. federal income tax regime for nonresident alien individuals, foreign corporations, and other foreign persons, and the U.S. federal gift and estate tax regime for nonresident aliens. These include references to certain rules respecting tax withholding and reporting, specific business enterprises conducted by foreign persons, and tax treaties. Certain aspects of state and local taxation relevant to such foreign persons also are noted.

Taxation of U.S. Source Nonbusiness Income

The United States generally taxes on a current basis the worldwide income of U.S. corporations, citizens and resident aliens, and other domestic persons as described in Chapter I. However, under the Foreign Investors Tax Act of 1966, in the case of a foreign person's income which is not effectively connected with the conduct of a trade or business within the United States — or, if a U.S. income tax treaty applies, not attributable to a U.S. permanent establishment — ("non-effectively connected income"), the sole bases of federal taxation are the U.S. source and the specific class of that income.[1] For example, both the receipt of a dividend from a U.S. corporation and the sale of goods where title passes within the United States may be taxed by the United States on the basis of the U.S. source of the income. The United States, however, generally restricts taxation of U.S. source non-effectively connected income to classes of such income which may be described as fixed or periodic. For example, dividends, interest, rents, royalties, and other fixed or periodic payments are subject to tax. Such taxable fixed or periodic income also may include certain distributions from estates or trusts, alimony payments, distributions of the value of a life insurance policy, regular commission payments, and the like. On the other hand, the occasional — *i.e.*, sporadic — sale of goods into the United States or the sale of U.S. nonbusiness assets by a foreign seller ordinarily is not subject to tax.

The statutory rate of tax on such income — subject to modification by a tax treaty if applicable — generally is 30% of the gross payment. This tax must be withheld by the last custodian of the income — *i.e.,* the withholding agent or agents — and paid over to the U.S. Internal Revenue

Service periodically. The foreign recipient generally is not required to file a federal tax return with respect to such income, unless he wishes to claim a tax refund. The liability to withhold income tax on certain items paid to or accrued by a foreign person is a separate liability from that of the owner of the income; the tax itself still is imposed on the owner. For example, if a U.S. payor owes $100 in interest to a nonresident alien lender and the U.S. payor contracts to assume the expenses of the U.S. withholding tax, then his combined payments to the lender and the federal government will be almost $143 rather than $130, since the tax is 30% of the total or grossed up amount taxable to the foreign lender.

Dividends and Interest

The receipt of a dividend out of current or accumulated earnings and profits of a U.S. corporation by a foreign person — if non-effectively connected income — generally is taxable at the statutory rate of 30% of the gross payment, unless this rate is modified by a tax treaty. The statutory rate is the same regardless of whether the dividend is paid to a person who holds one share of the corporation or to a 100% owner of the corporation, although under tax treaties lower rates may be provided for owners of higher percentages — for example, 90% or greater — of the corporation.[2] In that case, the corporation itself is a withholding agent. However, this tax does not apply to a dividend from a U.S. corporation if no more than 20% of its gross income during the most recent three full taxable years is from U.S. sources.

The United States also usually imposes this tax on a portion of each dividend even from a *foreign* corporation, if at least one-half of its gross income for the most recent three full taxable years is effectively connected income. This portion is the same fraction of each dividend as the effectively connected income is of the total gross income of the corporation. For example, in the case of a foreign corporation of which 80% of the gross income is derived from the conduct of a U.S. branch business, 80% of each dividend will be subject to U.S. withholding tax at the 30% rate. This tax, however, frequently is eliminated under tax treaties.[3]

The payment of interest to a person that is both a shareholder and a creditor of the corporation also may be characterized as a dividend when the corporation is thinly capitalized — *i.e.,* has little equity capital in proportion to its debt — especially if the debt to shareholders is substantially proportionate to their respective equity holdings in the corporation. Thin capitalization regulations defining whether corporate debt owed to shareholders is characterized as equity for federal income tax purposes may become effective during 1983 unless further postponed. These regulations have excluded international transactions involving debt owed to or from a foreign person; however, it seems likely that similar standards will be applied to such international loans, especially where a person subject to U.S. income tax is the borrower. Special exclusions also may be adopted for smaller businesses.[4]

The payment of loan guaranty fees or management service fees to a shareholder may be characterized as a dividend when the amounts are excessive or unnecessary, and the payment of royalties to a shareholder may be so characterized when the royalty computation is related more to net corporate earnings than to the arm's length value of the right on which the royalty has been based. In such event, not only will the withholding tax on a dividend be imposed, but the deduction for the payment by the corporation will be disallowed because dividends are not deductible.

It should also be noted that, for federal income tax purposes, the amount of a distribution of property other than money to a foreign corporate *or* noncorporate shareholder, if non-effectively connected income to the shareholder, is the fair market value of the property.[5]

Interest paid by a U.S. borrower — if non-effectively connected income — is taxable at the same 30% statutory rate, with the borrower being the withholding agent. The tax rate frequently is lowered in tax treaties — at times to zero.[6] There also are certain exceptions to the tax, largely for reasons of U.S. economic policy. For example, interest income received by a foreign person from deposits in a U.S. bank account ordinarily is not treated as U.S. source income. Nor is interest paid by a U.S. corporation which derives no more than 20% of its gross income from U.S. sources for the most recent three full taxable years.

Similarly to dividends, a portion of interest payments even by a *foreign* corporation may be subject to this U.S. tax, if at least one-half of its gross income for the most recent three full taxable years is effectively connected income, unless the tax is eliminated under a tax treaty.

A principal difficulty with respect to interest is the definition of the term. For example, deferred payments for purchase of property generally must bear minimum interest, or a portion of each installment payment will be treated as interest. Likewise, the purchase by a foreign person of a bond issued by a U.S. borrower for a term of more than six months at an original issue discount price may be treated as payment of interest in the amount of the discount because the discount represents a financing charge to be spread over the term of the bond under quite complicated rules.[7]

It should be noted that the exemption of bank deposit interest, and any treaty reductions in U.S. withholding taxes on other interest and dividends, override the general 10% federal withholding tax on such payments to an individual (domestic or foreign).[8]

Rents and Royalties

Rents, royalties, and similar payments which are non-effectively connected income are taxed at the same 30% statutory rate, unless reduced by tax treaty, although such payments quite commonly are effectively connected income of the recipient and so are taxed instead as described further below. However, there are important distinctions in determining the source of such a payment. In the case of a royalty for the use of intangible property — for example, patent rights, copyrights, secret industrial processes, and trade names — the source of the payment is the country where the property is used, *not* the location of the obligor or the place where the royalty agreement was executed. Royalties from U.S. mineral and other natural resource interests are considered U.S. source income. These payments also are subject to withholding by the payor — usually the lessee or licensee — even if the payor is a foreign person.[9]

In certain cases, it may be difficult to determine the nature of the payment. For example, if a foreign person enters into a partnership in the United States involving leasing of mineral rights, payments to the investor may under various circumstances be characterized as partnership business income, royalty payments, or fees for services. Each of these alternatives involves different source of income rules and possible U.S. tax rates. Tax treaties may furnish special guidance — for example, under certain treaties, equipment leasing income or film rentals constitute business income as opposed to rent or other periodic income.[10]

Personal Services Income

Income from personal services performed by a foreign person within the United States generally is treated as effectively connected income, but usually still carries a withholding responsibility for the payor. In the case of a nonresident alien employee, this is similar to that for U.S. employees' wage withholding; in the case of an independent contractor, this is a flat 30%. However, a statutory exclusion from tax applies if the services are performed by a nonresident alien for a *foreign* person not engaged in U.S. business (or a *foreign* office of a U.S. person), the earned amount during the taxable year does not exceed $3,000, and the individual is not present in the United States during the taxable year for more than 90 days. These limits frequently are increased or removed by tax treaties. Furthermore, an annuity paid to a nonresident alien from a U.S. qualified tax deferred pension or annuity plan may be subject to a 30% withholding tax on the annuity investment income, unless a tax treaty or statutory rule exempts the payment.[11]

Even the treaty exclusions ordinarily do *not* eliminate all unemployment insurance and social security contributions required with respect to U.S. employment. However, it should be noted that the United States has begun to enter into separate social security tax agreements under which, *inter alia,* an individual resident of the treaty country employed in the United States by an employer of the treaty country may be exempt from U.S. social security taxes.[12]

In addition, difficulty in characterizing income may arise particularly where the foreign person earns the income partly from services and partly from the investment of capital without an arm's length allocation of the income to each source.

Sales Income and Capital Gains

As noted above, the sale of goods or other personal property where title passes within the United States generates U.S. source income. However, an occasional such sale which generates non-effectively connected income usually is *not* subject to U.S. income taxation, unless the force of attraction problem discussed further below arises because the sale income is attributed to another U.S. business of the same investor. It may also be possible to avoid U.S. source income by having title to goods pass to purchasers outside the United States — for example, F.O.B. a foreign port — if this is done at least partly for business reasons and not only for tax avoidance purposes.

Long-term or short-term capital gain from sale within the United States of shares of corporate stock or other assets which is not effectively connected income generally is *taxfree* to a nonresident alien, foreign estate or trust, foreign corporation, or other foreign person. However, a nonresident alien present in the United States for at least 183 days during the taxable year of the sale is subject to a 30% tax on the entire gain. These rules usually apply even to the sale of shares of a collapsible corporation; the disposition of such a corporation by a foreign person is considered further in Chapter VI regarding new U.S. business enterprises.

The sale of U.S. real property, corporate distribution of such property, or sale of shares of a U.S. corporation owning such property usually generates income which is subject to special tax rules discussed in Chapter III.

Allocation and Other Special Provisions

Federal tax authorities may reallocate total income and deductions — whether or not effectively connected — among controlled enterprises either to prevent evasion of taxes or clearly to reflect income. The standard to be applied is that of uncontrolled enterprises dealing with one another at arm's length. If a foreign income tax has been paid by the foreign enterprise, a subsequent reallocation of the income as U.S. source income usually results in double taxation of the same income in the United States and abroad, subject to limited relief under certain U.S. administrative procedures and income tax treaties.

In this connection, any U.S. corporation or foreign corporation engaged in trade or business within the United States which is owned directly or indirectly at least one-half in voting power or value by a foreign person is required after 1982 to file with the federal tax authorities information identifying any other corporations which are similarly controlled by the same persons and with which it has any transactions during its taxable year, and describing its relationship to and transactions with each of such corporations.[13]

In the case of a foreign *or* U.S. corporation, if dividends, interest, or similar passive income constitute at least 60% of its gross income and more than one-half in value of its outstanding stock is owned by five or fewer individuals, the corporation's undistributed income may be subject to a federal personal holding company tax of 50%. However, in the case of a foreign corporation, generally only U.S. source income is considered. If the foreign corporation is owned at least 90% by nonresident aliens, this tax is limited to much smaller portions of such income. A tax treaty also may somewhat limit the tax on a corporation of the treaty country.[14]

In addition, a foreign or U.S. corporation which accumulates income in excess of its reasonable business needs — generally with a minimum allowance of $250,000 per year — may be subject to an accumulated earnings tax of 27½-38½% on such income. Again, in the case of a foreign corporation, usually only U.S. source income is considered, and an applicable tax treaty may somewhat limit the application of the tax.[15]

It should also be noted that a federal tax or so called toll charge may be imposed under regulations or a revenue ruling to permit certain taxfree reorganizations involving foreign corporations for U.S. tax purposes. Such a tax usually is not applicable where the only transferors are foreign persons. Nevertheless, the transaction may have to be reported to the U.S. Department of the Treasury to assure taxfree treatment.[16]

Taxation of Business Income

U.S. Trade or Business

The federal income tax statute does not provide an exhaustive definition of trade or business within the United States, but a foreign person generally may be considered to be engaged in such trade or business when assets located in the United States are employed in commercial activity.[17] These may include even personnel employed on behalf of the foreign person. The activity generally must be for a profit motive and conducted with continuity or regularity. Many definitions and related issues in this area remain unresolved. Of the two possible factors of assets and activities, the latter arguably should be more determinative because the conduct of a business depends on decisions of management and administration. For example, it may be more important where the decision to sell inventory is made than where the inventory physically is located.

However, a foreign person ordinarily will not be considered engaged in U.S. business solely on the basis of certain U.S. supervisory or shareholder functions for the foreign person as a shareholder of a U.S. subsidiary corporation, or of sporadic purchases of goods in the United States. In addition, largely to encourage foreign investment in U.S. securities, a foreign person generally may trade in securities and commodities in the United States through brokers or for his own account without being considered engaged in U.S. business.

Under most tax treaties, a resident of the treaty country — even if he is engaged in U.S. trade or business — will not be taxed on his U.S. industrial and commercial profits in the absence of a permanent establishment in the United States. Such a permanent establishment usually is defined to exclude certain activities which otherwise might be a trade or business — for example, maintenance of a warehouse or display office for goods, or a construction project of one year or less.[18]

Partners and Agents

A foreign person may cause U.S. activities to be carried out on his behalf either through his exclusive employee or other dependent agent, or through an independent agent who acts for more than one person. If the foreign person remains ultimately responsible for the obligations so incurred, such activities generally are treated as those of the foreign person for federal income tax purposes, except for special exceptions which may be provided in the definition of a U.S. permanent establishment under a tax treaty. Accordingly, the greater the degree to which employees, independent agents, or even attorneys in fact in the United States are given authority to obligate the foreign person, the greater the likelihood that that person will be considered engaged in business in the United States.

By contrast, for example, a foreign owner of U.S. real property may enter into a triple net lease under which the lessee assumes the property tax, insurance, and maintenance obligations; this ordinarily may not of itself cause the owner to be engaged in U.S. business. However, even a separate corporation created solely for a very limited purpose — for example, to borrow funds at the higher interest rates required by lenders where an unincorporated borrower cannot do so under state usury laws — may be considered an agent of its owners for tax purposes under narrow circumstances.[19]

If a foreign person who is not directly engaged in U.S. business is a partner in a U.S. or foreign partnership for federal income tax purposes and the partnership is so engaged (or, under a tax treaty, has a U.S. permanent establishment), then the foreign partner is considered to be so engaged (or to have such a permanent establishment) as to his portion of the income generated by the partnership. The same rule applies to a foreign person who is a beneficiary of a trust or estate that is engaged in

U.S. business. Furthermore, in the case of a *foreign* partnership with U.S. assets (and/or U.S. partners), even if the partnership's U.S. investments do *not* cause it to be engaged in a U.S. business and no federal tax return is otherwise due, if the partnership wishes to make an election that affects the federal tax computation of its income — for example, to step up the tax basis of its assets to reflect a higher price paid by a new partner to purchase his partnership interest — then a federal income tax return for the partnership containing the election often must be timely filed by the partnership or one of its partners.[20]

Characterization of Entities

The character of a U.S. *or* foreign entity as a partnership, corporation, or other type of entity for federal tax purposes depends on U.S. standards. Thus, notwithstanding the characterization of a foreign or other entity under foreign law, its attributes must be examined in light of these U.S. standards. For example, a German *GmbH* may be classified for U.S. federal tax purposes as an association taxable as a corporation, as a partnership, or as neither.[21]

This application of separate U.S. standards may raise several basic issues in connection with any effectively connected or other income. Foreign persons unwittingly may create a partnership for federal tax purposes, with certain special partnership tax consequences such as those noted above.

On the other hand, an apparent partnership, trust, or other unincorporated entity nonetheless may be treated as an association separately taxable as a corporation for federal purposes. Furthermore, an entity treated as a partnership for foreign tax purposes may be intentionally organized so as to be treated as an association taxable as a corporation under U.S. standards — or *vice versa* — in order to obtain different local tax or tax treaty benefits in each country.[22]

Income Effectively Connected with the U.S. Business

If a foreign person is engaged in trade or business within the United States — or, if a tax treaty applies, has a permanent establishment in the United States — then all of his income effectively connected with the conduct of that trade or business — or, under most treaties, his industrial and commercial profits attributable to that permanent establishment — generally will be subject to federal tax on net income at the usual rates payable by a U.S. person.[23] In the case of a foreign corporation, these are 15% (16% for 1982)-40% on the first $100,000 of taxable ordinary income and 46% on the balance, and 28% on long-term capital gains, as in the case of a U.S. corporation. In the case of a nonresident alien, foreign estate or trust, or other unincorporated entity, these are 0-50% (after 1981) on ordinary income and four-tenths of those amounts on long-term capital gains, as in the case of a U.S. citizen or resident. The minimum taxes on tax preference income also apply. A foreign person often may operate a business (or permanent establishment) in the United States on which tax is payable at usual domestic rates on net income and, at the same time, be subject to a 30% (or treaty rate) withholding tax on, for example, dividends from a nonbusiness investment in U.S. securities.

Certain fixed or periodic income such as interest or royalties, *or* capital gain, is considered effectively connected income if either of two criteria are met: (1) if the asset which generates the income is used in the U.S. business of the foreign person, or (2) if the U.S. business activities of the foreign person are material in producing the income. An example of the asset rule is that the capital gain from sale of a piece of farm equipment used in the taxable year of sale in a U.S. business which rents out heavy equipment usually will be considered effectively connected income. However, if the purchase price is made payable in installments, the foreign seller may be able to exclude installments received after the year of sale from effectively connected income if after the year of sale he is no longer engaged in a U.S. trade or business with which the installments may be connected.[24]

An example of the activity rule is that royalties received on a particular right usually will be considered effectively connected income where the foreign person engages in U.S. business activities which involve developing, marketing, and managing such rights. In such a case, the royalty income, less allocable expenses, is added to other income otherwise attributable to the U.S. business.

All *other* types of U.S. source income — principally from U.S. sales of goods — automatically will be attributed by the so called force of attraction principle to *any* U.S. trade or business in which the same person is engaged during the same taxable year. This may even cause such income which is received early in the taxable year to be attributed retroactively to the business of a partnership or other unincorporated enterprise in which the foreign person invests *later* in the year. To avoid this force of attraction problem, a foreign person may wish to segregate one unincorporated business from another in a separate foreign or U.S. corporation. Under most tax treaties, the automatic attribution of all such income to any U.S. permanent establishment is eliminated.[25]

A corollary of the taxation of net income is that most expenses — even those incurred abroad — which are connected with the U.S. effectively connected income may be allocated or apportioned to reduce that income, provided that a federal tax return claiming the same is timely filed. Detailed regulations apply to such expense allocations. In the case of a tax treaty, such interest and other expenses generally may be deducted as if the U.S. permanent establishment were a separate entity.[26]

One common problem arises where the U.S. business performs only part of the effort required to earn a particular item of income. For example, a foreign person may maintain both a foreign manufacturing facility and a U.S. sales office to sell the goods produced abroad. Whether these are organized in two separate enterprises, or in a single foreign enterprise, the U.S. business must be allocated a share of the profit generated on the ultimate sale of goods. If two separate enterprises are involved, this must generally be on the basis of an arm's length price between an unrelated manufacturer and distributor. If both the foreign manufacturing and the U.S. sales businesses are conducted by the same foreign enterprise, the U.S. operation's profit share often may be determined by, *inter alia,* accounting data on the cost of the effort by each of the two operations, or an equal split of profits.[27]

An important issue in the case of effectively connected income is that certain items generally considered *foreign* source income may nevertheless be taxable by the United States if attributable to a U.S. office or other fixed place of business. The specific types of such income which may be treated as effectively connected are limited essentially to income from certain sales of goods and other personal property; certain dividends, interest, and securities gains; and certain rents and royalties from intangible property. Such foreign source income may be considered effectively connected only if (a) the foreign person maintains a U.S. office or other fixed place of business during the taxable year *and* (b) that office plays a material role in the production of the item of income during that taxable year. For example, if a U.S. office were to take all necessary steps in one year to produce an item of Canadian source income for the U.S. business which arises in the next year and the U.S. office were closed before the beginning of that next year, then the Canadian source income would not be considered effectively connected.

Such a U.S. office or other fixed place of business which may give rise to effectively connected foreign source income often is similar to the permanent establishment referred to in U.S. income tax treaties. It must be managed by or include an employee or agent of the foreign person who has authority to negotiate and make contractual arrangements on his behalf and regularly exercises that authority, *or* who has a stock of inventory out of which he regularly fills orders for customers without referral to the home office abroad. The definition excludes the U.S. office of an independent agent acting for the foreign person and for others. Nor does the concept generally include a U.S. office in which incidental or occasional administrative activity takes place, or a U.S. display office, advertising office, or purchasing office.

Because only certain types of foreign source income may be so taxed, the definition of these types may become critical — especially where the payor and the payee are related. For example, the payment of a fee for personal services between related foreign parties may be considered a royalty and so become subject to such U.S. taxation.

A corollary of the taxation of foreign source income is that a credit against the U.S. tax is provided for any foreign income and related taxes with respect to such income.[28] It should be noted, however, that under certain tax treaties *no* foreign source income may be so attributed to a U.S. permanent establishment of a resident of the treaty country.[29]

The holding or operation of U.S. real property, and a sale or corporate distribution of such property or sale of shares of a U.S. corporation owning such property, usually are subject to special tax rules, as noted further above and discussed separately in Chapter III. Special rules also apply to certain industries such as foreign life insurance companies, and special exemptions apply to certain earnings from the U.S. operation of ships and aircraft, subject to tax treaty provisions. However, even the income of a foreign government and its controlled entities from U.S. commercial activities often is *not* exempt from tax.[30]

Treaty Abuse

U.S. income tax treaties in force at mid-1982 are listed in the Appendix to this chapter. The United States also has entered into a number of bilateral executive agreements covering the taxation of aircraft and shipping profits and similar limited items.

However, in all tax treaty planning the distinction between treaty use and abuse must be considered. This is particularly true where no valid business purpose other than tax saving is apparent in the choice of a particular investment structure or jurisdiction. This is most likely where an investment is made through a third country which imposes little or no taxes on the U.S. or other foreign income of a local corporation or other entity owned by foreign persons, or on the foreign owners themselves — *i.e.,* a tax haven — and use is made of a tax treaty between that country and the United States.

The United States and other countries are increasingly engaged in defining and limiting such abuse. First, legal challenges to the use of treaty benefits may be based on the intended beneficiaries of a treaty, the economic substance over legal form of a transaction, the correction of a material distortion of income of one entity, and other issues. In this connection, certain treaties may require a showing that the investment structure is not arranged or maintained primarily for tax reduction. Furthermore, the U.S. Department of the Treasury is to adopt by mid-1984 additional certification procedures, and possibly the use of withholding subject to tax refunds, to ensure that treaty benefits are used only by foreign persons entitled to such benefits.[31]

Second, under newer U.S. tax treaties, treaty benefits may be expressly denied to, for example, a corporation of the treaty country if it is not owned or controlled substantially by individual residents of the treaty country, or if it is subject to less tax on its income from abroad than on local income.[32]

Gift and Estate Taxation

The United States taxes the worldwide gifts and estates of U.S. citizens and of aliens who at the time of gift or death are domiciled in the United States, as described in Chapter I. However, in the case of an alien who is not domiciled in the United States, the sole basis of federal taxation is the U.S. situs of the property transferred.[33]

Gift Tax

A nondomiciled alien is subject to federal gift tax only on *tangible* property — real or personal — located in the United States. This generally excludes money as well as stock and other securities of even a U.S. corporation.[34]

The same tax rates as those described in Chapter I for U.S. donors apply to such a foreign donor. These rates apply to the cumulative taxable gifts, and a return must be filed for any calendar year in which such taxable gifts are made. However, *no* unified credit against the gift tax is permitted to such a foreign donor. The donor is entitled to the general exclusion of $10,000 in gifts each calendar year to each donee, and to a full deduction for gifts to U.S. charities, but *not* to the marital deduction for gifts to his spouse.

Estate Tax

In the case of an alien not domiciled in the United States at the time of death, federal estate tax applies to all property situated or deemed situated in the United States. This includes, *inter alia:*

(1) U.S. real property;

(2) Tangible personal property located in the United States at the time of death;

(3) Stock of a U.S. corporation, unlike the exclusion noted above for gift tax purposes;

(4) Bonds or other debt obligations of a U.S. corporation or political subdivision, again unlike the exclusion for gift tax purposes, but with certain exceptions noted below;

(5) The U.S. corpus of any revocable or grantor trust of the decedent;

(6) The beneficial interest of the decedent in the U.S. corpus of any trust;

(7) Probably currency physically located in the United States;

(8) Possibly any interest in a partnership engaged in trade or business within the United States, perhaps without provision for adjusting the U.S. share of the decedent's interest even where the partnership carries on only part of its business in the United States.

Such U.S. situs property specifically *excludes:*

(1) Debt obligations of a U.S. corporation whose income is mostly from foreign sources, or which has been used for certain foreign financings;

(2) All life insurance proceeds;

(3) Commercial bank, savings and loan, or interest bearing insurance company deposits.

Special tax rates apply to the estate of such a foreign decedent, as follows:

Taxable amount	Tax rate
Not over $100,000	6% of such amount
Over $100,000 but not over $500,000	$6,000 plus 12% of the excess over $100,000
Over $500,000 but not over $1 million	$54,000 plus 18% of the excess over $500,000
Over $1 million but not over $2 million	$144,000 plus 24% of the excess over $1 million
Over $2 million	$384,000 plus 30% of the excess over $2 million.

In addition, the federal gift and estate taxation of such foreign individuals is unified — similarly to that applicable to U.S. citizens and domiciliaries — so that these special rates apply based on the cumulative taxable gifts *and* taxable estate of the individual. For example, if a nondomiciled alien has made U.S. taxable gifts of at least $2 million during his lifetime, all of his U.S. taxable estate upon his death will be subject to federal estate tax at the top rate of 30%.

A credit of $3,600 is provided against the estate tax, which is far below the credit of up to $192,800 for U.S. citizens and domiciliaries. A credit also is available for certain state death taxes. The computation of the net amount subject to estate tax involves deduction of, *inter alia,* certain administrative expenses, debts of the estate, local taxes, and gifts to U.S. charities. Where the estate includes both U.S. situs and foreign situs property, the deductions generally must be allocated in proportion to the value of each part of the gross estate. However, *no* marital deduction for property passing to the decedent's spouse is permitted. The general federal rules described in Chapter I apply (with minor variation) to determine the recipient's basis for tax purposes in property received by gift or inheritance from such a foreign individual.

It should be noted that the United States has concluded several gift and estate tax treaties with other countries, and these frequently reduce or eliminate double taxation on transfer of the same property. Such treaties in force at mid-1982 are listed in the Appendix to this chapter.

State and Local Taxation

State and local property, sales or use, and most other taxes described in Chapter I apply identically to U.S. and foreign persons. The same generally is true for state income, gift, and inheritance or similar taxes, but certain aspects of such taxation which may be relevant to foreign persons should be noted.

Income Taxes

State income taxation often follows the model of federal taxation, including taxation of state individual residents on worldwide net income at graduated rates. However, a nonresident individual or unincorporated entity usually is taxed by each state — due to constitutional restrictions — only on income from sources within that state at the same rates as residents of the state. This applies to non-U.S. persons as well as out-of-state U.S. persons. Withholding of tax from payments to nonresidents also may be required of payors. However, interest on local bank deposits and income from other intangible property may not be taxable to nonresidents unless the deposits or other property are used in a business conducted in the state. Individuals generally should be treated as nonresidents for state income tax purposes so long as they enter the state only for a temporary or transitory purpose.

Contrary to the federal tax exemption of foreign persons on many non-effectively connected capital gains, all capital gains from local real property and other tangible property usually are subject to state tax. Indeed, for all persons capital gains may be taxed at ordinary income rates, or the tax rate or the amount of taxable gain may drop only as the property is held longer. An additional tax may be imposed on these and other tax preference items, similarly to federal taxation.

A local *or* foreign — non-U.S. or out-of-state U.S. — corporation usually is subject to a state franchise tax or income tax measured by net income from state sources. However, one of the most troublesome features of state income taxation concerning foreign investors has been the method whereby one state may determine the share of income allocable to that state. Nonbusiness or inactive investment income generally is wholly taxable in the corporation's state of organization. With regard to business income, as noted in Chapter I, in certain states a unitary formula based on the portion of worldwide assets, payroll, and sales in the state is used to determine the appropriate state share of income of a multistate corporation or group of affiliated corporations which are operated as a unit; this may include a share of an out-of-state corporation's worldwide business income, including in certain cases even dividends received from its foreign subsidiaries.[35] Such taxation has been attacked as particularly onerous and unjustified in the case of a *multinational* group of affiliated corporations of which one or more are operating in the state, and both income tax treaty and federal statutory limitations on unitary taxation of multinational groups have been considered; accordingly, further developments in this area should be followed.[36]

Other special state income tax problems may apply to non-U.S. persons or transactions. For example, a *state* tax or toll charge may be imposed under a revenue ruling to permit a taxfree reorganization involving a non-U.S. corporation, somewhat similarly to the federal provisions noted further above; or liquidation of a local corporation free of state tax may be denied if it is owned by non-U.S. persons. However, subjecting such a foreign corporation or shareholder to greater state tax burdens may run afoul of U.S. tax and other treaties or constitutional limitations.[37]

Many states attempt to attract non-U.S. investors by tax and other incentives. These are discussed further in Chapter VI which deals with the establishment of a new business enterprise in the United States.

Gift and Inheritance Taxes

Many states tax gifts by a nondomiciled individual if the property given is local real property, tangible personal property permanently in the state, or certain types of intangible personal property. As noted in Chapter I, the rates may be similar to those for the state inheritance tax and may include an exemption similar to the $10,000 per year per donee under federal taxation.

In addition, many states tax the heirs of a nondomiciled individual on their inheritance of local real property, tangible personal property permanently in the state, and certain intangible personal property having a situs in the state. If the decedent is a nondomiciliary of the United States, local bank deposits often may not be included for state tax purposes unless used in a business conducted in the state. However, even stock or other securities issued by a local corporation, or by a corporation with its principal place or the major part of its business there, may be subject to such tax. Other intangible personal property in the state — possibly including *any* corporate stock or other securities kept there — may be included for tax purposes.[38] Certain property may not be taxed if the foreign decedent's country has a similar exemption from its death tax for property there of the U.S. state's decedents.

Finally, it should be noted that current U.S. tax treaties do *not* alter state or local income, gift, or estate taxation of foreign persons, except generally to prohibit various types of discrimination between U.S. and treaty country residents.[39]

Appendix to Chapter II

U.S. Income Tax Treaties in Force

Australia
Austria
Belgium
Canada
Denmark
Egypt
Finland
France
Federal Republic of Germany
Greece
Hungary
Iceland
Ireland
Italy
Jamaica
Japan
Republic of Korea
Luxembourg
Malta
Morocco
Netherlands
Netherlands Antilles
New Zealand
Norway
Pakistan
Philippines
Poland
Romania
South Africa
Sweden
Switzerland
Trinidad and Tobago
Union of Soviet Socialist Republics
United Kingdom
U.K. overseas territories (see below)
Zaire

U.K. Overseas Territories and Former Territories:

Aden
Antigua
Barbados
Belize
Burundi
Dominica
Falkland Islands
Gambia
Grenada
Malawi
Montserrat
Rwanda
St. Christopher, Nevis and Anguilla
St. Lucia
St. Vincent
Seychelles
Sierra Leone
Zambia

U.S. Gift Tax Treaties in Force

Australia
France
Japan
United Kingdom

U.S. Estate Tax Treaties in Force

Australia
Canada
Finland
France
Greece
Ireland
Italy
Japan
Netherlands
Norway
South Africa
Switzerland
United Kingdom

Footnotes to Chapter II

1. Pub. L. 89-809 (Nov. 13, 1966), 80 Stat. 1541; *see generally* I.R.C. §§861-863, 871(a), (e), (f), 881, 894(b), 1441-1443; Internal Revenue Service Pub. No. 15. The standards for determining whether an alien is a resident or domiciliary for various federal tax purposes are discussed in Chapter XI covering tax planning for individual investors.

Where a foreign person wishes to challenge whether he is subject to U.S. tax on a particular item of income, rather than the amount of tax, he may be able to do so even in a U.S. federal district court, rather than only in the U.S. Tax Court, without first paying the tax. Ardalan v. United States, 534 F. Supp. 721 (D. Colo. 1982). *But see* Flora v. United States, 357 U.S. 63 (1960).

2. *Cf.* United States-France Income Tax Treaty of 1967, as amended ("U.S.-France Treaty"), Art. 9(2).

3. *Cf.* United States-Netherlands Income Tax Treaty of 1948, as amended, Art. XII.

4. *See, e.g.,* judicial and other decisions cited in Prentice-Hall, Inc., *Federal Taxes* §13,096; Treas. Reg. §§1.385-0 *et seq.* Thin capitalization tax issues are discussed further in Chapter III covering real estate and natural resource investments, Chapter VI dealing with the establishment of a new U.S. business enterprise, and Chapter VII covering the acquisition of an existing U.S. corporation.

5. I.R.C. §§301(b)(1)(A), (D).

6. *Cf.* United States-Sweden Income Tax Treaty of 1940, as amended, Art. VIII. A particular treaty may or may not extend this benefit to mortgage interest.

7. *See* I.R.C. §§483, 871(a)(1)(C), 881(a)(3); Treas. Reg. §§1.483-1 and -2.

8. *Cf.* I.R.C. §§3454(a)(2)(D)-(F), (b)(3)(C); *see generally* Chapter I *supra.*

9. *Cf.* U.S.-France Treaty, Art 11; Rev. Rul. 80-362, 1980-2 C.B. 208.

10. *Cf.* United States-United Kingdom Income Tax Treaty of 1975 ("U.S.-U.K. Treaty"), Art. 7(7).

11. *See* I.R.C. §§861(a)(3), 864(b)(1), 871(a), (f), 1441-1443, 3121, 3401-3404, 3508, 3509; *cf.* U.S.-France Treaty, Art. 1.

12. *See* I.R.C. §§1401(c), 3101(c), 3111(c); 42 U.S.C.§433; Rev. Proc. 80-56, 1980-2 C.B. 851; Chapter I *supra; cf.* United States-Italy Social Security Totalization Agreement of 1978 and subsequent similar agreements with the Federal Republic of Germany and Switzerland.

13. *See* I.R.C. §§482, 6038A; Treas. Reg. §§1.482-1 and -2; Rev. Proc. 82-29, 1982-18 I.R.B. 13; Rev. Proc. 65-17, 1965-1 C.B. 833; Rev. Proc. 65-31, 1965-2 C.B. 1024; Rev. Rul. 72-437, 1972-2 C.B. 660; Rev. Rul. 82-80, 1982-2 I.R.B. 7. Forms for new I.R.C. §6038A are expected in 1983.

14. *See* I.R.C. §§541-547, especially §§545(a), (d); Porto Rico Coal Co. v. Comm'r, 126 F.2d 212 (2d Cir. 1942); Rev. Rul. 68-127, 1968-1 C.B. 287; *cf.* U.S.-France Treaty, Art. 13(1)(b)(i). The foreign investment company provisions, which tax certain gain on a sale or exchange of stock in such a foreign corporation as ordinary income rather than capital gain, appear to apply in the case of a foreign shareholder only to U.S. source (or foreign source effectively connected) gain on such a stock sale — which usually can be eliminated. *See* I.R.C. §§1246-1247. The controlled foreign corporation and foreign personal holding company provisions which are discussed in Chapter VIII do not impose federal tax on the corporation itself or on foreign shareholders.

15. *See* I.R.C. §§531-537; *cf.* U.S.-France Treaty, Art. 13(1)(b)(ii); U.S.-U.K. Treaty, Art. 10(6). The allowance of $250,000 is reduced to $150,000 per year in the case of certain personal service corporations. This tax may apply even to a U.S. or foreign corporation owned in turn by a foreign corporation, rather than directly by a foreign individual. In the case of a foreign corporation, the tax may apply also to *foreign* source income attributable to a U.S. office or other fixed place of business of the corporation; this income is discussed generally further below in the text. *See* Prop. Treas. Reg. §§1.532-1(a), (c).

16. *See* I.R.C. §§367(a), (b); Temp. Treas. Reg. §§7.367(b)-1 through -12; Chapter VIII *infra.*

17. *See generally* I.R.C. §864(b).

18. *Cf.* U.S.-U.K. Treaty, Arts. 5(2)-(3), 7(1). In the case of a foreign professional individual, certain tax treaties require a fixed base rather than a permanent establishment for local taxation of the individual's professional services and certain other income, but this term is not yet common in U.S. tax treaties.

19. *See* Chapter III *infra*; *cf.* Joseph A. Roccaforte, 77 T.C. No. 22 (1981).

20. I.R.C. §875; *cf.* Donroy, Ltd. v. United States, 301 F.2d 200 (9th Cir. 1962); Rev. Rul. 75-23, 1975-1 C.B. 290; Letter Rul. 8029005; *see also* I.R.C. §§743,754; Letter Rul. 8142017.

21. *See* Treas. Reg. §§301.7701-2 through -4; Rev. Rul. 73-254, 1973-1 C.B. 613; Rev. Rul. 79-106, 1979-1 C.B. 448; *cf.* Rev. Rul. 77-214, 1977-1 C.B. 408; Letter Ruls. 7743060, 7743077, 7747083, 7748038, 7802012, 8221136; *see also* Letter Rul. 8006086 (Saudi Arabian limited partnership classified as corporation). *But see* Letter Ruls. 7806055-7806058, 7806062 (prior Letter Rulings on German *GmbH* and other foreign entities revoked). For further discussion and an example in connection with U.S. real estate investments, see Chapter III *infra.*

22. It may be difficult to obtain an advance ruling from the U.S. Internal Revenue Service that a foreign entity will be characterized for federal tax purposes as a partnership, *or* differently from the way it is characterized in its country of organization. *See* Rev. Proc. 80-22, 1980-1 C.B. 654; Rev. Proc. 81-10, 1981-1 C.B. 647. In addition, it should be noted generally that a private Letter Ruling (as opposed to a published Revenue Ruling or Procedure) cannot be used to bind the federal tax authorities by persons other than those for whom it was specifically issued.

23. *See generally* I.R.C. §§864(c), 871(b)-(d), 873, 874, 882; Chapter I *supra.*

24. *See* I.R.C. §453; Treas. Reg. §1.864-3(a).

25. *See* Treas. Reg. §§1.864-4(a), (b), 1.875-1; Alberto Vitale, 72 T.C. 386 (1979); *cf.* U.S.-France Treaty, Art. 6(1). If a tax treaty applies, income which is *not* effectively connected under the federal statute is likewise treated as not attributable to a permanent establishment under the treaty. I.R.C. §894(b).

26. I.R.C. §§873, 874, 882(c); Treas. Reg. §§1.861-8, 1.882-5; *cf.* Rev. Rul. 79-186, 1979-1 C.B. 238; U.S.-U.K. Treaty, Arts. 7(2), (3).

27. *See* I.R.C. §863; Treas. Reg. §§1.863-1 through -6; note 13 *supra.*

28. I.R.C. §906.

29. *Cf.* United States-Ireland Income Tax Treaty of 1951, Art. III(1); United States-Switzerland Income Tax Treaty of 1951, Art. III(1)(a).

30. *See* I.R.C. §§897, 6039C; 819, 4371-4374; 883(a)(1); 892, 893, 895; Treas. Reg. §§1.892-1 and -2.

31. *Cf.* Johansson v. United States, 336 F.2d 809 (5th Cir. 1964); Aiken Industries, Inc., 56 T.C. 925 (1971); Perry R. Bass, 50 T.C. 595 (1968); Compagnie Financière de Suez et de L'Union Parisienne v. United States, 492 F. 2d 798 (Ct. Cl. 1974); Rev. Rul. 79-65, 1979-1 C.B. 458; Rev. Rul. 79-40, 1979-1 C.B. 13; Rev. Rul. 75-23, 1975-1 C.B. 290; Letter Ruls. 7723035, 7739080, 7742048, 7742058, 7933080, 7936070, 8151023; United States-Netherlands Income Tax Treaty of 1948, as amended and presently in force between the United States and the Netherlands Antilles, Art. VII(1); *see generally* U.S. Dep't of the Treasury, 1 *Report to the Congress on Foreign Portfolio Investment in the United States* 42 (1976); R. Gordon, *Report to the Commissioner of Internal Revenue, et al. on Tax Havens and Their Use by United States Taxpayers: An Overview* (1981); Pub. L. 97-248 (Sept. 3, 1982), §342.

32. *Cf.* United States-Iceland Income Tax Treaty of 1975, Art. 27; United States-Jamaica Income Tax Treaty of 1981, Art. 17; U.S.-U.K. Treaty, Arts. 4, 16; proposed Model U.S. Income Tax Treaty of 1981, Arts. 4.1, 16.

33. *See generally* I.R.C. §§2101-2108, 2501-2524. As noted above, the standards for determining whether an alien is a resident or domiciliary for various federal tax purposes are discussed in Chapter XI covering tax planning for individual investors.

34. The possible application of federal *income* tax to a gift of stock of a U.S. corporation owning U.S. real property is noted in Chapter III in connection with disposition of real estate and natural resource investments.

35. Exxon Corp. v. Wisconsin Dep't of Revenue, 447 U.S. 207 (1980); Mobil Oil Corp. v. Comm'r of Taxes of Vermont, 445 U.S. 425 (1980). *But see* ASARCO, Inc. v. Idaho State Tax Comm'n, 50 U.S.L.W. 4962 (U.S. Sup. Ct. 1982); F. W. Woolworth Co. v. New Mexico Taxation & Revenue Dep't, 50 U.S.L.W. 4957 (U.S. Sup. Ct. 1982) (dividends from foreign subsidiaries not includable in unitary business income of out-of-state corporations).

36. A provision in the recently negotiated U.S.-U.K. Treaty in effect limited the application of the unitary method as to certain corporations and other enterprises controlled by U.K. residents. However, this provision of the treaty was not accepted by the U.S. Senate.

37. *E.g.,* California; *see* note 16 *supra*; proposed Model U.S. Income Tax Treaty of 1981, Art. 24; Chapter I *supra.*

38. Keeping U.S. *or* foreign corporate stock or other property in, for example, a U.S. bank safe deposit box also may permit readier access to such contents by federal tax authorities. *Cf.* United States v. New England Merchants Nat'l Bank, 465 F. Supp. 83 (D. Mass. 1979).

39. *Cf.* U.S.-France Treaty, Art. 24.

Chapter III

Real Estate and Natural Resource Investments

Nonresident alien individuals, foreign corporations, and other foreign persons have substantially increased their investments in U.S. real estate and other natural resources in recent years. Such investments have been facilitated in part by concentrations of available funds abroad, by U.S. dollar devaluations, by low U.S. purchase prices in comparison to real estate prices in many other countries, and by the continuing relative economic strength and political and legal stability of the United States. For foreign developers and other active investors, these factors frequently offer rapid profitability. For less active institutional or individual foreign investors, real estate and similar property often provides a tangible investment which generally will retain or increase its value as a limited commodity, can be managed in part by a U.S. representative or partner, and may provide a physical residence or occupation in case a nonresident alien owner moves to the United States by choice or necessity.

This chapter outlines certain basic structures for such foreign investments, focusing principally on the holding of U.S. income producing real property, property acquired for development, and property held for appreciation and on the sale or other disposition of property, including the use of tax treaty jurisdictions. Selected aspects peculiar to investments in U.S. agricultural property, timber property, and certain other natural resources also are described. The objective is to highlight important regulatory, income tax, estate planning, and related considerations affecting such investments.

General Federal and State Regulation

Federal Regulation

As noted in Chapter I, the United States generally does not regulate investments from abroad, although certain broad federal restrictions apply to foreign investors residing or organized in countries hostile to the United States and investors may wish to plan for the transfer of U.S. real estate and similar resources to neutral persons in case of such hostilities. Particularly in the case of a foreign government investment, review by the U.S. interagency Committee on Foreign Investment also may be involved.[1]

In the case of real estate and other natural resources, it should be noted that more than one-third of the approximately 3.5 million square miles of land in the United States — including the District of Columbia — is owned by the federal government. Limited restrictions on foreign ownership apply generally to certain unincorporated and unplatted portions of such federal lands; these may possibly be avoided by establishing a U.S. corporation or other entity to hold title to the property.[2] Special restrictions on foreign ownership and exploitation of federally owned grazing land, homestead land, mineral interests, and geothermal steam and related resources are noted further below in connection with specific types of properties.

However, real estate and similar property investments may be viewed by the federal government as providing particularly strong links between foreign owners and U.S. economic and/or political policies. In addition, as noted generally in Chapter I, restrictions on such investments may be limited by equal protection and other rights under the U.S. Constitution. Alternatively, they may be subject to treaty rights of foreign persons from specific countries under, for example, a treaty of friendship, commerce, and navigation which grants the right to acquire or to lease certain real estate on the same basis as by U.S. persons, or which grants such rights as are afforded the most favored nationals of any other country. However, such treaties often expressly exclude or limit rights with specific regard to U.S. real estate and other natural resources.[3]

In addition to such general federal restrictions, foreign direct investment *reports* to the U.S. Department of Commerce are required from the foreign investor, the U.S. enterprise, and certain U.S. intermediaries and brokers upon, *inter alia*, the establishment or acquisition of a U.S. business enterprise whose total assets — including real estate or similar property — exceed $1 million *or* include 200 acres or more of U.S. land. The U.S. enterprise itself also may have to report or claim exemption, no matter how small the investment. Furthermore, while limited partners in a real estate or other limited partnership are not considered to have a direct investment in the partnership, the partnership may have responsibility to report their interests under portfolio investment reporting regulations of the U.S. Department of the Treasury.

Under the Agricultural Foreign Investment Disclosure Act of 1978,[4] additional special reporting is required in the case of almost any acquisition or transfer of interest in U.S. agricultural property — *i.e,* land used for agricultural, forestry, or timber production — by a nonresident alien or foreign trust, corporation, government, or other foreign person. A report to the U.S. Department of Agriculture by such foreign person generally is required within 90 days after each such acquisition or transfer.

As noted generally in Chapter II, after 1982 any U.S. real estate or other corporation — or foreign corporation engaged in U.S. trade or business by, for example, holding income producing property through an unincorporated U.S. branch — which is owned at least one-half by a foreign person is required to file a return with federal tax authorities covering its transactions during each taxable year with other corporations in the same controlled group.

In addition, the Foreign Investment in Real Property Tax Act of 1980, as described further below, requires reporting of direct and indirect investments in U.S. real estate and natural resources to the U.S. Department of the Treasury.

All of these reporting requirements for real estate and natural resource investments from abroad are discussed more fully in Chapter XII.

State Regulation

State laws generally restricting foreign interests in real estate may be divided into two principal categories: (1) those applicable to ownership by foreign persons, and (2) those applicable to inheritance by foreign persons. Over 30 of the states have one or both of such restrictions.

First, as to state ownership restrictions, the varied details of these laws have been analyzed fairly recently elsewhere and may be ascertained there.[5] In general, a foreign investor may hold real property except as follows:

(a) Several states — such as Iowa, Kentucky, Minnesota, Missouri, North Dakota, Oklahoma, Pennsylvania, South Dakota, Wisconsin, and in certain circumstances Arkansas — in effect prohibit substantial ownership by *nonresident aliens* of agricultural property or, in infrequent cases, any real property in excess of a specified area. However, such ownership indirectly through the corporate form may be permitted.

(b) Investment in any real estate of any size by or through a *foreign corporation* which takes title to the property may be prohibited by the statutes of a few states. However, these usually simply condition any out-of-state corporation's power to hold property on reciprocity in the foreign jurisdiction. The judicial common law of certain other states also may be interpreted to extend their prohibitions against nonresident alien ownership to such a foreign corporation.[6]

(c) Investment in agricultural property by or through any *foreign or U.S. corporation* may be prevented by the family farm laws of a number of states — such as Iowa, Kansas, Minnesota, Missouri, North Dakota, Oklahoma, South Dakota, and Wisconsin. These generally prohibit ownership of such property by corporations that are held by numerous shareholders or engage in substantial nonagricultural activities. The latter type of corporation may be barred under most circumstances even if owned by as few as one or two individuals.

The states also have special bodies of law similar to federal laws restricting foreign ownership, lease, and exploitation of state owned lands, mineral interests, geothermal steam, and similar resources. Such laws, which are also noted further below in connection with specific types of properties, should be examined prior to any such investment within a particular state from abroad.[7]

In connection with enforcement of their restrictions on ownership, states increasingly impose *reporting* requirements on nonresident aliens and foreign or U.S. corporations with respect to real estate and other natural resource investments, as discussed further in Chapter XII.

Existing state restrictions on ownership of real estate and other natural resources by nonresident (as opposed to resident) aliens generally have been upheld even under the U.S. Constitution's Fourteenth Amendment, unless based on an investor's race or country of origin. While such state restrictions may be inconsistent with treaty rights of foreign persons from many countries, as noted above in connection with federal restrictions, such treaties often expressly recognize *state* land laws.[8] However, additional state legislation in this area — particularly if it discriminates among investors from different countries — may be invalid under the foreign relations and foreign commerce provisions of the U.S. Constitution.

Except as noted above with regard to agricultural property, these laws often have only nuisance value. For example, Oklahoma's prohibition on alien land ownership has been interpreted not to apply to a foreign corporation once it has qualified to do business in the state.[9] Certain state restrictions also possibly may be avoided by establishing a limited partnership (or a land trust) and having the partnership or a qualified general partner (or the trust) hold title to the property, because the foreign investor then may hold only an interest in personal rather than real property under the state's own law.

Second, as to state inheritance restrictions, these are described generally in Chapter I and usually are based on deprivation abroad of the foreign heir's enjoyment of the property, or on lack of foreign reciprocity. They may not only restrict one method of foreign acquisition of U.S. real estate or other natural resources, but generally discourage investment by any nonresident alien who may wish to bequeath his real estate or similar holdings to other foreign persons.

However, as noted generally in Chapter I, such restrictions may be modified by treaty rights of foreign persons from specific countries. In addition, the use of a foreign or other corporation to hold the nonresident alien's real estate or other natural resource interest may make local state probate laws less likely to apply to that interest. It should also be remembered that, as noted in Chapter I, in spite of a state restriction on foreign ownership of real estate or natural resources, a foreign heir may have a substantial period under the state law to dispose of the property.

Regardless of foreign ownership, the development and operation of U.S. real estate and other natural resources also require compliance with local zoning, subdivision, and building codes, as well as applicable local, state, and federal environmental protection regulations, which are described generally in Chapter I.

Holding of Unimproved Property for Appreciation

In connection with the structuring of various types of real estate investments, the following hypothetical facts will provide a useful basis for much of the discussion below: A foreign corporation is contemplating a number of real estate investments in the United States. Its principal investment criteria include well established present property value, likely substantial appreciation over the next three to five years and, in most cases, current cash flow from the property sufficient to meet interest and operating expenses together with a return of 8-10% per year on invested cash. The United States and the foreign corporation's country of organization recently entered into an income tax treaty. In addition, a group of individuals who are citizens and residents of another foreign country propose to engage in several U.S. real estate investments with the corporation. None of these individuals is or ever has been a citizen or resident of the United States. There are no tax treaties between their country and the United States.

Direct Ownership

Perhaps the simplest structure for a proposed investment in unimproved property to be held for appreciation is the direct ownership of such property by the foreign corporation and the nonresident aliens. Such property may be held by the investors as tenants in common, so that in the event of an individual investor's death, his interest should not pass to the other investors but to his own heirs.

During the holding by the investors, what will be the U.S. federal income tax consequences to them?[10] It should be noted that, although there is assumed to be an income tax treaty between the United States and the foreign corporation's home country, under most U.S. tax treaties the income from holding of direct real estate investments in the United States continues to be taxed by the United States in accordance with many of the basic statutory provisions applicable to nontreaty investors. An investment in unimproved property generally will not entail the conduct of a trade or business within the United States by the investors. Thus, no deductions or capitalization of real estate taxes, interest, or other carrying charges will be permitted to the investors, since these usually are permitted to them only to the extent the charges are allocable to income effectively connected with the conduct of a U.S. trade of business ("effectively connected income").

One alternative is the use of a statutory or treaty election to have income of the investors from their U.S. real property interests taxed on a net basis as effectively connected income. Alternatively, the property may be owned through a U.S. corporation (or possibly a U.S. trust) which is permitted to deduct or capitalize such charges as a domestic taxpayer. Other advantages and difficulties with these approaches are analyzed further below in connection with the holding of income producing property.

Partnership

Alternatively, the foreign corporation and the nonresident aliens may form a U.S. or foreign partnership to own their unimproved property. Since, for U.S. income tax purposes, such a partnership is not a separate taxable entity, the overall tax treatment of the investors should not differ substantially from that in the case of direct ownership described above.

However, if the partnership is engaged in U.S. trade or business, each of the partners — even limited partners — then will be considered to be so engaged. The same rule applies to the foreign beneficiary of a trust or estate engaged in U.S. business. Each partner also may separately make the statutory or treaty election to have income from his U.S. real property interests taxed as effectively connected income, as discussed further below in connection with income producing property.[11]

The characterization of a U.S. *or* foreign entity as a partnership or other type of entity for federal tax purposes will depend on U.S. standards. This may often be an issue either (1) where foreign investors in a joint venture unwittingly create a partnership under such U.S. tax standards, or (2) where an apparent partnership or trust nonetheless has attributes similar to those of a U.S. corporation. It should also be noted that the members of an investment partnership which is not used for the active conduct of a business may, under a narrowly interpreted exception, elect generally not to be taxed as a partnership under federal law.[12]

Foreign Corporation

A major additional factor in planning foreign investments in U.S. real estate is the impact of federal gift and estate taxes on individual investors. A gift by a nonresident alien of his interest in U.S. real estate, whether owned directly or through a partnership, likely will be subject to even greater U.S. gift tax than that applicable to a U.S. citizen or resident. Likewise, upon the death of such a nonresident alien, U.S. estate tax generally will apply to his interest in U.S. real estate owned directly or through a partnership.

Accordingly, it may be wise for the nonresident aliens to form — either directly or through another foreign corporation, trust or other entity — a foreign corporation to hold their interests in unimproved U.S. real estate. This may be a corporation organized in a country which imposes little or no taxes on the corporation itself or the individual shareholders — *i.e.,* a tax haven. In this situation, no U.S. federal gift tax will apply to transfers of shares of the foreign corporation's stock by the nonresident aliens to, for example, other members of their families. Nor will U.S. estate tax apply to the foreign corporation's stock upon the death of any of the nonresident aliens.[13]

Such a corporation may help satisfy any valid state law ownership or inheritance limitations on foreign persons as noted further above. Separate corporations also help segregate the liabilities of each U.S. property from any other property of the same investor, whether the investor is an individual, trust, corporation, or other legal entity. Furthermore, a tax haven corporation may be useful in accumulating income to minimize home country taxes or other regulation of the foreign investors.

The tax haven's own income, gift, and estate or inheritance taxes also must be examined and minimized, of course. In addition, any tax treaties between the United States and the tax haven, or between the tax haven and the individual investors' home country, must be examined carefully for their impact on the use of such a foreign corporation. The use of such treaty jurisdictions is discussed in greater detail futher below.

Additional Issues

The structure of the hypothetical investors' U.S. real estate investments also will depend on valid federal and state law ownership and inheritance requirements as noted further above. State income, gift, and inheritance or similar taxes applicable to the foreign corporate investor and to the nonresident aliens must be considered; in many states, as described in Chapter II, such foreign investors are treated approximately the same as out-of-state U.S. investors. Property and other local taxes and assessments should be examined as well; as described in Chapter I, these taxes generally will vary with the state in which the real estate is located or other activities of the investors are carried on.

Holding of Income Producing Property and Property Acquired for Development

Direct Ownership or Partnership

Rental income from an office building, apartment building, shopping center, or similar income producing property which is received by the foreign corporate investor and the nonresident aliens either directly or through a partnership usually will be effectively connected income for federal tax purposes. The same is true of sales proceeds from U.S. property developed and held for sale by the investors, such as from sales of condominiums or other subdivided property.[14] Such effectively connected income will be taxable by the United States to each of the nonresident aliens on a net basis at the ordinary 0-50% rates paid by a U.S. citizen or resident. Such income similarly will be taxed to the foreign corporate investor on a net basis at the ordinary rates paid by a U.S. corporation — 15% (16% for 1982)-40% of the first $100,000 of taxable income and 46% of the balance.

In this connection, it should be noted that most new or used real estate improvements placed in service by the taxpayer after 1980 are to be written off over 15 years, and other such capital equipment over shorter periods, by deductible depreciation allowances under the accelerated cost recovery system. Additional such deductions apply to low-income rental housing. However, if depreciation more accelerated than 15-year straightline cost recovery is used for real estate improvements, then at disposition of the property *all* gain up to prior allowances usually is recaptured as ordinary income rather than as capital gain; in the case of residential property only the excess over straightline is so taxed. In addition, the excess deduction each year over straightline cost recovery is subject to the 15% or 20% minimum tax. All other equipment's shorter period allowances also are recaptured as ordinary income.

The investment tax credit of up to 10% is increased to up to 35% of rehabilitation expenses for older buildings, and an additional investment tax credit of 10% or more — *i.e.,* a total of 20% or more — may apply, *inter alia,* before 1983 to new building heat recovery equipment and non-oil or gas heating equipment — but often with a reduction in tax basis for depreciation purposes equal to one-half or all of the credit. Generally, construction period interest and real property taxes must be capitalized and amortized over 10 years or more rather than deducted currently, except as to residential property of a corporation. However, interest on industrial development bonds of a state or its political subdivision whose proceeds are used for a residential project to be occupied at least 15% — or 20% in certain cases — by low- or moderate-income individuals, and on mortgage subsidy bonds whose proceeds are used for single family residence purchases at least 20% of which are in low-income areas, is exempt from federal income tax.[15]

In certain cases where little or no business activity is carried on in the United States by the foreign investors or their resident agents, the income may not constitute effectively connected income. This is particularly likely where net lease arrangements for the property provide that all property taxes, insurance, maintenance, and other activities and expenses are to be undertaken by the tenant rather than the foreign owner. In the case of rental income, such treatment usually is undesirable because the income will be subject to a withholding tax of up to 30% of the gross amount — including even those amounts paid by the tenant for the owner — without any deductions. This tax may not be reduced even under a tax treaty, so that the tax often will equal or exceed the net income from the property.[16]

If such taxation appears likely, either the foreign corporate investor or any of the nonresident aliens may make a special election to have his share of the income taxed on a net basis as effectively connected income. Where net leased property such as an industrial warehouse, grazing land, or a private house leased to a single tenant is involved, the use of the election may be convenient to permit lower net income taxation of rentals. However, in the case of a nonresident alien, the general limitation on an individual's deduction of interest incurred to purchase or carry property held for investment only — including property subject to a net lease — still must be considered. Such an election must apply to all U.S. real property interests of an electing foreign corporation and to all such interests held for the production of income by an electing individual. Once made and not modified within the three-year period generally available for amending the original year's tax return, the election remains in force for all subsequent years unless revoked by the taxpayer with the federal tax authorities' permission. In case of such revocation, a re-election generally may not be made for another five years without further permission.[17]

The election may be made from year to year under certain tax treaties, the use of which is discussed further below. This can be helpful where expenses of a passive investment fluctuate so that in certain years a U.S. tax of, for example, 46% on net income is less than a 30% tax on gross income, while in other years the opposite is true.

Another alternative is ownership of the property through a U.S. corporation (or possibly a U.S. trust) which is permitted deductions as a domestic taxpayer.

It should be noted that failure to make the statutory or treaty election will *not* make gain on the *sale* of property taxfree, as discussed further below.

Foreign Corporation

As in the case of unimproved real property, the interest of each of the nonresident aliens in U.S. income producing property or property acquired for development, if owned directly or through a partnership, likely will be subject to federal gift tax upon a gift by the individual. His interest also will be subject to federal estate tax upon his death. In order to avoid such taxes, the individual investors may wish to organize directly or indirectly a foreign corporation in a tax haven to own their interests in the property, since no federal gift or estate taxes will apply to their transfers of stock in the corporation itself. In addition, such a corporation may help satisfy valid state law ownership or inheritance limitations as noted further above.

However, the use of such a foreign corporation by the nonresident aliens is somewhat more difficult in the case of income producing or development property than in the case of unimproved property. First, the income of the foreign corporation from the property usually will be effectively connected income subject to federal taxation on a net basis at the ordinary 15-46% rates paid by a U.S. corporation, which may be higher than the rates if the individuals received the income directly.

Second, and more important, the individual foreign shareholders of the corporation ordinarily will wish to receive personally or through intermediary holders of the stock — either immediately or eventually — the proceeds from operation or sale of the property. If this is accomplished by way of dividends from the foreign corporation, the profits often will be subject twice to federal income tax — once at the corporate level, and once by a withholding tax at the payment of dividends. If the U.S. profits are instead accumulated in excess of the reasonable business needs of the foreign corporation, a substantial accumulated earnings tax may be imposed on the corporation.[18]

Alternatively, the shareholders may receive certain income by way of interest charges on loans they make to provide part of the corporation's investment and operating funds. As a general rule, where debt to shareholders is substantially proportionate to their respective equity holdings in the corporation, the ratio of shareholder loans to equity probably should not exceed three to one and the ratio of total corporate debt to equity should not exceed 10 to one; otherwise, the shareholder loans may be treated as equity so that, for example, interest payments will be treated as nondeductible dividends. It seems likely that similar thin capitalization standards will apply to international loans owed to (and possibly from) a foreign person. The interest for each year also usually should be paid not later than two and one-half months after the close of the taxable year of the corporation if it deducts expenses on the accrued basis and is majority owned by one individual or family. In addition, the interest charges should be at arm's length rates.[19] Such interest will be deductible by the corporation if connected with its U.S. income. However, the interest payments to the shareholders often will be subject in turn to a large withholding tax.

These U.S. withholding taxes on the dividends and interest paid by the foreign corporation are likely because, if at least one-half of the foreign corporation's gross income for the most recent three full taxable years is effectively connected income, a like proportion of any dividends or interest paid by the corporation will be subject to a U.S. withholding tax of 30% of the gross amount paid.[20]

However, under various tax treaties, this U.S. withholding tax in certain circumstances is not imposed on dividend or interest payments by a foreign corporation. The use of such treaty jurisdictions is discussed in greater detail further below.

U.S. Corporation

The foreign corporate investor or the nonresident aliens may wish to organize a U.S. corporation to own their income producing property, property acquired for development, or even unimproved property as described further above. Such a corporation may, for example, help satisfy valid federal or state law ownership or inheritance limitations as noted further above. It may also assist in obtaining additional local financing for the purchase or development of the property, provide a local organization to manage or develop the property, or simply provide a local identity which is helpful in dealing with federal or state agencies, contractors, or other U.S. businesses.

From a federal tax planning standpoint, ownership of the property through such a corporation may have certain benefits, especially for the nonresident aliens, but usually also will have substantial disadvantages. On the positive side, the nonresident aliens will be able to make gifts of their stock in the U.S. corporation without the imposition of federal gift tax. However, such stock still will be subject to federal estate tax in the event of an individual investor's death. This latter problem in turn may be met by the U.S. corporation's stock being owned by a foreign holding or other corporation whose stock alone is held directly or beneficially by the nonresident aliens. Of course, the income, gift, and estate or inheritance taxes of the holding corporation's country also must be examined and minimized. In addition, as noted earlier, the U.S. corporation will be permitted to deduct or capitalize its expenses rather than possibly having to rely on a statutory or treaty election to be taxed on a net basis as in the case of a foreign person.

On the negative side, the rental or any other income generated by the property will be taxed on a net basis at the rates ordinarily applicable to any U.S. corporation. It should be possible for the U.S. corporation — as in the case of the foreign corporation noted above — to take deductions for reasonable interest charges payable to its foreign shareholders. However, such interest payments will be subject to U.S. withholding tax of 30% of the gross amount paid. In addition, any dividends paid by the

U.S. corporation out of its current or accumulated earnings and profits will be subject to a further withholding tax of 30% of the gross amount paid. Excessive accumulation of profits also may result in imposition of the penalty tax alluded to above in the case of a foreign corporation. This contrasts with direct ownership of the property, where the foreign investors pay only one tax at ordinary rates on the effectively connected income realized directly by them from the property.

However, under many tax treaties, the U.S. withholding tax on such interest payments may be eliminated or reduced to 10% or less of the gross amount, and the withholding tax on such dividends may be reduced to 5-15% of the gross amount. In the case of interest, a particular treaty may or may not extend this benefit to mortgage interest. Again, the use of such treaty jurisdictions is discussed further below.

If the foreign investors wish to avoid these tax difficulties with a U.S. corporation owning the property — or taxation upon sale through a U.S. corporation as discussed further below — it may be wise to consider organizing such a U.S. corporation not to own the property — if this is possible under valid federal or state law — but to perform development or management services for the property. The corporation's income from such services may be kept as low as consistent with arm's length dealings between the corporation and its foreign shareholders or a related foreign corporation owning the property. The U.S. corporation then can provide liaison with local agencies and businesses, with the property itself providing all or most of the security required for any additional local financing for the property on behalf of the foreign owners.

Additional Issues

Whether direct ownership, a partnership, or a foreign or domestic corporation is used for U.S. income producing property or property acquired for development, valid federal and state law ownership and inheritance limitations on foreign persons as noted further above must be considered, just as in the case of unimproved real property. State income, gift, and inheritance or similar taxes also must be examined. Property, sales, gross receipts, and other local taxes often will affect ownership and operation of the property.

In the case of income producing or development property, it will also generally be necessary to qualify the foreign investors, or the legal entity they employ, to conduct business in the applicable state jurisdiction as described in Chapter I.

Sale or Other Disposition of Property

The Foreign Investment in Real Property Tax Act of 1980 with certain technical amendments adopted in 1981 ("FIRPTA") significantly altered U.S. federal income taxation of the sale or other disposition of interests in U.S. real estate and other natural resources by foreign persons.[21] These legislative provisions and the initial Department of the Treasury regulations interpreting them, together with their general application to dispositions of such U.S. real property interests, are summarized below.

Legislative Provisions

Basic provisions. First, FIRPTA taxes any disposition of a U.S. real property interest by a nonresident alien or foreign corporation after June 18, 1980. Second, in the case of a disposition between related parties after December 31, 1979, the purchaser's basis is reduced by the amount of nontaxed gain. Third, the disposition of shares of stock or other interests in a U.S. real property holding corporation ("U.S. RPHC") is similarly taxed. Fourth, gain on the disposition of U.S. real property interests held in a *foreign* corporation is taxed upon the distribution (whether or not in liquidation) of the real property interest by the foreign corporation. Thus, upon the disposition of shares of a foreign corporation, tax is due not when the foreign owner sells the stock, but when the corporation is liquidated by the purchaser. Moreover, the tax is due from the liquidating foreign corporation, which is then owned by the purchaser.

Rates of tax. Gain of a nonresident alien or foreign corporation from the disposition of a U.S. real property interest (net of most U.S. real property losses) is taxed as if the same were effectively connected income at graduated capital gain and ordinary income tax rates substantially as in the case of a U.S. taxpayer. In the case of a nonresident alien, however, there is a minimum tax of 20% of the gain up to $60,000.

It should be noted that neither the purchaser nor any broker, attorney, or other person involved in the purchase of a U.S. real property interest from a foreign person is required by the 1980 provisions to withhold a portion of the purchase price to ensure that the seller's tax liability is paid. However, such a supplementary provision has been considered and foreign investors, purchasers, and others involved in such purchases should follow developments in this area.

Definitions of U.S. real property interest and U.S. RPHC. A U.S. real property interest includes any interest in U.S. real property (including a mine, well, or other natural deposit), a leasehold of U.S. land or improvements thereon, an option to acquire such land or improvements, and all personal property associated with the use of the real property. A loan is interpreted to be included in its entirety if the lender has any right to share in the value of the borrower's U.S. real property interests. However, the taxable gain upon disposition of such an asset arguably should be limited to that attributable to the equity participation (if any) by the lender in the asset's appreciation, such as the gain under a so called shared appreciation mortgage in excess of arm's length interest. The term also includes any interest (other than solely as a creditor) in any domestic corporation, unless the taxpayer establishes in accordance with regulations that the corporation is not, *and* has not been on certain determination dates (usually December 31) while the taxpayer owned the interest during the five years prior to disposition, a U.S. RPHC.

A domestic corporation is a U.S. RPHC if the fair market value of its U.S. real property interests is at least 50% of the aggregate fair market value of (1) its real property interests wherever located and (2) any of its other assets used or held for use in a trade or business (thus excluding excess cash or other assets not so used). This is to be calculated on the basis of gross asset values, rather than net values after subtracting debt against each asset, and excludes foreign assets acquired for the principal purpose of affecting the corporation's status. Dispositions of stock which is regularly traded on an established securities market are not covered, except those by a person who has held (directly or through special attribution rules) at any time while the corporation was a U.S. RPHC during the previous five years more than five percent of the class of stock sold.

Where another domestic *or* foreign corporation holds control (defined as 50% or more of the value of all classes of stock) of the U.S. RPHC, the controlling corporation is treated as owning a portion of each asset of the controlled corporation equal to the percentage of the fair market value of the stock of the controlled corporation represented by the stock held in it by the controlling corporation, for determining in turn whether the controlling corporation is treated as a U.S. RPHC.

U.S. real property interests and other assets held by a partnership, trust or estate also are treated as owned proportionately by its partners or beneficiaries.

The regulations provide further details for these definitions and ownership rules.

Distributions. Gain generally is to be recognized by a *foreign* corporation on any distribution (including a liquidating or redemptive distribution) of a U.S. real property interest. Such gain is the excess of the fair market value of the interest at the time of distribution over its tax basis. However, no gain is recognized if the distributee has a carryover basis in the property received and will be taxable upon the subsequent disposition of the property. In addition, the provision for nonrecognition of gain at the corporate level where the corporation sells its assets and liquidates within a 12-month period does not apply to any sale or exchange of a U.S. real property interest by a foreign corporation. These rules apply whether the foreign corporation is owned by foreign *or* U.S. persons.[22]

If a *domestic* corporation distributes a U.S. real property interest to a nonresident alien or a foreign corporation, the tax basis of the interest for the distributee remains the predistribution tax basis increased only by any gain recognized by the distributing corporation and any U.S. tax paid by the distributee.

Taxfree reorganizations and exchanges. Notwithstanding the above rules, general nonrecognition provisions continue to apply to permit, for example, a taxfree exchange of a U.S. real property interest for another such interest or a corporate or partnership reorganization — but only *if* the subsequent sale of the interest received in the transaction still will be taxable by the United States. Regulations may further limit such taxfree transactions. Even the transfer of a U.S. real property interest as a contribution to the capital of a foreign corporation may be taxable.

Special rules also are provided to tax sales of interests in partnerships, trusts and estates, and distributions by real estate investment trusts.

Election by foreign corporation to be treated as domestic. A foreign corporation with a U.S. real property interest may, if an applicable treaty accords nondiscriminatory treatment with respect to that interest, elect — generally within 90 days after it first holds a U.S. real property interest — to be treated as a domestic corporation for purposes of these disposition provisions. However, all owners of interests (other than solely as a creditor) in the foreign corporation must consent to the election and agree to taxation of any gain from disposition of such interests after June 18, 1980, even if the gain would otherwise be taxfree under a U.S. tax treaty. Regulations govern further the making and revocation of this election.[23]

Reporting requirements. First, any nonpublic *U.S. corporation* which at any time during the calendar year or during the four preceding years was a U.S. RPHC, and during the calendar year has one or more foreign shareholders,.must file an information return with federal tax authorities on Form 6659 for that year.

Second, any *foreign corporation,* whether or not its stock is publicly traded — and any *foreign or domestic partnership, trust, or estate* — which at any time during the calendar year has a substantial investor in U.S. real property must file a return for that year on Form 6660 with information concerning the entity itself and the interests held in it by the substantial investor. A substantial investor usually is a foreign person whose *pro rata* share of the fair market value of the foreign corporation or other entity's U.S. real property interests exceeds $50,000 — again, on a gross assets basis — at any time during the calendar year.

Third, *any foreign person* who is not engaged in a U.S. trade or business during the calendar year, but whose U.S. real property interests exceed $50,000 in value at any time during the year, must file an information return on Form 6661 for that year.

Each of these filing requirements is waived, however, if a security agreement for any potential federal capital gain or other income tax liability on the appreciation in value of the U.S. real property interests is entered into with federal tax authorities and renewed, usually each year. As noted further above, all of these reporting and security requirements are discussed further in Chapter XII. The reporting forms are expected to be available by early 1983. They may, however, become less significant if withholding of tax by purchasers and/or other agents is later adopted to ensure collection of the tax.

Treaty override. Treaties between the United States and foreign countries which may reduce or eliminate the tax under FIRPTA generally are to be overridden after December 31, 1984. If after 1980 and before 1985 a new treaty is signed to resolve such a conflict, the old treaty may by its terms be extended for up to two years after the signing.

As noted above, in a disposition between related parties after 1979, the purchaser's basis is reduced by the amount of any nontaxed gain; this is true even if the gain is exempt from taxation because of treaty provisions.

Application to Dispositions

The application of FIRPTA may be illustrated by several examples, in terms of the hypothetical investors described previously, as follows:

Direct ownership. In the case of property owned directly or through a partnership by the foreign corporate or individual investors, an investment in unimproved property or net leased property often does not entail the conduct of a U.S. trade or business, as noted further above. Capital gain realized by such foreign investors on sale of assets not used in a U.S. trade or business usually is taxfree (unless, in the case of a nonresident alien, he is present in the United States at least 183 days during the taxable year in which the sale occurs). However, gain on the direct sale or other disposition of real property even if *not* used in a U.S. trade or business — as well as of income producing property or property developed by the investors — generally will be taxed as if the same were effectively connected income at capital gain or ordinary income tax rates substantially as in the case of a U.S. taxpayer. For example, long-term capital gain will be taxed to a foreign corporate investor at the rate up to 28% applicable to such capital gain derived by a U.S. corporation, and will be taxed to nonresident aliens at the rates — four-tenths of the graduated amounts for ordinary income up to a maximum of 20% — applicable to long-term capital gains derived by U.S. citizens or residents. In the case of a nonresident alien, however, such property gain is subject to a minimum tax of 20% of the gain up to $60,000. Any long-term capital gain usually will be further subject to the 15% or 20% minimum tax on certain tax preferences. Losses from other U.S. real property interests held for profit, or otherwise effectively connected with the conduct of a U.S. trade or business, apparently including net operating loss carryovers from other years, may be used to offset the gain.[24]

Even if the purchase price is made payable in installments and the foreign investor is no longer engaged in a U.S. trade or business after the year of sale, the installments should remain taxable as effectively connected income. Furthermore, taxation of the seller on the installment basis may not be available if the property is sold to a related person who then resells it within two years. Likewise, if depreciable property is sold to the seller's spouse or an entity owned at least 80% by the seller, installment basis taxation usually is not available, *and* any gain of the seller is treated as ordinary income even if it would otherwise be taxed as capital gain.[25]

As an alternative, the foreign investors or their partnership may be able to exchange the property wholly or partly for other U.S. property of like kind. In that case, the currently taxable gain will be limited to the sum of the money, any net reduction of indebtedness because the second property includes less unpaid debt than the original property, and the fair market value of other property not of like kind — if any — which is received by the investors in the exchange. If attractive property for the exchange is not immediately available, it may even be possible to negotiate a deferred exchange under which the purchaser acquires the foreign investors' property immediately, subject to an agreement to purchase one or more other properties for delivery to the investors if the same are located within a specified period. It may also be possible to so exchange a general partner's interest in the property for a similar general partner's interest in another property of substantially identical type. However, this nonrecognition provision is unlikely to be available in an exchange for foreign property which subsequently could be sold taxfree by the foreign investors — unless an investor is a resident alien when the exchange is made, and later gives up U.S. residence before resale of the foreign property.[26]

It should be noted that even a gift or other *nonsale* disposition of a U.S. real property interest may be interpreted to be subject to income tax under FIRPTA. However, in the case of a gift the amount of gain which is recognized and thus may be taxable to the donor generally should be limited to economic benefits retained by the donor — for example, accrued expenses for which the donor was liable that are assumed by the property's recipient; the principal amount of a nonrecourse loan on the property to the extent it was used by the donor personally rather than invested in the property, or to the extent it resulted in additional cost recovery allowance deductions for the donor by increasing his tax basis in the property improvements; and any gift tax paid for the donor by the recipient in excess of the donor's tax basis in the property.[27] In the case of ownership of stock in a U.S. RPHC rather than direct ownership of property, few of such benefits are likely to have been received by the donor, so that a gift of the stock should not be likely to result in income recognition under FIRPTA.

Foreign corporation. In the case of property owned through a foreign corporation formed to hold the property — perhaps in a tax haven — if the foreign corporation itself directly sells the property, gain on the sale will be taxable as noted above. Even if the foreign corporation is formed in a country with which the United States has an income tax treaty, *no* protection from application of the FIRPTA provisions generally is provided for direct investment in property by a treaty country resident, except as noted further below in the discussion of certain treaty jurisdictions.

Moreover, the foreign corporation ordinarily may not sell the property and liquidate pursuant to a 12-month plan of liquidation without U.S. federal income tax on the corporation itself, as noted further above.

Distribution of the sale profits as a dividend from the corporation possibly may be subject to a U.S. withholding tax of 30%, as noted further above in connection with the holding of property when the corporation's recent gross income is substantially effectively connected income, unless a treaty eliminates such a U.S. withholding tax on the foreign corporation's dividend; however, FIRPTA itself apparently was not intended to affect such taxation of dividends or other nondisposition income, at least where the sale income would not be effectively connected except for the act. The alternative of a liquidating distribution of the sale proceeds should be taxfree to the foreign shareholder — as discussed in the case of a distribution of property immediately below — but will likely trigger taxation of the corporation itself on the balance of any installment obligation of the purchaser under the provisions noted above in connection with installment dispositions of directly owned property.

If the foreign corporation distributes the property to its foreign shareholders in exchange for all or part of their stock or in complete or partial liquidation of the corporation — or distributes property constituting only part of its assets to them as a dividend — *before* the sale negotiations, they may obtain a stepped-up basis in those assets equal to their fair market value and may subsequently negotiate sale of the property themselves with little or no further capital gain. This step-up often will be taxfree to the shareholders themselves, except that a dividend (including treatment as a dividend to the extent of the corporation's current and accumulated earnings and profits in the case of a partial liquidation to a corporate shareholder after August 1982) may be subject to a U.S. withholding tax of 30% where the distributing corporation's recent gross income is substantially effectively connected income, unless a treaty eliminates such a U.S. tax. In any event, however, the distribution of the property by the foreign corporation also will trigger U.S. capital gain or ordinary income taxation of the corporation itself on the excess of the property's fair market value over its tax basis for the distributing corporation.[28]

Both the prohibition on use of a 12-month plan of liquidation and the taxation of the foreign corporation triggered by distribution of the property as described above may be eliminated if the foreign corporation is permitted, due to a nondiscrimination clause in the tax treaty between the United States and its country of organization, to elect to be treated as a domestic corporation. However, its liquidation or distribution then becomes taxable similarly to that of a U.S. corporation discussed further below.

As an alternative, the foreign corporation may engage in a like kind exchange of the property for U.S. real property, in which event its currently taxable gain will be limited to any money, debt reduction, and the value of any other unlike property received in the exchange. As in the case of direct ownership noted above, this is unlikely to be available in an exchange for foreign property.

Alternatively, the foreign corporate or individual investors generally may sell their stock of the foreign corporation for taxfree capital gain. However, the purchaser must liquidate the acquired corporation — or, for a corporate purchaser of at least 80% of the foreign corporation's stock after August 1982, must elect to have the acquired corporation treated as having sold its assets and liquidated — in order to make the purchaser's tax basis in the property equal to the purchase price for the stock. In that event, gain will be recognized by the corporation equal to the excess of the fair market value of its property over its own tax basis in the property. This may be eliminated if the foreign corporation is permitted, due to a nondiscrimination clause in the tax treaty between the United States and its country of organization, to elect to be treated as a domestic corporation *and* the selling shareholders consent to taxation of their own gain.[29] Where the foreign corporation's own tax basis in the property has been reduced by straightline cost recovery allowances or other deductions below the selling shareholders' basis in their stock, this election usually will result in less tax.

Even where these requirements for taxfree liquidation of the foreign corporation are not met, sale of its stock taxfree may continue to be feasible if the purchaser does not require a prompt step-up in tax basis in the property by liquidating the corporation or making the election described above as to the corporation or making the election described above as to the corporation — for example, where the foreign corporation owns nondepreciable U.S. agricultural property.

U.S. corporation. In the case of property owned by the foreign investors through a U.S. corporation, if the corporation itself sells the property, gain on the sale will be fully taxable at the usual U.S. corporate rates of 15-46% for ordinary income and up to 28% for long-term capital gain. Distribution of the sale proceeds to the foreign shareholders also generally will constitute a dividend to the extent of the corporation's current or accumulated profits and be subject to an additional U.S. withholding tax of 30% or to a lesser treaty rate.

If the U.S. corporation sells the property and liquidates pursuant to a 12-month plan of liquidation, this will avoid most federal income tax on the corporation, except as to recapture of personal property and more accelerated real property cost recovery allowances and investment tax credits taken by the U.S. corporation. However, income tax generally will be imposed on distributions to the foreign shareholders, since they are considered to receive the proceeds of sale of the property in exchange for their stock. If they receive from the corporation installment obligations of the purchaser, they may still be entitled to the installment sale U.S. tax treatment referred to above for direct sale of property. This 12-month arrangement is not available where the U.S. corporation qualifies as a collapsible corporation, which is particularly likely where the corporation has been used to develop the property. Nor is it generally available if another corporation — such as the foreign corporate investor in the hypothetical situation here — owns at least 80% of the U.S. corporation's stock.[30]

If the U.S. corporation instead distributes the property to its foreign shareholders in exchange for all or part of their stock or in complete or partial liquidation of the corporation — or distributes property constituting only part of its assets to them as a dividend — before sale negotiations, their tax basis in the property will remain the predistribution tax basis of the U.S. corporation increased only by (1) any gain recognized by the corporation and (2) any U.S. tax paid by the shareholders on the distribution. Such gain usually will be recognized by the distributing corporation if after August 1982 it uses appreciated property to redeem the stock of a corporate shareholder or the stock of a less than 10% noncorporate shareholder. The U.S. tax payable by the shareholders usually will be capital gain tax on redemption of their stock in a U.S. RPHC (except that treatment as a dividend applies to the extent of the corporation's current and accumulated earnings and profits in the case of a partial liquidation to a corporate shareholder after August 1982), or ordinary income tax in the case of stock of a collapsible U.S. RPHC Alternatively, in the case of a dividend, they will be subject to a U.S. withholding tax of 30% or a lesser treaty rate. In any event, resale of the property by the shareholders will be taxable to the extent of any gain over their own tax basis in the property, as described further above in the case of dispositions of directly owned property.[31]

As an alternative, the U.S. corporation itself — as in the case of a foreign owner noted above — may engage in a like kind exchange of the property for other real property, in which event its currently taxable gain will be limited to any money and the value of any other property not of like kind received by the corporation in the exchange. In the case of a U.S. corporation, this may be possible even in an exchange for foreign real property, unless the value of that property would cause the U.S. corporation to cease to be a U.S. RPHC so that its stock could be sold taxfree by the foreign shareholders.

Alternatively, the foreign shareholders may be able to sell the stock of their U.S. corporation. A purchaser unrelated to the selling shareholders generally may then obtain a new tax basis in the property for cost recovery allowances, resale, and other purposes which equals the purchase price for the stock by liquidating the acquired corporation, which liquidation usually will be taxfree in the case of a U.S. acquired corporation — or, for a corporate purchaser after August 1982, by electing to have the acquired corporation treated as having sold its assets and liquidated, which usually also will be taxfree except as to recapture of personal property and more accelerated real property cost recovery allowances and investment tax credits.

However, the selling shareholders' own gain from disposition of the shares owned at any time while the corporation was a U.S. RPHC generally will be taxed as effectively connected income as described further above. This will include ordinary income rather than capital gain taxation in the case of stock of a collapsible corporation. Even in the case of capital gain taxation, minimum taxes as in the case of a U.S. person may apply.

Alternatively, in case of a loss on the sale or other disposition of such stock, a nonresident alien — similarly to a U.S. individual shareholder — may be able to treat such a loss on certain stock of a U.S. small business corporation as ordinary rather than capital loss.

A foreign selling shareholder may avoid these taxes if the U.S. corporation has not been a U.S. RPHC at any time within the past five years — for example, by ensuring that its assets are comprised less than one-half of U.S. real property interests for the previous five years. A foreign shareholder's disposition of U.S. stock also may be taxfree if the stock is regularly traded on an established securities market and the seller has not held (directly or through special attribution rules) at any time while the corporation was a U.S. RPHC during the previous five years more than five percent of the class of stock sold. It may also be taxfree if the stock disposition is made before 1985 by a person entitled to the benefits of a U.S. tax treaty which eliminates U.S. federal income tax on gains from dispositions of capital assets. The use of such treaty jurisdictions is discussed in greater detail below.[32]

Additional Issues

The sale or other disposition of interests in U.S. real estate and other natural resources by the hypothetical investors also may be subject to state income taxes as described generally in Chapter II. In particular, gain on the direct sale of property by a nonresident alien or a foreign or U.S. corporation usually is taxed by the state where the property is located.

Use of Tax Treaty and Other Foreign Jurisdictions

The Netherlands Antilles and British Virgin Islands

As noted above, nonresident aliens often may find it advantageous to organize a foreign corporation to own their interests in U.S. real estate in order to minimize federal gift and estate taxes on their holdings. In addition, such a corporation may help satisfy valid state law ownership or inheritance limitations as noted further above. Moreover, both foreign corporate and individual investors may find such a foreign corporation in a tax haven useful in accumulating income to minimize home country taxes or other investment regulations.

However, as noted above, where such a foreign corporation is used to own income producing property or property acquired for development which generates effectively connected income, part or all of the dividend or interest payments by the corporation to its foreign corporate or individual shareholders may be subject to additional federal withholding tax of up to 30% of the gross amount paid. In addition, the foreign corporation's country of organization may impose its own income, gift, and estate or inheritance taxes, even though most of such taxes may be low enough to qualify the jurisdiction as a tax haven.

These difficulties often may be avoided by utilizing a Netherlands Antilles corporation to own U.S. real estate investments, because of the benefits under the U.S. income tax treaty with the Netherlands as extended to the Antilles and under local Antilles tax laws.[33] In this situation, the U.S. property commonly is owned by an Antilles corporation organized as a *Naamloze Vennootschap* ("*N.V.*"), the stock of which is issued to the foreign corporate or individual investors or to another foreign corporation, trust, or other entity established by them. The basic tax treatment of such an investment structure may be summarized as follows in terms of the hypothetical investors described previously:

(1) Ownership of the U.S. real estate by the *N.V.* avoids U.S. federal gift tax upon transfers of the corporate stock by the nonresident aliens and U.S. federal estate tax upon the death of any of such individuals.

(2) The *N. V.* may elect from year to year to be taxed on a net basis on its income even from unimproved or other less active property, which may facilitate U.S. deduction or capitalization of its expenses in certain years and U.S. taxation at a lower 30% rate on gross income in other years.

(3) Reasonable interest charges — as described previously in connection with holding of property generally — may be made by the corporate or individual shareholders of the *N. V.* on loans to the *N. V.* to provide part of the funds to acquire or develop the property, which charges may be deducted by the *N. V.* from gross income generated by the property for U.S. federal tax purposes.

(4) No U.S. federal withholding tax generally is imposed on interest paid by the *N. V.* or on dividends to the *N. V.*'s foreign shareholders, even where one-half or more of the *N. V.*'s gross income is effectively connected income.

(5) No Antilles income taxes are imposed on U.S. real estate income of the *N. V.* or on dividends or interest paid by the *N. V.* to its non-Antilles shareholders or lenders.

(6) No Antilles gift, estate, or inheritance taxes are imposed on transfer or inheritance of the *N. V.*'s stock by the non-Antilles individuals or their successors.

(7) Upon sale of the U.S. real estate, the *N. V.* should be able to elect to be treated as a U.S. corporation, provided the selling shareholders consent to tax on their own gain under FIRPTA. This will permit sale of the stock of the *N. V.* and its prompt liquidation taxfree by the purchaser — or, in the case of a corporate purchaser after August 1982, the purchaser's election to have the acquired corporation treated as having sold its assets and liquidated, usually taxfree except as to recapture of certain accelerated cost recovery allowances and investment tax credits — in order to obtain a tax basis in the property equal to the stock's purchase price. Where the *N. V.*'s own tax basis in the property has been reduced — for example, by straightline U.S. cost recovery allowances — below the selling shareholders' basis in their stock, this election to have the selling shareholders taxed usually will result in less current tax on the disposition. No Antilles tax will be imposed at the shareholder level upon sale of the *N. V.*'s stock and its liquidation if Antilles corporate liquidation requirements are complied with and the *N. V.* has been organized and maintained under Article 14A of the Netherlands Antilles Profits Tax Ordinance.

However, the U.S. income tax treaty applicable to the Antilles does *not* override FIRPTA to permit taxfree sale by the *N. V.* itself of U.S. real property interests *or* of the stock of a U.S. RPHC. Likewise, interest on a purchaser's installment obligation to the *N. V.*, if secured by a mortgage on U.S. property, generally will be subject to 30% withholding tax.

This tax treaty also is being renegotiated and many of its U.S. benefits may be eliminated or reduced.

As one alternative to such a Netherlands Antilles corporation, a British Virgin Islands corporation often has been used to own U.S. real estate investments, because of the benefits under the prior U.S. income tax treaty of 1945 with the United Kingdom as extended to the British Virgin Islands and under local B.V.I. tax laws. However, these are likely to be altered substantially by the treaty recently negotiated and thereafter being renegotiated between the United States and the British Virgin Islands.[34] Unlike the Antilles treaty, the B.V.I. treaty has not specifically exempted U.S. real estate income of the B.V.I. corporation from local B.V.I. tax. However, a Type-D B.V.I. corporation currently is not taxed there on, for example, rental income unless remitted to the country. In addition, an election of U.S. net income taxation may be made, but under the new treaty is likely to be binding for all subsequent years unless terminated with the U.S. tax authorities' permission. More significantly, under a new treaty interest and dividends paid by a B.V.I. corporation whose gross income is at least one-half effectively connected income — for example, from U.S. income producing property — may well be subject to the U.S. withholding tax of 30% of the gross amount paid.

Any new treaty's benefits also possibly may be denied to a B.V.I. corporation if it is not owned substantially by individual residents of the British Virgin Islands. In the meantime, the prior treaty was terminated by the United States in mid-1982 without a new treaty to replace it.

The same alternatives for sale of the property as in the case of an Antilles corporation generally are available in the case of a B.V.I. corporation, except the election to be treated as a domestic corporation due to lack of a treaty. Furthermore, in the British Virgin Islands, absence of exchange controls and local director requirements, use of English common law and the U.S. dollar, and slightly more rapid access to the United States than from the Netherlands Antilles may be helpful. Individual foreign investors may be troubled by the absence of bearer corporate stock. As to this last matter, a trust or other nominee holder of stock may offer one alternative in any investment structure.

The Netherlands

If a foreign investor wishes to take advantage of the delay in the treaty override under FIRPTA described further above because most of his disposition gain from property will be realized before 1985, then the use of a Netherlands holding corporation should be considered.[35] In this situation, the U.S. property commonly is owned by a U.S. corporation, the stock of which is owned in turn by a Netherlands holding corporation organized as a *Besloten Vennootschap* ("*B.V.*"). The *B.V.* should be owned in turn by a person qualifying under a Netherlands treaty for elimination of the Netherlands' own withholding tax of 25% on dividends; a Netherlands Antilles parent corporation usually can be used for this purpose. The basic tax treatment of such an investment structure may be summarized as follows in terms of the hypothetical investors described previously:

(1) Ownership of the stock in the Antilles or other foreign parent corporation by the nonresident alien investors avoids U.S. federal gift tax upon transfers of the stock and U.S. federal estate tax upon the death of any of such individuals.

(2) Reasonable interest charges — as described previously in connection with holding of property generally — may be made by the *B. V.* on loans to the U.S. corporation to provide part of the funds to acquire or develop the property, which charges may be deducted by the U.S. corporation from gross income generated by the property for U.S. federal tax purposes. Under the U.S. income tax treaty with the Netherlands, no U.S. federal withholding tax is generally imposed on interest paid by the U.S. corporation to the *B. V.*

(3) The U.S. federal withholding tax on dividends paid out of earnings of the U.S. corporation to the *B. V.* generally is reduced to five percent (or 15% if the *B. V.* owns less than 25% of the U.S. corporation) rather than the usual 30% U.S. rate.

(4) No U.S. federal withholding tax generally is imposed on interest or dividends paid by the *B. V.* to its Antilles parent, even where one-half or more of the *B. V.*'s gross income is effectively connected income.

(5) No U.S. federal income tax under FIRPTA should apply currently before 1985 to sale of the U.S. corporation's stock by the *B. V.* or, if the U.S. corporation is not a collapsible corporation and generally is owned less than 80% by one or more affiliated corporations, possibly to a 12-month sale of the property and liquidation of the U.S. corporation by the *B. V.* Even if an installment sale is used, mortgage interest from the U.S. purchaser usually should be exempt from U.S. federal withholding tax under this tax treaty. However, the *B. V.* should file a U.S. federal income tax return for the year of disposition of the U.S. subsidiary. If sale installments may continue after the lapse of treaty protection from the FIRPTA provisions, the *B. V.* should elect out of the installment sale U.S. tax treatment referred to further above on a timely filed return. Moreover, as suggested further above in connection with sales generally, sale to a purchaser related to the *B. V.* or its shareholders may prevent the election by a corporate purchaser of a stepped-up tax basis in the property of the U.S. corporation, or may limit the availability of installment sale treatment.[36]

(6) The *B. V.* should obtain a ruling from the Netherlands tax authorities — a so called participation exemption — to exempt from

income tax there the dividends and disposition gains from its investment in the U.S. corporation. Such rulings apparently are available currently only where the U.S. corporation is actively engaged in a trade or business such as development of commercial or residential property, and not in the case of more passive investments such as holding of unimproved property for appreciation or an investment only as a limited partner. Interest from the U.S. corporation may be subject to Netherlands tax, but should be nearly offset by deductible interest payments to the Antilles parent corporation which generally are free of Netherlands withholding tax.

(7) No or very low Antilles income taxes are imposed on dividends or interest received by the Antilles parent corporation, or on dividends or interest paid by it to its non-Antilles shareholders or lenders.

(8) No Antilles gift, estate, or inheritance taxes are imposed on transfer or inheritance of the Antilles parent corporation's stock by the non-Antilles individuals or their successors.

It should be noted that any attempted transfer of property which has appreciated in value, or of the shares of a U.S. or foreign corporation owning such property, into a holding corporation entitled to protection from FIRPTA under the Netherlands or another treaty is unlikely to qualify for U.S. federal income tax purposes as a taxfree reorganization or exchange, as opposed to a taxable sale on arm's length price and other terms.[37]

In addition, the current treaty with the Netherlands is being renegotiated and certain of its U.S. tax benefits may in the future be reduced, or be denied to a Netherlands corporation not owned substantially by individual residents of the Netherlands.

Other Treaty and Nontreaty Jurisdictions

A number of other countries are parties to older U.S. income tax treaties containing a U.S. tax exemption for gains from dispositions of capital assets, somewhat similarly to the Netherlands treaty described above. Although these are generally not tax havens for foreign investors, the exemption may be useful for sale before 1985 of the stock of a U.S. RPHC owned by a resident of such a treaty country. However, if the treaty exemption is interpreted to apply only to capital gains — rather than all gains from dispositions of capital assets, whether taxed as ordinary income or capital gains, which are not attributable to a U.S. permanent establishment of the seller — then the exemption may not apply to the sale of stock of a U.S. collapsible corporation.[38]

The treaty of 1966 with Canada even exempts from U.S. tax the gain from sale of most U.S. property held directly by a Canadian resident, if the resident has no permanent establishment at all in the United States. This may be useful for non-Canadians if property is owned by an individual that becomes a Canadian resident — or a corporation that becomes such a resident for Canadian tax purposes by shifting its management and control to Canada — since the property generally is considered for Canadian income tax purposes to have a basis equal to its value upon taking up such residence and may be resold promptly with little Canadian tax. However, this basis step-up does not apply to inventory under Canadian tax principles, which may include even unimproved land. Furthermore, the U.S. taxfree reorganization limitations noted above in connection with use of the Netherlands treaty may make such a reorganization in the case of a corporation with appreciated property difficult without U.S. tax, and it is also arguable that the Canadian treaty was not intended to benefit a corporation which recently shifted residence.

Various other treaty countries may be useful for U.S. real estate investments in certain circumstances. For example, if resale of the property before 1985 is not anticipated, but interest payments or dividends to foreign persons are anticipated, then a foreign corporation organized in any country with a tax treaty which eliminates part or all of the U.S. withholding tax on such payments by the foreign corporation should be considered.

Alternatively, if unimproved property is producing little or no income, or the U.S. statutory net income election results in sufficient cost recovery allowances and other offsetting deductions without interest payments to foreign persons which may be subject to U.S. withholding tax, then a foreign corporation organized in a nontreaty country may be just as useful in minimizing federal gift, estate, and income taxes as a treaty country corporation.

It may also be possible for a U.S. or foreign corporation to establish permanent residence in the U.S. Virgin Islands by conducting all significant business operations and all directors' and shareholders' meetings there. Generally it will then be taxed by the V.I. authorities only on its V.I. source income. However, under the Revised Organic Act of the Virgin Islands of 1954, all persons with V.I. permanent residence apparently satisfy their U.S. federal income tax obligations by paying V.I. tax on worldwide income.[39] The FIRPTA provisions described above have been extended to tax the sale or other disposition of U.S. and V.I. real property interests held through a V.I. or V.I. resident corporation.[40] However, such a foreign corporation's rental or other nonsale income from U.S. real estate and other transactions and investments may escape most U.S. federal and V.I. taxation. The U.S. federal withholding tax of 30% still may apply to dividends and interest paid by the corporation if at least one-half of its gross income is U.S. effectively connected income, as noted generally further above, but this also may be eliminated by a tax treaty between the United States and the foreign corporation's country of organization. Judicial authorities have not resolved issues involved in such a foreign corporation's establishing V.I. permanent residence — contrary to the U.S. Internal Revenue Code's general taxation of corporations based not on residence but on country of organization — as well as other potential interpretive questions under the Organic Act.

U.S. Holding Corporation

The FIRPTA provisions described further above — unless they are amended — override after 1984 even those treaties referred to above as to sales or other dispositions of U.S. real estate and other natural resource interests. If nonresident alien investors are willing to hold their interests directly in spite of U.S. gift and estate tax difficulties, or if a trust through which they are not treated as owners of the property for U.S. estate and gift tax purposes (as discussed generally in Chapter XI) is used to hold such interests, the U.S. federal long-term capital gain rates may be limited to a maximum of 20%. Even if a foreign or U.S. corporation is used, the U.S. corporate long-term capital gain rate of 28% may not be considered excessive.

However, for investments producing ordinary income — such as most subdivisions of property — or investments producing short-term capital gains, adaptation of U.S. tax planning employed by U.S. domestic investors in real estate and other natural resources may be appropriate. One possible structure to facilitate such planning is the use of a U.S. holding corporation owning U.S. subsidiary corporations for various projects and activities, which may be owned in turn by a foreign parent corporation organized in a country with which the United States has an income tax treaty. There may be several favorable elements in this structure for the hypothetical foreign investors described previously, including the following:

(1) Ownership of the stock of the foreign parent corporation (or of a further entity owning the parent) by the nonresident alien investors avoids U.S. federal gift and estate taxes for them.

(2) Reasonable interest charges — as described previously in connection with holding of property generally — may be made by the foreign parent corporation on loans to the U.S. corporations to provide part of their funds to organize or develop properties and other investments. This interest should be free of most or all U.S. withholding tax under the U.S. income tax treaty with the parent's country.

(3) The use of tax losses and the transfer of excess cash among the U.S. subsidiaries and their respective properties are facilitated because the subsidiaries may qualify as a consolidated group for U.S. income tax purposes where they are controlled by one U.S. holding corporation. Interest deductions from loans to any of the U.S. corporations from abroad may be used to reduce the entire group's consolidated taxable income.

(4) Taxfree corporate reorganizations involving the U.S. subsidiaries and taxfree exchanges of property for other U.S. property may provide substantial U.S. tax deferral opportunities.

(5) Dividends from the U.S. holding corporation to the foreign parent corporation generally should be subject to U.S. withholding tax of only 5-15% under the U.S. tax treaty with the parent's country.[41]

In all such tax treaty structuring of U.S. real estate and similar investments, the distinction between treaty use and abuse must be considered, particularly because the definition and limitation of such abuse may be of increasing importance for U.S. and other tax authorities. For example, the U.S. Department of the Treasury initially was instructed in 1978 to study the tax treatment of sale of U.S. real estate by nonresident aliens and foreign corporations in part because of the apparent use of the annual net income election as noted above under certain tax treaties. The report of the Department has been followed not only by the FIRPTA provisions described further above with respect to real estate disposition gains of foreign investors, but also by current and proposed tax treaty negotiations to eliminate treaty clauses inconsistent with the FIRPTA provisions *and* to limit the use of a treaty generally by investors who are not residents of the treaty country.[42]

Investments in Agricultural and Ranch Property

For investments from abroad in U.S. agricultural or ranch property, timber property, or oil, gas, or other mineral interests, certain additional aspects should be considered beyond the regulatory, tax, and other considerations outlined above that apply generally in structuring U.S. real estate investments. While it is not feasible here to describe the many federal and state considerations applicable generally to each type of property, selected aspects relevant to foreign investors are noted here.

U.S. agricultural and ranch property — dairy and poultry farms; cotton, wheat, feed grain, fruit and vegetable, and specialty crop farms; and livestock ranches — have been of increasing interest to foreign investors in recent years. Possibly as much as one-fifth of all such property recently sold in the United States has been purchased by such investors. Somewhat similarly, an influx of European nobility and money occurred in the U.S. western states a century ago. In the current wave of interest, not only concentrations of available funds abroad, U.S. dollar devaluations, and the continuing relative economic strength and political and legal stability of the United States — as in the case of other U.S. real estate investments — but in particular high farmland prices abroad and potential further value increases in agricultural property in view of worldwide food needs may cause foreign investors to be willing to pay high prices at low initial rates of return for such U.S. property.

Such foreign investments have been the subject of increasing federal and state attention. For example, the FIRPTA provisions described further above with respect to general real estate disposition gains of foreign investors were prompted initially by desires to eliminate potential U.S. tax benefits for foreign investors in U.S. agricultural property. This is due in part to the relatively high visibility of foreign ownership in less densely settled and more confined rural areas, the use of such agricultural property for domestic food supplies, possibly higher general farming expenses following price increases, and recurrent concern with any corporate or limited partnership or other absentee farming — domestic or foreign. Accordingly, a potential foreign investor in such property must follow further regulation in this area, especially at the state level.

Federal reporting requirements for foreign investments in agricultural and other property are noted further above and described in greater detail in Chapter XII. In addition, grazing permits for federal ranch land generally may be issued only to U.S. citizens (or aliens who have declared their intentions to become U.S. citizens), partnerships or other associations of such citizens, or U.S. corporations. Under applicable regulations, such a U.S. corporation usually must be directly or indirectly controlled — or, for forest land grazing permits, must be owned at least 80% — by U.S. citizens.[43] Such permits may be significant where adjacent federal land is required to make grazing of livestock economical. However, an unqualified foreign owner may lease his own property to a qualified U.S. person or enter into a management or operating agreement for his property with such a person, who then may be able to obtain a grazing permit for federal land. Often federal laws restrict the foreign acquisition of homesteads within federal territories — relatively insignificant now — and limit benefits in the case of foreign persons under other federal agricultural programs such as loans under the Farmers Home Administration and emergency disaster relief.[44] It should also be noted that a controversial federal law generally limiting any person to 160 acres for which certain federal dam or other project water may be used is being amended to increase this limit and to permit purchase of additional such water at higher prices.[45]

State laws, as described further above, often especially attempt to restrict foreign ownership or inheritance, or corporate ownership, of agricultural and similar property. Leasehold interests in agricultural or state owned property may be subject to similar restrictions. In addition, state law may prohibit any agricultural or state owned property lease from extending for more than a specified term — for example, two or three years. As noted above and in Chapter XII, broad state reporting requirements may be triggered by such an investment. A potential foreign investor also should note that special farm labor laws may apply to agricultural workers.

On the other hand, state tax and other incentive programs for out-of-state or foreign investors — discussed more generally in Chapter VI respecting new U.S. business enterprises — may apply to certain farm operations and should be investigated in the state involved.

One alternative if federal or state restrictions limit ownership or leasing of agricultural or other property, and the foreign investor is concerned primarily to obtain the agricultural or other products for use or sale, is simply to enter into a long-term contract for the output of the property. Here only the broad federal restrictions on transactions with investors from countries hostile to the United States and possible U.S. export restrictions will be applicable.[46]

From a federal tax planning standpoint, numerous special gross income calculation, deduction, investment tax credit, capital gain, tax accounting, and other income tax rules, as well as tax curbs on certain limited partnerships and other farming syndicates, apply generally to agricultural and similar property. Special federal income tax — as well as antitrust — exemptions and rules apply to agricultural cooperatives.

In addition, several significant tax aspects should be noted in the case of foreign investment in such property. First, federal estate tax rules providing special valuation reductions for certain farms and closely held business real estate are *not* available to the estate of a nonresident alien decedent.[47]

Second, a nonresident alien, foreign corporation, or other foreign person often will wish to have the seller of agricultural property or another unrelated or related party enter into a farming or grazing lease or a management or operating agreement for the property in order to relieve the absent foreign owner from operating responsibilities. For federal income tax purposes, as noted further above, if a net lease is used the foreign owner may not be engaged in U.S. trade or business. However, federal taxation of the lease rental on a net income basis and potential federal gift and estate taxes on transfers by an individual foreign owner may be important. In that case, one approach is to have the property owned and leased out by a foreign corporation owned by the foreign investor and organized in a country such as the Netherlands Antilles which has a tax treaty with the United States permitting an annual net income election.

Third, if the use of a foreign corporation to take title to such property is prohibited by applicable federal or state law, the property may be able to be owned instead by a U.S. corporation which is permitted deductions as a domestic taxpayer, and which is owned in turn by a foreign holding corporation organized in a country such as the Netherlands that has a tax treaty with the United States permitting interest, dividends, and possibly (until 1985) gain on sale of the U.S. corporation's stock to be paid free of most or all U.S. federal income taxes.

Fourth, sale of the stock of a foreign corporation taxfree may be feasible if the purchaser does not require a prompt step-up in tax basis in the property by liquidating the corporation — or, for a corporate purchaser, by electing to have the acquired corporation treated as having sold its assets and liquidated — because, for example, the agricultural property is both nondepreciable and unlikely to be resold in the near future at a gain.

Investments in Timber Property

Millions of acres of commercially valuable U.S. timber property remain in the hands of governmental and noncommercial private owners. However, because large adjacent acreages may be required to make timberland operations economical, a potential foreign investor may have to give particular attention to restrictions limiting foreign leasing or ownership of federal forestry land and state public and private timberland. For example, a prohibition such as that of South Carolina on certain foreign investment in more than 500,000 acres of any real estate (approximately 780 square miles, 2,000 square kilometers, or 200,000 hectares) — which is generally of little concern — might be significant for a foreigner with a substantial undivided fractional interest in a large such property.[48]

From a federal tax planning standpoint, special cost depletion and other deductions and income tax rules apply generally to timber property. In addition, brief examples of aspects relevant to foreign investment in such property may be noted here. First, as to most timber cutting profits, any owner generally may elect to treat as capital gain the part of such profits attributable to the timber's standing value on the first day of the taxable year of the cutting itself, or will treat as capital gain the profits from timber sold under a cutting contract with another person under which the owner retains an economic interest in the timber after cutting until it is sold. However, under the latter approach, gain to a nonresident alien or foreign corporation from such a cutting contract expressly is subject to a U.S. withholding tax of 30%, which may be unattractive to the parties, unless the gain is taxable as U.S. effectively connected income.[49]

Second, even regular thinning and selling of the timber in the course of good forest husbandry may result in the foreign owner being engaged in U.S. trade or business and so subject to federal net income taxation as in the case of a U.S. person.[50] However, even if the foreign owner enters into a net lease of the property with another party who remains responsible for all maintenance and similar expenses of the property, the owner still may wish to be taxed in most years on a net income basis. Alternatively, the use of a U.S. corporation to take title to the property may be required by applicable federal or state law, yet potential federal estate taxes may be important. For these issues, the use of U.S. and/or foreign corporations similar to those noted above in connection with agricultural property should be considered.

Investments in Oil, Gas, and Mineral Interests

Federally owned lands generally may be leased for exploration and exploitation of oil, gas, oil shale, coal, phosphate, potassium, or sodium to U.S. citizens, partnerships or associations of such citizens, and U.S. corporations. Such a U.S. corporation may be controlled by aliens, unless their country prohibits U.S. citizens or corporations from leasing its public lands for mineral development. In addition, generally no individual, association, or corporation directly or indirectly may so lease more than a specified acreage.[51] Geothermal steam and related resource development leases of federal land likewise may be issued to such U.S. persons (and state and local governmental units), subject again to specified acreage limits, but in such case the U.S. corporation may be owned by aliens from any country.[52] Any uranium or thorium recovery, transportation, sale, or use within the United States requires a federal government license.[53] Further, development of certain federally owned metallic minerals generally is limited to U.S. citizens (or aliens who have declared their intentions to become U.S. citizens) and apparently U.S. corporations regardless of foreign stock ownership.[54] It should be noted, however, that the United States did undertake to develop jointly with the Federal Republic of Germany and Japan a facility to produce fuel oil from U.S. coal.

Federal leases for all minerals of the U.S. outer continental shelf beyond the three-mile limit of general state regulation may be issued, under applicable regulations, to U.S. citizens or resident aliens or U.S. corporations regardless of foreign stock ownership. Foreign investors have made extensive use of U.S. subsidiary corporations for such offshore leasing. In addition, any person may be licensed to conduct mere geological or geophysical operations in the same area.[55]

In the case of any gas — but *not* oil — produced from federal lands or otherwise committed to interstate commerce, certain federal pricing regulations also apply.[56]

Under state laws, mineral interests usually are treated as interests in real estate subject to the same general restrictions on foreign ownership, lease, or inheritance. However, in several states special additional laws, restrictions, and reporting requirements apply to state owned lands, onshore and offshore oil and gas, and other mineral interests and these should be investigated by a potential foreign investor. Severance or production taxes also may be imposed on mining or oil, gas, or other natural resources production within the state.

From a federal tax planning standpoint, myriad special tax issues arise generally in oil and gas investments. These include, for example, deductions for cost depletion and percentage depletion — dropping to 15% after 1983 — investment tax credits, special rules for offshore operations, limits on advance royalty deductions, recapture of intangible drilling cost deductions, and curbs on use of tax benefits by limited partnerships and other investment syndicates. Additional special taxes often apply, including the windfall profit excise tax of 15-70% where crude oil sale is involved, and the crude oil spill tax.[57]

In the case of geothermal resources, percentage depletion and intangible drilling deductions similar to those for oil and gas recently were added. Special depletion, tax curb, and other rules also apply generally to coal and other mineral investments — even to soil.[58]

Certain tax aspects relevant to foreign investment in such property may be noted briefly. First, as discussed generally below in connection with joint ventures, much federal income tax planning of mineral and other real property investments for U.S. persons, and especially U.S. limitations on such tax shelters, are not applicable to tax needs of foreign investors because they have little other U.S. effectively connected income against which to use excess writeoffs. Furthermore, they may look more to *foreign* tax benefits from such investments.

Second, payments to a foreign investor selling or leasing such a U.S. mineral interest may be characterized as a royalty under certain circumstances and, if not effectively connected income, will be subject to a federal withholding tax of 30% of gross amount (or a lesser tax treaty rate), which may be unattractive to the parties.[59]

Third, the necessity of using a U.S.corporation to hold federal — and possibly state — mineral interests may raise concern with federal estate taxation of a nonresident alien owner on the stock of that corporation. If so, the use of a foreign holding corporation similar to that noted above in connection with agricultural and timber property should be considered.

Additional Joint Venture Considerations

In addition to the basic partnership taxation and other considerations noted above, joint investments in U.S. real estate and other natural resources — particularly between foreign and U.S. investors — may involve more complex considerations. In terms of the hypothetical investors described previously, the foreign corporate investor or the nonresident aliens may wish to joint venture a U.S. real estate or similar investment with domestic investors or a domestic developer.

An appropriate vehicle may be a limited or general partnership between the U.S. party and — if possible under valid federal or state law limitations — a separate foreign or U.S. corporation owned by the foreign investors. Such a partnership may be used, for example, for investment in improved property or development property by a small group of foreign investors in a private offering structured by a U.S. partner who will manage the day to day operation of the U.S. investment. Partnerships for domestic investors in real estate and other natural resources — as in many other types of investments — have been oriented historically toward providing investors with initial tax deductions which substantially exceed immediate taxable income of the partnership, which may then be used to offset other taxable income of the investors. However, such excess writeoffs have come under increasing attack by federal tax authorities and have been limited in certain respects by amendments to the federal tax laws.[60] For foreign investors, excess writeoffs for U.S. tax purposes often may be unnecessary, since they may have little or no other U.S. effectively connected income against which to apply them. Such investors often are more concerned to spread available deductions over several years in order to reduce future taxable income from the same property or group of properties.

Since the domestic and foreign investors may have different income goals or be subject to different tax treatments, special partnership allocations between them should be considered. For example, ordinary income from operating the property and excess deductions from cost recovery allowances for buildings and other improvements might be allocated to the U.S. partner. However, where long-term holdings are anticipated — particularly beyond 1984 when even treaty protected taxfree dispositions of property will likely be unavailable — foreign investors should be cautious about relinquishing excess deductions which may be carried forward or otherwise used to offset operating or sale profits. The foreign or U.S. corporate partner owned by the foreign investors also might arrange to receive interest income on a loan to the partnership which is taxfree under a U.S. tax treaty, or is in turn mostly offset by interest owed to its shareholders subject to little or no U.S. federal withholding tax under a U.S. tax treaty. Similarly, among the foreign investors themselves — whether they are individuals or corporations — different income goals or applicable foreign tax laws may dictate special allocations or participations in the project. However, such partnership allocations must have a substantial economic effect in order to be effective for federal income tax purposes — generally by being reflected in charges and credits to the partners' capital accounts which determine their ultimate participations in partnership revenues.[61]

Whether or not a special allocation of partnership income or deductions is made, the U.S. partner or another party may wish to purchase the partnership interest of the foreign investors on arm's length price and other terms during holding, operation, or development of the property by the partnership. If the foreign investors' partnership interest is held by a U.S. or foreign corporation, as noted further above generally in the case of dispositions by foreign investors, the U.S. partner or another party unrelated to the foreign shareholders may wish to purchase the stock of their corporation for gain which may be taxfree to them. The purchaser then may be able to obtain a new tax basis in the acquired corporation's partnership interest which equals the purchase price for the stock by liquidating the corporation or, in the case of a corporate purchaser, by electing to have the acquired corporation treated as having sold its assets and liquidated.[62]

Alternatively, the use of excess accelerated cost recovery allowances or other deductions may be provided to U.S. investors by having the foreign investors lend funds to the U.S. investors under debt instruments convertible into equity interests later. The deductions attributable to full ownership of the property should be available to the U.S. investors until the debt is converted if the debt is not treated as additional equity initially. Under various U.S. income tax treaties as noted above, the interest payments — even if the loan is secured by a U.S. mortgage in the case of certain treaties — may be free of U.S. withholding tax. However, gain on disposition of such a convertible instrument in excess of arm's length interest rates may be taxable under FIRPTA because attributable to a U.S. real property interest.[63]

Another possible joint investment vehicle is the U.S. real estate investment trust which, upon compliance with requirements of the Internal Revenue Code, is not itself subject to federal income tax. Dividends paid by the trust to foreign shareholders are subject to U.S. withholding tax, and property disposition gains passed through to the foreign holders usually will be effectively connected income to them and so will not escape U.S. tax. However, if less than one-half of the trust's value is held by foreign persons, then sale by foreign holders of their interests in the trust generally will be taxfree. Such a trust must have at least 100 shareholders, and foreign investors may join with U.S. shareholders in a new or existing trust.[64]

In the event that U.S. persons wish to join with foreign investors as shareholders in a foreign corporation to invest in U.S. property — especially to participate in U.S. income tax advantages of the foreign corporation — the federal accumulated earnings tax, controlled foreign corporation, foreign personal holding company, and personal holding company provisions should be examined carefully.[65]

The use of privately and publicly held entities — including offshore investment companies — for portfolio investments in U.S. real estate and similar property often involves securities laws and other issues which are discussed further in Chapter IX in the context of stock and securities investments. In the particular case of limited partnerships, even a call for additional capital from the limited partners, whether foreign or domestic, may be considered a new securities offering subject to U.S. securities law requirements.[66]

Any foreign or U.S. person acting as a finder or broker in U.S. real estate investments by foreign persons also should be careful to comply with, or avoid falling within, state real estate broker licensing requirements, or federal or state investment adviser or securities broker licensing requirements, as described in Chapter I.

Furthermore, establishment of a joint venture involving a foreign person for a U.S. real estate investment probably will require foreign investment reporting to federal and/or state authorities as noted earlier in this chapter and discussed further in Chapter XII.

Foreign Tax and Legal Factors

In addition to U.S. regulatory, tax, and other considerations, taxes and legal requirements in the foreign investor's home country may alter the structure of an investment in U.S. real estate or other natural resources, whether made by the investor alone or in a joint venture. For example, in terms of the hypothetical investors described further above, no tax may be imposed on the original foreign corporate investor by its country of organization or on the nonresident aliens by their home country in the case of capital gain on the sale of unimproved U.S. real estate. Similarly, such gain generated abroad may not be subject to tax until remitted to the home country.

On the other hand, substantial home country taxation of such U.S. gain may be an additional factor favoring use of a foreign corporation organized in a tax haven by the nonresident aliens or even by the corporate investor in order to accumulate the sale proceeds outside the home country's tax jurisdiction and permit their reinvestment abroad without current tax costs. Other factors such as foreign exchange or investment limitations in the home country also may affect the availability or value to the investors of using such a foreign corporation.

Clearly, it is not feasible here to analyze the many applicable foreign tax and other laws and their probable impact on the variety of possible structures for U.S. real estate and other natural resource investments.

However, two brief examples may illustrate the importance of these factors:

(1) Under the U.S. income tax treaty with the Federal Republic of Germany, German investors generally are not subject to German taxation on U.S. real estate and certain related interest income. However, U.S. losses may be considered in determining the German tax rate applicable to a German investor. In the case of oil and gas exploration or development or other property investments which constitute an active trade or business under German tax principles — but excluding most rental property — such U.S. losses alternatively may be deducted directly from the investor's income under the German Foreign Investment Law. Accordingly, when U.S. real estate or other natural resource investments produce tax losses, German investors have often formed a U.S. limited or other partnership for German tax purposes to hold the property directly and be allocated all or part of such losses.

The same legal entity may be organized so that, under differing U.S. standards, it is considered a domestic corporation for U.S. federal tax purposes. In that case, pursuant to the treaty — in addition to the German tax exemptions referred to above — interest payments from the corporation to German lending investors are deductible by the corporation for U.S. tax purposes and subject to no U.S. withholding tax. Furthermore, dividends from the corporation's property earnings and profits to the German shareholders are subject to a reduced 15% U.S. withholding tax, and capital gain from any German shareholder's sale of the corporate stock held for more than six months generally will be free of U.S. tax before 1985.

Alternatively, where German tax principles may reduce the use of U.S. losses in Germany from direct ownership of U.S. property, using a U.S. corporation also under *German* tax standards may permit (a) a German corporation owning at least 25% of the U.S. corporation's voting shares to receive dividends from the U.S. corporation free of German income tax and subject only to the 15% U.S. withholding tax or (b) a German individual owning not more than 25% of the U.S. corporation's voting stock to sell his shares free of German income tax.[67]

(2) Several countries — such as Canada, Germany and Japan — tax their residents more harshly on certain passive and other so called tainted income derived through tax haven corporations or similar entities, which may restrict use of such a corporation for a U.S. real estate or similar investment. Likewise, other countries may exempt capital gain from a direct U.S. real estate investment, but not such gain from stock of a tax haven or other corporation used to hold the investment.

In summary, the structuring of foreign investments in U.S. real estate and other natural resources requires consideration of special regulatory, income tax, estate planning, and related issues affecting the holding and disposition of the property. These issues and structures will vary with the character of each property or other resource investment, the income and other objectives of the foreign investors and possible U.S. joint venturers, and the specific foreign taxes and other laws involved.

Footnotes to Chapter III

1. *See generally* Chapter I *supra.*

2. Alien Land Act of 1887, as amended, 48 U.S.C. §§1501 *et seq.*

3. *Cf.* United States-Netherlands Treaty of Friendship, Commerce and Navigation of 1956, Arts. VII, IX.

4. 7 U.S.C. §3501; *see also* 7 C.F.R. Part 781.

5. *See, e.g.,* F. Morrison, Chapter I *supra,* note 75; W. Weber, *id.* note 76; H. Brodkey, "Foreign Investment in U.S. Real Estate: The Role of State Restrictions in Structuring the Transaction," in *Lawyer's Supplement to the Guarantor* (Chicago Title Ins. Co. 1978); G. Spinner, "State-by-State Survey of Limitations on Foreign Investment," in *Foreign Investment in the United States* (D.C. Bar Ass'n 1980); U.S. Dep't of Agriculture, *Report to the Congress on State Controls and Reporting Requirements for Foreign-Owned Real Estate in the United States* (1980).

6. *See* Society for the Propagation of the Gospel v. New Haven, 8 U.S. 464, 489-491 (1823).

7. *E.g.,* the state constitutions and/or statutes of Alaska, Arizona, California, Idaho, and Oregon; *see generally* H. Brodkey, *supra* note 5.

8. *Compare* Terrace v. Thompson, 263 U.S. 197 (1923); Porterfield v. Webb, 263 U.S. 225 (1923); Shames v. Nebraska, 323 F. Supp. 1321 (D. Neb. 1971), *aff'd,* 408 U.S. 901 (1971); and Lehndorff Geneva, Inc. v. Warner, 74 Wis. 2d 369, 246 N.W.2d 15 (1976); *with* Sei Fujii v. State, 38 Cal. 2d 718, 242 P. 2d 617 (1952).

9. State v. Hillcrest Investments, Inc., 630 P.2d 1253 (S. Ct. Okla. 1981).

10. *See generally* I.R.C. §§871-874, 881-884; Chapter II *supra.*

11. I.R.C. §875; Treas. Reg. §1.871-10(d)(3); *cf.* Rev. Rul. 75-23, 1975-1 C.B. 290. The same rule may be applied to determine whether a partner has a U.S. permanent establishment to which its partnership income is attributable under a U.S. income tax treaty. *Cf.* Donroy, Ltd. v. United States, 301 F. 2d 200 (9th Cir. 1962).

12. I.R.C.§761(a); *cf.* John B. Hynes, Jr., 74 T.C. 1266 (1980); Estate of Levine, 72 T.C. 780 (1979): Rev. Rul. 78-371, 1978-2 C.B. 344; *see generally* Chapter II *supra.*

13. *See generally* I.R.C. §§2101-2108, 2501-2524; Chapter II *supra.* For the possible application of federal *income* tax to a gift of a U.S. real property interest, see the discussion of dispositions further below.

14. I.R.C. §864(c); *see generally* Chapter II *supra.* With regard to treatment of income from subdivided property as ordinary income or capital gain, see also I.R.C. §1237.

15. I.R.C. §§46-48, 57(a)(2), 103(b)(4), 103A, 168, 189, 196, 1245(a), 1250. More rapid cost recovery allowances after 1985 were repealed in 1982.

16. *Cf.* Evelyn M. L. Neill, 46 B.T.A. 197 (1942); Treas. Reg. §1.1441-2(a)(2); Rev. Rul. 73-522, 1973-2 C.B. 226. Net leasing of several properties by the same taxpayer may change this treatment.

17. I.R.C. §§871(d), 882(d); *see* I.R.C. §163(d).

18. I.R.C. §§531-537; *see also* Chapter II *supra.*

19. *See generally* Treas. Reg. §§1.385-0 *et seq.*; I.R.C. §§267, §482; Treas. Reg. §1.482-2(a); *see* Chapter II *supra.*

20. I.R.C. §§861(a)(1)(D), 861(a)(2)(B), 871(a)(1), 881(a); *see* Chapter II *supra.*

21. Pub. L. 96-499 (Dec. 5, 1980), 94 Stat. 2599, §§1121-1125; Pub. L. 97-34 (Aug. 13, 1981), 95 Stat. 172, §831; I.R.C. §§897, 6039C; *see also* I.R.C. §862(a)(8); Temp. Treas. Reg. §§6a. 897-1 through -4, 6a.6039C-1 through -5.

22. The consequence for a U.S. owner in the case of a 12-month liquidation is one tax on the foreign corporation upon sale of its assets and another tax on the U.S. shareholder upon liquidation. *But see* I.R.C. §897(*l*) designed to relieve the burden of the foreign corporation's tax if the U.S. owner already held the stock on June 18, 1980, when FIRPTA generally became effective.

23. Temp. Treas. Reg. §6a.897-3. *But see* I.R.C. §897(k) and Temp. Treas. Reg. §6a.897-4 generally permitting without taxation of selling shareholders the election, and consequent taxfree

liquidation and step-up in tax basis under I.R.C. §334(b)(2), in the case of a foreign corporation whose stock was purchased between January 1 and November 25, 1980, when the FIRPTA provisions taxing distributions by foreign corporations were initially publicly proposed.

24. I.R.C. §§897(a), (b); *see generally* Chapters I, II *supra*; I.R.C. §§55-58, 291, 172.

25. I.R.C. §§453, 1239; *compare* Treas. Reg. §§1.864-3(a), 1.871-8(c) *with* I.R.C. §897(a). The special reduction of the maximum rate of imputed interest in the case of smaller installment sales or exchanges of land between family members does not apply where any of the parties is a nonresident alien. I.R.C. §483(g).

26. I.R.C. §§1031, 897(e); *cf.* Starker v. United States, 602 F.2d 1341 (9th Cir. 1979); Arthur E. Long, 77 T.C. No. 71(1981); Gulfstream Land & Dev't Corp., 71 T.C. 587 (1979); Estate of Meyer, Sr., 58 T.C. 311 (1972); *see also* Biggs v. Comm'r, 632 F.2d 1171 (5th Cir. 1980) (taxfree like kind exchange may be accomplished by exchange of seller's real property for buyer's contract right to purchase other property of like kind); Chapter XI *infra*. However, the U.S. Internal Revenue Service may challenge the use of a deferred exchange; *cf.* Letter Rul. 8046122. This is also true as to an exchange of general partner interests; *cf.* Rev. Rul. 78-135, 1978-1 C.B. 256.

The taxfree rollover or reinvestment within two years of gain on sale of a U.S. principal residence for another principal residence under I.R.C. §1034 (and one-time exclusion of such gain for older individuals under I.R.C. §121) depends on the U.S. residence being the owner's principal residence, which usually is not applicable in the case of a nonresident alien.

27. *See* I.R.C. §897(a)(1); *cf.* Diedrich v. Comm'r, 50 U.S.L.W. 4647 (U.S. Sup. Ct. 1982); Estate of Levine v. Comm'r, 634 F.2d 12 (2d Cir. 1980).

28. I.R.C. §§301(b)-(d), 302, 331(a), 346, 871(a), 881, 897(d); *see* note 20 *supra; cf.* United States v. Cumberland Public Service Co., 338 U.S. 451 (1949). *But see* Comm'r v. Court Holding Co., 324 U.S. 331 (1945).

29. I.R.C. §§331(a), 338, 897(i).

30. I.R.C. §§337, 1245, 1250, 331(a), 453(h), 453B(d)(2), 341; *see* I.R.C. §337(c)(2)(B) also allowing partial use of taxfree disposition under §337 where parent corporation has acquired its stock in the liquidating corporation by purchase. The general application of U.S. collapsible corporation tax provisions to foreign investors is discussed further in Chapter VI in connection with disposing of a U.S. business.

A further possible alternative in the case of a U.S. corporation — again, if it is not a collapsible corporation — is a one-month liquidation in which the shareholders are taxed only on the greater of the accumulated profits of the corporation or money and certain securities received by them. However, the corporation remains taxable on any preliquidation gain from the sale of its property and the distribution of such profits also may be subject to a dividend withholding tax. In the alternative event of distribution of the property itself in the liquidation, even the domestic shareholders' tax basis remains the same as their stock basis rather than being adjusted to equal the fair market value of the property; for foreign shareholders, the tax basis of U.S. real property interests generally should remain the predistribution tax basis of the U.S. corporation increased only by any U.S. redemption or dividend tax. Thus this alternative is not widely used. *See* I.R.C. §§333, 334(c), 897(f). It is also apparently not available for a foreign corporation electing to be treated as a domestic corporation under a tax treaty nondiscrimination clause. Temp. Treas. Reg. §6a.897-3(a).

31. I.R.C. §§897(f), 311(d)-(e), 336, 346, 302 (b)(4), 301(c)(3), 341. This means that a second tax on any gain, reduced only by a *deduction* from the gain for any tax paid by the foreign shareholders on the distribution, usually may be imposed on resale of the property by the shareholders. A dividend out of the U.S. corporation's current or accumulated earnings and profits is subject to U.S. withholding tax based on the fair market value of the property. I.R.C. §§301(b)-(d), 871(a), 881. A distribution in excess of the corporate earnings plus the shareholders' basis in their stock is taxed to the shareholders as gain from the sale of property, *i.e.,* from sale of their stock. I.R.C. §301(c)(3).

32. I.R.C. §§331(a), 338, 897(c)(3), 341, 55-58, 873, 897(b), 1244; Pub. L. 96-499, *supra* note 21, §1125(c). For an example of a taxfree disposition by foreign owners of the stock of a U.S. corporation with real estate assets before FIRPTA and, by analogy, where an exception to FIRPTA now applies, see Letter Rul. 7806032.

33. *See generally* United States-Netherlands Income Tax Treaty of 1948, as amended and presently in force between the United States and the Netherlands Antilles ("U.S.-Antilles Treaty"), Arts. V, X, XII.

34. *Compare* United States-United Kingdom Income Tax Treaty of 1945, as amended and extended to the British Virgin Islands, Arts. IX, XV; *with* proposed United States-British Virgin Islands Income Tax Treaty of 1981, Arts. 6, 10, 11, 13.

35. *See generally* United States-Netherlands Income Tax Treaty of 1948, as amended

("U.S.-Netherlands Treaty"), Arts. VII, VIII, XI, XII. However, it should be noted that the U.S. income tax treaty with the Netherlands — or other treaties referred to below — may be renegotiated to provide an earlier termination date for treaty protection from the U.S. FIRPTA provisions. *Cf.* Pub. L. 96-499, *supra* note 21, §1125(c); Pub. L. 97-34, *supra* note 21, §831(h).

36. I.R.C. §§338(h)(3), 453(e), (g); *see also* Pub. L. 96-499, *supra* note 21, §1125(d); Treas. Reg. §1.6012-2(g); Temp. Treas. Reg. §15a.453-1(d)(3).

37. I.R.C. §§897(d), (e), (j).

38. *E.g.,* Belgium, Canada (1966 treaty), Egypt, Finland, France, Federal Republic of Germany, Hungary, Iceland, Israel (pending), Japan, Republic of Korea, Morocco, Poland, Romania, and Sweden. *Compare* I.R.C. §341(a) *with* same provision before 1977. Several exceptions to collapsible corporation treatment are noted in Chapter VI in connection with disposing of a U.S. business.

With respect to the Canadian treaty of 1966 discussed below, see especially Art. VIII. *But see* Treas. Reg. §519.103(c) under this treaty; proposed United States-Canada Income Tax Treaty of 1980, Arts. VI, XIII.

39. 48 U.S.C. §1642; *cf.* Rev. Rul. 80-40, 1980-2 C.B. 175.

40. I.R.C. §§897(c)(1)(A)(i), 862(a)(8), 6039C(f).

41. I.R.C. §§163, 172, 243, 1501-1564; *cf.* U.S.-Netherlands Treaty, Arts. VII, VIII.

42. *See* Revenue Act of 1978, Pub. L. 95-600 (Nov. 6, 1978), 92 Stat. 2763, §553; U.S. Dep't of the Treasury, *Report on Taxation of Foreign Investment in U.S. Real Estate* (1979); *cf.* U.S.-Antilles Treaty, Art X; United States-Norway Income Tax Treaty of 1971, as amended, Arts. 12(1)(b), (c); Chapter II *supra.*

43. 43 U.S.C. §§315 *et seq.*; 43 C.F.R. §§4121.1-1(a)-(c).

44. *See, e.g.,* 43 U.S.C. §161; 43 C.F.R. §2511.1.

45. 43 U.S.C. §431.

46. *See* Chapter I *supra,* Chapter VIII *infra.*

47. I.R.C. §2032A.

48. S.C. Code Ann. §§27-13-10, -30(1976).

49. I.R.C. §§631(a)-(b), 871(a)(1)(B), 881(a)(2), 1441(c)(5). If the timber is to be exported, election of the former approach under §631(a) also may substantially reduce tax benefits under the Domestic International Sales Corporation provisions discussed in Chapter VIII regarding the United States as a base for foreign operations. *See* Longview Fibre Co., 71 T.C.357 (1979).

50. *Cf.* Huxford v. United States, 441 F. 2d 1371 (5th Cir. 1971). For an extensive discussion of these and other aspects of such investment, see W. Knight, Jr. & W. Wilkins, "Planning for Foreign Investments in U.S. Timberlands," 78-5 Tax Mgt. Int'l J. 3 (1978).

51. 30 U.S.C. §§181, 184, 241, 352. The United Kingdom, for example, meets this reciprocal rights requirements; so do Canada and approximately 38 other countries. Certain federal coal lands also may be sold only to U.S. citizens. Moreover, certain federal coal leases are set aside for small businesses.

52. 30 U.S.C. §1015. However, regulations require any shareholder owning 10% or more of the U.S. corporate lessee to file a statement showing his ownership and citizenship. 43 C.F.R. §3202.2-1(b).

53. 42 U.S.C. §2092.

54. 30 U.S.C. §22.

55. 43 U.S.C. §§1337(a), 1340; 43 C.F.R. §3300.1.

56. 18 C.F.R. Parts 152 *et seq.*; E.O. 12287, 3 C.F.R. (1981).

57. *See* Chapter I *supra.* With respect to tax issues posed by drilling equipment brought into and removed from the United States by foreign persons, see, *e.g.,* I.R.C. §§47(d)(1), 48(a)(2); Rev. Rul. 76-339, 1976-2 C.B. 251.

58. Similarly to timber, profits to a nonresident alien or foreign corporation from certain coal sold under a mining contract with another person are treated as capital gain subject to a federal withholding tax of 30%. I.R.C. §631(c); note 49 *supra.* Soil and loam are subject to the allowance for cost depletion but not percentage depletion. I.R.C. §611; Rev. Rul. 79-411, 1979-2 C.B. 246.

59. *See* Chapter II *supra.*

60. I.R.C. §704(b)(2).

61. *Cf.* I.R.C. §§172, 189, 278, 464, 465.

62. I.R.C. §§734, 754, 755.

63. *Cf.* U.S.-Netherlands Treaty, Art. VIII.

64. I.R.C. §§856-860, 897(h). By contrast, the stock of a state chartered general stock ownership corporation which is formed (before 1984) to invest in properties, and whose income — somewhat similarly to that of a real estate investment trust — must be distributed annually and is taxed directly

to its shareholders under I.R.C. §§1391-1397, must be issued only to residents of the state of its organization.

65. *See* Chapter II *supra,* Chapter VIII *infra.*

66. *Cf.* Goodman v. Epstein, 582 F.2d 388 (7th Cir. 1978), *cert. denied,* 440 U.S. 939 (1979); *see generally* Chapter I *supra.*

67. *See generally* United States-Federal Republic of Germany Income Tax Treaty of 1954, as amended, Arts. VI, VII, IXA, XV; F.R.G. Treaty Reg. §20; Rev. Rul. 76-435, 1976-2 C.B. 490; Chapter II *supra.*

Chapter IV

Licensing Activities

This chapter summarizes for a foreign investor the major considerations which influence the decision to licence technology into the United States, the most frequently used techniques in locating a suitable U.S. licensee, and the clauses generally used in U.S. technology and trademark license agreements. The chapter also includes examples of the impact of U.S. federal antitrust laws on such license agreements and describes certain aspects of U.S. federal taxation particularly applicable to a foreign licensor.[1]

Factors Influencing the Decision to License in the United States[2]

The United States represents the largest consumer market in the world, particularly with respect to the sale of technologically oriented innovations: accordingly, it must be considered by a foreign investor seeking maximum economic return. One simple method to exploit proprietary technology in the United States is through U.S. import sales, which often can be set up in a relatively simply fashion, such as by appointing a U.S. sales representative or distributing agent. Other methods include establishment of a branch, a wholly or partially owned subsidiary corporation, or a joint venture for the manufacture and sale of goods within the United States or for the export from the United States.[3] These methods provide the greatest control of expenses by the foreign investor. They have the disadvantage, however, of requiring a large initial investment and of subjecting that investment to the operation of extensive U.S. laws.

The third possible method of exploiting technology in the United States is the licensing of the technology. Certain benefits may flow from licensing, as compared with other methods of exploiting technology, such as the following:

(1) No capital investment is required in the United States by the licensor.

(2) No permanent staff need be maintained by the licensor in the United States.

(3) Any compulsory licensing requirements of U.S. law probably will be met automatically through the license itself.

(4) It may be possible to obtain a minority equity position in the licensee enterprise in exchange for the licensing of the technology.

(5) Licensing is feasible where U.S. importation of goods is not — for example, if the licensed products are too heavy or bulky to make shipping them over long distances practical or competitive, or where tariff or non-tariff barriers exist.

Locating a Suitable U.S. Licensee

Often a foreign licensor will know through the operation of its own business which enterprises in the United States would make good licensing partners. For example, ICI in the United Kingdom might know that DuPont in the United States would make a suitable licensing partner or joint venture partner in many areas of ICI's technology. However, caution must be exercised in such transactions between large enterprises because U.S. antitrust laws or foreign — for example, European Economic Community — competition laws may preclude a mutually beneficial licensing arrangement, depending on the license terms and conditions, as discussed in certain respects further below.

For the smaller and medium-sized foreign licensors, particularly those entering the U.S. licensing arena for the first time, a problem frequently arises in locating suitable license partners. What steps can such a licensor take to find a suitable partner? The following are certain methods used successfully by various licensors:

(1) Engagement of a reputable international licensing consultant or broker who can locate appropriate partners through his contacts;

(2) Contact with trade associations that represent U.S. enterprises within the field of the projected license agreement, since such trade associations, particularly if they are efficient ones, often know almost all of the U.S. businesses operating within their area of expertise;

(3) Use of a friendly firm in the United States to locate, through its expert knowledge of its own country, a suitable partner;

(4) Contact with international organizations, such as the International Chamber of Commerce, the Organization for Economic Cooperation and Development, or various United Nations organizations or the United Nations Conference on Trade and Development, for information about suitable licensees;

(5) Use of commercial banks or U.S. offices of foreign banks to provide valuable and detailed information about possible partners;

(6) Attendence at international licensing or trade fora, which in recent years have offered valuable opportunities for licensors and licensees to make contact with one another.[4]

License Clauses[5]

This section summarizes the clauses generally used in U.S. technology and trademark license agreements, and addresses certain potential U.S. antitrust and other issues in connection with such clauses. The general requirements for protection of patents, trade secrets, trademarks, and other intellectual property in the United States — which should be understood before U.S. licensing is undertaken — and the general federal antitrust laws are covered in Chapter I describing the basic U.S. legal system.

Parties

Practically every U.S. license agreement begins with a paragraph identifying the parties to the agreement, *i.e.*, the licensor and the licensee. This initial paragraph generally also recites the principal locations and the state or country of incorporation of each of the parties. It is usually convenient to designate the parties in this first paragraph as being thereafter referred to as LICENSOR and LICENSEE; for example, "the ABC Corporation (hereinafter LICENSEE)." When this is done, it then becomes possible to use standard form of agreement when many licensees are contemplated, with only the first paragraph having to be modified. All of the remaining paragraphs in the agreement will appear with the standard terminology.

Similarly, it is helpful to use full capital letters for each term that is defined in the license agreement to have a specific meaning. By this system, the terms stand out in the clauses and provisions in which they appear and an overall economy of words is achieved.

Recitals

Introductory recital clauses, often referred to as "whereas" clauses, are not anachronistic in a modern license agreement and can serve various purposes. For example, they can often assist in presenting the agreement in its best aspect from the viewpoint of avoiding U.S. antitrust problems that might otherwise occur.

Definitions

Three very useful defined terms to be included in license agreements are the following:

Licensed products. This term is typically defined as a product that incorporates, is covered by, or is made, in whole or in part, by the use of any of the licensed patents, or by the use of any of the data or information constituting part of the licensed know-how described elsewhere in the agreement.

Licensed patents. This term generally can be defined as all patents listed in a Schedule A to the agreement, any patents issuing from patent applications listed in Schedule A, and any patents which cover inventions that are within the scope of and constitute improvements on any patents referred to in Schedule A, which are owned or controlled by the licensor. This provides a concise way of referring repeatedly in the agreement to LICENSED PATENTS and embracing within that short term the full definitions as first set forth.

Licensed known-how. This term is frequently defined to mean all the unpatented data, trade secrets, and similar information which are or have been furnished by the licensor to the licensee under the agreement. Again, the term LICENSED KNOW-HOW then forms a convenient term of reference for later use in the agreement.

Grant Clause

The grant clause is a very important part of any license agreement. It sets forth in broad terms the basic rights that are being granted under the license. Therefore, particular care must be devoted to the drafting of this clause. Typically, a grant clause would include the following provisions:

(1) A delineation of whether the license is exclusive or nonexclusive;

(2) A license to manufacture or make, and the area or territory in which this license may be exercised, together with any reservations of rights that may be made by the licensor;

(3) A license to use and sell, and a demarcation of the territory throughout which the license is granted;

(4) A right to sublicense, if agreed by the parties, particularly where the grant is of an exclusive license. If the licensee is given the right to grant sublicenses, the parties must be careful that the licensor reserves no veto power over the licensee's selection of sublicensees: such a provision generally is considered a violation of the U.S. antitrust laws if the licensor and licensee are competitors and enjoy substantial shares of the market.[6]

Income received from sublicensing can be divided in different ways between the original licensor and the original licensee. Many agreements provide that all income received from sublicensing operations shall be divided equally between the licensor and licensee. Other agreements may provide that three-fourths of the income shall be paid to the licensor and only one-fourth to the licensee. Different divisions of income also can be provided with respect to down payments, licensing fees, minimum royalty payments, and regular running royalties.

Royalties[7]

Measurement. There are many different ways to measure royalty payments under license agreements, but certain problems recur with respect to measuring royalties, such as the following:

(1) *Royalty base.* The royalty base is the item used as the base against which the royalty rate — usually a percentage royalty — is applied to determine the total royalty due. Generally, no problem arises when the royalty base is the same in scope as the licensed technology. Problems can arise, however, when the royalty base is not reasonably related to the licensed technology.

For example, if a licensed patent covers only a portion or part of a machine, and the total sales price of the machine is used as the royalty base, the effective royalty may be higher than the apparent royalty recited in the agreement. Thus, if a licensed patent covers only 25% of the parts that make up the total value of a machine, and the royalty is five percent applied against the total price of the machine, then the effective royalty rate is really 20%.

Alternatively, if the licensed patent covers, for example, certain electronic circuits for television sets which are manufactured by the licensee but does not cover *all* of the electronic circuits used for television sets manufactured by the licensee, and the licensee is required to pay a percentage royalty on all television sets sold by him, the agreement is referred to as a total sales royalty agreement. If the licensor imposes a mandatory royalty base on the licensee and that royalty base exceeds the scope of the licensed technology, such activity constitutes a patent misuse and possibly also an antitrust violation. If, however, the licensee voluntarily agrees as a matter of convenience to pay royalties determined against a royalty base that exceeds the scope of the licensed technology, there will be no patent misuse or violation of the antitrust laws.[8]

(2) *Lump sum.* Many potential problems with royalties can be avoided if the licensee is willing to pay the royalty in one lump sum at the beginning of the license agreement. However, most licensees are not willing to pay royalties in this manner, and most licensors do not favor receiving royalties measured in this rather arbitrary fashion. Both the licensor and licensee in a typical agreement usually prefer to measure the royalties on some basis that is tied to, or consonant with, the degree of use of the licensed technology by the licensee.

(3) *Running royalty.* Running royalties are by far the most common and accepted manner of paying for licensed technology under a license agreement. Running royalties may be computed on a percentage or on a straight monetary basis, such as one cent per pound, five cents per square yard, or 25 cents per barrel. Percentage royalties are generally favored as a percentage of the net sales price of the licensed products, particularly at

times of world-wide inflation. Although a royalty of one cent per pound may appear attractive at the beginning of a 10-year license agreement, it may become much less attractive during the latter years of the agreement if a great deal of inflation has taken place.

(4) *Net Sales Price.* The most common arrangement for measuring a running royalty is as a percentage of the net sales price of licensed products. Thus, it is important to define *exactly* what amounts are included in this term. Such items as taxes, credits for returned products, quantity discounts, freight allowances, cash discounts, and agents' commissions are normally omitted from the net sales price.

(5) *Graduated scale.* In license agreements where a running royalty is measured against sales of licensed products and the quantity of licensed products sold and the amount of royalty paid are expected to reach high figures, it is fairly common practice to use a graduated royalty scale. Under this approach, after a stipulated volume of licensed products has been sold, the royalty rate is reduced until another stipulated level of sales is reached, and the royalty may then be reduced again. For example, a five percent royalty might be paid against the first 100,000 licensed products sold per year, a four percent royalty paid against the next 100,000, a three percent royalty up to a total of 500,000 licensed products, and so on.

Graduated scales are helpful to the licensee in reducing the impact of the royalty if its volume use of the licensed technology is high. At the same time, they provide an incentive to the licensee to increase its volume of sales of the licensed technology.

(6) *Different royalties to different licensees.* Frequently, where a licensor has a number of nonexclusive licensees or different licensees for different fields of use, different royalties are charged to the various licensees. For example, a licensee in one location may be willing to pay a higher royalty than a licensee in another location. A licensee who takes a license after the licensed technology has been proven may be willing to pay a higher royalty than a licensee who took a license for the technology before its commercial value was clearly established. Similarly, a licensee for a field of use having high profit margins normally will be willing to pay a higher royalty than a licensee in a field having low profit margins.

However, it is now part of developing U.S. antitrust law that, if different royalties are charged to different licensees, there must be business reasons justifying the distinction. If it can be shown that the different royalties were arbitrary and unjustifiable, the licensor may be exposing himself to liability for imposing discriminatory royalties upon one licensee when compared to another.[9] This is particularly so where it can be shown that the differing royalties have an adverse effect on the high paying licensee's ability to compete with other enterprises.

(7) *Valuation of patents and know-how.* Where a number of different

patents and a variety of know-how and trade secrets comprise the licensed technology in a license agreement, it may become important to assign values to the various patents and know-how. There are several reasons why this may be a good practice.

If one of the patents is declared invalid, or if some of the know-how or trade secrets enter the public domain, it is essential that the licensor be able to show that the remaining patents and know-how have a measurable value. This will enable the licensor to continue to collect royalties based on the proportionate value that the remaining patents and know-how bear to the original total value of the licensed technology.

Also, whenever the licensor is offering a package license — in the United States, a package license is any license that contains more than one patent, or patents and know-how — the licensee should be given the opportunity to take a license under less than the full package offered. If the licensee takes significantly less than the full package, he should pay a lower royalty than another licensee who secures rights under the entire package. Present U.S. antitrust law generally requires *not* that the royalty charged be exactly proportionate to the values assigned to the respective patents and know-how but, instead, that a reasonable adjustment be made not totally disproportionate to the amount of technology that one licensee receives with respect to another licensee.[10]

Minimum royalties. It is a frequent provision in exclusive license agreements to require the licensee to pay a minimum royalty per year, regardless of the amount of use of the invention. Such a provision protects the licensor by ensuring that the licensee makes a good faith effort to exploit the licensed technology and that, if the licensee chooses not to exploit the technology, the licensor will receive at least the minimum royalty.

Devaluation and revaluation. Because wide fluctuation of world monetary exchange rates is now commonplace, it is prudent in international license agreements to protect the foreign licensor against devaluation or revaluation of currency, *inter alia,* by specifying adjustment of the royalty to correspond to the devaluation or revaluation, as the case may be, or by selecting a more stable currency as the means of payment. The agreement also should specify the date within a given royalty period which will determine the applicable rate of exchange for the royalties due in that period.

Taxes. License agreements should provide for the handling of withholding taxes which the United States imposes on the foreign licensor, as discussed further below. However, an income tax treaty between the United States and the country of the licensor may eliminate or greatly reduce such U.S. taxes on royalties and other types of income received by the foreign licensor. If there is no tax treaty, the foreign licensor may lose as much as half his royalties to federal and state taxes; it is therefore important that he be forewarned that his real royalty may have to be determined as a *net royalty after taxes* and not the full royalty set forth in the agreement.[11]

Inspection and reporting. All agreements providing for a running royalty should include a provision that requires a licensee to keep complete and accurate books and records with respect to the licensed products sold by him or by his sublicensees. These books and records should be opened during business hours at specified intervals during the year to the inspection of independent public accountants selected for the purpose of verifying the royalty statements rendered by the licensee to the licensor.

Delivery of Know-How[12]

Initial data and information. Many licensing agreements provide for an initial transfer of a substantial body of know-how. Typically, the first portion of the agreement recites the initial data and information being transferred to the licensee. More often than not, there may be a special fee charged by the licensor for the transfer to the licensee of this valuable know-how.

Improvement data and information.[13] In a typical agreement, there will also be a provision for the continuing transfer of data and information with respect to changes and improvements which the licensor adopts in its designs of machinery and equipment or in its methods of manufacture for production of licensed products. The licensee also may wish to secure the right to use future patents generated by the licensor in connection with the licensed technology. The licensee may require that the licensor communicate all such improvements to the licensee and give the licensee the right to use these improvements under the terms of the agreement or under other specified terms. Such provisions are often referred to as flow-through or flow-forward clauses.

Technical Assistance

Almost all important international license agreements provide that the licensor will render technical assistance to the licensee. It may be very important for the licensee to have access to such technical assistance since, in the design, construction, and operation of a complex facility — such as a petroleum refinery — it is essential for the licensee to have detailed, specific, and personal assistance from the licensor in order to operate the licensed technology successfully. Normally, the license agreement contains separate provisions for initial and follow-on assistance and a clear indication of which party is responsible for the salaries and expenses of technical personnel furnished by the licensor. Many agreements also provide for visits by the licensee's staff to the licensor's plant and for training of the licensee's staff. The licensee also may wish to call the licensor's staff to the licensee's plant for short visits to assist in correcting minor problems.

Other Special Clauses

Limitations on use of know-how[14]

(1) *Field of use.* Where the licensed technology — whether a patent or other know-how — can be used in more than one field or area of endeavor, the licensor often will grant exclusive licenses to various licensees with restrictions as to fields of use. For example, if the licensed technology comprises a new type of rotary engine, the engine may be valuable for a number of different uses — for automobiles, for trucks, for aircraft, for earth moving equipment, for small marine craft, for large ships, for railroad trains, for gardening equipment such as lawnmowers, and for a variety of other uses.

In the United States, it is generally considered a possible violation of the antitrust laws to employ an exclusive field of use licensing structure to divide relevant markets among enterprises that would otherwise be competitors.[15] Accordingly, in carving out distinct fields of use from one bundle of license technology, it is important that the exclusive licensees in each field are not competitors such that significant competition between them in relevant markets will be substantially affected.

(2) *Territory.* Many licensors attempt to restrict the territory within which licensed technology may be used. Under U.S. law, certain territorial restrictions within the United States or between the United States and other countries may be accepted as legal. Territorial restrictions are so complex, however, that a detailed analysis of the particular proposed clauses is required.[16]

(3) *Duration.* The duration of a use restriction on a licensee should be no greater in years than the amount of time that it would take the licensee *independently* to develop the licensed technology without the assistance of the licensor.[17] Usually, the best way to measure this is by the amount of time it took the licensor to generate the licensed technology in the first place.

(4) *Production quantity.* Production or other quantity limitations on a licensee are of questionable legality in the United States, and it is possible that in the future almost all such restrictions will be found to be illegal.

(5) *Pricing.* For practical purposes, with certain exceptions, it is *per se* illegal under U.S. antitrust law — *i.e.,* no economic rationale, no matter how persuasive, will justify such an arrangement — for a licensor to attempt to fix the price at which a licensee may sell products made under the licensed technology.[18]

(6) *Know-how from others.* It is generally illegal in the United States

for a licensor to restrict in any way a licensee's freedom to deal with others — even in the field of the licensed technology — except as to limitations on disclosure of licensed confidential information.[19]

(7) *Purchases from and sales to others.* Under U.S. law a licensor cannot restrict his licensee from purchasing unpatented components and spare parts from third parties unless the licensor can show convincingly that it would not be possible for a third party to meet the specifications required to supply components and spare parts that will work properly in the licensor's equipment.[20] It is usually very difficult for a licensor to establish that third parties are unable to meet specifications for components and spare parts. As a practical matter, most licensees will wish to purchase their components and spare parts from the licensor voluntarily, unless these items are priced exorbitantly.

It is quite clearly illegal, however, for a licensor to attempt to restrict his licensee from purchasing raw materials from others, since these seldom require any specifications that would be difficult for a third party to meet. It is also illegal in the United States to require a licensee not to deal in a competitor's products that are similar or even identical to the licensed products. Such a restriction often is referred to as a tie-out.[21]

Similarly, a licensor generally cannot require his licensee to buy unpatented materials or equipment from him as a condition of the license. Such a restriction is referred to as a tie-in and is illegal except in fairly limited circumstances..[22]

(8) *Resale of licensed products.* In the United States it is potentially illegal for a licensor to attempt to place restrictions on the resale of licensed products.[23] Once the first sale has been made — either by the licensor to a purchasing licensee or by a manufacturing licensee to others — the licensor or licensee, as the case may be, generally is deemed to have parted with all authority over the sold product. Similarly, under U.S. *patent* law the principle of exhaustion by first sale holds that the exclusive right of the patent is exhausted once the patent owner or his licensee has made the first authorized sale, on the theory that the patent owner's or licensee's reward is secured from the proceeds of such sale.[24]

Limitations on disclosure of know-how. In a know-how license agreement, the licensor and licensee usually agree, for their mutual protection, to terms and provisions such as the following:

(1) The licensee agrees not to disclose the licensed know-how to any third parties without the specific written consent of the licensor.

(2) Necessary disclosure to customers of the licensee will be permitted upon specific approval by the licensor.

(3) Necessary disclosure by the licensee to his sublicensees will be permitted on the same terms.

(4) The licensee shall have the right to disclose the know-how in the following instances:

(a) if the licensee can show that the know-how was in his possession prior to entry into the license agreement;

(b) if the licensee can show that the know-how is in the public domain through action by others;

(c) if confidential know-how is disclosed to the licensee by a third party who has the right to disclose it to him;

(d) without restriction after a specified period of years, on the rationale that almost all know-how becomes obsolete with time and that, with certain exceptions, there is no economic reason for preserving confidentiality for unlimited or very long periods.

Marking of licensed products. Many license agreements will require the licensee and sublicensee to mark all licensed products to show that they were manufactured under license from the licensor.

Improvements made by licensee. If a licensee makes improvements — including inventions and know-how — within the field of the licensed technology, the licensor will wish to have access to those improvements. The licensor thereby avoids the risk of being shut out of the practice of his own licensed technology. In the United States the most the licensor can safely insist on is a nonexclusive worldwide license to the improvement technology.[25] This type of provision or arrangement is referred to in the United states as a grantback, since it is literally a granting back of technology from the licensee to the licensor. From the antitrust standpoint in the United States, the safest form of grantback provides that, if the licensee grants back technology which the licensor wishes to have the right to use, the licensor will pay a reasonable royalty for the use of the licensee-developed technology.

Licensee to promote demand. The licensor should always insist on securing the licensee's agreement to use his best efforts and due diligence to promote demand for the licensed product. As explained further above, if the licensee is an exclusive licensee, the requirement of a minimum royalty payment may also be used to help insure that the exclusive licensee exercises his best efforts in promoting demand for licensed products.

However, even with a nonexclusive licensee, it is helpful for the licensor to have a best efforts clause. If the licensee then does little or nothing to promote sale of licensed products, the licensor may have legal grounds for cancelling or terminating the agreement.

Licensee's responsibilities in case of third party infringement.[26] The licensor and licensee should provide for their respective duties and responsibilities under the agreement if a third party infringes one or more licensed patents. Questions that should be settled include, for example: who sues, the licensor or the licensee; how litigation expenses will be borne; if there is a substantial recovery of damages for the infringement, how the recovery should be divided between the licensor and licensee; and, if the licensor refuses to bring suit for infringement, whether the licensee acquires the right to sue in the name of the licensor.

Licensee challenge to validity of patents. In the United States it is a wasted effort for a licensor to secure an obligation from the licensee not to challenge the validity of a licensed patent. Moreover, such an obligation may be held to be a misuse of the patent, rendering the patent unenforceable in a court. In addition, it may constitute an antitrust violation to insist that a licensee include such a provision in an agreement.[27]

Duration and Termination[28]

In all license agreements it is important to delineate the intended life of the agreement and procedures for terminating the agreement either before or at the end of its normal term; the following are typical of such provisions:

(1) The term of the agreement should be specifically provided. Five or 10 years is a fairly typical period for the length of a know-how agreement, or a mixed patent and know-how agreement.

(2) The agreement should set forth any options of the licensee either to renew or to extend the agreement and should specifically state how these options may be exercised.

(3) The agreement should give the licensor the right to terminate the agreement if the licensee defaults in any major obligation under the agreement. Similarly, the licensee should have the right to terminate if the licensor should default in a major obligation under the agreement.

(4) The agreement should specify what rights and obligations continue for each party after termination. This can be particularly important where equipment or know-how is to be returned to the licensor after termination. Likewise, the licensee may be required to pay royalties on sales made after termination as to licensed products manufactured (or processes used) *prior* to termination.

Particular care should be taken *not* to include an obligation to pay royalties on acts occurring *after* expiration of licensed patents because, under U.S. antitrust law, such post-expiration royalties are illegal.[29]

Miscellaneous Provisions

Warranties.[30] From the licensor's viewpoint, the safest warranty clause to place in a license agreement is one to the effect that the licensor warrants he has good title to the licensed patents, the documents containing the know-how accurately reflect the best knowledge of the licensor, and no other warranty of any nature express or implied is made.

In specific situations, a licensee may insist that the licensor make additional warranties, but licensors should be wary of entering into specific warranties on such intangible property rights.

Disclaimers. The parties to a license agreement may wish to disclaim that either party shall have any recourse against the other for any loss, liability, damage, or cost which may be suffered or incurred by utilizing any of the rights or licenses granted by the agreement. They may also disclaim any liability arising from any lawsuit brought against one of the parties by reason of its exercise of rights under the agreement. Similarly, the parties may disclaim any representation with respect to the validity or scope of any licensed patents.

Infringement of third party patents or trademarks. In the event that the licensee is sued by a third party for infringement of a patent or trademark, the licensor may be willing to help defend the licensee. If possible, however, the licensor will wish to place the responsibility for defending against charges or suits for infringement directly on the licensee.

Performance guarantees. In international agreements licensing rights to use commercial processes — such as processes used in petroleum refining — the licensor often will give the licensee a performance guarantee. For example, the licensor may guarantee that, when the licensed technology is used as prescribed, a refinery will produce so many barrels of a certain grade of gasoline from a specified number of barrels of crude oil of a certain grade and quality. A licensee investing millions of dollars in setting up a complex plant almost always insists on such performance guarantees.

However, the licensor usually will insist on limiting liability so as not to exceed the total royalties paid by the licensee, if the plant cannot meet performance guarantees. In the United States, attempts have been made recently to hold the licensor liable for sums greater than the royalties paid, but no definitive decisions have yet been rendered.

Patent applications. Ordinarily, the licensor will be responsible for the prosecution of patent applications within the field of a licensed technology. However, the parties may wish to provide that the licensee will be responsible for the prosecution of certain applications.

The agreement also should set forth what consequences will result if a patent fails to issue or is held invalid — for example, a reduction in royalties to be paid to the licensor.

Most favored licensee. Many license agreements provide that a licensor will notify his licensee of any further licenses granted under the licensed technology within the licensee's territory. The licensor may further agree to a most favored licensee provision, so that, if the licensee feels that a license granted to another licensee contains terms more favorable than those of his license, he shall have the option to accept the more favorable agreement, including *all* of its terms and provisions, not just the more favorable provisions. The agreement should state whether the most favored licensee provision is to operate with respect only to subsequently granted licenses or to both previously and subsequently granted licenses.

Government approvals. Unlike most other countries, the United States does not normally require any government approval of license agreements where the licensor is a foreign enterprise and the licensee is a U.S. enterprise. Accordingly, although it is common in many international license agreements for the licensor to require the licensee to secure any government approvals of license agreements that are required by law, this provision usually is not needed where technology is being licensed *into* the United States.

However, it should be noted that, under the federal Foreign Assets Control Regulations pursuant to the Trading with the Enemy Act, all U.S. transactions with persons of listed countries require approval from the U.S. Department of the Treasury. A foreign licensor may also wish to consider plans for the transfer of licensed technology or trademarks to neutral persons in case of hostilities between the United States and the licensor's country.

In any event, the U.S. licensee may have to comply with U.S. Department of Commerce reporting requirements with respect to royalties and fees paid to the foreign licensor.[31]

Export controls. The U.S. government controls the export of technical information and goods from the United States under a variety of statutes and regulations administered by the Departments of Commerce, State and Treasury.[32] A foreign licensor contemplating export of technical information or goods by a U.S. licensee as part of a license agreement must carefully review these controls with the appropriate authorities.

Force majeure.[33] Each party to the agreement should be excused under an appropriate clause for failures and delays in performance caused by catastrophes or events beyond its control. Specific items frequently falling under such clauses include the following:

(1) Wars, riots, and insurrections;

(2) Laws, proclamations, ordinances, and governmental regulations;

(3) Strikes and lockouts; and

(4) Floods, fires, and explosions.

Such a clause also usually provides that no party shall be excused for failure or delay in making any payment of money required under the agreement.

Choice of law. The agreement should state that the law of a particular country or of a state of the United States shall be applied in construing and interpreting the agreement.

It will also frequently provide that, if the parties litigate a dispute under the agreement, the law of a particular country or state shall govern the dispute. In practice, such agreements are difficult to enforce because almost all national courts are reluctant to apply and enforce the law of a foreign jurisdiction. As a practical matter, the complaining party usually is forced to sue the defending party in the country or state where the defendant resides and the courts there will tend to apply their local laws to settle the dispute.[34]

Arbitration.[35] The parties may provide that any dispute under the agreement will be submitted to a panel of arbitrators for resolution. Many agreements provide that the arbitration rules of the International Chamber of Commerce shall be followed, since they have been developed from vast experience over many years and are likely to be as foolproof as possible under current knowledge and circumstances. Often the arbitration is stipulated to take place in a neutral or mutally convenient jurisdiction, such as Switzerland.

Arbitration clauses generally work quite well when the matter in dispute is *relatively minor.* If the dispute involves important rights and large sums of money, almost invariably the losing party will try to contest the arbitration decision in a court of law, usually on the ground that one or more of the arbitrators were biased or prejudiced or that the party did not receive a full and fair hearing before the arbitration panel. Accordingly, the parties should not rely on such clauses to resolve all — and particularly the most serious — disputes.

Furthermore, as a result of the interplay between U.S. antitrust and patent laws, U.S. judicial decisions — particularly in recent years — often have adopted the principle that the arbitration of patent validity or patent infringement is against public policy because — like antitrust issues generally — such monopoly issues are affected with a public interest and accordingly should be decided by a court of law rather than a panel of arbitrators.

Applicable language. In an international license agreement, it is advisable to provide that the version of the agreement in a certain language is the official version that will ultimately govern the rights of the parties. Because English is rapidly becoming the closest alternative to a world language, many license agreements provide that the English version is the official version — particularly, of course, where one of the parties is a U.S. enterprise and many of the activities under the license are to take place in the United States.

Right of first refusal. The parties may wish to provide that, if the licensor withdraws from the business and sells the assets in which the licensed technology is used, the licensee shall have the right of first refusal to purchase such business and assets for a specified period of time.

Assignability. Frequently, a foreign licensor may wish to limit the assignability of the U.S. license by providing that the rights granted to the licensee under the agreement are personal to the licensee and may not be assigned or transferred without written consent of the licensor. A further clause may then be included, which states that any attempted assignment without such consent shall be void and at the licensor's option shall automatically terminate all the rights of the licensee under the agreement.

If the licensor had no strong objection to the assignment of a nonexclusive license by a licensee, the licensee nevertheless should furnish the licensor with reasonable assurance that the assignee will comply with the terms of the agreement, and the licensee may be required to remain responsible for such compliance.

Amendment. The agreement should state that it can be amended only by the consent of both parties clearly expressed in writing and signed by both parties.

Integration. A provision that the terms set forth in the agreement constitute the entire agreement between the parties prevents either party from asserting that there are other agreements, either in writing or oral, that modify the terms set forth in the license agreement itself.

Notices and correspondence. The agreement should set forth the official addresses of the licensor and licensee and state that all notices and communications under the agreement must be delivered or mailed to these addresses. Generally, such clauses further provide that any notice or correspondence so addressed and mailed with postage prepaid will, in the absence of clear contrary evidence to be established by the addressee, be deemed to have been received on the date on which it would in the ordinary course of the mails have been delivered or on a specified number of days after mailing.

Place of payment. Particularly in an international license agreement, the place at which royalties are to be paid should be specified. For example, the licensor may wish to be paid in his own country.

Execution and effective date. The agreement should end with a provision that each of the parties has caused the agreement to be executed in duplicate originals by its duly authorized officers or representatives. It may also be advisable to state that each of the parties has caused its corporate seal (if applicable) to be affixed to the agreement. Many agreements also provide for authentication of the signature of a corporate officer through an attesting signature, usually by the secretary or attesting secretary of the corporation.

It is also advisable for an effective date to be specified in the license agreement itself, because the date of execution of the agreement by the parties or of duplicate originals by one party may be different from the intended effective date. In the body of the agreement, this effective date should be referred to for the creation or duration of important rights. For example, the licensee's option to secure a license under another patent may run for three years from the effective date of the agreement.

Trademark License Clauses[36]

A trademark serves two principal functions: (1) it distinguishes the goods and services of the owner from those of competitors; and (2) it protects the consuming public by informing them of the origin of the goods, thereby implying that a certain standard of quality had been met. Under a trademark license, the owner of the mark permits a licensee to use his mark but retains ownership of the mark. This is to be distinguished from an assignment whereby the trademark owner transfers all right, title, and interest in the mark to the assignee. The discussion in this section of the chapter is limited to provisions essential and unique to the licensing of a trademark in the United States by a foreign owner.

Form and use of trademark. To avoid the danger of losing the licensor's own rights in the trademark, the license agreement should carefully describe the form of the trademark and detail the manner in which the mark is to be used. The trademark or marks which are the subject of the license should be clearly identified in the grant clause and included within the definitions set out at the beginning of the license agreement. An illustration or drawing of the trademark also may be included in a schedule appended to the license agreement.

The manner in which the license is to use the licensed mark should specify, *inter alia,* the goods or services with which it it to be used as well as the proper means of displaying the mark — for example, with the symbol ®, the letters "TM" or the abbreviation "Reg. U.S. Pat. Off." The agreement should state that no other mark may be used in conjunction with the licensed mark. Typically, where an extensive trademark licensing program is involved, the licensor will have an instruction booklet on how the licensed mark is to be used; this will be incorporated into the license agreement. Frequently, the licensee must obtain the licensor's approval of advertising copy, labels, and the like.

Territorial restrictions are often considered desirable by both the licensee and licensor. However, extreme caution should be exercised when imposing such restraints on a licensee because of the serious antitrust implications involved.[37] In general, restricting a licensee's use of a mark to the United States is acceptable under U.S. law, provided the restriction does not amount to a simple division of world markets.

Quality control. Under U.S. law, quality control of products and services by the licensor of a trademark is mandatory in all trademark licenses, because the owner of a trademark has a responsibility to the public to ensure that certain minimum standards of quality will be met by the products and services bearing the owner's mark. If the licensor does not exercise sufficient control over such quality, he may be held to have abandoned and forfeited all rights to the mark.[38] The quality control provisions of the license should at least specify:

(1) The licensor's right to supervise and inspect the licensee's production facilities;

(2) Minimum standards and specifications for all final products bearing the licensed mark;

(3) Specifications for the components and raw materials used in producing the goods; and

(4) The consequences of the licensee's failure to observe the quality control provisions of the agreement — for example, termination of the license.

Care should be taken not to impose unreasonable requirements on the licensee. For example, requiring the licensee to purchase all or certain supplies from the licensor or an approved source has, in many situations, been held to be an illegal tie-in.[39] The licensor can minimize the risks by limiting such arrangements to those items for which specifications cannot be practically supplied, or to products involving trade secrets.

Obligation of licensee to use trademark. In the United States, use is a prerequisite to registration of a trademark, whereas many other countries confer substantive rights upon registration and permit the first registrant to enjoin a prior user. To avoid possible loss of rights in the trademark, the licensor should impose a use obligation on the licensee sufficient to support continued U.S. ownership of the mark by the licensor. Even use by a controlled licensee will inure to the benefit of the licensor.[40]

Notice of licensor's ownership. While the use of a trademark does not necessarily indicate ownership of the mark by the user,[41] it is often advisable to require the licensee to indicate on the goods involved that the mark is being used under a license from the owner. This indication reaffirms the licensor's ownership of the mark, prevents a third party infringer from arguing that the owner of the mark is the licensee, and clarifies the origin of the products so marked.

Similarly, a separate clause in which the licensee recognizes the licensor as owner of the trademark, disclaims any interest or rights in the mark, and agrees to refrain from contesting the validity of the mark may be desirable to fortify the licensor's position *vis-à-vis* his licensee. Under such a clause the licensee is prohibited from challenging the validity of the mark and the licensor's ownership of the mark.[42]

Reversion of rights in trademark. The termination provision should explicitly state that: (1) all rights, legal or equitable, in the licensed mark revert to the licensor; and (2) the licensee will discontinue any use of the mark after termination of the license. If leeway is permitted the licensee for disposition of inventory bearing the licensed mark, the termination provision should specify the period of time within which the licensee must dispose of the marked goods in his hands at the termination of the agreement.

U.S. Taxation of the Foreign Licensor[43]

Chapter II describes the basic structure for the U.S. federal taxation of foreign persons, including foreign licensors, particularly distinguishing between (1) U.S. source nonbusiness income generally subject to withholding tax at a flat 30% of gross income without any allowance for deductions, or not taxed at all, and (2) business income taxed at usual domestic graduated rates on net income. With particular regard to royalty income, two tests determine whether the income is in the latter cateogory, *i.e.,* is effectively connected with the conduct of a U.S. trade or business:

(a) whether the income arises out of assets used or held for use in the conduct of a trade or business within the United States; or

(b) whether the activities of such a U.S. trade or business are a material factor in the realization of the income.[44]

If the foreign licensor maintains a U.S. office or other fixed place of business, certain foreign source income attributable to the office also is considered connected with the U.S. business, subject to a foreign tax credit with respect to such income.[45]

The following examples illustrate these basic principles with respect to a foreign licensor, but do *not* take into consideration the varied effects of U.S. income tax treaties:

(1) If the foreign licensor is not engaged in any U.S. trade or business, license royalties received by the foreign licensor from U.S. sources will be subject — except for specific tax treaty exemptions — to a flat 30% withholding tax, with no deductions. It is important to remember that even a *foreign* licensee of U.S. patents or other U.S. property must withhold the tax from its payments to a foreign licensor.[46] However, capital gains — for example, from assignment of a patent that is a capital asset — will not be taxed by the United States.

(2) If the foreign licensor has a U.S. trade or business, but no U.S. office, only U.S. source income effectively connected with the conduct of that business will be taxed at graduated rates on net income. Absent treaty exemption, royalties from a license agreement not negotiated through the U.S. business will be taxed at a flat 30%. Capital gains, such as from assignment of a patent that is a capital asset, will not be taxed if the U.S. business has little or no involvement in the transfer, but will be taxed at

usual domestic capital gain rates if the assignment takes place through the U.S. business.

(3) If the foreign licensor is engaged in a U.S. trade or business through a U.S. office or other fixed place of business, even royalties received for the use of patents, trade secrets, trademarks, and the like in a country outside the United States will be taxed by the United States at usual graduated rates on net income if derived from the conduct of the U.S. trade or business, and if the license giving rise to the royalties is made through the U.S. office. A fixed facility regularly used constitutes a U.S. office and continuous use is not necessary. In this connection, the use of substantial U.S. quality control facilities by a foreign licensor to supervise U.S. licensees should be handled carefully.

Where an income tax treaty is in force between the United States and the country of the foreign licensor, U.S. withholding tax on royalties usually will be reduced or eliminated. In addition, even if the foreign licensor has a U.S. permanent establishment whose profits are taxable by the United States, this may not include foreign source income attributable to the establishment. The licensed technology may be owned initially by a treaty country corporation or other resident or be contributed or otherwise transferred to it by a related party. The treaty country also may be one which imposes little or no local tax on the royalty income, or permits deductible payments in turn by the local resident to another country without substantial withholding tax. However, in all such tax treaty arrangements, the distinction between treaty use and possible abuse must be considered.[47]

In summary, the foreign licensor should be aware of the principal U.S. license clauses commonly used and of the most likely U.S. antitrust and other legal issues under such clauses. In addition, the foreign licensor should be alert to the U.S. tax consequences of alternative licensing structures.

Footnotes to Chapter IV

1. The authors of this chapter gratefully acknowledge the assistance of Horacio Rangel O. in the preparation of the second edition of this chapter.

2. *See generally* 1 L. Eckstrom, *Licensing in Foreign and Domestic Operations* §1.03 (3d ed. 1981); 1 M. Finnegan & R. Goldscheider, *The Law & Business of Licensing* Part II (1980); 1 J. Gilson, *Trademark Protection and Practice* Ch. 6 (1982); G. Pollzien, "Introductory Remarks About International Licensing," in *International Licensing Agreements* (2d ed., G. Pollzien & E. Langen eds., 1973).

3. *See generally* Chapters V, VI, VIII *infra.*

4. One of the first and most successful of these expositions was the KNOW-HOW '72 international forum held in Oslo, Norway, in November 1972. Other international expositions following somewhat the same format were KNOW-HOW '74; TECHNO '73 TOKYO, held in Japan in November 1973,TECHNO '75 TOKYO, and TECHNO '77 TOKYO; INOVA '73, INOVA '75,

and INOVA '77, all held in Paris; and TECHTRANSFAIR '78 held at Utrecht in the Netherlands.

5. For sample license agreements, see 2 L. Eckstrom, *supra* note 2, Ch. 18.

6. *See* United States v. Besser Mfg. Co., 96 F. Supp. 304 (E.D. Mich. 1951), *aff'd,* 343 U.S. 444 (1952).

7. *See generally* 1 H. Einhorn, *Patent Licensing Transactions* Ch. 3 (1980).

8. *See, e.g.,* Zenith Radio Corp. v. Hazeltine Research, Inc., 395 U.S. 100 (1969).

9. *See* Laitram Corp. v. King Crab, Inc., 244 F. Supp. 9, *modified,* 245 F. Supp. 1019 (D. Alas. 1965); Bela Seating Co. v. Poloron Prods., Inc., 438 F. 2d 733 (7th Cir. 1971), *cert. denied,* 403 U.S. 922 (1971).

10. *Cf.* Hazeltine Research, Inc. v. Zenith Radio Corp., 388 F. 2d 25 (7th Cir. 1967), *modified,* 395 U.S. 100 (1969) (disproportionate rates charged for patents contained within a package license must be reasonable in light of commercial realities).

11. *See generally* Chapter II *supra.*

12. *See generally* 1 L. Eckstrom, *supra* note 1, Ch. 4; 1 H. Einhorn, *supra* note 7, §1.06.

13. *See generally* 1 L. Eckstrom, *supra* note 1, §9.02[5]; R. Nordhaus, *Patent License Agreements* §35 (1981).

14. *See generally* 8 J. von Kalinowski, *Antitrust Laws and Trade Regulation* §59.06 [4] (1981).

15. *See* United States v. Glaxo Group Ltd., 410 U.S. 52 (1973); United States v. Timken Roller Bearing Co., 83 F. Supp. 284 (N.D. Ohio 1949), *modified,* 341 U.S. 593 (1951).

16. *See generally* United States v. General Elec. Co., 82 F. Supp. 753 (D.N.J. 1949); Dr. Miles Medical Co. v. John D. Park & Sons Co., 220 U.S. 373 (1911); 8 J. von Kalinowski, *supra* note 14, §59.06 [4][a][ii]; Chapter I *supra.*

17. *See* U.S. Dep't of Justice, *Antitrust Guide for International Operations* 34 (1977).

18. *See* 8 J. von Kalinowski, *supra* note 14, §59.06 [4][a][i].

19. *Cf.* National Lockwasher Co. v. George K. Garrett Co., 137 F.2d 255 (3d Cir. 1943)(a patentee's right does not extend to the use of patents to purge market of competing unpatented goods except through process of fair competition).

20. *Cf.* International Business Machines Corp. v. United States, 298 U.S. 131 (1936) (quality control defense rejected by the court in holding a tie-in of an unpatented product with a patent license agreement illegal). *But cf.* Continental T.V., Inc. v. GTE Sylvania, Inc., 433 U.S. 36 (1977) (quality control may be a legitimate reason for a manufacturer to exert control over the manner in which his products are sold and serviced).

21. *See* National Lockwasher Co. v. George K. Garrett Co., 137 F. 2d 255 (3rd Cir. 1943); Morton Salt Co. v. G. S. Suppiger Co., 314 U.S. 488 (1942). *See also* 1 H. Einhorn, *supra* note 7, §7.01(1).

22. *Cf.* B.B. Chem. Co. v. Ellis, 314 U.S. 495 (1942) (exercise of control over unpatented product held *per se* illegal even though patent could not otherwise be exploited); *see also* Chapter I *supra. But see* Rohm & Haas v. Dawson Chem. Co., 599 F. 2d 685 (5th Cir. 1979), *aff'd,* 448 U.S. 176 (1980) (sale of unpatented herbicide held to be contributory infringement under 35 U.S.C. §271).

23. *See* United States v. Glaxo Group Ltd., 410 U.S. 52 (1973); United States v. Arnold, Schwinn & Co., 388 U.S. 365 (1967), *overruled by* Continental T.V., Inc. v. GTE Sylvania, Inc., 433 U.S. 36 (1977).

24. *See, e.g.,* United States v. Univis Lens Co., 316 U.S. 241 (1942).

25. *See, e.g.,* United States v. Huck Mfg. Co., 227 F. Supp. 791, 804 (E.D. Mich. 1964), *aff'd,* 382 U.S. 197 (1965); United States v. Wisconsin Alumni Research Foundation, [1970] Trade Cas. (CCH) §73,015 (W.D. Wis. 1970).

26. *See generally* R. Nordhaus, *supra* note 13, §30.

27. Lear, Inc. v. Adkins, 395 U.S. 653 (1969). *See* Panther Pumps & Equip. Co. v. Hydrocraft, Inc., 468 F. 2d 225 (7th Cir. 1972), *cert. denied,* 411 U.S. 965 (1973);Bendix Corp. v. Balax, Inc., 421 F. 2d 809 (7th Cir. 1970), *cert. denied,* 399 U.S. 911 (1970). *But see* Coast Metals v. Cape, 205 U.S.P.Q. 154 (D.N.J. 1979) (assignee estoppel); *compare* Aronson v. Quick Point Co., 440 U.S. 257 (1979) (neither the holding nor the rationale of *Lear* controls when no patent has been issued and no ideas have been withdrawn from public use). For treatment accorded similar agreements dealing with trademark licensing, see Heaton Distrib. Co. v. Union Tank Car Co., 387 F. 2d 477 (8th Cir. 1967); Beer Nuts, Inc. v. King Nut Co., 477 F. 2d 326 (6th Cir. 1973), *cert. denied,* 414 U.S. 848 (1973) (an agreement wherein the alleged trademark infringer recognized the validity of a trademark precluded him from claiming that trademark was merely descriptive).

28. *See generally* 1 L. Eckstrom, *supra* note 2, §§10.05 [18], 10.08.

29. *See* Brulotte v. Thys Co., 379 U.S. 29 (1964).

30. *See generally* R. Nordhaus, *supra* note 13, §25.

31. *See* Chapter XII *infra.* Government approval provisions exist in most countries — for example, Argentina, Brazil, Japan, and Mexico.

32. *See generally* Chapter VIII *infra.*

33. *See generally* 1 H. Einhorn, *supra* note 7, §4.05.

34. *Id.* §2.17.

35. *See generally* 1 L. Eckstrom, *supra* note 2, Ch. 11; 1 H. Einhorn, *supra* note 7, §5.02[3][i].

36. *See generally* 3 R. Callmann, *The Law of Unfair Competition, Trademarks and Monopolies* §78.2(3d ed. 1981); 1 J. Gilson, *supra* note 2, Ch. 6; L. Meville, *Forms and Agreements on Intellectual Property and International Licensing* Ch. 6 (1981); E. Offner, *International Trademark Protection* 106-137 (1965); Poms & Harris, "Problems in International and Domestic Trademark and Copyright Licensing," in *Current Trends in Domestic and International Licensing* 207-246 (M. Finnegan & R. Goldscheider eds., 1976).

37. *See, e.g.,* United States v. Sealy, Inc., 388 U.S. 350 (1967).

38. *See, e.g.,* E. I. duPont de Nemours & Co. v. Celanese Corp. of America, 167 F. 2d 484 (C.C.P.A. 1948).

39. *See, e.g.,* Siegel v. Chicken Delight, Inc., 448 F. 2d 43 (9th Cir. 1971), *cert. denied,* 405 U.S. 955 (1972) (subsequent cases, however, have questioned the reasoning of *Chicken Delight*); Susser v. Carvel Corp., 332 F.2d 505 (2d Cir. 1964). *But see* Principe v. McDonald's Corporation, 463 F. Supp. 1149 (E.D. Va. 1980), *aff'd,* 631 F.2d 303 (4th Cir. 1980), *cert. denied,* 451 U.S. 970 (1980) (where the challenged aggregation is an essential ingredient of the franchised system's formula for success, there is but a single product and no tie-in exists as a matter of law).

40. *See, e.g.,* Capital Tie Rak, Inc. v. Tie Rack Stores of Ill., Inc., 150 U.S.P.Q. 357, 360 (N.D. Ill. 1966); La Chemise La Coste v. Alligator Co., 374 F.Supp. 52 (D. Del. 1974).

41. *See* Zephyr America Corp. v. Esterbrook Pen Co., 135 U.S.P.Q. 84 (T.T.A.B. 1962). *But see Ex parte* C.B. Donald Co., 117 U.S.P.Q. 485, 487 (Comm'r Pat. 1958).

42. While *Lear, Inc. v. Adkins,* 395 U.S. 653 (1969), abolished the doctrine of licensee estoppel in patent licensing, it did not affect the estoppel doctrine for trademark licensees. *See* Beer Nuts, Inc. v. King Nut Co., 477 F.2d 326 (6th Cir. 1973), *cert. denied,* 414 U.S. 848 (1973).

43. *See generally* J. Bischel, *Taxation of Patents, Trademarks, Copyrights and Know-How* §7.3a (1976); Chapter II *supra.*

44. I.R.C. §864(c)(2).

45. I.R.C. §§864(c)(4), 906.

46. I.R.C. §§861(a)(4), 871(a)(1), 881(a), 1441-1443; Rev. Rul. 80-362, 1980-2 C.B. 208.

47. *See* Chapter II *supra.*

Chapter V

Import Activities

A foreign investor's U.S. involvement often includes importation and distribution of goods and related items within the United States. This chapter summarizes selected aspects of such activities including U.S. customs laws and related import limitations, as well as certain U.S. income tax aspects relevant to a foreign investor. In this connection, however, it should be noted that most enterprises which import extensively into the United States find it necessary to obtain the services of a licensed customs broker. In addition, the services of legal counsel in customs and international trade matters, as well as those of other specialists in this area, frequently may be necessary to guide imports through the maze of technical customs and other requirements.

Government Agencies Dealing with Imports

U.S. Customs Service

The U.S. Customs Service is an agency of the Department of the Treasury and has the most substantial governmental responsibility for dealing with imports. It supervises the unlading of vessels, land vehicles, and aircraft, and the entry of merchandise, its classification, and valuation. It also administers quotas, laws prohibiting importation of certain items and smuggling of contraband, and numerous health, safety, environmental, and commercial restrictions on imports. The Customs Service is headquartered in Washington, D.C., but was divided into 46 customs districts as of the beginning of 1982 and numerous ports of entry and customs stations within these districts. The districts are grouped into nine regions, each of which is headed by a Regional Commissioner of Customs.

Trade Reorganization Agencies

Under the mandate of the Trade Agreements Act of 1979,[1] the President has placed various trade responsibilities in the following agencies:

The U.S. Trade Representative has primary responsibility, with the advice of the interagency Trade Policy Committee, for developing and coordinating the implementation of U.S. international trade policy and, to the extent related to trade policy, direct investment matters. The Trade Representative advises the President on trade policy, conducts international trade negotiations, and provides policy guidance to other government agencies on basic trade issues in designated areas.

The Department of Commerce has operational responsibility for major nonagricultural international trade functions, including export development, commerical representation abroad, the administration of the antidumping and countervailing duty laws discussed below, and trade adjustment assistance to firms and communities injured by imports.

The International Trade Administration, established in the Department of Commerce under the supervision of the Under Secretary for International Trade, determines the applicability of antidumping or countervailing duties.

International Trade Commission

The U.S. International Trade Commission (the "ITC"), which prior to 1975 was the U.S. Tariff Commission, conducts studies on import trade for the U.S. Congress and for the executive branch of the federal government and develops statistics on imports under various statistical classifications. In connection with tariff negotiations and other international trade agreements, the ITC investigates, holds hearings, and makes reports on the probable effect of such agreements on the U.S. economy. It is also charged with determining whether imports are injuring or threatening to injure domestic industry. These include cases under the Trade Act of 1974 as amended,[2] and the antidumping and countervailing duty laws discussed below. Similarly, it is charged with determining whether imports produced in communist controlled countries cause U.S. market disruption.

Other Agencies

Other U.S. agencies with responsibilities relating to imports are:

The Department of Agriculture which initiates investigations of the need for and administers import quotas on various agricultural commodities and processed agricultural products necessary to protect domestic agricultural support programs and groups of American producers from injury from import competition. With respect to the supervision and development of international standards for imports and exports, the Secretary of Agriculture has substantially the same responsibility for agricultural products as the Secretary of Commerce has for nonagricultural products.

The Department of Defense and ***the General Services Administration***

which apply the Buy American Act and the exceptions to that act discussed below.

The Department of Energy which administers imports of petroleum and petroleum products.

The Department of Labor which provides adjustment assistance to workers found to be injured by imports.

Import Procedures

The Customs Procedural Reform and Simplification Act of 1978[3] extensively amended various import procedures, which have been clarified and amplified by implementing regulations. The principal procedures as revised may be summarized as follows:

Entry

When items are brought into the United States from abroad or withdrawn from a bonded warehouse, import procedures commence with the filing of an entry document to secure immediate delivery, followed within a maximum of 10 days by an entry summary document for consumption or warehouse. Certain items are not dutiable but, in any event, entry documents must be filed. The entry summary document describes the items being imported, states the value thereof, and specifies the provision of the U.S. Tariff Schedules referred to below which is applicable to them. Estimated duty must be deposited at the time of making entry or with the entry summary. Various other documents must be filed accompanying or within 10 days after entry, such as the bill of lading, a customs bond to cover payment of duty, a power of attorney, and the like.

Classification

The duty on an imported item is dependent on its tariff classification and, usually, its value. The classification of imports is determined by the provision of the U.S. Tariff Schedules[4] under the Tariff Act of 1930, as amended, which most specifically describes them. These Tariff Schedules have three main divisions: (1) the General Headnotes and Rules of Interpretation, (2) Schedules 1 through 8 which contain descriptions of approximately 5,000 items, and (3) an Appendix. The General Headnotes contain statutory provisions and principles to determine which of two or more tariff classifications apply to a particular imported item. An item should be classified under that provision which most specifically describes it. Also, classification by use is governed by the use made of the item in the United States immediately prior to the date of importation. If an item is classified instead by actual U.S. use, then that use must be intended when imported, such use must be made of the item after importation, and proof of such use must be made within three years after the article is entered.

Valuation

The valuation of imported items is a highly technical procedure. Even where duties are not based on value but, for example, a specific amount per unit of import, the Customs Service is required to value the items for statistical purposes.

Valuation of all articles exported to the United States in or after July 1980 (except certain rubber footwear) now is made in accordance with the Customs Valuation Standards enacted by the Trade Agreements Act of 1979. These standards follow the Valuation Code in the Agreement on Implementation of Title VII of the General Agreement on Tariffs and Trade adopted during the so called Tokyo Round of Multilateral Trade Negotiations ("MTN") and approved by Congress in the Trade Agreements Act. The new valuation law provides for five bases for appraising imported merchandise, the first being the primary and preferred basis:

(1) The transaction value of the imported merchandise;

(2) The transaction value of identical merchandise;

(3) The transaction value of similar merchandise;

(4) The deductive value;

(5) The computed value.

Each basis is to be used only if the preceding basis cannot be determined; and, in the case of the first basis, even if the transaction value of the imported merchandise can be determined, that basis may not be used if any of certain disqualifications applies. However, the importer may timely elect to have the merchandise appraised on the basis of computed value rather than deductive value. If none of the five bases can be used, appraisal is to be on the basis of a value derived from one of the bases, with the methods being reasonably adjusted as necessary to arrive at a value.

The pre-existing law[5] continues to apply to the valuation of all articles exported prior to July 1980. Prior exports placed in warehouses may remain there up to five years, and those previously brought into foreign trade zones may remain there indefinitely. Whenever such prior exports are entered for consumption, they must be valued under the pre-existing law.

Liquidation

After the entry document and related papers have been filed, the final process in the determination of duty is liquidation of the entry. This is the determination by the Customs Service of the proper dutiable value of the items, the applicable rate of duty and, as a result, the amount of duty due and payable. If this amount is the same as the amount deposited at the time the entry documents were filed, the entry is endorsed liquidated without change as entered. If the liquidated duty is more than that which was deposited at the time of entry, the importer is billed for the difference and, if less, he is given a refund in the amount of the difference.

The official notice of liquidation is posted in the form of a bulletin in a conspicuous place in the Customs House in the port of entry. An informal Courtesy Notice also may be provided. An entry not liquidated within one year after entry is considered liquidated as asserted by the importer, unless notice of an extension for a permitted reason is given by the Customs Service — which in turn expires four years after entry unless liquidation then is suspended by statute or court order. If the importer does not agree with the determination in the liquidation, he may file a protest in writing within 90 days from the posting of the notice of liquidation. The District Director of Customs first considers the protest. If he denies it, the protest may be transferred by the importer either to the Regional Commissioner of Customs or to the Commissioner of Customs at Customs Service headquarters in Washington, D.C. A protest must be fully disposed of — by being allowed or denied in whole or in part — within two years after the date filed.

Judicial Review

If the importer still does not agree with the final determination on his protest, he may within 180 days after its denial in whole or in part file a summons in the U.S. Court of International Trade[6] for a judicial determination. Appeal may be taken from a decision of the Court of International Trade to the Court of Appeals for the Federal Circuit (before October 1982, the Court of Customs and Patent Appeals), which usually is the final arbiter in customs matters. The U.S. Supreme Court has, but rarely exercises, discretionary jurisdiction to hear appeals from decisions of this latter court.

Penalties and Forfeitures

Numerous statutory sections provide in case of violation of U.S. customs laws for forfeiture of the vessel, vehicle, or item involved in the violation, or for various penalties including a penalty equal to the value of that item.[7] Section 592 of the Tariff Act of 1930 — a highly controversial provision — originally provided that, in the case of imports fraudulently or falsely introduced into the United States, the items or the value thereof were subject to forfeiture. The penalty could be applied to each violation in a series of entries with the result that total penalties assessed could reach astronomical amounts. However, under 1978 amendments, negligent, grossly negligent, and fraudulent erroneous entries are subject to differing civil penalties generally ranging from 20% of the dutiable value to the entire domestic value of the items.

An individual arriving in the United States who fails to declare an article being imported may be subject to forfeiture of the merchandise *and* a penalty of the value of the forfeited merchandise. It should be noted that only returning U.S. residents are allowed the general duty-free entry of up to $300 in value for articles acquired abroad.

After a penalty or forfeiture has been assessed, a petition may be filed with the Commissioner of Customs for the remission or mitigation thereof. Once the amount of a fine, penalty, or forfeiture has been reduced under a final administrative decision, the importer has the choice of accepting the decision or defending against a civil action for the amount of the penalty. In an action for a penalty assessed under Section 592, however, the court may modify the penalty.

Special Limitations on Imports

Quotas

Quotas are of two types: absolute quotas and tariff-rate quotas. An absolute quota designates a maximum quantity of a commodity which may be imported in a stated period. It may apply globally, or to imports from specified countries. A tariff-rate quota permits the entry of a specified quantity of imports over a specified period at a preferential or reduced rate of duty, with imports above the specified quantity being subject to a higher rate of duty.

The bulk of U.S. quotas are administered by the Customs Service and cover a wide range of products from cattle to whisk brooms. A report issued by the Customs Service during the first week of each calendar month shows the status under the various quotas established in the Tariff Schedules. Most such quotas are on a first-come, first-served basis so that, if an entry is not filed before the quota amount is filled, the importer must wait until the opening of the next quota period — which may be annual, semi-annual, or quarterly.

Certain quotas are administered by or require licenses from other agencies and departments of the U.S. government. For example, to preclude imports from interfering with the operation of related domestic programs, quotas covering butter, various cheeses, and various dried milk products are proclaimed by the President on recommendation by the Department of Agriculture and a finding by the ITC of interference by the imports with the agricultural program; to make entries under these quotas one must have a license issued by the Department.[8]

Controls which are the equivalent of quotas are applied on cotton, wool, and man-made fiber textiles and textile products, under bilateral textile agreements between the United States and specific foreign countries. These are usually administered by licenses issued by the exporting country itself, but may be administered by the U.S. Customs Service under direction of the Office of Textiles in the Department of Commerce.

Special quotas apply to watches and watch movements from insular possessions of the United States.[9] Finally, the importation of petroleum and petroleum products is governed by an elaborate system of quota-like controls.[10]

Transactions with Specified Countries

The Office of Foreign Assets Control of the Department of the Treasury administers regulations generally prohibiting — other than pursuant to license — trade and other transactions with listed countries, as described in Chapter I. Such transactions by persons subject to the jurisdiction of the United States are prohibited whether they take place within or outside the territorial United States. The limitations on trade with the People's Republic of China have been lifted but, as to the other countries, the regulations are tantamount to an embargo on trade. Accordingly, imports from the countries mentioned and imports of products of those countries are prohibited except pursuant to license.

The further application of these and related regulations to *exports* from the United States is described in Chapter VIII, which deals with use of the United States as a base for foreign operations.

Buy American Restrictions

Pursuant to the Buy American Act,[11] generally only articles, materials, and supplies produced in the United States may be acquired by the federal government for public use. Moreover, in construction contracts for the federal government, contractors and suppliers may use only articles, materials, and supplies produced in the United States. Any contractor violating these requirements may be blacklisted and thereby rendered ineligible for future contracts with the federal government.

Exceptions to these restrictions apply in the case of items which are not mined, produced, or manufactured in the United States in sufficient and reasonably available quantities of a satisfactory quality, or if the prices of such domestic products are unreasonably high. In addition, the restrictions do not apply to the acquisition of articles, materials, and supplies for use by the federal government outside the United States.

Certain Buy American restrictions on federal government procurement now may be selectively waived under the Trade Agreements Act of 1979, which approved the MTN Agreement on Government

Procurement to permit products and supplies of reciprocating signatory countries to be treated no less favorably than domestic products or supplies in specified areas of procurement. The waiver authority is confined to procurement by designated government agencies of goods (not services) over a threshold value determined by the U.S. Trade Representative, from countries designated as eligible by the Trade Representative. The Customs Service makes advisory rulings and final determinations on questions concerning the country of origin of particular products. Judicial review of the final determinations is provided for in the Trade Agreements Act. The U.S. General Services Administration has provided temporary procurement regulations governing solicitation and procurement procedures under this waiver authority effective after 1980.[12]

Prohibited Items[13]

The Tariff Schedules contain various absolute prohibitions on the importation of certain items; the list is lengthy and includes specified fur skins from the U.S.S.R., the feathers or skins of various wild birds, white phosphorous matches, and so forth. Any investor preparing to engage in import and distribution activities in the United States *must* check the Tariff Schedules for such prohibited items.

The investor likewise should check with the Customs Service for so called Special Classes of Merchandise, entry of which is restricted or prohibited by other statutes. Importation of toxic substances such as chemicals also may require advance notice to, for example, the U.S. Environmental Protection Agency.

A statutory prohibition applies to importation of so called immoral articles. These include books and printed matter advocating treason or insurrection or forcible resistance to U.S. laws, or containing personal threats; obscene books, writings, and illustrations; drugs or medicine for causing unlawful abortion; and lottery tickets. Another provision prohibits importation of items mined, produced, or manufactured by convict, forced, or indentured labor.

Finally, any contract of sale of U.S. foreign surplus property must contain a provision which forbids its importation into the United States except under authorization from the Secretary of Agriculture in the case of agricultural commodities, or from the Secretary of Commerce in the case of other items.

Marking, Trademarks, and Copyrights

Generally all imported items must be marked with the country of origin. In addition, special marking, labeling, certification, and similar requirements are applied to certain imports in order to protect U.S. health and welfare. The applicable statutes and regulations contain lists of items which are exempt from these marking requirements.[14]

The Customs Service administers laws prohibiting importation of a foreign item if the item or its label, sign, or wrapper bears a trademark owned by a U.S. citizen or corporation, provided a copy of the certificate of registration has been filed with the Secretary of the Treasury. This prohibition does not apply if written consent to importation has been obtained from the owner of the trademark and is produced at the time of entry or if the article is brought in by an arriving individual for his personal use and is within the limits of type and quantity determined by the Secretary of the Treasury.

In addition, the owner of a patent may file a complaint with the ITC in case of possible infringement of the patent by imports, whereupon the ITC can require exclusion of such imports. Similar provisions exist for the protection of tradenames, trademarks, and copyrights. Customs regulations contain detailed procedures which must be followed to invoke these provisions.[15]

Provisions Against Foreign Competition

A number of remedies are provided by U.S. law to deal with unfair and other foreign competition, and the federal government recently has been quite vigilant in pursuing these remedies.

Antidumping Law

The current U.S. antidumping provisions of the Tariff Act of 1930[16] were added by the Trade Agreements Act of 1979. The revisions were intended to expedite investigations and assessment of duties and to ensure conformity with the MTN Antidumping Code approved by the Trade Agreements Act. The new provisions became effective January 1, 1980.

Under this law, an additional customs duty may be assessed when goods are dumped in the United States — that is, sold at a price less than that at which they are sold in the seller's foreign home market, or in certain cases in third country markets — and such sales threaten or cause injury to or prevent establishment of a domestic industry that manufactures or sells a like product. The Department of Commerce determines whether dumping has occurred, after which the ITC decides the question of injury to domestic industry. If an affirmative decision is rendered, the Department publishes a finding of dumping and through the Customs Service collects an antidumping duty equal to the difference between the import (or so called United States) price and the home market price after certain adjustments, referred to as the dumping margin.

It is the importer who pays the additional antidumping duty, even if the importer is not the foreign producer who is selling at an inordinately low price. An independent importer should contract with the foreign producer or exporter to indemnify the importer against antidumping duty, and should follow the daily U.S. Federal Register for notices of commencement of antidumping investigations. Once an investigation is started, further orders should be stopped until it is completed.

Sale at Less than Cost of Production

As initiated in the Trade Act of 1974, where sales in the foreign home market have been made at less than cost of production over an extended period of time, in substantial quantities, and at prices which do not permit recovery of all costs within a reasonable period of time, the Secretary of Commerce can in an antidumping proceeding disregard such sales in determining the foreign market value. If the remaining sales provide inadequate information for the proceeding, a constructed value may be used for comparison with the U.S. sale price. Such constructed value is derived by using the best evidence available to estimate the cost of producing the items and adding a reasonable margin for general expenses, profit, and the cost of preparing the merchandise for shipment to the United States.

This provision was used to develop what is referred to as the trigger price mechanism in antidumping proceedings against imported steel products. In the initial 1978 case, following antidumping complaints by the domestic steel industry, the Department of the Treasury (then so empowered) determined that the bulk of sales of steel to the United States from Japan had been made at prices below the cost of production over a substantial period of time. Accordingly, the Department determined constructed values and published a series of so called trigger prices for basic types and forms of steel, plus add-on prices for extras. Under Department of Commerce administration, sales of imported steel products from major steel producing countries at prices below the trigger prices were assumed to be at less than the cost of production and the importer was required to post a bond in the amount of the difference to cover possible future assessment of an antidumping duty.[17] However, the importer and the foreign producer could submit evidence to establish that prices charged in any given shipment were not lower than the cost of production. This procedure was followed throughout 1981 in the case of shipments of steel to the United States by all major producing countries, but was suspended as to most steel imports early in 1982.

In the future, where foreign producers make substantial inroads on the U.S. market for other items at prices well below U.S. producers' prices, the Department of Commerce may resort to the trigger price mechanism for several reasons: first, it is a simple technique compared to the extended processing and investigation in connection with an antidumping complaint; second, it makes possible much faster relief to domestic industry; and third, it provides relief from certain foreign competition without as strong an appearance of protectionism as under other techniques.

Countervailing Duty Law

The revisions to the Tariff Act of 1930 added by the Trade Agreements Act of 1979 provide a new U.S. countervailing duty law[18] consistent with the MTN Agreement on Subsidies and Countervailing Measures approved in the Trade Agreements Act. The new law applies to exports from a country under that agreement or which has assumed equivalent obligations, or which are determined by the President to fall in a defined category. The new provisions became effective beginning with 1980.

Exports from countries not covered by the new law remain subject to the old countervailing duty law.[19] The significant difference is that under the new law material injury determinations by the ITC are required with respect to dutiable as well as nondutiable imports in a countervailing duty proceeding. However, the old law was also amended by the Trade Agreements Act to include some of the procedural remedies and requirements contained in the new law.

The new and old countervailing duty laws provide in effect that, where a foreign country subsidizes exports, a countervailing duty equal to the amount of the foreign subsidy is required to be imposed. Again, the duty is assessed against and collected from the importer whether or not the importer receives the subsidy. If there is a question whether the foreign country is making any form of direct or indirect subsidy available to its exporters, an independent importer should contract for indemnification in case a countervailing duty is assessed.

The administering authority, originally the Department of the Treasury and now the Department of Commerce, has held a variety of foreign government actions to constitute indirect subsidies prompting countervailing duties. For example, a series of foreign measures to promote investment in a factory — including tax exemption, a grant of land, and low interest loans — amounted to a subsidy within the meaning of the countervailing duty law on the production of tires for export to the United States.[20] Likewise, the rebate of certain indirect taxes by the Italian government in connection with the export of steel transmission towers to the United States constituted such a subsidy.[21] However, the U.S. Supreme Court found that the nonexcessive remission of a Japanese commodity tax upon export did not constitute such a subsidy.[22]

Section 301 of the Trade Act

The Trade Act of 1974 included a new and very broad provision in Section 301, developed procedurally by the Trade Agreements Act of

1979, which gives the President authority to retaliate against foreign discrimination against U.S. trade.[23] For example, if a foreign country discriminates against U.S. exports by unreasonable tariff or other import restrictions, the President may impose duties or other import restrictions on the same or other products of such a foreign country when they enter the United States. Also, if a foreign country subsidizes exports to a third country and such subsidized exports substantially reduce the sale of a competitive U.S. product, the President may impose duties or other import restrictions on products of the original country. However, the President may determine that retaliatory measures are not appropriate or feasible or consistent with the purposes of the Trade Act.

Section 301 is administered by the U.S. Trade Representative who operates through an interagency Section 301 Committee which investigates complaints and provides for public hearings. The Trade Representative consults with the foreign government concerned and utilizes, if needed, the dispute settlement procedures of the General Agreement on Tariffs and Trade. His semiannual reports to Congress covered 21 cases through the first six years.

Section 337 of the Tariff Act

Section 337 of the Tariff Act of 1930[24] was strengthened by amendments contained in the Trade Act of 1974 and the Trade Agreements Act of 1979. This provision declares generally that unfair methods of competition and unfair acts in the importation of items into the United States are unlawful if their effect or tendency is to destroy or substantially injure an industry in the United States which is efficiently and economically run, to prevent the establishment of such an industry, or to restrain or monopolize trade and commerce in the United States. It is administered by the ITC, which can issue either a cease and desist order demanding that the unlawful acts be stopped, an exclusion order prohibiting continued import of items, or both. Any such order does not become final for 60 days, during which time the President may review and reverse it.

Where the unlawful acts complained of amount to dumping or subsidy, the antidumping and countervailing duty acts take precedence. This was made mandatory by the Trade Agreements Act. Of over 100 cases before the ITC, most have concerned alleged infringement by imports of U.S. patents. But Section 337 action has been instituted based on various anticompetitive charges such as trademark and copyright infringement, price fixing, attempts to monopolize, palming off, and predatory pricing.

The ITC makes its determination on the basis of a full hearing under the Administrative Procedure Act. If a violation is found, it must consider the effects of any remedial actions on the public health and welfare, competitive conditions in the U.S. economy, the production of like or directly competitive U.S. articles, and U.S. consumers. During the 60-day period for review by the President of an ITC order, the U.S. Trade Representative invites public comment on the domestic or foreign policy issues involved and makes recommendations to the President. The President so far has rejected only two ITC orders.[25] A final order of the ITC is subject to appeal to the Court of Customs and Patent Appeals.

Other Anticompetition Provisions

Under certain provisions of the Trade Act of 1974, as amended by the Trade Agreements Act of 1979, the President can — without any allegation of unfair competition — place restrictions on imports entering "in such increased quantities as to be a substantial cause of serious injury or threat thereof" to domestic industry.[26] This was referred to under previous law as the escape clause mechanism. The President is authorized to act on the basis of an investigation and recommendation by the ITC to provide relief in the form of additional duties or other import restrictions, such as quotas, if he considers the same to be in the national economic interest. However, the President alternatively may provide various forms of assistance to industry and employees; this course of action has been followed in most cases to date. The President must report to Congress a decision to provide or deny import relief and, if the decision differs from the ITC recommendation, the reasons therefor. If Congress disapproves the President's decision within 90 days, the President must proclaim the increase in or imposition of any duty or import restriction recommended by the ITC.

Incorporated in the Trade Act of 1974 is another provision, similar to the escape clause mechanism, which offers protection against market disruption by imports from communist controlled countries. If a petition is filed with the ITC alleging that imports of specified items from such countries cause market disruption, the ITC will investigate and report to the President its determination whether such market disruption is occurring and, if so, what action should be taken by the President to impose or increase a duty or otherwise restrict such imports. Such countries include "any country dominated or controlled by Communism."[27]

Laws to Facilitate Imports

Generalized System of Preferences

The Trade Act of 1974 established a Generalized System of Preferences under which for the 10-year period beginning January 1, 1975, the President may grant duty-free treatment to imported items from developing countries.[28] Approximately 112 independent countries and 29 dependencies currently are entitled to receive such preferences, including most countries of South and Central America, the Caribbean, Africa, and Southeast Asia, island territories, and Hong Kong, India, Indonesia, Israel, Portugal, Romania, Taiwan, and Yugoslavia. The current country list appears in Section 3(c) of the annotated General Headnotes and Rules of Interpretation of the Tariff Schedules. It includes associations of countries eligible for treatment as one country under a Trade Agreements Act of 1979 amendment. The President has by executive order listed almost 3,000 items which, when imported from one of the specified countries, are to be admitted free of duty.[29]

However, there are certain limitations on the use of this procedure. The President may add or delete countries annually. A country also can be removed from the list if imports of an eligible item exceed a specified amount based on the gross national product during the year or, above a minimum value, constitute one-half or more of the total U.S. imports of that item during the year. Items also may be added to the list. Listed eligible items are given duty-free treatment only if they are imported directly into the United States from the developing country or eligible association of countries and either they were wholly grown, produced, or manufactured there or at least 35% of the appraised value was added there.

Foreign Trade Zones

There are numerous foreign trade zones in or adjacent to ports of entry of the United States. They are isolated, enclosed, and policed areas furnished with facilities for loading, unloading, handling, storing, manipulating, manufacturing, and exhibiting items and for reshipping them by land, sea, or air. Items may be manufactured, exhibited, stored, packaged, graded, cleaned, mixed, or otherwise manipulated in a foreign trade zone and, as long as the items remain in the zone, no duty is payable. Thus, merchandise may be placed in such a zone for various operations and subsequently shipped abroad without the necessity of paying duty.[30]

The statutory authority for these zones also has been interpreted to permit assembly of items from abroad into items which then can be imported into the United States at lower duty than if the components had been directly imported, since higher duties often are imposed on components to protect U.S. parts producers. Alternatively, items may be transformed in the zone into merchandise which is subject to U.S. quotas less restrictive than those for the original items. The zones in any event permit deferral of duty until the manufacture or sale or other use of items has been accomplished and completed products are ready for U.S. importation and sale. Special purpose subzones at individual manufacturing plants have been granted by the Foreign Trade Zones Board, and are of interest even to U.S. owned companies.

Drawback on Exported Items

If exported items manufactured or produced in the United States are to include components or raw materials previously imported subject to U.S. customs duty, either of two techniques may be used to recover all or most of such duty. First, parts or materials may be imported without duty by posting of temporary importation bonds.[31] However, the particular merchandise must be traced to the exported items and, if this is not possible, at least double the ordinary duty will be required. In addition, intentional failure to re-export the imported items may result in civil and/or criminal penalties.

Second, the importer may apply for drawback — *i.e.*, refund of 99% of the duty paid upon importation — by asking for a drawback rate from U.S. customs officials prior to exportation.[32] Tracing of particular imported parts or materials to the exported items is required, but domestic parts or materials of the same kind and quality may be substituted in equivalent amounts and values for imported items and used in the exports. Such drawback also is allowed on imported items not conforming to samples or required specifications upon their return to customs officials for exportation.

Refund of duty in full also is provided under certain conditions. For example, when imported items are found not to be entitled to admission into the United States, they may be exported or destroyed under supervision of the Customs Service. Duty also is refundable under certain conditions on imported items used for the maintenance or repair of vessels or aircraft.

Items Exported and Returned

The basic rule is that articles exported from the United States are dutiable when they are returned to the United States. However, there are four major exceptions to this rule. The first permits duty-free re-entry of U.S. products which have been exported and have not been advanced in value or improved in condition abroad by any process of manufacture or other means.[33] Samples sent abroad for approval, rejected shipments, prototypes, and the like can be returned under this exception. Further, certain operations may be performed abroad which are not considered to advance items in value or improve their condition. For example, loose items — such as fishhooks — may be sent abroad in bulk for sorting and packaging and returned.

A foreign investor also may wish to export U.S. items temporarily for limited processing or for assembly abroad — for example, in an area with lower wage rates such as the Mexican border zone facilities — and return them for sale or use within the United States. In this connection, a second provision permits duty-free re-entry of items which have been sent abroad for repairs or alterations.[34] In this case, import duty is payable only on the repair or alteration accomplished abroad and *not* on the entire value of the item.

Similarly, under a third exception, manufactured articles of base metal exported for further processing abroad may be returned for additional processing subject to customs duty only on the value of the processing abroad.[35]

Fourth, any U.S. fabricated item may be exported ready for assembly and for activity strictly incidental to assembly such as cleaning, lubricating, or painting and, upon its return, the value of the original item sent abroad is deducted from the dutiable value of the returned item.[36]

Trade Fairs

The Trade Fair Act of 1959[37] permits importation of items free of duty and taxes for use and display in connection with fairs, exhibitions, and expositions. These privileges are available in connection with any fair which has been designated by the Secretary of Commerce as a qualified trade fair. The Customs Service administers the program to assure that items are not imported in evasion of duty requirements. Within three months after the fair's closing, items entered free of duty must be removed. They may be exported, transferred to another qualified fair, destroyed, abandoned to the U.S. government, or entered for consumption in the United States. If they are entered for consumption, the duty must be paid at that time.

Articles Conditionally Free of Duty or Subject to Reduced Rates

The Tariff Schedules authorize temporary importation of certain items such as exhibition displays, theatrical effects, and articles brought in by professional artists, lecturers, or scientists for use for professional purposes. Also, certain items are conditionally free of duty or subject to a reduced rate such as articles for educational, scientific, and religious institutions, works of art and antiques, supplies and equipment for vessels, products of American fisheries, and certain others.[38]

U.S. Taxation of the Foreign Investor's Import and Distribution Activities[39]

If a foreign investor engages in importation and/or distribution of goods and related items within the United States, whether manufactured abroad by the investor or purchased from others, he must consider — in addition to the U.S. customs laws and import limitations described above — the following issues: (1) the U.S. protection of patents, trademarks, and other intellectual property, as described in Chapters I and IV, with respect to the imported items; (2) the restrictions of U.S. antitrust laws on his agreements with U.S. distributors or possible competitors, as described in Chapters I and IV; (3) the product liability, security interest, and other standard terms of his contractual arrangements with U.S. purchasers and other persons, certain of which matters are discussed in Chapter VI dealing generally with new U.S. business establishments; and (4) the U.S. income and other tax aspects of such import and/or distribution activities. In this section, certain federal income and related tax aspects are reviewed briefly.

Isolated Sales

One approach is simply to respond to solicitations by potential U.S. customers by having the foreign investor's corporation or other business enterprise abroad ship goods directly to the United States through independent importers, although the foreign enterprise may not maintain its own U.S. office. For example, buyers for major U.S. department stores may visit Europe frequently to look over the wares of various fashion houses and decide what to buy, and the goods may be shipped directly into the United States to various customers by the foreign enterprise. If the enterprise passes title to the goods outside the United States — for example, F.O.B. a foreign port — for business reasons and not only tax avoidance purposes, the sales income will be foreign source income. This *foreign* income will not be taxed by the United States if it is not attributable to a U.S. office or other fixed place of business of the foreign enterprise or, if an income tax treaty applies, it is not attributable to a U.S. permanent establishment of the enterprise. In addition, as noted generally in Chapter II covering U.S. taxation of foreign investors, under certain tax treaties no foreign source income may be so attributed to a U.S. permanent establishment.

If the enterprise keeps title to the goods until they arrive in the United States, the sales income generally will be *U.S. source* income. However, the issue remains whether the foreign enterprise itself is engaged in trade or business in the United States or, under an income tax treaty, has a U.S. permanent establishment. In the case of sales of goods in the United States — even though title may pass in the United States and thus U.S. source income is involved — if the foreign enterprise does not engage in U.S. trade or business or, under a tax treaty, does not have a U.S. permanent establishment, then the sales income is not taxed at all by the United States. If the enterprise does not have a U.S. agent with contracting authority or a store of inventory and all orders arise in its own country through representatives of U.S. buyers or other independent importers soliciting sales abroad, quite likely the foreign enterprise will not be engaged in U.S. trade or business or have a U.S. permanent establishment.

On the other hand, such U.S. sales income automatically is

attributable to *any* U.S. trade or business of the foreign investor — even from an unrelated business. However, this is not true under most U.S. income tax treaties. In addition, under many tax treaties, even a warehouse or showroom in the United States — if the U.S. personnel are without authority to conclude contracts — will not constitute a permanent establishment whose U.S. sales income can be taxed by the United States.

U.S. Office or Joint Venture

If the foreign enterprise decides to establish its own office in the United States directly soliciting and concluding contracts with U.S. customers for its own account — whether or not contemplating eventual manufacturing or final assembly in the United States — sales income from such an operation generally will be effectively connected with the conduct of a U.S. trade or business or, in terms of U.S. tax treaties, will be attributable to a permanent establishment in the United States. While the two concepts are not identical, in the present case they are roughly analogous and have similar U.S. income tax effects. The principal effect is that the sales income no longer will be free of U.S. tax, but will be subject to tax on a net basis at the same rates applicable to a domestic U.S. taxpayer. In the case of a foreign corporation, this rate currently is 15-40% of the first $100,000 of taxable ordinary income and 46% of the balance. A number of other issues are raised by such a U.S. office or permanent establishment and must be explored by the foreign investor in the context of his specific operations — for example, as to foreign sales income that might be attributable to the U.S. operation (even if a tax treaty applies between the United States and the foreign investor's country), and as to the allocation of expenses between the U.S. office and the home office in the foreign country.

The foreign enterprise may not have the expertise to enter the U.S. market on its own, but still may want to be involved in a U.S. enterprise rather than simply contracting with independent parties. It may prefer to establish an unincorporated joint venture or partnership, perhaps with a U.S. enterprise already engaged in a related business. Aside from antitrust problems, there may be important U.S. income tax effects of such an arrangement. The United States does not treat a partnership as a separate taxable entity. However, in determining whether the foreign enterprise is engaged in a U.S. trade or business, the United States determines whether the partnership itself is so engaged in business. Even if only the U.S. partner carries on substantial U.S. activities on behalf of the partnership, that generally will put the partnership itself into a U.S. trade or business. Thus, even if the foreign enterprise does not itself engage in business within the United States, by reason of such a partnership arrangement it may be subject to tax on its share of the partnership earnings as effectively connected with the conduct of a U.S. trade or business.

U.S. Subsidiary

Another alternative is to establish a U.S. subsidiary corporation. There may be quite valid nontax reasons for creating such a subsidiary in connection with a U.S. sales operation — for example, to insulate the foreign parent enterprise from activities involving potential U.S. liabilities or other jurisdictional problems. In addition, the foreign enterprise may wish customers to consider it a U.S. entity or may be able to obtain local financing more readily as a U.S. enterprise. Furthermore, U.S. activities of the separate subsidiary generally will not cause income of the foreign parent enterprise or affiliates to be considered effectively connected with the conduct of a U.S. trade or business.

However, there may be tax costs in using such a structure. First, such a U.S. corporation generally will be subject to tax by the United States on its worldwide income, like other U.S. enterprises, at the usual 15-46% rates.[40] In addition, however, when the accumulated income is paid to the foreign shareholder as a dividend — perhaps to avoid an accumulated earnings tax — the dividend will in the absence of a tax treaty be subject to U.S. withholding tax of 30% of the gross amount. Under many U.S. tax treaties this tax is substantially reduced; either there may be a treaty between the United States and the jurisdiction of the foreign enterprise, or a separate foreign subsidiary to own the U.S. corporation may be created in a jurisdiction that does have such a treaty with the United States, if the tax in that second jurisdiction is not substantial.

The foreign parent enterprise also may lend funds and charge interest at an arm's length rate to the U.S. subsidiary, which can deduct the interest on its U.S. tax return. Generally there will be a 30% withholding tax on such interest payments to the foreign enterprise. However, a tax treaty may apply to reduce or eliminate this tax.

In all such tax treaty planning for U.S. importing and related activities, the distinction between treaty use and abuse must be considered, particularly because the definition and limitation of such abuse may be of increasing importance for U.S. and other tax authorities.[41]

Pricing between the foreign parent enterprise and the U.S. subsidiary also may raise problems. For example, the foreign enterprise may manufacture and the U.S. subsidiary may buy and resell the goods into the United States. If the transfer price is too high, arbitrarily reducing the income to the U.S. subsidiary for U.S. tax purposes, then U.S. tax authorities may reallocate the income between the two enterprises to increase the U.S. income, without a credit for foreign taxes on the same income. Somewhat less strict standards for such pricing may apply to U.S. imports manufactured by a Puerto Rico corporation.[42]

On the other hand, a potentially valuable tax aspect of using such a U.S. (or foreign) subsidiary is that, if the foreign enterprise wishes to sell out, it may simply sell the subsidiary's stock and usually generate taxfree capital gain on the sale. This is because even U.S. source capital gains are taxfree to a foreign corporation, or to a nonresident alien if he is not present there at least 183 days in the taxable year of sale, if the gains are not effectively connected with the conduct of a U.S. trade or business. The foreign enterprise's gain on the stock would not be so connected simply because the separate subsidiary has been carrying on the U.S. business.

In addition, if a foreign parent corporation wishes later to liquidate the U.S. subsidiary, or reorganize or merge it into a foreign corporation in a taxfree transaction, regulatory compliance or a ruling from the U.S. Internal Revenue Service may not be needed in spite of a foreign corporation's involvement in the transaction. However, there may be difficulties in using the U.S. corporation in certain of such transfers quite as freely as if it were part of a wholly domestic group of enterprises.[43]

If at least one-half of the fair market value of a U.S. subsidiary's assets is (or has been within five years prior to the sale) attributable to U.S. real property interests, of if a foreign subsidiary holds such interests — which may include even a warehouse owned or leased — then disposition or reorganization of the subsidiary may involve special U.S. taxation and planning as described in Chapter III covering U.S. real estate investments.

Tax Haven Subsidiary

The use of offshore tax haven enterprises, often considered for investing from abroad in the United States, raises certain issues in the context of import sales operations. The foreign enterprise may, for example, create a separate foreign subsidiary corporation in a tax haven to do business in the United States partly to accumulate income outside the parent enterprise's home country tax jurisdiction.[44] It may also be attractive for nontax reasons, as in the case of a U.S. subsidiary, to segregate the U.S. sales operations in a separate corporation for liability and jurisdictional advantages. Furthermore, U.S. activities of the separate foreign subsidiary generally will not affect — nor be affected by — the U.S. taxation of affiliated enterprises on other activities and income.

As to the U.S. income tax consequences of using such a foreign subsidiary, the subsidiary itself will be treated as any other foreign corporation with tax problems of effectively connected income and the like as noted above. In addition, when accumulated earnings are to be removed from the corporation — because, for example, reinvestment is unnecessary or an accumulated earnings tax is possible — this may be accomplished primarily by paying dividends to the foreign parent enterprise. U.S. taxation can again be significant at this point: if at least one-half of the foreign subsidiary's gross income has been effectively connected with its conduct of a U.S. trade or business — for example, carrying on sales operations in the United States — then dividends paid by the subsidiary will be subject in the same proportion to a further withholding tax by the United States, even though the foreign corporation is paying the dividends to its foreign shareholder. This additional U.S. tax normally is 30% of the gross dividend. However, U.S. tax treaties with specific countries may reduce or eliminate this tax.

The foreign parent enterprise also may lend funds to its foreign subsidiary and charge interest on the loan. The interest generally will be deductible by the foreign subsidiary from its U.S. taxable income, if all of its business is in the United States and the interest is at an arm's length rate. However, the interest still will — except under certain tax treaties — be subject to a U.S. withholding tax of 30% similar to that on dividends.

As in the case of a U.S. subsidiary, pricing between the foreign parent enterprise and the foreign subsidiary may raise reallocation of income problems. Furthermore, if the foreign parent enterprise wishes, for example, to liquidate or reorganize the foreign subsidiary, regulatory compliance or a ruling similar to that referred to further above may be required for certain transactions involving a U.S. person.

Additional Tax Issues

Any foreign (or U.S.) importer should note that, if a foreign country maintains certain types of import restrictions or engages in discriminatory acts unjustifiably restricting U.S. commerce, the President may deny the U.S. investment tax credit — of usually up to 10% — for the purchase of property manufactured in that country unless the property is completed in the United States and at least one-half of its tax basis is attributable to value added in the United States.[45]

The variety of potential state and local income and other taxes also should be explored in planning U.S. import and/or distribution activities in a particular locale. For example, state income tax rates now may reach 9-11%.

State and local property and inventory taxes also may apply to imported goods even though they are still held by the importing party.[46] However, many states have so called free port laws that exempt from property taxes goods — usually those from outside the state — which are stored in a warehouse awaiting shipment to a destination outside the state.[47]

Footnotes to Chapter V

1. Pub. L. 96-39 (July 26, 1979), 93 Stat. 144; *see* 19 U.S.C. §§2501 *et seq.*; E.O. 12188, 3 C.F.R. 131 (1980).
2. Pub. L. 93-618 (Jan. 3, 1975), 88 Stat. 1978; *see* 19 U.S.C. §§2101-2465.
3. Pub. L. 95-410 (Oct. 3, 1978), 92 Stat. 888; *see* 19 C.F.R. Parts 141-144.
4. Tariff Schedules of the United States ("T.S.U.S."), 19 U.S.C. §1202.
5. 19 U.S.C. §§1401a, 1402 (1976 ed.). For a discussion, see Bureau of National Affairs, Inc., *U.S. Import Weekly,* Reference File §25. The regulations issued by the Customs Service recognize the limited continuation of the pre-existing law, referred to as the old value law, by amending the appraisement regulations in 19 C.F.R. Part 152, Subpart C, to provide that the value of merchandise exported to the United States prior to July 1980 will be determined under that Subpart. The regulations to cover the new valuation standards have been added as Subpart E of 19 C.F.R. Part 152. They restate the relevant provisions of the 1979 Act and amplify them with interpretive notes from the Statement of Administrative Action on Customs Valuation presented to Congress with the MTN Valuation Code.
6. Name changed from U.S. Customs Court by Customs Courts Act of 1980, Pub. L. 96-417 (Oct. 10, 1980), 94 Stat. 1727.
7. Ten such provisions are found in the Tariff Act of 1930, 19 U.S.C. §§1526, 1527, 1581, 1584, 1585, 1586, 1587, 1588, 1592, and 1595(a), as amended.
8. 7 U.S.C. §624.
9. *See* Headnote 6(b), Schedule 7, Part 2, Subpart E, T.S.U.S.
10. Federal Energy Administration Act of 1974, 15 U.S.C. §§761 *et. seq.*; E.O. 11790, 3 C.F.R. 882(1971-1975 compilation); 10 C.F.R. Part 213.
11. 41 U.S.C. §§10a-10d.
12. G.S.A. Temp. Proc. Reg. 57.
13. *See* 19 U.S.C. §§1305, 1307; 40 U.S.C. §512; 15 C.F.R. Part 302; 40 C.F.R. Part 720.
14. 19 U.S.C. §1304(a); 19 C.F.R. §134.33.
15. *See generally* 19 U.S.C. §§1337, 1337a, 1526; 19 C.F.R. Part 133; *see also* Chapter I *supra.*
16. 19 U.S.C. §§1673 *et seq.*
17. The trigger prices were based on Japanese cost of production because Japan is deemed to be the most efficient steel producer in the world. Trigger prices were revised each calendar quarter to become effective in the next quarter. *See U.S. Import Weekly, supra* note 5, Reference File §37.
18. 19 U.S.C. §§1671 *et seq.*
19. 19 U.S.C. §1303.
20. T.D. 73-10, 7 Cust. Bull. 24(1973); Michelin Tire Corp. v. United States, 15 Cust. Bull. No. 47 (U.S. C.I.T. 1981).
21. T.D. 67-102, 1 Cust. Bull. 212(1967).
22. Zenith Radio Corp. v. United States, 437 U.S. 443(1978).
23. 19 U.S.C. §2411.
24. 19 U.S.C. §1337.
25. *In re* Certain Welded Stainless Steel Pipe and Tube, No. 337-TA-29 (1977); *In re* Certain Headboxes and Papermaking Machines, etc., No. 337-TA-82 (1981).
26. 19 U.S.C. §§2251-2253.
27. 19 U.S.C. §2436.
28. 19 U.S.C. §§2461-2462.
29. E.O. 11888, 3A C.F.R. 207(1976), as amended annually effective on or about March 1; *see* 15 C.F.R. Part 2007.
30. 19 U.S.C. §§81a-81u; 19 C.F.R. Part 146. However, a *state* statute exempting from local property or inventory taxes goods brought into the state for transshipment elsewhere only if the origin or destination is a foreign country, rather than another state of the United States, is of doubtful federal constitutionality under the prohibition on discrimination against interstate commerce. *See* Sears, Roebuck & Co. v. County of Los Angeles, 449 U.S. 1119 (1981), *aff'g by evenly divided vote* 85 Cal. App. 3d 763, 149 Cal. Rptr. 750 (1978); Walter Fleisher Co., Inc. v. County of Los Angeles, 449 U.S. 608 (1981).
31. 19 C.F.R. §§10.31-10.40.
32. 19 U.S.C. §1313; 19 C.F.R. Part 22.
33. Item 800.00, T.S.U.S.

34. Item 806.20, T.S.U.S.
35. Item 806.30, T.S.U.S.
36. Item 807.00, T.S.U.S. A somewhat similar issue is raised where articles such as truck parts — which are ordinarily subject to U.S. excise tax — are sold taxfree for export under I.R.C. §4221 (a)(2); upon their return to the United States unused and undamaged, the importer may be liable for excise tax.
37. 19 U.S.C. §§1751-1756.
38. *See* Items 862.10, 864.65, 864.70, 851.60, 850.70, 854.10, 765.03-30, 766.25, T.S.U.S.; 1900 U.S.C. §1309(a); Item 180.00-20, T.S.U.S.
39. *See generally* Chapter II *supra.* This section is the responsibility of the general author and editor of the volume, rather than the chapter author.
40. This is not true, except as to certain income, if the U.S. subsidiary qualifies under the strict definition of a Possessions Corporation. *See* Chapter VIII *infra.*
41. *See* Chapter II *supra.*
42. *See* I.R.C. §482; Treas. Reg. §§1.482-1 and -2; Chapter II *supra.*; Rev. Proc. 63-10, 1963-1 C.B. 490; Rev. Proc. 80-57, 1980-2 C.B. 852.
43. *See* I.R.C. §367; Chapter II *supra*, Chapter VIII *infra.*
44. This may even be a foreign subsidiary of a U.S. corporation owned in turn by the foreign parent enterprise; however, this may raise special controlled foreign corporation and related issues. *See,* Chapter VIII *infra.*
45. I.R.C. §48(a)(7). The denial of investment tax credits has been raised with regard to, for example, imports from Japan.
46. *See generally* Chapters I, II *supra*; *cf.* Michelin Tire Corp. v. Wages, 423 U.S. 276(1976). *But see* Japan Line Ltd. v. County of Los Angeles, 441 U.S. 434 (1979) (local property tax prohibited on cargo containers owned by foreign shipping companies and used on vessels sailing exclusively in foreign commerce).
47. *E.g.,* California, Florida, and Texas. However, for possible difficulties with such statutes if they are limited to international rather than any U.S. interstate shipments, see note 30 *supra.*

Chapter VI

Establishment of a New Business Enterprise

A foreign investor often will become involved in the United States through a series of gradual steps, such as the licensing or import activities described in Chapters IV and V, eventually reaching the point where a more extensive U.S. business enterprise or joint venture is appropriate. A common reason for such investments is the desire of foreign investors — including a growing number of medium size enterprises as well as large multinational corporations and foreign banks — to increase their access to the substantial U.S. market for goods, services, and technology and its plentiful raw materials, as well as to the apparent economic and political stability of the U.S. free enterprise system. This affirmative goal often is supplemented by concern that foreign exports to the United States may be priced out of the U.S. market by the increased value of foreign exchange in U.S. dollars and increased labor and other costs abroad, or perhaps will be excluded by U.S. tariff or other barriers.

This chapter outlines various legal and tax considerations in the establishment of such a new U.S. business enterprise by a nonresident alien, foreign corporation, or other foreign person. These include the federal and state regulation of foreign investment in certain fields, and selected aspects of establishing, operating, and disposing of a U.S. branch, subsidiary corporation, or joint venture. It should be noted that real estate and other natural resource investments, often constituting the initial U.S. involvement of individual and certain corporate and other foreign investors, are covered separately in Chapter III.

Federal and State Regulation of Foreign Direct Investments

Substantially Unrestricted Activities

The United States traditionally has welcomed foreign investment and this attitude is reflected in the general absence of restrictions even on foreign direct investments — *i.e.,* investments in which the foreign investors control or participate significantly in the operations of the U.S. enterprise. Foreign investors are free to establish a U.S. branch or subsidiary without substantial control or review by any government authority. The general absence of foreign exchange controls also facilitates such investments. Foreign investors may even qualify for one of several federal and state investment incentive programs.

Liberal attitude toward foreign investment. As noted in Chapter I, there is no general system of licensing foreign direct or other investments in the United States. Existing restrictions are limited to specific fields that are deemed to be sensitive or related to national security, such as communications or defense. This liberality may reflect in part the dominant role played by foreign financing in the development of the United States, particularly in the nineteenth and early twentieth centuries. Nonetheless, most of such foreign financing was in the form of loans or portfolio equity investment — *i.e.*, investment that did not give the foreign investor significant participation in the operations of the U.S. enterprise. Perhaps two-thirds of the book value of all current foreign investment in the United States is portfolio investment, while only one-third of U.S. investment abroad is in that form.

Direct investment may be viewed with greater suspicion locally since it appears to involve partial loss of local control over the economy. For example, it may be suggested that a foreign employer will be more likely to terminate unprofitable operations in the United States or that a foreign controlled enterprise may act in the interest of a foreign government. This fear may be particularly strong where the foreign investor is a government or government controlled enterprise whose decisions might be made to further the political objectives of the foreign government. Nonetheless, it seems unrealistic to believe that the United States would be powerless in the face of a decision by a foreign government controlled U.S. enterprise contrary to the political interest of the United States. Indeed, new business establishments and similar investments may provide rather strong links between foreign owners and U.S. economic and political policies. The United States generally exercises no greater control over foreign government controlled investors than over privately owned foreign investors, except — as noted in Chapter I — to review through the federal interagency Committee on Foreign Investment primarily major investments by such foreign governments.

The acquisition of an existing U.S. enterprise by a foreign investor can be even more sensitive. A new investment may clearly create new opportunities and jobs and often may bring with it new technical and managerial know-how. In the case of an acquisition, however, a major objective may be to gain access to U.S. managerial skill or technology rather than to make a new contribution. With a few exceptions, U.S. laws generally do not distinguish between acquisitions and new investments. However, foreign takeover attempts may be resisted in part through informal government action, particularly on the state level in industries subject to state regulation.

Establishment of a branch or subsidiary. A foreign investor may establish a new business in the United States through either a branch or a U.S. subsidiary with an ease unknown in many other countries. There is no federal regulation or limitation of branches of foreign corporations or other business enterprises except in a few special situations and restricted sectors of the economy such as those discussed below. Moreover, direct participation in the U.S. economy by foreign persons often is guaranteed under bilateral treaties of friendship, commerce, and navigation and, to a lesser extent, under the U.S. Constitution and civil rights statutes as noted generally in Chapter I.

No foreign corporation, including even a U.S. corporation formed under the laws of another state, has the right to conduct business in a state without obtaining a license from that state. Nonetheless, applications for qualification to conduct business are subject to little or no state administrative control or review beyond confirmation that no other corporation is operating under the same name and that the business in which the corporation proposes to engage is one permitted to general business corporations. The fact that the foreign corporation is organized under a law that differs substantially from U.S. corporate law usually will not of itself prohibit qualification. However, in the case of a foreign corporation that seeks to conduct business in a regulated industry such as banking or insurance, state qualification may be subject to more substantial restrictions.

A U.S. subsidiary may be organized by a foreign investor even more quickly and possibly less expensively than a branch. No state corporate law restricts foreign ownership of shares in general business corporations. However, such restrictions may appear with respect to regulated industries such as insurance or banking, or with respect to certain specialized corporations such as the Texas international trading corporation or fish marketing corporations established under the laws of a few states. Likewise, the stock of a state chartered general stock ownership corporation, which is not subject to federal income tax if it distributes to its shareholders substantially all of its profits each year, must be issued only to residents of that state.[1] A few states require that incorporators be citizens or residents of that state. This is not a substantial impediment, because a local person other than the party who will actually own and operate the business may act as incorporator, obviating even the need for individuals from abroad to be present in the United States at the incorporation. In addition, most state corporation laws permit shareholders' meetings to be held anywhere, although a few require the annual meeting to be held within the state of incorporation or within the United States. This latter requirement is merely an inconvenience for the foreign investor.

A few states require that at least one director must be a resident of the state. This could constitute a nuisance to investors who prefer that all of the directors be foreign citizens and residents, but such a provision may be avoided by establishing the subsidiary in another state — such as Delaware — and then qualifying that subsidiary to do business in the state in question. No state imposes any citizenship or residency requirement on officers.

Absence of exchange controls. The United States has traditionally avoided exercising any significant control over or licensing of foreign exchange transactions. Thus, a foreign investor is free to establish a branch or subsidiary in the United States without obtaining any formal approval from financial authorities. The investor is free to invest or lend such capital as is required and may make other financial arrangements, such as loans from U.S. or foreign banks, as it deems appropriate. Most importantly, the investor is able freely to remit profits abroad and to repatriate capital. In addition, interest and royalty rates charged to the corporation may be freely established, although such matters will come under the scrutiny of U.S. tax authorities.

Individuals traveling into and from the United States are required to disclose to U.S. Customs Service agents when they carry into or out of the country more than $5,000 in currency or other monetary instruments. Furthermore, the U.S. Department of the Treasury requires substantial reporting of transactions and holdings in foreign currencies by U.S. bank and nonbank enterprises and their foreign affiliates. These include reporting or record keeping of each transaction in excess of $10,000 in U.S. or foreign currency by a bank, broker-dealer in securities, or other financial institution in the United States. Whatever banking and other administrative inconveniences may be involved in complying with these requirements, they fall far short of substantive exchange controls.[2]

Access to federal and state benefits. Foreign investors may not qualify for certain government benefits. Federal subsidies in the shipping and fishing industries, for example, are available only to enterprises controlled by U.S. citizens. Majority U.S. stock ownership also may be required for any corporation that seeks Overseas Private Investment Corporation insurance against expropriation of non-U.S. investments. As discussed further below, foreign banks may not become members of the Federal Reserve system, although the impact of this distinction has recently been reduced.

On the whole, however, foreign controlled and operated U.S. enterprises are not at a substantial disadvantage under such federal laws. For example, federal policy in the area of exports is designed to make U.S. manufactured products competitive abroad; thus, the focus is on the place of production rather than on the ownership of the producer. Accordingly,

Foreign Credit Insurance Association and Export-Import Bank financing programs look more to the place where the exports are produced than to the nationality of the producers. Moreover, federal investment incentives such as Small Business Administration guarantees for loans to small enterprises — generally those with a net worth of less than $25 million — and Economic Development Administration loans and loan guarantees for industrial investments in economically depressed areas are available to otherwise qualified U.S. subsidiaries of foreign enterprises. Federal tax incentives such as the investment tax credit are applicable generally to the income of any U.S. subsidiary or to the income effectively connected with the conduct of a U.S. trade or business of any branch of a foreign enterprise.[3]

Free access to state and local benefits and incentives appears to be the rule rather than the exception for foreign controlled enterprises. In fact, substantial foreign investment in the United States seems to have been viewed more as an opportunity than as a threat by many state governments, as indicated by the fact that over 20 states maintain permanent representatives in Europe and in certain cases elsewhere, as with the State of Illinois office in Hong Kong, one of whose chief functions is to attract foreign direct investments. Such officials and their counterparts at each state capital can provide data and special services to ease the entry of a foreign enterprise into the state.

In addition, most states have adopted a number of financial incentives for new enterprises — generally industrial — which locate within their borders. Substantially all states offer tax incentives in the form of exemptions from state taxes, including real estate taxes, state income taxes, personal property taxes, and sales taxes on newly purchased capital equipment. A few states even offer an exemption from the state personal income tax for the investor's employees. Such incentives have not always proved to be effective in attracting out-of-state investors, perhaps because so many states have adopted them.

A number of states also offer direct financial assistance. Certain states have created institutions which will loan funds on a favorable basis to new enterprises. Even more common — as discussed further below in connection with financing of a U.S. subsidiary — is the use of state or municipal industrial development bonds. Under the federal (and issuing state's) income tax laws, most interest received from state or municipal bonds is not subject to tax. Thus, municipalities and states are able to offer their bonds at lower than the market rate of interest since the lender will enjoy a substantial tax benefit. Plants and equipment may be financed through such bonds, subject to various limitations, with repayment made through leasing the facility to the new industrial investor. Such programs generally are available to foreign investors.[4]

Restricted Investments

General regulation and reporting.[5] Notwithstanding the absence of general U.S. licensing of foreign direct or other investments, certain broad federal restrictions apply to foreign investors residing or organized in countries hostile to the United States as described in Chapter I, and investors may wish to plan for the transfer of U.S. business establishments to neutral persons in case of such hostilities. Particularly in the case of a foreign government investment, review by the U.S. interagency Committee on Foreign Investment also may be involved.

In addition, federal foreign direct investment *reports* to the U.S. Department of Commerce generally are required under the International Investment Survey Act of 1976 upon, *inter alia,* the establishment or acquisition of a U.S. corporation or unincorporated business enterprise (including a branch or partnership) owned at least 10% by foreign persons, whether newly established or acquired. However, usually just an exemption claim is required if the U.S. enterprise's assets do not exceed $1 million. Additional real estate investment disclosure requirements apply under these provisions if the enterprise owns 200 acres or more of U.S. land, under the Agricultural Foreign Investment Disclosure Act of 1978, and under the Foreign Investment in Real Property Tax Act of 1980. Even license fees, royalties, and similar payments to (or from) foreign persons may have to be reported. As noted generally in Chapter II, after 1982 a U.S. corporation, or a foreign corporation engaged in U.S. trade or business, which is owned at least one-half by a foreign person also is required to file a return with federal tax authorities covering its transactions during each taxable year with other corporations in the same controlled group. Furthermore, the federal Foreign Agents Registration Act should be examined in connection with the U.S. agents for the foreign enterprise. All of these and certain other reports are discussed in Chapter XII.

The principal general state law restrictions affecting direct investments from abroad in new U.S. business enterprises and similar assets are those on inheritance by foreign persons, as described in Chapter I. These may encourage use of a foreign or other corporation to hold the U.S. business, so that state probate laws will be less likely to apply to a nonresident alien decedent's interest.

With respect to certain restricted industries, these general regulation and reporting requirements are supplemented by further special requirements, many of which are discussed immediately below.

Pattern of regulation for restricted industries.[6] With respect to restricted industries, certain patterns of federal and state regulation are apparent from the specific rules, including those which are described further below in greater detail in connection with particular fields.

First, the federal government does regulate foreign investment in certain sectors of the economy that are considered particularly sensitive — for example, radio or television broadcasting, domestic air or maritime transportation, and fishing. Certain of these restrictions may be avoided by incorporating a U.S. subsidiary. However, many federal laws also look to the nationality of the owners, the nationality of management, or a combination thereof in determining whether even a U.S. corporation is qualified.

Federal limitations on ownership usually are in the form of a mechanical percentage of ownership test. Traditionally, foreign ownership in a restricted industry has been limited to 25% or less and, in some cases, to 20% or less. The recent trend has been to lower the percentage deemed to constitute control, and the Foreign Investment Study Act of 1974 treated direct investment as a holding of 10% or more. Federal regulations generally do not restrict investments from abroad in the form of loans or licenses to U.S. enterprises, though such relationships have come under close scrutiny in other countries such as France. The principal exception to this rule is found in the Department of Defense guidelines for defense contractors, where license and loan arrangements with a foreign enterprise are included among the factors that will determine whether the foreign enterprise is likely to exercise undue influence over the U.S. enterprise.

Federal laws also occasionally limit foreign participation in management of even U.S. owned corporations. For example, not less than a majority of the directors of a national bank owned by a foreign bank must be U.S. citizens, and a U.S. corporation wishing to register a vessel under the laws of the United States must have substantially U.S. management.

Second, a number of industries are regulated heavily at the state level, such as banking, insurance, and public utilities. Many states prohibit direct foreign (non-U.S.) participation in these industries, particularly in the banking field, and may restrict foreign ownership or management of local corporations participating in these industries. Although formal restrictions of this kind are relatively rare, state administrative authorities may exercise considerable discretion in performing their licensing functions. In certain cases, this discretion has been exercised to restrict or eliminate foreign participation.

State authorities also have been particularly sensitive to foreign acquisition of existing banks, insurance companies, and the like and the informal discretionary authority exercised by state officials has been quite effective in blocking certain such foreign entry.

Third, certain state and federal laws impose a reciprocity requirement on foreign investment, permitting such investment only if the investor's country of origin admits U.S. enterprises on the same or similar terms. For example, a foreign bank is permitted to establish a branch in the central business district of Chicago only if it is organized under the laws of a country that permits Illinois banks to establish branches — thereby excluding Canadian banks, among others. Federal laws regulating communications and international air transport incorporate a reciprocity standard, as do laws governing foreign participation in certain mineral interests on federal lands as described in Chapter III. A sense of fairness is only one basis for such reciprocity; a second basis is a need to facilitate the operations of local citizens and corporations abroad. For example, one of the principal reasons for the enactment of reciprocal state banking legislation may be to facilitate the operations of local banks abroad.

Federal and state laws and regulations restricting foreign direct investment in selected fields are summarized below.

Banking and financial activities.[7] A substantially complicated situation exists in the area of government control over foreign investment in banking and financial activities, due in part to the existence of regulation on both the federal and state levels. Moreover, while many federal restrictions preclude participation in restricted industries by foreign corporations, a foreign bank has the choice of conducting business in the United States through a branch, a U.S. subsidiary, or both, a decision that can carry considerable significance.

(1) *Branches of foreign banks.* A foreign bank wishing to conduct depository banking directly in the United States (a) must receive permission to do so from a federal or state authority, (b) must be subject to regular examination by the banking authorities of the jurisdiction granting permission, and (c) must publish periodic reports of its financial condition. Such a branch includes for most purposes an agency which can accept credit balances and make loans, whereas a representative office which only maintains correspondent bank relations and gathers information must register with the Secretary of the Treasury but is not otherwise substantially regulated. Until recently, the National Bank Act of 1864 required domestic incorporation in order to obtain a bank charter from the federal government, and there was no federal regulation or examination of branches of foreign banks. Therefore, a foreign bank wishing to operate through a branch had to seek state permission. However, the International Banking Act of 1978 provides for federal chartering of foreign bank branches for the first time. Such a federal branch may be established in any one state, which serves as the bank's so called home state, under federal or state law to engage in a general banking business. Branches in additional states may only accept deposits from abroad and engage in international banking activities, although they may extend commercial and industrial loans without being limited to such an international purpose. All federal and state branches which accept deposits of less than $100,000 are required to obtain deposit insurance from the Federal Deposit Insurance Corporation.[8]

A foreign branch bank may not join the Federal Reserve system, since membership is open only to banks incorporated within the United States. Lack of membership had meant that foreign branch banks were not legally subject to the reserve requirements and interest rate limitations of the Federal Reserve Board, although the Board had been able to secure informal compliance with its policies from most foreign branch banks. Now, federal branches and agencies are expressly made subject to such reserve requirements as well as interest rate limitations. Effective September 4, 1980, state branches and agencies also were made subject to such requirements and limitations. At the same time, they were given many of the benefits of Federal Reserve membership, including access to Federal Reserve services and borrowing.

A foreign branch bank also may form an Edge Act corporation, since a majority of the stock of such a corporation no longer need be owned by U.S. citizens. This act permits federal incorporation to carry on a solely international banking business, which may even include certain investment advisory and management services for foreign customers or investments. This has been a principal method by which a U.S. bank can maintain offices outside the state of its incorporation or principal place of business. However, a branch or agency established outside a foreign bank's home state is essentially the equivalent of the Edge Act corporation for most purposes. In addition, beginning in December 1981, both U.S. banks and U.S. branches and agencies of foreign banks may establish international banking facilities in the United States to accept deposits from and make loans to foreign persons, free of Federal Reserve requirements as to reserves and interest rate limits.[9]

Foreign branch banks are not subject to the Glass-Steagall Act which prohibits a corporation from carrying on both depository and investment banking — for example, securities underwriting — activities.[10] While a U.S. branch of a foreign bank may not engage directly in both such activities within the United States, a foreign bank may operate a banking business through a branch and own a subsidiary that engages in investment banking. Several foreign banks operate in this manner.

(2) *Subsidiaries of foreign banks.* If a foreign bank decides to enter the United States market indirectly by establishing or acquiring a U.S. subsidiary, it will be faced with quite a different set of regulations and issues. Like a domestic investor, it may choose to establish either a national or a state bank. However, the choice of a national or state bank will have little or no effect on the scope of the bank's operations in the United States because, under present U.S. banking law, national banks are *not* national in operation and must conform with state restrictions that generally confine their banking operations to a single state or, in a few states, to even a certain portion of the state. State banks are similarly restricted in the scope of their banking operations. In addition, although

there is no direct limitation on foreign stock ownership of a national bank, the National Bank Act requires that at least a majority of the directors — but not officers — be U.S. citizens.[11] This latter requirement has been viewed by many foreign banks as a significant disadvantage and there has been a tendency for foreign banks to incorporate U.S. subsidiaries as state rather than national banks.

If a foreign bank decides to establish or acquire a state bank, it will normally be required to obtain the consent of the state banking authorities involved. Most state laws do not formally prohibit foreign investors from owning or controlling depository banks, although Florida amended its law in 1972 to prohibit foreign control of banks. It is generally understood in many states, however, that the administrative authorities charged with granting bank charters are reluctant to permit foreign investors to own or control depository banks. The important commercial states of California, Illinois, and New York generally permit foreign investors to establish new banks, and New York law expressly grants foreign investors this right.

An acquisition of an existing state bank may be treated differently. Barclays Bank attempted to acquire Long Island Trust Company in 1972, but its application was rejected by the New York State Banking Department, allegedly on the grounds that the acquisition would injure competition. This injury to competition was somewhat hard to perceive since Barclays had no operations on Long Island, but the banking authorities looked to Barclays' worldwide, rather than local, operations. Barclays was later permitted to acquire the First Westchester National Bank, a somewhat smaller bank. By contrast, Lloyds Bank acquired First Western Bank and Trust Company in Los Angeles, California, with the approval of the Federal Reserve Board without objection from California authorities, although First Western was substantially larger than Long Island Trust Company. When the application by Hong Kong and Shanghai Banking Corp. to acquire Marine Midland Banks, Inc., was opposed by the New York state banking authorities, the problem was circumvented by having Marine Midland convert from a state to a national bank.

The acquisition of a *national* bank also may run afoul of state policy. In 1973, the Royal Trust Company of Montreal, Canada, attempted to acquire Inter National Bank of Miami, Florida. Although the Federal Reserve Board originally approved the acquisition, it reversed its decision at the request of the Florida Banking Commissioner and the Florida Bankers Association, indicating that the Board might defer to state policy even where the acquisition of a national bank was concerned. However, recent trends, including the Marine Midland acquisition noted above, indicate that the Board now gives less deference to state authorities in such cases.

A foreign corporation that seeks to acquire control of a national *or* state bank or to establish a domestic bank subsidiary also must comply with the federal Bank Holding Company Act of 1956.[12] This act requires the filing of detailed information with the Federal Reserve Board and the obtaining of the Board's consent prior to acquisition of control or establishment of a subsidiary. The act creates a presumption of control if 25% or more of the voting shares are acquired. The act's requirements generally mean that a foreign (or domestic) owner may not have banking subsidiaries in more than one state. However, the Board has approved acquisitions of savings and loan (or so called thrift) institutions by bank holding companies within the same state, and recently approved such an interstate acquisition by Citicorp, where a financially troubled thrift needed capital. In addition, the Board will grant its approval for a U.S. bank subsidiary only if it is satisfied that the foreign parent will not have substantial equity participation in domestic commercial — *i.e.,* nonbank — businesses where such participation would not be permitted for domestic bank holding companies. However certain limited exemptions have been made available pursuant to amendment to Federal Reserve Regulation K; in addition, as noted in Chapter XII regarding foreign operations from the United States, a bank holding company may operate a U.S. export trading company. These limitations also should not apply if the newly established or acquired U.S. subsidiary eliminates or spins off its commercial lending function, because it is then generally no longer considered a bank for purposes of the act as currently drawn.

On the other hand, *no* divestiture of a foreign bank holding company's foreign commercial subsidiaries will be required so long as the foreign subsidiaries' U.S. activities are only incidental to their foreign activities. Several Japanese bank holding companies — whose relationship with trading companies is somewhat undefined but generally considered to be very close — have been granted Federal Reserve Board permission to establish subsidiaries in both California and Illinois. However, this remains an area that could cause serious difficulties for foreign owners of a U.S. bank subsidiary.

In cases where no filing is required under the Bank Holding Company Act, either because the acquiror or owner is an individual or because less than 25% of the voting shares are acquired, information may still have to be filed under the Change in Bank Control Act of 1978. A detailed filing must be made with the appropriate federal supervisory agency of the national or state bank at least 60 days prior to the acquisition of control. Regulations under this act create a presumption of control where as little as 10% of the voting shares are acquired, if that is the largest single holding in the bank. A merger of banks also may be subject to administrative approval under the federal Bank Merger Act of 1960, as well as to general federal and state antitrust laws.[13]

The establishment of a national or state banking subsidiary also will subject a foreign bank or other owner to the limitations of the Glass-Steagall Act and it may be required to divest itself of any investment banking or securities businesses in the United States. However, the Federal Deposit Insurance Corporation has indicated that state banks which do not belong to the Federal Reserve system (and are not owned by bank holding companies regulated by the Federal Reserve Board) may have securities subsidiaries. Furthermore, Security Pacific National Bank of Los Angeles has been permitted to create a discount securities brokerage subsidiary of its banking unit by the U.S. Comptroller of the Currency (rather than seeking approval as a bank holding company regulated by the Board).

As noted further above, many foreign banks choose to operate in the United States through both a branch *and* a U.S. subsidiary. For example, a foreign bank holding company also may form an investment company, which is not deemed to be a bank and so is not subject to the federal Bank Holding Company Act. However, as described earlier, even such foreign branch banks are now subject to substantial restrictions on establishing additional branches or acquiring interests in banks outside the home state. Such additional branches or subsidiaries generally may only accept deposits from abroad and engage in international banking activities. Thus, foreign banks are now subject to restrictions on nationwide full service banking similar to those applicable to U.S. banks.

(3) *Other financial activities.* Many U.S. enterprises — whether foreign or domestically owned — look to the U.S. public investment market as a source of capital by issuing either stock or various forms of debt securities. Securities underwriters, brokers, and other parties involved in such activities within the United States are subject to licensing and strict regulation under federal and state securities laws, which are described generally in Chapter I. Foreign persons seeking to engage in such U.S. activities may be subject to special scrutiny or reporting requirements. However, access to U.S. securities exchange membership by foreign owned corporations was broadened in 1975. Foreign owned entities also may register as broker-dealers under the Securities Exchange Act of 1934 and become members of the National Association of Securities Dealers.[14]

Of course, any corporation or other person, domestic or foreign, that seeks to issue stock or other securities in the United States may do so only in conformity with extensive federal and state securities laws. These are described generally in Chapter I, and certain special forms and rules for *foreign* issuers are referred to in Chapter VII in connection with the use of stock or other securities to acquire an existing U.S. corporation.

In recent years, U.S. enterprises also have looked to the leasing of equipment and the like as a source of financing. Rather than purchasing data processing equipment, copying equipment, or even production machinery, the enterprise may lease such equipment from the manufacturer or, more often, from a specialized leasing company. The economic effect of a leasing arrangement is somewhat similar to that of the purchase of the equipment with borrowed funds. The leasing company advances the funds necessary to purchase the equipment and then leases it to the user on terms that are calculated to return to the lessor the cost of the equipment plus a reasonable return on its capital investment. From the point of view of the lessor, investment tax credits and deductible accelerated cost recovery allowances may provide additional benefits. From the point of view of the user, such a lease may have substantial tax benefits since the lease payments may be deductible on a current basis for tax purposes. If the equipment were purchased on an installment basis or through a loan, only the interest portion of the payments would be currently deductible, although the total cost of the equipment also could be depreciated for tax purposes over a period of time. Lease commitments of this kind have increasingly come to be treated as a form of debt for purposes of financial reporting by the lessee.[15]

Leasing companies generally are unregulated in the United States; thus, a foreign investor may enter this sector without being subject to the federal and state restrictions applicable to banking.

Insurance. Insurance underwriting in the United States is not regulated by the federal government, but is largely governed by state law. Each state has established an insurance commission or the like to regulate the activities of both domestic and foreign — either out-of-state or non-U.S. — insurers. State insurance laws require that an insurer obtain a license before engaging in the insurance business in that state. A number of requirements must be satisfied before a license may be obtained, including participation in a fund designed to insure that adequate resources will be available to satisfy the claims of policyholders, minimum capital and surplus requirements and, occasionally, a mandatory deposit of funds with state officials. This general pattern of regulation may restrict to a certain degree the ability of non-U.S. insurers to enter the U.S. market either directly through a branch or indirectly through establishment of a U.S. subsidiary or acquisition of an existing insurer.

(1) *Branch.* Certain state requirements to carry on an insurance business may be applied more stringently to foreign insurers. Substantially all states impose minimum capital and surplus requirements, but most states apply the same requirements to both domestic and foreign insurers. A few states, however, impose on all out-of-state insurers — or, in certain cases, all non-U.S. insurers — higher such requirements than are applied to locally organized insurers. In addition, a majority of states impose a deposit requirement only on non-U.S. insurers or require a substantially

larger deposit from such insurers. An insurer also may be required to demonstrate that it has operated over a period of time before it will be admitted to the state, which requirement may be applied more stringently against non-U.S. insurers.

Moreover, a number of states have reciprocity requirements whereby a foreign insurer may be admitted to the state only if it can demonstrate that its own domicile does not impose higher standards or requirements on foreign insurers seeking to obtain a license there. Otherwise, the higher or more difficult requirements of the insurer's own domicile will be applied. In practice, it is often difficult to determine the domicile of a foreign insurer, since it may be the place where its principal business is located or the jurisdiction in which it first operated. In certain cases, once a non-U.S. insurer is licensed to conduct business in one state, it may thereafter qualify as domiciled in that state for purposes of such reciprocity requirements.

Finally, a number of states restrict participation in the insurance business by insurers that are owned or controlled by foreign governments.

(2) *Subsidiary.* A local insurance subsidiary normally will be formed under the general business corporation laws of the state in question. No state has imposed a citizenship or residency requirement on shareholders in insurance subsidiaries, although a number do require that the annual shareholders' meeting be held within the state. On the other hand, a number of states have imposed citizenship and residency requirements on incorporators and directors of such a subsidiary — for example, that a certain percentage of the board of directors be residents of the state or that a minimum number of directors be residents. However, none requires that a majority of the board be domestic citizens or residents.

A few states permit a foreign insurer which has been licensed to engage in the insurance business in the state to become domesticated by, in effect, merging into a local subsidiary, thereby becoming a corporation organized under the laws of that state. This permits a continuity of the insurance business previously conducted in branch form, since the resulting corporation is entitled to all of the prior local rights and benefits and subject to all of the prior local liabilities of the foreign insurer.

Many states regulate the acquisition of control of an insurer by foreign investors, with control often being presumed upon acquisition of a relatively small percentage of voting securities. State laws usually require notice to the state insurance commission prior to completion of the transaction. Approval of the acquisition by the insurance commission usually is subject to mandatory financial disclosure concerning the acquiror.

In spite of the foregoing branch and subsidiary restrictions, a large number of non-U.S. insurers have been licensed to underwrite insurance in the United States, many of them operating in substantially all states. In

Illinois, for example, at least 22 non-U.S. insurers — mostly European — are licensed to write property and liability insurance, while half of such insurers — mostly Canadian — are authorized to write life insurance. In connection with such operations, it should be noted that New York recently has allowed specially licensed insurers in the state's insurance free-trade zone to write primary policies on large corporate and unusual risks without prior state approval of rates and policy provisions, with possible state tax concessions on non-U.S. risks.

State insurance authorities generally contend that (except where required by local statute) they do not impose more difficult requirements on non-U.S. insurers to obtain a license to underwrite insurance directly or to establish a local subsidiary. Nonetheless, a somewhat different attitude may be encountered in the case of non-U.S. acquisition of a substantial existing local insurer. For example, Illinois insurance authorities rejected a bid by a Swiss insurer to acquire control of CNA Financial Corporation, in spite of the fact that the acquisition promised to provide a source of much needed capital.

Government contracts. Foreign persons are, in principle, free to bid on federal government contracts. Suppliers to the Department of Defense, however, normally will require access to classified materials which is prohibited to almost all foreign persons — the exception being that citizens of Canada and the United Kingdom are permitted limited access to such materials under certain circumstances. In addition, no security clearances may be granted to a facility which is under foreign ownership, influence, or control.[16] This means that the contractor must be domestic *and* its management must not be under foreign control.

A foreign equity interest of more than five percent will create a presumption of foreign control, although the Department then may look to other factors, especially whether the enterprise is publicly or privately held. The Department is concerned primarily with the degree of control actually exercised by foreign persons and thus will also consider the presence of interlocking directorates (especially if the directors in question are in fact appointed by foreign shareholders), technology licenses from foreign licensors (especially those with a requirement that the licensee disclose innovations), and indebtedness to foreign lenders (especially the percentage of corporate net worth affected and the nature of any collateral pledged). Even the nature of the foreign shareholder is important. A foreign bank as a shareholder may be ignored, but a foreign defense contractor may be prohibited regardless of the percentage of stock owned.

On the other hand, disqualification of even a wholly foreign owned U.S. corporation may be avoided by having foreign shareholders put their stock in a voting trust. This is particularly useful when foreign investors acquire a corporation of which a relatively minor subsidiary is engaged in

U.S. defense work. Because of the sensitive nature of the matter, defense contractors recently have been advised to report even preliminary discussions with potential foreign investors. However, of 720 cases of foreign involvement in defense contractors reviewed by the Department from 1968 to mid-1975, most were successfully concluded and a facility clearance issued.

More generally, federal *and* state Buy American statutes — described also in Chapter V respecting imports — may require items produced in the United States to be acquired for public use by the federal or the state government, unless the quantity, quality, or price of available U.S. items is unreasonable. However, these generally look more to the place of manufacture rather than to the ultimate ownership of the producer, because they often reflect U.S. labor union concern for local employment. They may still be onerous for a foreign investor, because a foreign owned U.S. enterprise may have to use a U.S. item even where a foreign parent or other affiliate produces a similar item. In addition, the use of a prohibited foreign item in a building construction project or other relatively irreversible manner may place the contractor in a poor financial and bargaining position if final payment is therefore delayed.

It should be noted that Buy American restrictions on *federal* government procurement may now be selectively waived under the Trade Agreements Act of 1979.[17]

A foreign investor should be careful not to violate federal or state prohibitions on illegal payments to government officials or agencies; these are also discussed in Chapter VIII respecting U.S. rules affecting foreign operations.

Other industries

(1) *Communications and power.* A Federal Communications Commission ("FCC") license to participate in radio and television broadcasting is denied to foreign individuals, corporations, and governments. Limited exceptions are made for the operation of a radio in an aircraft, amateur radio operators, and the like. Foreign investors also are limited as to indirect entry, since an FCC license is denied to any domestic corporation with a foreign officer or director or in which more than 20% of the stock is owned or voted by foreign persons. The FCC also exercises control over the transfer of licenses either directly or indirectly by transfer of the licensee itself. Foreign shareholder participation in the Communications Satellite Corporation is limited to 20%, and all directors and officers of that corporation must be U.S. citizens.

There is no general federal regulation of foreign participation in the telephone or telegraph industries. However, the acquisition by consolidation or merger of a foreign interest of more than 20% in a telegraph carrier is prohibited without FCC approval.

A number of states restrict any out-of-state corporation from engaging in telephone or telegraph communications, or from exercising the power of eminent domain as a public utility. However, control over the citizenship or residency of the owners of such domestic corporations is quite rare.

No federal or state control is exercised over foreign participation in other communications media. However, limitations on foreign government participation in various media have been proposed from time to time.

Foreign ownership or control of nuclear power facilities is prohibited under federal law and the rules of the Nuclear Regulatory Commission. However, hydroelectric power facilities, for example, may be owned by a U.S. corporation controlled by foreign persons under rules of the Federal Power Commission and Federal Energy Regulatory Commission.

(2) *Domestic and foreign transportation.* Federal law limits foreign participation in both domestic maritime and air transportation, and certain state laws limit such participation in railroad transportation.

(a) *Maritime transport.* Coastal and fresh water shipping is restricted to vessels which are built and registered in the United States and owned by U.S. persons. For this purpose, a corporation will qualify as a U.S. person only if it is organized under domestic law; its chief executive, chairman of the board, and the majority of a quorum of its board of directors are U.S. citizens; and not less than 75% of its equity is owned and controlled directly or indirectly by U.S. citizens. By contrast, there is no general prohibition against foreign owned or registered vessels operating to or from U.S. ports in the international transport of goods or persons.

Federal subsidies for the construction and operation of vessels likewise may be granted only to U.S. persons as defined above.

Federal law also prohibits the transfer of U.S. registered vessels *or* U.S. ship construction facilities to foreign persons without government consent. As a corollary, a mortgage on a vessel or on shipbuilding facilities directly in favor of a foreign lender is void.

(b) *Air transport.* Domestic air transport of passengers and goods is limited to domestically registered aircraft. Aircraft — including a private executive craft — may be registered by U.S. citizens, partnerships in which all partners are U.S. citizens, and U.S. corporations in which the chief executive officer and two-thirds of the directors are U.S. citizens and 75% of the stock is held or controlled by U.S. citizens. The Civil Aeronautics Board ("CAB") must approve all acquisitions of more than 10% of a domestic carrier's shares.

The CAB does have the authority to grant foreign registered aircraft the right to transport goods and persons between points within and without the United States, if it finds the carrier technically qualified and such transport in the public interest. Such public interest normally is found if there is a treaty or other international agreement with the country of registration providing for such service, or if the country of registration affords reciprocal privileges to aircraft registered in the United States. Foreign charter operators, air freight forwarders, and shippers may only have to register with the CAB.

(c) *Railroads.* Federal law does not prohibit or restrict foreign ownership or operation of railroads in the United States, but many state laws restrict any out-of-state railroad from directly operating within the state. Only Vermont restricts foreign ownership of a railroad corporation, but a number of states impose restrictions on the nationality or residence of incorporators or directors of railroad corporations.

(3) *Towing, salvaging, and dredging.* Vessels engaged in U.S. towing and salvaging operations also must be registered under U.S. law, registration being available only to U.S. persons including corporations that meet the same management and ownership requirements as those applied to participants in coastal and fresh water shipping. The U.S. Commissioner of Customs may grant exceptions if no U.S. vessels are available. Similar restrictions are imposed on corporations that wish to engage in domestic dredging operations.

(4) *Fishing.* Only vessels registered in the United States may fish within the three-mile limit of U.S. waters or, absent an international convention, land catches in U.S. ports. As noted above, such U.S. registration of a vessel is limited to U.S. persons including corporations organized in the United States whose management and ownership largely are composed of U.S. citizens. Activities of foreign fishing vessels within the 200-mile or other continental shelf limit of exclusive U.S. fishery management are governed by the Department of Commerce.

Regulation of foreign investments in real estate and other natural resources is described separately in Chapter III. In addition, special national limitations on imports are covered in Chapter V.

Branch Operations

Advantages of a Branch

There are a number of possible advantages to a foreign corporation or other business enterprise operating directly in the United States through a branch. Although customers and other parties may be dealing with an unfamiliar entity, this will usually not present substantial problems so long as the U.S. operation remains fairly modest. For example, many foreign manufacturers use a branch to operate a U.S. purchasing office or sales and service office, while most assembly and manufacturing operations are carried on through a U.S. subsidiary. From the foreign investor's point of view, it may be more comfortable to operate through a familiar entity with usual controls by the head office, so that a branch operation is administratively simpler than a subsidiary.

A branch operation also may simplify compensation arrangements for non-U.S. executives. There are relatively few mandatory social contributions required of employers in the United States and so it is often economically feasible for the foreign investor to continue to make appropriate social contributions on behalf of its non-U.S. executives in the country of origin. This may be simpler to arrange if the executive is employed by a branch of the foreign parent rather than a U.S. subsidiary. Such arrangements should be reviewed with the investor's U.S. tax adviser to be certain that they are in accordance with the requirements of U.S. income tax laws.

The new U.S. business is unlikely to produce immediate profits and it may be possible for the foreign enterprise to take advantage of start-up expenses in the United States to reduce its taxable income in its country of origin. Remittances to the head office also normally should be free of U.S. withholding taxes.

In certain cases, as noted above, U.S. regulations — such as in banking — may make a branch operation advantageous. However, government regulations also may prohibit direct entry through a branch in restricted industries.

Registration of a Corporate Branch

As noted further above in connection with regulation of investments, there is no federal requirement for a foreign corporation to register a U.S. branch. Every state, however, requires any foreign corporation — including one formed under the laws of another state *or* country — to qualify by registration before doing business in that state. The procedure for registration of a branch of a foreign corporation under state law is not onerous. However, it may involve sufficient disclosure, delay, expense, and potential U.S. taxation to prompt an initial inquiry whether such registration is required for a particular operation.

Definition of doing business. A number of activities in which a corporation may engage generally will *not* constitute doing business and so will not require qualification. For example, many foreign corporations, particularly banks, maintain representatives or representative offices in the United States. So long as such representatives have no authority to accept orders or otherwise bind the corporation, no qualification should be required.

A number of other activities may require qualification in one state and not another, and many state statutes are ambiguous. For example, owning real property may require qualification under the laws of a number of states. Many other state laws are silent here, although state authorities tend to insist on qualification if the matter comes to their attention even in the absence of a specific provision. Many states have enacted laws permitting foreign corporations to lend money to residents of the state without qualifying, even if the loan is secured by real or personal property located in the state. This remains an open question in other jurisdictions, however. The owner of personal property leased to another and used in a state generally is not required to qualify in that state, at least if the lease is executed outside the state.

A number of common activities clearly *do* require qualification in most states. The maintenance of an office for the purpose of purchasing or selling products on an ongoing basis generally will require qualification, as will maintaining a stock of goods out of which delivery is made to customers located in the state. The performance of a construction or engineering contract in a state also will require qualification under most circumstances, as will the performance of other services through a fixed place of business.[18]

Procedure. As described generally in Chapter I, in order to qualify to do business in a state, a foreign corporation will be required to submit an application for a license to the appropriate state authorities, usually the Secretary of State, including the name of an agent for service of process within the state in case of a legal action against the corporation. The application form itself usually must be executed on behalf of the applicant corporation by the president or vice president and the execution attested by the secretary. Many non-U.S. corporations do not have officers with these specific titles, but usually it will suffice to have the application executed by the corresponding personnel — for example, the execution may be attested by the employee charged with the maintenance of corporate records. In most states the application also will have to be notarized — *i.e.,* an individual licensed by the state must certify as to the identity of the person signing the documents and, occasionally, that the statements contained therein were the subject of an oath. If the qualification documents are executed by individuals physically present in the United States, notarization will present little problem. On the other hand, if the documents are executed outside the United States, this formality requires certification by the nearest U.S. consul, which can be a considerable inconvenience. Certification by a foreign *notar* or *notaire,* for example, usually will *not* be acceptable. However, under the Hague Convention Abolishing the Requirement for Legalization for Foreign Public Documents which became effective for the United States in 1981, execution of an *apostille* by designated foreign officials in the treaty country should be sufficient.

The application normally must be accompanied by a certificate of good standing from an appropriate official in the country of incorporation, and often by a copy of the articles of incorporation. Since foreign corporate articles such as *Statuten* tend to be quite lengthy and must be translated into English, it is often more expeditious to obtain an extract of the articles from the local commercial register and present the extract in translation. This abbreviated version is closer to the U.S. concept of articles of incorporation and generally is accepted. State officials often will require that the translation itself be certified by the local U.S. consul or other appropriate official.

The application must be accompanied by a registration fee and, usually, the first year's franchise tax. Although these initially are not usually large, if they will continue to be calculated on the basis of that portion of the foreign corporation's total operations attributable to the state, it may be appropriate at the time of registration to so estimate in a conservative fashion.

Penalties. The principal penalty for failure to qualify to do business in a state where the foreign corporation's activities normally require qualification is denial of the corporation's right to institute a legal action in that state. In most cases, this disability can be cured by filing a late application and paying all current *and* past franchise taxes. In a few states, however, the disability is permanent and locally executed contracts will be considered to be void. In addition, corporations that fail to qualify may be subject to monetary penalties of various kinds. Such fines vary substantially from state to state and may be in the form of a flat fee or a given amount per day, month, or year of delay in qualifying. A few states also impose penalties on the officers and directors of unqualified corporations.

Operating the Branch

Management. Foreign investors often encounter difficulties in selecting an appropriate managerial arrangement for a U.S. branch. One of the principal concerns expressed by management in the country of origin is defining the authority to be exercised by a U.S. representative and choosing an appropriate means of controlling his activities while, at the same time, cloaking the representative with sufficient authority that he is able to deal effectively with other parties in the United States, particularly customers. If the representative is a long-term employee of the investing enterprise, this may not be a serious problem. In practice, however, the representative often will be relatively new to the foreign enterprise. Moreover, since moving to a foreign country requires a certain flexibility, foreign representatives often are relatively young. This lack of a long prior relationship may be exacerbated if the representative is a U.S. citizen.

One approach is to draft a detailed power of attorney for the U.S. representative, carefully delineating his authority and its limits. However, the representative is likely to want a title of the kind that is customary in the United States. Under U.S. practice, a substantial foreign branch of a U.S. corporation normally would be headed by at least a vice president and often by an individual designated as president of the foreign branch. This terminology does not describe a legal position as such, since an officer of the foreign branch in fact may not be an officer of the corporation itself. However, U.S. persons are accustomed to dealing with a representative who holds such a position. Aside from internal problems of granting the title of vice president to a relatively new or young employee, such a title also may convey an impression of greater authority than is desired by the investor. It is unlikely that persons dealing with the U.S. branch will ask to review any limiting power of attorney, at least in day-to-day transactions. In addition, the lack of a federal or state commercial register means that there is no effective means of notifying third parties of any such restrictions. Thus, this is not a completely satisfactory solution.

In practice, this problem often is exaggerated by the parties at the outset of operations. As time passes, the parties tend to work out an acceptable means of dealing with each other and the problem generally recedes into the background. It is therefore advisable not to allow this matter to consume too much time when the U.S. branch is being established.

Tax and financing considerations.[19] A number of U.S. income tax problems may arise in connection with the operation of the branch. First, if foreign goods are supplied by the home office or another affiliated enterprise, they will have to be valued for U.S. customs purposes. Moreover, such goods will have to be priced in order to determine the cost of goods sold by the U.S. branch, which may partly establish its income for federal and state tax purposes. These values and prices usually should be consistent, because both customs and tax authorities have the right to demand evidence supporting the valuation.[20]

The principal factor for tax purposes will be the arm's length price charged to unrelated persons in the United States or, in the absence of any sales in the United States, in other countries. The foreign investor may be reluctant to disclose this information, but the only alternative may be an arbitrary assessment by the tax authorities. Since such an arbitrary assessment would not be binding on the tax authorities of the country of origin, there is a risk that the authorities in each country would place a different value on the goods, with the result that a certain portion of the total income would be subjected to double taxation. This problem may arise even if the selling price to other countries is disclosed. Under many U.S. income tax treaties, there is a procedure for resolving such differences through a conference between the tax authorities of the respective jurisdictions, although resort to such a procedure can be time consuming.

It may also be possible for federal income tax purposes to use last in first out (LIFO) accounting — which usually reduces income if later inventory is more costly — even if the foreign investor's home country accounting rules require the first in first out (FIFO) method.

Second, in addition to the cost of goods sold, other expenses — for example, of the home office abroad — may be allocated to the branch to reduce its U.S. taxable income. These expenses generally must be connected with branch business income — *i.e.,* income effectively connected with the conduct of a U.S. trade or business or, under a tax treaty, attributable to a U.S. permanent establishment. They may include personnel training, advertising and promotion, and research and development costs. Under the theory that money is fungible, even interest expenses of the foreign enterprise worldwide are allocated to reduce U.S. taxable income. This is generally modified in determining U.S. taxable income of a foreign branch bank — and even of a foreign nonbank enterprise's U.S. branch where the worldwide operation is conducted in more than one currency — by applying to the U.S. branch's share of the enterprise's worldwide liabilities only the interest rate paid separately by the U.S. branch for its own funds, to determine its allocable share of the worldwide interest.

If *foreign* sales or certain other income is subject to federal tax because it is attributable to a U.S. office or other fixed place of business, a foreign tax credit also may reduce the U.S. tax. However, under certain tax treaties *no* foreign source income may be so attributed to a U.S. permanent establishment of a resident of the treaty country — for example, foreign interest income on loans booked out of a U.S. office of a Swiss bank.

Third, one of the principal tax advantages of a branch operation is that remittances to the country of origin generally are not subject to federal withholding tax since such intracompany transfers are not dividends. In the event, however, that at least one-half of a foreign corporation's gross income is effectively connected income as noted above from U.S. branches, a like proportion of dividends paid by it even to other foreign persons will be subject to a federal withholding tax of 30%. This tax is eliminated under many U.S. tax treaties.

Furthermore, it should be noted that state unitary income taxation of the branch may require onerous reporting of worldwide assets, payroll, and sales of the home office and possibly affiliated enterprises to determine the state's share of worldwide income.

With respect to financing the establishment or expansion of the branch, reference should be made to the financing of a new U.S. subsidiary discussed further below. Several of the considerations and techniques discussed there frequently are relevant to new branch financing.

Third country subsidiary. Certain of the advantages of both branch and subsidiary can be obtained by establishing a subsidiary in a third country and registering a branch of that subsidiary in the United States, particularly if the country of origin does not have a tax treaty with the United States. The third country subsidiary may insulate the foreign investor from U.S. jurisdiction and liability to the same extent as a U.S. subsidiary. The third country subsidiary also may be able to take advantage of a narrow tax treaty definition of permanent establishment in determining whether it is subject to U.S. federal taxation on industrial and commercial profits. For example, a construction project which does not exist for more than one year may not be subject to such U.S. taxation. Moreover, even if a permanent establishment is found, only the third country subsidiary will be so subject to tax in the United States.

If a correct treaty country is chosen, dividends and interest remitted to the country of origin also will not be subject to any local withholding tax, nor to any U.S. withholding tax since the tax treaty may preclude such a tax even if most of the subsidiary's income is U.S. business income.

Investors from tax treaty countries often will have similar advantages available, however, and it may be more beneficial for them to invest through a new subsidiary formed in the home country. Moreover, as noted further below in connection with tax treaty planning for a U.S. subsidiary, the principle of treaty abuse may be used increasingly to limit such U.S. treaty benefits for a third country subsidiary.

Commercial Law Considerations

It is advisable for any foreign enterprise selling goods in the United States — whether produced abroad or domestically — to review its standard terms and conditions of sale to see that they comply to the greatest possible extent with the requirements of U.S. laws. So long as the seller has no establishment of any kind in the United States, a U.S. or other court may consider the sale to be an international transaction and there is a reasonable possibility that the law of the country of origin will govern, except as to federal or state product safety standards and product liability for personal injury resulting from use of the goods in the United States. Once the foreign enterprise establishes even a sales office in the United States, however, this situation is likely to change. Customers who deal with such a U.S. branch are more likely to view the transaction as one coming under U.S. laws and practices. Moreover, any legal action begun against even a foreign manufacturer then is more likely to be brought in a U.S. court and that court is more likely to view the transaction as governed by U.S. laws. This change indicates a need for the adoption of sales forms and other documents adapted to U.S. laws and also may require new credit arrangements with U.S. customers.

For example, under U.S. laws governing sales of goods,[21] a warranty that the goods sold are merchantable is implied in connection with every sales contract unless expressly excluded. This means that the seller warrants to the purchaser that the goods are of a quality that is normal for items of the kind. Because this standard is subject to varying interpretations, it is customary for U.S. sellers to exclude this warranty in their standard terms and conditions of sale and substitute an express warranty — usually to the effect that the goods are warranted to be free of defects at the time and place of delivery and that the seller will honor claims resulting from any such defects for a limited period of time, often one year from the date of sale. In addition, a warranty that the goods are fit for the particular purpose intended may be implied in any case in which the seller is aware of the use to which the purchaser intends to put the goods. Again, it is customary to exclude this warranty in the seller's standard terms and conditions of sale.

A seller also may be liable for any consequential damages suffered by the purchaser that were reasonably foreseeable at the time of sale. These are damages that result from any nonperformance or defective performance by the seller. For example, it is conceivable that a seller could be liable for the loss of profits suffered by the purchaser because an entire assembly line broke down due to a defect in a component of that assembly line supplied by the seller, at least in circumstances indicating that the loss was a foreseeable consequence of the defect. It is the general practice in the United States expressly to exclude consequential damages in the seller's standard terms and conditions of sale.

In the case of consumer goods, in spite of such exclusions in the contract of sale, a manufacturer may be liable for personal injury from the use of defective goods in the United States — even to an individual other than the original purchaser. Accordingly, special product liability insurance may be appropriate. In addition, favorable federal income tax deductions apply to product liability losses and claims.[22]

Another change in the relationship of the foreign manufacturer or seller with its U.S. customers that may result from the establishment of a sales office is a reluctance on the part of customers to provide a letter of credit, even though they may have done so routinely in the past. Customers who deal with a local sales office will typically view sales as domestic rather than international and insist on paying on an open account basis. U.S. laws provide excellent tools for ensuring that a seller receives payment for its goods through retention of a security interest in the goods sold. Such security interests are extremely flexible, but are subject to strict formalities with which the seller must comply. In addition, the seller must confirm that the goods sold do not become subject to security interests held by others, such as banks or other financial institutions. Such information may be obtained from public registers.

Furthermore, it is advisable to determine any applicable federal and state requirements for the advertising or performance of express and implied warranties, product safety standards, usury limits, and finance charge disclosures, particularly in the case of consumer products — either goods or services furnished to the public — as described in Chapter I.

Personnel

A foreign enterprise which registers a branch in the United States typically will have few employees, of whom most will be foreign individuals provided by the home office. In many cases, it is possible to continue providing retirement and other social benefits to such employees in the country of origin. As noted in Chapter I, there are mandatory unemployment insurance and social security payments in the United States, except in the limited cases of certain foreign employees covered by a U.S. social security tax agreement as noted in Chapter II. However, U.S. benefits are relatively modest by, for example, European or Japanese standards. Since foreign employees are unlikely ever to be in a position to take advantage of these benefits, it is usually preferable to continue home country benefits at the same time.

For a foreign employee, nonresident status has a number of U.S. federal tax advantages. For example, if the employee maintains a home outside the United States, all of his unreimbursed living expenses, including room and board, in the United States should be deductible for federal income tax purposes. Moreover, under many tax treaties, a nonresident employee who remains in the United States for less than 183 days in any one taxable year will be exempt from any federal income tax on his U.S. earnings. Even if subject to federal tax on income earned in the United States, as noted in Chapter II regarding the general U.S. taxation of foreign persons, the nonresident usually will not be subject to tax on earnings or pensions for services outside the United States or other foreign income.

An alien present in the United States as a business visitor or on another nonimmigrant visa generally is presumed to be a nonresident for federal tax purposes. However, if a foreign employee remains in the United States for more than a year or is otherwise present on a more permanent basis, he may become subject to U.S. income and other taxes on a worldwide basis.[23] In many cases, the foreign enterprise may wish to pay a portion of the employee's salary outside the United States. If the employee is considered to be a U.S. resident for tax purposes, all such income will be — regardless of where paid — subject to U.S. taxation even if earned through services performed by the employee for the home office outside the United States and not for the U.S. branch. Failure to declare such income may be considered to be tax fraud punishable by criminal penalties, so that split salary arrangements can be dangerous.

A married foreign employee who becomes resident in the United

States may wish to file a joint return with his spouse in order to gain substantial U.S. tax advantages, including a lower tax rate on income. However, a married couple usually may file such a joint return only if each of the individuals has been a U.S. resident (or citizen) — or has elected to be so treated — for the entire taxable year. This difficulty may be avoided possibly by having the employee elect a taxable year other than the calendar year — generally considered permissible for a new resident — so as to have an extremely short initial taxable year ending, for example, one month after taking up residence in the United States. The employee therefore will be resident for the entire second taxable year and all subsequent tax years without U.S. tax on prearrival foreign income.[24]

Numerous other arrangements in the United States, such as owning a home rather than renting, may produce substantial personal tax benefits for a resident foreign employee and should be explored at an early point.

Formation and Operation of a U.S. Subsidiary

Advantages of a Subsidiary

Formation of a U.S. corporation is relatively simple and subject to little administrative review, so that such formation is likely to take less time and possibly be less expensive than registration of a foreign branch. A subsidiary also will insulate the foreign owner from liability for many of the debts incurred by the subsidiary. A foreign manufacturer generally will remain responsible, however, for U.S. product liability claims arising out of defects in its goods, even if it maintains a separate selling subsidiary in the United States. Since a manufacturer generally is strictly liable for personal injuries resulting from the use of its goods, the only practical protection for a foreign manufacturer is to obtain adequate U.S. product liability insurance. In addition, it may be necessary to provide financial support from abroad for the subsidiary, perhaps in the form of a formal bank guarantee.

In certain restricted industries, as noted further above in connection with regulation of investments, use of a U.S. subsidiary will be the only practical means of investment, since direct participation by the foreign enterprise will be prohibited. However, even use of a U.S. subsidiary may not satisfy such requirements.

A U.S. subsidiary also offers considerable flexibility in setting up financial and other arrangements. The potential advantages of using shareholder loans, licenses, and leasing arrangements are discussed in greater detail below. Moreover, in the absence of other activity in the

United States by the foreign investor, only the subsidiary will be subject to U.S. business income taxation. Although dividends paid to the parent may be subject to U.S. withholding tax at the rate of 30%, this normally is reduced if a tax treaty is in effect.

Finally, operating through a U.S. corporation means that persons who deal with the corporation in the United States will be dealing with a familiar entity. Although this may not be of overriding importance, it can be beneficial in dealing with customers. More importantly, if one is establishing a manufacturing or assembly operation, it will be necessary to deal with U.S. employees who may be reluctant to be employed by a foreign corporation.

Formation of the Corporation

Formalities. The requirements and procedures for the formation of a U.S. corporation are described generally in Chapter I. Regulation of the formation and operation of such corporations is left largely to the individual states. Unlike the European practice of requiring a company to be formed under the laws of the jurisdiction in which its principal place of business is located, a U.S. corporation may be formed under the laws of one state and have its principal place of business elsewhere so long as it qualifies to do business in each state in which it operates, as noted above in the case of a branch of a foreign corporation. This means that investors may choose the state law that best fits their needs. Although there is substantial uniformity among the states, Delaware corporate law is particularly flexible, which is reflected in the fact that many U.S. corporations are organized in Delaware.

The incorporator's role can be carried out conveniently by a local person because it is in all states limited and temporary, ending with the organization of the corporation or the appointment of the board of directors. Since the incorporator does formally appoint the initial board of directors in certain states, including Delaware, it is often advisable not to use the U.S. representative of the investor as incorporator: this could result in embarrassment, since the principals of the new corporation would seem to depend on their employee for election to office as directors.

A corporate name will be available only if there is no other corporation operating under a substantially identical name in the state of incorporation *or* in any other state in which the corporation will be registered to do business. This may be determined by telephone calls to the appropriate states' officials — usually the Secretary of State — and the corporate name chosen may be reserved for a limited period of time.

It will also be necessary to determine the amount of capital that will be contributed to the new corporation, the names of the officers and directors, the fiscal year, and the bank at which corporate accounts may be opened. The concept of capital in a U.S. corporation is both more flexible and less important than in many other countries. Persons dealing with a U.S. corporation rely on its net worth as indicated by its balance sheet rather than on its stated capital, and a corporation's capital is not stated on its letterhead as may be the case, for example, in France.

Once the above matters are determined, the corporation may be formed and activated very quickly, often within a matter of days.

Tax and financing considerations. Neither a U.S. corporation nor its controlling foreign or other shareholders generally recognize taxable gain on the contribution of property to the corporation solely in exchange for its stock, even if the property in question has increased substantially in value over the original cost, nor will a contribution of cash to the corporation result in any gain to the contributing party or to the corporation. This is true, *inter alia,* if U.S. branch assets are contributed to a new U.S. subsidiary. The corporation will be considered to have the same tax basis in the contributed property as the contributing shareholder. Thus, if the corporation subsequently disposes of contributed property, it will generally recognize that portion of any gain that was not recognized at the time the property was contributed to the corporation. Alternatively, a controlling shareholder may contribute cash to the corporation and cause the corporation to use the cash to purchase the property at an arm's length price. In that event, the shareholder generally will recognize a taxable gain equal to the difference between his basis in the property and the price at which it is sold to the corporation, and the corporation will have a basis in the property equal to the cash price paid. However, if the shareholder is a foreign person whose gain on such a sale may not be taxed by the United States or abroad, this sale may permit a taxfree increase in tax basis for the corporation. Losses on such a sale by a controlling individual generally are not recognized.[25]

Transfer taxes and registration fees on the transfer of both real and personal property are, in most cases, rather modest in the United States. With the exception of Florida, real property may be contributed to a corporation at little or no tax cost, and personal property may be so contributed in all states. However, if at least one-half of the fair market value of the U.S. corporation's assets is *or* has been at any time within the previous five years attributable to U.S. real estate or natural resource interests — which may include even a factory or warehouse owned or leased — then the disposition of the corporation's stock or assets may be subject to substantially greater U.S. income taxation than otherwise, as discussed further below and in Chapter III. Thus, it can be valuable to avoid having such assets even temporarily comprise one-half of the new subsidiary's value as it is being formed or capitalized.

It will often be advantageous in establishing a U.S. corporation to advance only a portion of its capital needs in the form of equity and to contribute the balance as a loan, either directly from the shareholders themselves if that is permitted under the foreign exchange control laws of the country of origin, or from an outside financing source in the country of origin or in the United States. Unlike the practice in some foreign countries, dividends paid to shareholders are not deductible in determining a corporation's U.S. taxable income. By contrast, interest payments are deductible — even interest paid to shareholders. There are certain limitations on the use of loans, however. For U.S. tax purposes — and occasionally for corporate law purposes as well — a corporation must have an adequate level of equity investment or tax authorities will treat shareholder loans as disguised equity, with the result that interest payments are treated as dividends and consequently are denied as deductions in determining corporate taxable income. As a general rule, where debt to shareholders is substantially proportionate to their respective equity holdings in the corporation, the ratio of shareholder loans to equity probably should not exceed three to one and the ratio of total corporate debt to equity should not exceed 10 to one. It seems likely that similar thin capitalization standards will apply to international loans owed to (and possibly from) a foreign person. The interest for each year also usually should be paid not later than two and one-half months after the close of the taxable year of the corporation if it deducts expenses on the accrual basis and is majority owned by one individual or family.

Shareholder loans are subject to other restrictions under U.S. tax laws. The Internal Revenue Service can require that interest be set at an arm's length level equal to that which would be available in a transaction between unrelated parties. The Service publishes from time to time minimum and maximum interest rates which are presumed to be arm's length, reflecting fluctuations in commercial rates. Interest of between 11 and 13% per year on the unpaid principal balance currently is considered acceptable. In addition, deferred payments for purchase of property generally must bear at least nine percent annual interest, or a portion of each installment principal payment will be taxed as interest. However, there is no other general government control over private interest rates.[26]

As described in Chapter II, such interest paid to foreign persons by a U.S. corporation is subject to a federal withholding tax of 30%. If the interest is paid to a resident of a country having a tax treaty with the United States, however, this rate will be reduced — often to zero. If the investor is not a resident of such a tax treaty country, or if interest received in the country of origin would be subject to tax at a high rate, it may be advantageous to use a third country subsidiary as a financing entity. For example, arm's length interest paid to a foreign owned Netherlands Antilles lender currently is usually subject to no U.S. withholding tax and to exemptions that reduce the tax in the Antilles to a very low rate. Funds then distributed to the foreign owner as dividends should not be subject to withholding tax in the Antilles or in the United States.[27] In many countries, dividends received from foreign subsidiaries are subject to no tax or to a lower rate of tax than other forms of income such as interest. Thus, the use of such a finance subsidiary results in interest payments, deductible in the United States, being taxed favorably as dividends when received in the country of origin.

Other favorable financial arrangements may be provided from a third country. For example, if a U.S. manufacturing subsidiary is established, it is often advisable to license foreign technology, trademarks, and the like to the subsidiary. Royalties are subject to the same federal withholding tax of 30%, but this is reduced or eliminated under many tax treaties if the technology is owned by a treaty country corporation or other resident.

Another useful arrangement for financing a U.S. subsidiary is the leasing of real estate or equipment from abroad. The net leasing of real or personal property in the United States generally will not cause the foreign lessor to have a U.S. permanent establishment under most tax treaties, and it may not then be subject to U.S. tax on rents paid by the subsidiary. Leases may have to be carefully structured, however, if they are to be treated as leases rather than installment purchases by the U.S. subsidiary.

However, in all such tax treaty planning for a U.S. subsidiary, the distinction between treaty use and abuse must be considered, particularly because the definition and limitation of such abuse may be of increasing importance for U.S. and other tax authorities.[28]

It should be noted that the use of a U.S. subsidiary also may involve special problems of pricing or valuation of foreign goods purchased by the subsidiary from foreign affiliates, similar to those noted above in connection with a U.S. branch.

Many other U.S. tax and financing issues involving a U.S. subsidiary are common to domestic and foreign investors. For example, a newly formed U.S. corporation is entitled to make a number of U.S. tax elections. Perhaps the most important such election is the choice of a fiscal year for tax and other purposes. Although it is often useful to choose the same fiscal year as the foreign owner, this choice should be made carefully because it may involve substantial tax benefits in the country of origin.

In addition, a U.S. corporation is entitled to file a consolidated federal income tax return with affiliated U.S. corporations owned by a common U.S. parent corporation having a common fiscal year. This generally causes the various corporations to be treated as a single taxable entity and eliminates intercorporate transactions. If the foreign investor already has other profitable corporations in the United States, structuring the U.S. holding corporation to permit the filing of a consolidated return may allow the investor to use initial U.S. losses and/or interest payments on financing to shelter income earned by the other U.S. corporations. If initial losses cannot be so utilized, it is possible to carry them forward for up to 15 subsequent taxable years.[29] Dividends also can flow to the U.S. holding corporation free of U.S. tax for use elsewhere in the U.S. affiliated group.

The use of a U.S. holding corporation may help insulate foreign entities' income from state taxation based on unitary business operations. Likewise, the use of different U.S. subsidiaries to conduct businesses in different states or different industries may help reduce the application of unitary tax provisions to all of the investor's U.S. operations.

In connection with domestic financing of the U.S. subsidiary, it should be noted that a corporation or other person that invests in certain U.S. tangible property may receive a federal income tax credit in the amount of up to 10% of the amount invested, or more for certain energy saving and other property. It is also entitled to accelerated cost recovery allowances over 3-15 years for capital equipment and real estate improvements, thereby creating additional deductions for federal income tax purposes. As noted further above in connection with financial activities generally, these U.S. investment tax credits and depreciation deductions may be able to be transferred from the user of property to an unrelated domestic or foreign corporation which can better take advantage of them, by having the latter purchase and lease the property to the user. In a so called leveraged lease, additional purchase funds may be borrowed so that the lessor may be able to obtain extra tax benefits attributable to the additional amounts invested. However, all such so called safe harbor financing leases after June 1982 are subject to certain limitations as to the fraction of the lessor's tax liability which can be reduced by such benefits, the use of accelerated cost recovery and the spreading of investment tax credits over several years, deductible interest paid by the lessor to the lessee in a sale and leaseback to the seller, the term of the lease, application primarily to new property, the fraction of the lessee's property which can be so leased, and other matters. Finance leases after 1983 are subject to further limitations as to these items, as well as the minimum price at which the lessee can purchase the property from the lessor and other matters.

Another U.S. financing technique for domestic projects — as noted further above in connection with government benefits generally — is the issuance by local governments of industrial development bonds whose interest is at lower rates because it is free of federal (and the issuing state's) income taxes. The bond proceeds may be used to finance facilities which are leased or sold to a foreign investor or its U.S. subsidiary, or perhaps to tax oriented investors who lease them to the user under a leveraged lease as described above; however, for most property so financed after 1982, only straightline depreciation deductions are allowed and the bonds' maturity cannot exceed by more than 20% the reasonably expected economic life of the financed facilities. Only interest on small issues of bonds up to $1 million issued before 1987 is exempt from federal tax, but these often may be aggregated up to $10 million for one user. The bonds generally are not subject to securities registration requirements of the U.S. Securities and Exchange Commission, although the issuance of letters of credit or other security by a bank or other unrelated private party for payment of the bonds may require registration. In addition, most issues of such bonds after 1982 must be approved by local elected government officials after a public hearing, or by a local voter referendum, and be reported promptly to federal tax authorities by the issuer.[30]

Reference also should be made to Chapter VII which deals with financing structures for the acquisition of an existing U.S corporation, certain of which frequently are relevant to new U.S. subsidiary financing.

Management of the Corporation

The control of a U.S. corporation rests in the shareholders, the board of directors, and the officers. The functions of each are summarized in Chapter I. In the case of a U.S. corporation owned by foreign investors, certain management considerations should be noted:

Shareholders. In comparison with many other legal systems, the shareholders in a U.S. corporation play a rather limited role, principally electing the board of directors and approving a few extraordinary changes in the corporation. The shareholders have no power to declare dividends and are not required to approve the corporation's balance sheet or the actions of the board of directors. Shareholders generally do not elect internal auditors or controllers of the corporation, since that institution is not legally required in the United States. However, shareholders of publicly held corporations generally approve the appointment of independent outside accountants. The shareholders are required to meet at least once a year, although they may act through proxies — *i.e.,* essentially revocable powers of attorney — or through a resolution by written consent — *i.e.,* a written document embodying a resolution executed by all or part of the shareholders. In Delaware, for example, such resolutions need be executed only by a majority of shareholders. The use of such written resolutions is a considerable convenience where a wholly owned subsidiary is involved, since it avoids holding a formal meeting by the sole shareholder.

Board of directors. The board of directors exercises all corporate powers not reserved to the shareholders. Although the directors often delegate authority to the officers, all significant corporate actions — for example, substantial loans or the acquisition or sale of substantial assets — generally must be authorized by a board resolution. Unlike European practice, for example, directors in U.S. corporations act only as a board — *i.e.,* individual directors do not represent the corporation and there is no office of managing director. In practice, a director often will be an officer as well and may represent the corporation in that latter capacity.

There is *no* requirement that a director be a shareholder and therefore no requirement for qualifying stock of a director. Although a corporation often will have more than one director — three or five being the number most commonly specified — many states provide an exception allowing only one or two directors, as well as other simplified procedures, where there are but one or two shareholders. There is only one board of directors, unlike the dual board arrangement in, for example, a German *Aktiengesellschaft*.

Directors normally act through regular meetings at places and times in accordance with the by-laws. Directors' meetings are not required by state laws to be held within the state. Notice requirements for special meetings are very short — often 24 hours — but foreign investors typically specify longer periods where directors are located abroad. Such notice may be waived in writing or by a director's presence at a special meeting. A majority of the directors will constitute a quorum and directors' resolutions will be adopted by a simple majority of the directors present and voting, unless otherwise specified in the articles of incorporation or elsewhere as permitted by state law.

Directors also may act through a written consent similar to that described for shareholders, although usually all directors must so sign. Thus, a formal meeting of the directors need never be held even in connection with the organization of the corporation — a considerable convenience for foreign investors. In many states, directors' meetings also may be held by a single conference telephone call. However, a director generally may not delegate his vote at meetings by a power of attorney or other means.

One of the early decisions that must be made by a foreign investor is the composition of the board of directors. In connection with branches, attention often is given to such matters as the title and authority of U.S. representatives. In the case of a U.S. subsidiary, since few states impose any residence or citizenship requirements on directors, generally there is no requirement that a U.S. representative be appointed to the board. Moreover, the customary lack of direct contact between customers or other persons and members of the board means that there may be no strong business reason to include a U.S. representative as a board member. However, under the laws of the United Kingdom and similar jurisdictions, even a U.S. corporation may be considered a local resident subject to worldwide income taxation abroad if it is managed or controlled in that country. Accordingly, it may be wise to ensure that a majority of the board members are U.S. residents or other nonresidents of such a country.

Officers. The day-to-day affairs of a U.S. corporation are managed by its officers, generally consisting of a president, one or more vice presidents, a secretary and a treasurer. U.S. customers and other persons may expect to be dealing with at least one officer; thus, it is generally worthwhile to have the U.S. representative hold a title such as president or vice president. The actual authority granted to the representative as an officer normally must be delineated in the by-laws or specific directors' resolutions of the corporation; this also may be done in a power of attorney. However, any attempt to limit the authority of an officer to less than the powers that normally would be exercised by an individual holding that title may be ineffective as to outside parties. It is therefore appropriate for the foreign investor to avoid attempting an unusual curtailment of such an officer's powers.

The next most important officer is the secretary. The secretary generally is charged with maintaining all corporate records. In addition, in any important document calling for authority beyond that customarily exercised by the president or a vice president, the attestation of the secretary also will be required. This attestation is not an additional signature binding the corporation, but is a certification by the secretary that the person executing on the part of the corporation is duly authorized to execute the same either by the by-laws or by special resolution of the board of directors. For this reason, an attorney on the corporate staff often will act as secretary, although this is not required.

Personnel

Certain considerations for foreign individual personnel have already been noted further above in connection with branches. Similarly to branch operations, split payroll arrangements are equally objectionable here, since a U.S. subsidiary's foreign personnel who are resident in the United States also are subject to U.S. income tax on their worldwide income, including income paid by a separate parent enterprise even if such payments are for services performed outside the United States for the parent. U.S. visas also usually should be no more difficult to obtain for foreign employees of a U.S. subsidiary than for those of a branch.[31]

However, a U.S. subsidiary may have a more substantial number of U.S. personnel than a branch, especially if a manufacturing operation is contemplated. Such U.S. employees may be treated quite differently from those in other countries. For example, in Japan an employee often is considered to have life tenure and it is quite unusual for him to change employers. The United States is quite different in this respect and generally neither the employee nor the employer owes such a degree of loyalty one to the other.

Furthermore, many European investors may have had difficult experiences with labor unions in their own countries and so make an effort to avoid having to deal with unions in the United States. Labor unions are weaker in some sections of the United States than in others. The industrial northeast and north central states tend to have the strongest unions, while unions are relatively weak in both the southeast and the southwest: this has been a significant factor in the choice of plant location by a number of European investors. Such apprehension is probably unwarranted, however. In the first place, many employees are not unionized and many nonunion plants operate even in the industrialized northern sections of the United States. As noted in Chapter I, unions currently represent less than 25% of all U.S. employees and lose more than half of the certification elections. Moreover, labor unions in the United States tend to be apolitical and, for the most part, nonmilitant. Unauthorized strikes that stop production in many foreign countries are relatively rare in the United States. Finally, the southeast and southwest are likely to become more unionized as industrialization spreads. In this connection, the competition from and exploitation of illegal alien workers in the southwest and other sections of the United States have been subjects of increasing federal concern.

In addition, as noted in Chapter I, there may be difficulties under U.S. employment antidiscrimination laws if the U.S. subsidiary discriminates in favor of the foreign investor's home country nationals (or in favor of male employees or other special groups) in hiring or promotion. This issue also may be present in a U.S. branch, but it is less likely to be raised there because fewer employees are needed, and those are often from the foreign investor's country and share many of the same employment attitudes.

Employment compensation in the United States usually includes both basic salary or wages and fringe benefits of several types. An employer is required to withhold both federal and state income, social security, and other taxes from salaries or wages paid to employees, as described in Chapter I. However, by comparison to many European and other countries, social security and public health program benefits are rather limited. Accordingly, it is customary for U.S. employers to provide private pension plans for their employees. Federal law sets maximum vesting standards — *i.e.,* the maximum period after which an employee must be considered to have a vested right to receive private pension benefits, even if he changes employment — and requires that private pension funds be established in a manner calculated to insure their solvency and that such pension benefits be fully and adequately disclosed to employees. Each employee also may be able to contribute tax deductible sums to an individual retirement account. Many employers also provide group medical insurance plans to underwrite part or all of the cost of medical care.[32]

Partnerships and Joint Ventures

A foreign investor may decide to establish a new U.S. business enterprise in conjunction with another investor — usually a U.S. corporation or other person — for a number of reasons. The foreign investor may feel the need to associate with one who knows the U.S. market and way of doing business. Although expertise in the market may be acquired by hiring an experienced executive, an existing enterprise may have well established marketing ties with potential customers and also may have immediately available manufacturing or service facilities. Even if an experienced individual is hired, it may be necessary to offer such an individual equity participation in the new enterprise in order to attract a highly qualified executive. A joint arrangement also may spread the risk for the new investor, and may provide an additional source of financing.

The structure of the joint arrangement will depend on the nature of the enterprise to be undertaken. In certain cases, an unincorporated joint venture may be formed for the purpose of carrying out a single undertaking or a series of undertakings of relatively short duration. Where the operation of an ongoing business is contemplated, the parties are more likely to form a partnership or perhaps a jointly owned corporation. The choice between the unincorporated and incorporated joint venture often will turn on such considerations as limitation of liability, management considerations, and tax planning.

Unincorporated Joint Venture

An unincorporated joint venture, as described in Chapter 1, most often is used in connection with a specific construction or similar project. For example, a project bid may be entered in the name of one of the participants and the existence of others may or may not be disclosed. Thus, the relationship between the parties may resemble that of contractor and subcontractor, although the parties will share profits and losses. In any event, a written joint venture agreement should be executed by the parties.

The agreement first should define the scope of the venture and provide that one party is not entitled to bind the others outside that scope. In certain cases, the parties may want expressly to avoid any power of representation. The agreement also should provide for the initial contribution of working capital and the circumstances, if any, in which additional capital must be contributed. Typically, there will be no binding commitment to make future contributions, but any party will be permitted to make such an advance, which advance may be treated as a loan to be repaid on a preferred basis. Such a loan also may be treated under the agreement as a liability of the noncontributing parties. In addition, each party's contribution in kind — in the form of equipment, labor, or expertise — should be specified as well as the right, if any, of each party to the return of contributed equipment and other materials upon termination of the venture. Title to contributed equipment often will remain in the name of the contributing party. The share of each party in the profits and losses of the venture also should be stipulated.

The supervision and management of an unincorporated joint venture usually is simple in form. A project manager often will be nominated by one of the parties, and his assistant by another. The assistant may have a separate field of responsibility, reflecting the area of expertise of the party that he represents. He also may have a veto power over certain actions by the project manager. Normally, the concurrence of both such representatives is required for any amendment to the joint venture agreement.

Partnership

The general requirements for the formation and operation of a general or limited U.S. partnership are described in Chapter I.[33] Although it is possible for a foreign investor to operate in the United States through a limited partnership, a limited partner ordinarily may not participate in the management of the partnership and most joint ventures involving ongoing U.S. businesses are conducted as general partnerships. The principal exceptions are limited partnerships for foreign direct investments in U.S. real estate and other natural resources, as noted in Chapter III. In any case, a written partnership agreement should be used.

The partnership agreement will have to provide for many of the matters noted above in the case of the unincorporated joint venture. Thus, the partners will have to agree on their present and future capital contributions, their shares of profits and losses, and the like. The partnership will be more formal than the unincorporated joint venture and normally will own property in its own name. Each partner has a right to object to the admission of new partners and no partner has the right to have an assignee of his interest in the partnership admitted as a partner with voting power, unless otherwise provided in the agreement. In addition, unless otherwise agreed, no partner has the right to the return of specific property upon partnership dissolution and any contrary desire should be set forth in the agreement.

The foreign investor should remember that all partners in a general partnership have the right to participate in management and, as a result, can bind the partnership and indirectly the other partners. This right may be restricted in the agreement as among the partners — for example, by designating a managing partner. However, there is no convenient way to put outside parties on notice as to such restrictions. A U.S. general partnership — unlike a limited partnership — is not registered, so there exists no commercial register in which appropriate restrictions may be listed. Furthermore, the general partnership may be dissolved upon the election of any one partner, although it is customary to provide for contractual liability to the other partners in such event.

Incorporated Joint Venture

A joint venture in U.S. corporate form offers a number of advantages over other joint venture forms, particularly for an ongoing business. A corporation is a more formal entity and its continuity does not depend on any of the owners. At the same time, the corporation permits sufficient flexibility to accomplish practically any managerial objective that may be accomplished through an unincorporated joint venture or partnership.

Shareholder agreement. Where the U.S. corporate form is chosen for a joint venture, it is customary to have an underlying joint venture agreement among the shareholders. This agreement will cover many of the items that would be covered in a partnership agreement, such as the initial and subsequent capital contributions of the parties, as well as the value to be placed on any contribution other than cash. Once the valuation of a contribution in kind is approved by the corporation's board of directors, that valuation is binding on outside parties in the absence of fraud and no independent appraisal is required.

The agreement also should provide for the right of each party to have its representatives elected as directors. Voting agreements among shareholders are enforceable in most states, although their duration may be limited. In Delaware, for example, the duration of such a shareholders' agreement is limited to 10 years. During the period of validity, such agreements may be specifically enforced in a court of equity — *i.e.,* in the event that one shareholder fails to vote his stock in the manner provided by the agreement, the other shareholders have the right to request that a court itself vote the recalcitrant shareholder's stock to elect the appropriate directors. Although discretionary with the court, this extraordinary remedy — largely unknown in civil law countries — normally is available in the absence of a showing of bad faith on the part of the petitioning shareholder.

As an alternative to the shareholder voting agreement, the corporate laws of most states recognize voting trusts. A voting trust is an arrangement under which one party is given legal title to the stock in a corporation, including the right to vote that stock, while another party remains the beneficial owner of the stock enjoying the right to all dividends and other economic benefits. This separation of legal and equitable ownership of shares is consistent with the general common law recognition of a trust and such arrangements are not subject to any particular limitations, except that they are often limited by law to the same duration as shareholder voting agreements.

The voting power of each party in such a joint venture need not be identical to its economic interest. There are a number of ways in which this may be accomplished. The corporate laws of many states permit the issuance of nonvoting stock, so it is possible to establish two or more classes of stock with certain classes carrying voting rights and others not. Even in those states that require that all stock carry certain voting rights, the voting power need not be in proportion to the value of the shares. A corporation also may have stock that enjoys a preference as to distribution of dividends, distribution of assets upon liquidation, or both. Such preferred stock may or may not carry voting rights. If one party is contributing a disproportionate share of the capital and yet it is not considered desirable to have that contribution in the form of a loan, the use of such preferred stock may be appropriate.

Management. One of the key decisions in organizing a U.S. corporate joint venture is the choice of a chief executive officer, normally the president. Since the president generally has authority to conduct the day-to-day affairs of the corporation and there is no U.S. commercial register, it may be difficult to limit day-to-day powers of the president as to outside persons, although the parties may wish to give the nominee of one shareholder a veto power over a president who is the nominee of another shareholder. Nonetheless, most significant acts of the corporation will require a resolution of the board of directors and attestation by the secretary, who therefore may play a significant protective role in a joint venture. The president and other officers of the corporation are removable at any time by decision of the board of directors. However, an agreement among the shareholders with respect to the election of particular persons as particular officers generally is enforceable.

It should be noted that the Delaware Close Corporation Act[34] permits a corporation with a small number of shareholders to avoid the use of a formal board of directors by providing in its by-laws that the corporation will be managed directly by the shareholders. Participation in management will not expose the shareholders to liability beyond their investment in the subsidiary. While this may appear convenient under certain circumstances, the use of this device often is inadvisable because the board of directors is an institution familiar to outside persons who may deal with the corporation, and because foreign shareholders may find such direct management inconvenient.

Restrictions on transfer of stock. Stock in a U.S. corporation ordinarily is freely transferable, subject to compliance with federal and state securities laws as described in Chapter I, but it is unlikely that parties in a corporate joint venture will be willing to permit the substitution of a new investor without their consent. Generally, an absolute right to prohibit a stock transfer is not enforceable. At a minimum, however, a shareholder who wishes to transfer an interest in part or all of his stock should be required first to offer the same to the corporation and/or the other shareholders, either at the price offered by a *bona fide* purchaser or at a reasonable price determined under the agreement. To the extent that this right of first refusal is not exercised by the parties, the selling shareholder will be free to transfer his remaining stock to the proposed purchaser. Normally an exception to the right of first refusal is made for transfers among affiliated entities or within an individual's family.

Under Delaware law, one may provide that stock be transferred only with the consent of a specified percentage of the shareholders or directors. Such a provision is enforceable, subject to a requirement that this power be exercised in good faith. The corporate laws of other states often do not expressly provide for such a restriction and a provision of this kind in a shareholders' agreement may be denied enforcement.

It is also possible to prohibit transfers to designated persons or classes of persons, such as competitors, in both Delaware and a number of other states.

These restrictions may be included in the articles of incorporation or by-laws of the corporation, or in the joint venture agreement itself. Regardless of where the restriction appears, however, it may not be binding on outside parties unless a notation or legend indicating the existence of the restriction on transfer is included on the face or reverse side of each stock certificate. The absence of a commercial register in the United States means that there is no other means of effectively notifying outside parties of such a restriction.

Termination. Most U.S. corporations have no specified duration and may continue for an indefinite period of time unless dissolved by vote of the shareholders. However, most state corporate laws require at least a majority vote for dissolution. As a result, grounds for termination of the joint venture and dissolution of the corporation should be included in the joint venture agreement. Among other matters, the agreement should provide for termination and dissolution upon a substantial default by one of the parties or upon the bankruptcy, death, or dissolution of one of the parties.

In addition, provision for termination of the venture in the event of dissatisfaction of one party — even in the absence of default by another — often is included. For example, the agreement may provide that one party may notify another of his intent to sell his own stock or buy the stock of the other at a fixed price. The offeree then may have the option either to acquire the seller's interest or to sell his own interest at that price. In the absence of a decision by the offeree shareholder, the offeree may be considered under the agreement to have chosen to sell his stock. There are many other variations on the same buy-sell agreement. This provides a means for resolving deadlocks among the parties without resort to dissolution of the corporation or judicial action and therefore may operate in the interest of all parties, at least if all have relatively equal financial capacity.

Tax and Financing Aspects

An unincorporated joint venture generally will be treated as a partnership for federal tax purposes.[35] If such an unincorporated joint venture or general or limited partnership is conducting business in the United States, the foreign partner likewise will be treated as engaged in such trade or business through a branch in the United States for federal income tax purposes. Accordingly, many of the tax and financing considerations noted above in connection with branch operations should be considered.

Furthermore — as described in Chapter III respecting real estate joint ventures — special allocations of any partnership's ordinary income, deductions, and capital gains between the foreign and U.S. partners (and/or among the foreign partners) may be appropriate. These often are used to attract financial partners for tax benefits in, for example, research and development (including the federal income tax credit of 25% of increases in such expenditures before 1986), cable television, and film and art production activities, provided they have substantial economic effect and do not run afoul of tax shelter rules applicable to certain businesses.

If the joint venture is conducted in U.S. corporate form, the corporation itself will be taxed in the same manner as any other U.S. corporation. However, dividends paid to the foreign co-owner will be subject to a federal withholding tax of 30%. Most tax treaties reduce this withholding tax, *but* they may reduce it to a lesser extent where — as in a joint venture — the foreign recipient owns less than, for example, 95% of the payor corporation.[36]

It is generally disadvantageous for an investor to leave funds tied up in a jointly operated corporation and most investors prefer to have joint venture corporations pay dividends whenever possible. In addition, the United States imposes a federal tax on excess accumulated earnings of a corporation. However, use of a U.S. or foreign intermediary corporation held by one or a few individual foreign investors to receive distributed funds can have disadvantageous tax effects in the United States, because dividends — as well as interest, royalties, and certain other passive income — are considered personal holding company income for U.S. tax purposes. If such a subsidiary is established to act as shareholder in — or lender or licensor to — the U.S. joint venture corporation, and engages in no other significant activity, the holding corporation may be considered a personal holding company whose undistributed income is subject to heavy taxation, unless it is a foreign corporation wholly owned by nonresident aliens directly or through other foreign entities. In addition, any corporation that accumulates earnings from the venture may itself be subject to the federal accumulated earnings tax, if the accumulated earnings are not required for the reasonable needs of the corporation's business; since the only active business is to be conducted through the joint venture, a holding corporation generally may have no business need for such funds. In the case of a foreign holding corporation, these issues will apply only to its U.S. source income.

Accordingly, it may be advantageous to use a foreign subsidiary in a tax treaty country as the holding corporation for the foreign investor's U.S. corporate shares, because under a treaty such a foreign corporation may be less subject to the U.S. personal holding company or accumulated earnings penalties even on U.S. source income or, more likely, may receive and pay out income to avoid such penalties without substantial U.S. withholding taxes. At the same time, funds may be able to be accumulated outside the country of origin in a parent corporation or trust which owns the foreign subsidiary and is organized in a low tax jurisdiction and, if desired, may even be maintained in a bank account in the United States.[37]

Antitrust and Reporting Aspects

The formation of a joint venture for a new U.S. business enterprise is subject to scrutiny under federal and state antitrust and similar laws, which are described generally in Chapter I. In addition, the formation of a corporate or other joint venture may be subject to federal requirements for notices to the Federal Trade Commission and the Antitrust Division of the Department of Justice, similar to those in the case of a corporate acquisition described in Chapter VII.[38] In general, however, small and medium size enterprises with sales or assets of less than the equivalent of $15 million should only rarely encounter U.S. antitrust problems with joint ventures in the United States.

It should be noted that, as described in Chapter XII, in the case of a joint venture with a foreign person, the U.S. person entering the venture or the venture itself may be required to make a foreign direct (or portfolio) investment report even if the foreign venturer does not do so.

Disposing of the U.S. Business

Liquidating a Business

The procedures to be followed in liquidating a U.S. business enterprise will depend in part on the form of the investment. If a foreign enterprise has operated through a branch, it may withdraw from those states in which it is qualified to do business. Alternatively, it may simply discontinue payment of annual franchise taxes and filing of annual reports which, in most states, will result in a revocation of the license to do business in the state. No further formality generally is required, although the foreign enterprise will of course remain liable for any obligations incurred by the branch prior to withdrawal.

In the case of an unincorporated joint venture, no formalities will be required. The joint venture agreement itself normally will provide for the disposition of assets held upon termination. The party contributing certain equipment and the like often will have the right to recover that equipment, and title to the equipment often will have remained in the name of that party rather than in the name of the venture itself. Claims of any creditors of the venture will have to be satisfied, and a venturer may have the right to claim contribution from the other venturers in the event that the venture has suffered losses, if provided in the venture agreement.

In the case of a U.S. partnership or corporation, certain formalities will be required which are described generally in Chapter I. In the case of a partnership, dissolution usually will terminate all authority of any partner to act for the partnership except insofar as may be necessary to wind up partnership affairs and to complete transactions begun but not finished at the time of dissolution. The assets of the partnership ordinarily are first applied to pay outside creditors, then to repay debts owed to partners, then to repay partners' capital accounts, and finally to distribute the partners' profits. If the assets of the partnership are not sufficient to pay its liabilities, each general partner will be responsible for such liabilities, subject to reimbursement by other partners in accordance with the partnership agreement, and dissolution will not of itself discharge such a partner from this responsibility.

In the case of a wholly owned or joint venture U.S. corporation, dissolution usually will require the consent of the holders of a majority of its stock. A corporation may be continued for a short period following dissolution for the purpose of winding up its affairs or completing any legal actions that may be pending against it. The directors are charged with the obligation to distribute the corporation's assets in payment of any debts owing to creditors, who generally may include shareholders so long as the debt has been clearly reflected on the books of the corporation. The balance of the corporation's assets then are distributed to the shareholders, first on any stock which enjoys a preference upon dissolution, and then to holders of common stock. Except in an unusual situation, shareholders will not be required to make any further contributions even if the assets of the corporation are insufficient to pay its debts.

Sale or Merger of a Business[39]

A foreign investor may wish to sell or merge a U.S. business enterprise that is not insolvent and has an ongoing value.

Branch. If the U.S. enterprise is operated as a branch, it is possible to sell the business for cash. In that event, however, the proceeds generally will be subject to U.S. federal capital gain tax which, in the case of business assets of a foreign corporation held for more than one year, will be up to 28% of any gain, except as to recapture of tangible personal property and most accelerated (in excess of straightline) real property cost recovery allowances at ordinary income tax rates, together with taxation of such long term capital gain as a corporate tax preference item as noted generally in Chapter I.

There are, however, a number of ways in which one may dispose of a branch and avoid most of such U.S. taxation. For example, the business may be sold on an installment basis, with none or only a small portion of the purchase price received in the first year and the balance received in the second and/or subsequent years. Under installment sale treatment of the transaction, only that portion of the gain attributable to the portion of the purchase price received in the first year generally will be subject to U.S. capital gain tax because, when subsequent payments are received, the foreign investor will no longer be engaged in a U.S. trade or business, or under a tax treaty will no longer have a U.S. permanent establishment. However, such taxfree treatment of the seller on the installment basis may not be available if the assets are sold to a related person who then resells them in the same year. In addition, if assets which are depreciable property are sold to the seller's spouse or an entity owned at least 80% by the seller, not only is installment basis taxation usually not available, but the seller's gain will be treated as ordinary income even if it would otherwise be taxed as capital gain.[40]

Another alternative is to incorporate the branch as a U.S. or foreign subsidiary substantially prior to a disposition of the business. The contribution of branch assets to such a U.S. subsidiary by a foreign person, even if they have increased substantially in value, should be free of federal income tax as described further above in connection with formation of a U.S. subsidiary; however, in the case of such a contribution to a foreign subsidiary, the transaction may have to be reported to the U.S. Department of the Treasury to assure taxfree treatment as noted generally in Chapter II regarding U.S. taxation of foreign persons. If this transfer is not done independently of and prior to discussions with prospective purchasers, the entire transaction may be subject to treatment as a step transaction substantially equivalent to a sale of the assets. Properly structured, however, this transaction then can achieve the tax benefits discussed below in connection with sale or merger of a U.S. or foreign subsidiary.

State capital gain and other taxes also must be considered. However, as noted further above in connection with transfers to a new subsidiary, local transfer and registration taxes are relatively modest in most states, so there is relatively little such tax cost to the transfer of tangible or intangible business assets.

Partnership or joint venture. The sale of the business of a partnership or joint venture will require consent by all of the owners, unless otherwise provided in the partnership or venture agreement. The tax effects on the foreign investor of such a disposition generally will be similar to those upon disposition of a branch. Thus, for example, it may be advisable to incorporate the partnership or venture by contributing its business to a corporation, which may be accomplished substantially taxfree. If this is done coincidentally with the other partners' sale of their interests, however, substantial tax challenges may result.

Alternatively, an installment sale may be advisable. Since the U.S. income tax treatment of partnerships is extremely complicated, the potential tax consequences of any such transaction should be reviewed carefully.

Corporation. Significant tax benefits may be achieved upon sale or merger of a U.S. business operated through a U.S. subsidiary, or through a branch of a foreign subsidiary organized in the investor's country or in a third country, if careful planning is utilized. If the U.S. or foreign corporation sells the business for cash, any long-term capital gain on the transaction generally will be subject to a federal corporate tax of up to 28% and treatment as a corporate tax preference item. A further U.S. withholding tax may be imposed on distribution of the gain as a dividend to the foreign shareholders. However, this taxation may be avoided by, for example, the following techniques:

(1) The corporation's stock, rather than its assets, may be sold to the purchaser. Since the foreign shareholders usually will not be subject to U.S. taxation on such gain, all U.S. tax may be avoided. This should be true even for a sale of stock in a collapsible corporation, unless possibly the sale gives rise to U.S. source gain and the shareholder is engaged through a partnership or other activity in a separate U.S. trade or business to which the gain might be automatically connected by general force of attraction. From the point of view of the purchaser, however, there will be a strong preference for purchase of the assets themselves. Although such a transaction is more complicated, the purchaser can be more certain that it is not acquiring undisclosed liabilities. Moreover, the assets may have been substantially depreciated below their fair market value. If stock is acquired, the corporation itself will continue to enjoy only a limited basis from which to calculate depreciation, even if the purchase price of the stock is substantially in excess of the depreciated book value of the assets. This latter problem may be avoided, however, if the purchaser liquidates the corporation or, for a corporate purchaser of at least 80% of the acquired corporation's stock after August 1982, elects to have the acquired corporation treated as having sold its assets and liquidated promptly following purchase of its stock.

In case of a loss on certain stock of a U.S. small business corporation, an individual shareholder — including a nonresident alien — may treat the loss as ordinary rather than capital loss. However, this is generally unlikely to benefit a nonresident alien, because the loss is unlikely to be connected with his own conduct of a U.S. trade or business in order to permit federal income tax use of the deduction.[41]

(2) If it is necessary to sell assets rather than stock, this often may still be accomplished free of U.S. tax. The liquidating corporation may be entitled to adopt a plan of liquidation prior to selling its assets. If the assets are disposed of within a period of 12 months from the date of adoption of the plan, no federal income tax is imposed at the corporate level. In addition, the shareholders usually will not be subject to U.S. tax on the liquidating exchange of the sale proceeds (even installment obligations of the purchaser) for their stock. This arrangement is not available where the corporation qualifies as a collapsible corporation. This is most likely where the corporation has been used to develop real property or similar assets, or to purchase property held for sale to customers, with a view to selling the corporation's stock before it realizes a substantial part of its income from such property; even there, several exceptions apply. The 12-month sale arrangement also is often not available where another corporation owns at least 80% of the corporation's stock.[42]

(3) It may also be possible to distribute the assets to the foreign shareholders in exchange for all or part of their stock or in complete or partial liquidation of the corporation before the sale negotiations so that they generally obtain, without taxable effectively connected capital gain, a stepped-up basis in the assets equal to their fair market value at that time. Subsequently, they may negotiate the sale with little or no further taxable capital gain. However, several possible difficulties should be noted here. Such a step-up generally is not available in a complete liquidation of a subsidiary to a corporation owning 80% or more of the liquidating subsidiary. In addition, a partial liquidation to any corporate shareholder after August 1982 is treated as a dividend taxable as discussed immediately below — rather than as capital gain — to the extent of the distributing corporation's accumulated earnings and profits. Alternatively, if the corporation uses appreciated property to redeem the stock of a corporate shareholder or the stock of a less than 10% shareholder, the distributing corporation generally will be taxed on the appreciation. If the distributing corporation is collapsible, then the holding or resale of its inventory by a shareholder also possibly may cause the shareholder to be engaged in a U.S. trade or business in the same taxable year as he receives the assets for his stock (unless he receives the assets on the last day of his year), so that any U.S. source ordinary income from the collapse might be automatically connected to such business and taxed to him. In any event, such an advance distribution is often difficult to arrange practically, and may be challenged by U.S. tax authorities.[43]

(4) A further possible alternative is to distribute only part of the assets to the foreign shareholders as a dividend before the sale negotiations so that they generally obtain a stepped-up basis in those assets equal to their fair market value at that time. Again, they may subsequently negotiate the sale of those assets with little or no further taxable capital gain. However, the U.S. corporation's dividend will be subject to a 30% U.S. withholding tax unless it is owned by shareholders in a country with a U.S. tax treaty which reduces that tax. In the case of a foreign corporation's dividend, the foreign corporation usually must be organized in a country with a tax treaty which eliminates the potential 30% U.S. withholding tax on the corporation's own dividends. Furthermore, other substantial assets should be retained in the corporation to permit such dividend treatment, and corporate law limitations on the amount of dividends must be considered.[44]

(5) If the foreign investor desires to remain involved in the U.S. business, it may also be possible to merge the U.S. or foreign corporation with another corporation or utilize one of the other taxfree reorganizations provided for under U.S. tax laws, subject to appropriate reporting of the transaction to the U.S. Department of the Treasury especially where a foreign corporation is involved.[45] For example, the stock in the U.S. or foreign corporation wholly owned by foreign persons generally may be exchanged for stock in a purchasing corporation without immediate U.S. taxation. If the acquiring corporation is publicly traded in the United States, the acquired stock may then be disposed of taxfree at such time as the foreign investor deems appropriate. The investor usually will in effect have become a portfolio rather than a direct investor.

If a foreign corporation or other enterprise or partner disposes of *U.S. real estate or natural resource interests* or if at least one-half of the fair market value of a U.S. corporation's assets is (or has been within five years prior to the sale) attributable to such interests — *which may include even a factory or warehouse owned or leased* — then few of the above disposition techniques will be applicable. In this case, reference should be made to Chapter III covering such interests.

It is important not to ignore potential state taxation — as well as non-U.S. taxation — in planning for a corporate sale or reorganization.[46]

In addition to such tax planning, compliance with U.S. securities laws, antitrust laws, and corporate and related laws must be undertaken. In this connection, from the point of view of the foreign investor, the situation is substantially the reverse of that described in Chapter VII dealing with corporate acquisitions, since the investor is now acting as seller rather than purchaser. Reference should be made to that chapter for discussion of such issues.

Insolvent Business

In the event that a U.S. business enterprise becomes insolvent, the investor may wish to use one of the federal U.S. bankruptcy arrangements, as modified recently by the Bankruptcy Reform Act of 1978.[47] This is feasible if the investor has acted through a separate subsidiary organized in the United States or in another country: bankruptcy is not limited to corporations, or even to merchants, but it is not possible to place a U.S. branch alone into bankruptcy, and it is unlikely that one would want to place an entire foreign enterprise into bankruptcy in the United States. However, if a foreign enterprise is a limited partner in a partnership in the United States, the partnership itself may be placed in bankruptcy without requiring the foreign enterprise to be so subject.

If the U.S. enterprise is hopelessly insolvent, the owners will place it into what has been generally termed straight bankruptcy or liquidation. The purpose of such a proceeding is to provide for the orderly liquidation of the assets and the protection of creditors. A trustee will be appointed by the federal bankruptcy court to take charge of the assets. A creditors' committee also may be elected to consult with the trustee and make recommendations regarding the performance of the trustee's duties. In furtherance of the principle of equal treatment of all creditors, any payment of a pre-existing debt made to any creditor during the 90-day period (or one-year period in case of payment to a so called insider who also had reason to believe the enterprise was insolvent) prior to the declaration of bankruptcy will be treated as a preference to that creditor and the amount of such payment may be recovered by the trustee. All assets, tangible and intangible, including claims against third parties, then are liquidated. If outside parties are engaged in legal actions against the bankrupt enterprise, these actions may be brought under the jurisdiction of the bankruptcy court for disposition. Secured and other preferred creditors — *i.e.*, creditors having a valid lien on certain of the assets — will have first right to the proceeds from the liquidation of those assets. The federal income tax authorities also will have a lien on all assets. The balance of the assets then are distributed *pro rata* among the unsecured creditors.

Insolvency does not always have to lead to liquidation. The federal bankruptcy laws provide for reorganization proceedings designed to permit payment to creditors in order to preserve the business. The most common such procedure is that under Chapter XI of the Bankruptcy Act, which permits a stay of all legal actions while a plan acceptable to creditors is attempted. Such a plan may include partial or deferred payments to all creditors, or only to certain classes of creditors. If the plan is accepted by a majority of each proposed class, the plan is binding on all other creditors in that class.

Finally, either the debtor or the court may elect to convert a liquidation proceeding to a reorganization proceeding, or *vice versa,* provided certain conditions are met.

For U.S. federal income tax purposes, the discharge of indebtedness in bankruptcy or while the debtor is insolvent generally will reduce first the debtor's ordinary losses and prior carryovers of such losses, prior investment tax credit carryovers, capital losses and prior such carryovers, and then the debtor's basis in its property. Gain upon disposition after such reduction in basis will be taxed as ordinary income. Alternatively, the debtor may apply the discharge to reduce first its basis in depreciable property (or in realty held as inventory), thereby potentially increasing its taxable income from that property. Any debt discharge beyond the debtor's basis does *not* result in income or generally have other tax consequences.[48]

Footnotes to Chapter VI

1. I.R.C. §§1391-1397; *see* Chapter III *supra,* note 64.

2. *Cf.* 31 U.S.C. §§1051-1122; 31 C.F.R. Parts 103, 128, 129; 17 C.F.R. §240.17a-8; Chapter XII *infra.* The Interest Equalization Tax imposed in 1964 became inapplicable to many foreign investors in 1973 since it was no longer made to apply to issues of stock and debt obligations in connection with long-term direct investments in the United States, so long as such investments were substantially financed from abroad. In addition, the tax was reduced to zero in January 1974 — at which time the voluntary guidelines limiting bank credit to foreign borrowers also were eliminated — and it subsequently expired.

3. *See generally* Chapters I, II *supra.*

4. *See, e.g.,* Conway Publications, *Site Selection Handbook* (1977); R. Waldmann, *Direct Investment and Development in the U.S.: A Guide to Incentive Programs, Laws and Restrictions* (1981); text *infra* at note 30.

5. *See generally* Chapter I *supra,* Chapter XII *infra.*

6. *See generally* D. Phillips, "Legal Restraints on Foreign Direct Investment in the United States," in U.S. Dep't of Commerce, 7 *Report to the Congress on Foreign Direct Investment in the United States* (1976); P. McCarthy, "Government Regulation of Foreign Investment in the United States," *Current Legal Aspects of Foreign Investment in the United States* 84 (1976); G. Spinner, "State-by-State Survey of Limitations on Foreign Investment," *Foreign Investment in the United States* (D.C. Bar Ass'n 1980).

7. *See generally* J. Lichtenstein, "Foreign Participation in United States Banking: Regulatory Myths and Realities," 15 B.C. Indus. & Com. L. Rev. 879 (1974).

8. *See* 12 U.S.C. §§165, 3101 *et seq.* Even a representative office now must register with the U.S. Department of the Treasury. 31 C.F.R. §§123.1-123.7.

9. 12 U.S.C. §§611 *et seq.*; 12 C.F.R. Parts 204, 211, 217. Similar international banking facility exemptions apply to insured nonmember banks under Federal Deposit Insurance Corporation regulations. 12 C.F.R. Part 329. International banking facilities also may be excluded from state income taxation in, for example, California, Florida, Illinois, Maryland, and New York.

10. 12 U.S.C. §378.

11. 12 U.S.C. §72.

12. 12 U.S.C. §§1841 *et seq.*

13. 12 U.S.C. §§1817(j), 1828(c); 12 C.F.R. §§5.50, 303.15, 563.18(2); *see generally* Chapter I *supra,* Chapter VII *infra.*

14. *Cf.* 15 U.S.C. §78c.

15. *See, e.g.,* T. Lefevre, "The Tax Law of Lease Transactions Revisited," 53 Taxes 764 (1975); *see also* text *infra* at note 30.

16. 32 C.F.R. Parts 155 *et seq.*

17. Pub. L. 96-39 (July 26, 1979), 93 Stat. 144; *cf.* G.S.A. Temp. Proc. Reg. 57; *see* Chapter V *supra.*

18. A useful guide for attorneys to the standards for doing business in a state is *What Constitutes Doing Business,* revised periodically by CT Corporation System.

19. *See also* Chapter II *supra.*

20. *But see* Robert L. Brittingham, 66 T.C. 373 (1976).

21. *See generally* Uniform Commercial Code (except in Louisiana); *Williston on Sales* (4th ed., A. Squillante & J. Fonseca eds., 1973).

22. I.R.C. §§172(b), (i).

23. *See also* Chapter XI *infra.*

24. *Cf.* I.R.C. §§441, 879, 6013(a)(l), (g), (h); *see also* Chapter XI *infra*, note 28.

25. *See* I.R.C. §§118, 267, 351, 367; Chapter II *supra.*

26. I.R.C. §§385, 267, 482, 483; *see* Chapter II *supra.*

27. *See generally* United States-Netherlands Income Tax Treaty of 1948, as amended and presently in force between the United States and the Netherlands Antilles, Art. VII.

28. *See* Chapter II *supra.*

29. I.R.C. §§163, 172, 243, 1501-1564. For further information on U.S. corporate taxation generally, see B. Bittker & J. Eustice, *Federal Income Taxation of Corporations and Shareholders* (4th ed. 1979, cum. supp. 1981).

30. I.R.C. §§168(f)(8), (i), 103(b)(6), (k). As a further possible leasing alternative, a foreign lessor may be treated as the owner of property for depreciation or cost recovery allowances under its local tax law, but the user may be treated as the owner for U.S. credits and allowances, under a so called double dip lease.

In connection with development bonds, the standards for aggregating different bond issues so that the maximum permissible amount is exceeded have provoked controversy. *Cf.* Rev. Rul. 81-216, 1981-36 I.R.B. 6; Prop. Treas. Reg. §1.103-7(b). Even foreign branch banks in the United States, however, apparently may issue letters of credit and certificates of deposit in support of such bonds without federal securities registration.

With respect to mortgage subsidy bonds for single family residences, see I.R.C. §103A and Chapter III *supra.*

31. *See generally* Chapter X *infra.*

32. For further description of these and certain other aspects of U.S. labor and tax laws generally, see Chapter I *supra.*

33. The law governing the formation and operation of U.S. partnerships also is discussed in detail in S. Rowley, *Rowley on Partnership* (2d ed. 1960), and the taxation of such partnerships is discussed in A. Willis, *Partnership Taxation* (3d ed. 1981).

34. 8 Del. C. §§341 *et seq.*, especially §351.

35. *See* Treas. Reg. §301.7701-3. However, certain passive investment and property ownership ventures may elect out of such treatment. I.R.C. §761(a). In addition, federal taxation as a corporation is possible under certain circumstances. *See* Chapters II, III *supra.*

36. *Cf.* United States-Switzerland Income Tax Treaty of 1951, Art. VI. *But see* United States-France Income Tax Treaty of 1967, as amended ("U.S.-France Treaty"), Art. 9.

37. *See* I.R.C. §§531-537, 541-547, 861(a)(2)(B), 861(c), 881(a); Chapter II *supra; cf.* U.S.-France Treaty, Arts. 9, 13.

38. *See* Chapter VII *infra,* note 32. For guidelines as to research joint ventures, see U.S. Dep't of Justice, *Antitrust Guide Concerning Research Joint Ventures* (1980). For guidelines in the analogous situation of joint ventures in foreign operations by U.S. business enterprises, see U.S. Dep't of Justice, *Antitrust Guide for International Operations* (1977).

39. For the basis of most of the tax aspects discussed here, see Chapter II *supra. See also* R. Frei, "Tax Problems in Corporate Acquisitions Other than Reorganizations — from the Seller's Point of View," 52 Taxes 821 (1974); B. Bittker & J. Eustice, *supra* note 29; A. Willis, *supra* note 33.

40. I.R.C. §§453, 1239; Treas. Reg. §§1.864-3(a), 1.871-8(c).

41. I.R.C. §§331(a)(l), 334(b) (2), 341(a), 864(b), (c)(3), 871(a), 881; Chapter II *supra*; I.R.C. §§873, 1244. Income tax treaties containing a U.S. tax exemption for all gains from dispositions of capital assets if not attributable to a U.S. permanent establishment of the seller, whether ordinary or capital gains — as opposed to capital gains only — also should exempt the sale of stock in a collapsible corporation. *Cf.* United States-Jamaica Income Tax Treaty of 1981, Art. 13.

The general application of U.S. federal collapsible corporation tax provisions to foreign investors is discussed more extensively in R. deLap and J. Adams, "Applying the Collapsible Corporation

Provisions to Foreign Stockholders," 8 J. Corp. Taxation 308 (1981). However, in the case of a U.S. real property holding corporation, reference should be made to Chapter III *supra.*

42. I.R.C. §§337, 331(a) (l), 453(h), 453B(d)(2), 341; *see* I.R.C. §337(c)(2)(B) also allowing partial use of taxfree disposition under §337 where parent corporation has acquired its stock in the liquidating corporation by purchase. The principal specific exceptions to collapsible corporation treatment apply to a shareholder of no more than five percent of the stock's value during the production or purchase of the property, to gain of which less than 70% is attributable to the produced or purchased property, to gain realized more than three years after production or purchase of the property. I.R.C §341(d). Other more complex exceptions may apply for certain purposes where property whose sale would produce ordinary income is a small fraction of the corporation's net worth, or where the corporation whose stock is sold consents to be taxed on any later liquidating or other disposition of its property other than non-real property capital assets. I.R.C §§341(e), (f). Perhaps the simplest exception is for gain from the sale (or distribution in exchange) of stock which has not been held for more than one year. I.R.C. §341(a).

With respect to the further possible alternative of a one-month liquidation under I.R.C. §333, see Chapter III *supra,* note 30.

43. I.R.C. §§302, 311(d)-(e), 331(a), 332, 336, 346, 341(a), 864(c)(3); *cf.* United States v. Cumberland Public Service Co., 338 U.S. 451 (1949); Letter Ruls. 7838068, 8020003. *But see* Comm'r v. Court Holding Co., 324 U.S. 331 (1945).

44. I.R.C. §§301(b)-(d), 871(a), 881; *see generally* Chapter II *supra.* A distribution in excess of the corporation's current and accumulated earnings and profits plus the shareholders' basis in their stock is taxed to the shareholders as gain from the sale of property, *i.e.*, usually taxfree gain from sale of their stock. I.R.C. §301(c)(3).

45. *See generally* I.R.C. §§354-368; Chapter II *supra.*

46. *Cf.* Chapter II *supra* as to state taxation; Chapter III *supra,* Chapter VII *infra* as to examples of non-U.S. tax planning.

47. 11 U.S.C. §§101 *et seq.* This act applies to all cases filed after October 1, 1979. Prior cases are governed by the Bankruptcy Act of 1938, 11 U.S.C. §§1 *et seq.* For an introduction to U.S. bankruptcy law, *see* W. Collier, *Bankruptcy Manual* (3d ed. 1979).

48. *See, e.g.*, I.R.C. §368(a)(1)(G).

Chapter VII

Acquisition of a U.S. Corporation

This chapter describes the principal alternative techniques for the acquisition of a controlling interest in an existing U.S. corporation by a foreign investor and analyzes many of the U.S. tax and financing, securities law, antitrust, corporate law and related considerations involved in structuring and completing such an acquisition.

Foreign investors acquire U.S. corporations for many of the same reasons they establish new business enterprises as described in Chapter VI. They want to increase their access to the U.S. market, to benefit from the stability of the U.S. free enterprise system, and to reduce their reliance on exports to the United States which may be priced out of the U.S. market or excluded by other barriers. The acquisition approach is attractive because it enables investors to avoid many of the delays and risks associated with establishing a new U.S. enterprise and to gain access to technology owned by a U.S. corporation without incurring the expense of duplicating the technology abroad. Furthermore, the cost of such U.S. acquisitions may be reduced — possibly below asset values — due to increases in the value of foreign exchange in U.S. dollars or to reduced market prices of publicly traded U.S. corporate stocks. In connection with the latter situation, control of operating policies of a widely held U.S. corporation possibly may be obtained even where less than a majority interest is acquired. Finally, even small U.S. corporations and other business enterprises may be of interest to a nonresident alien individual seeking U.S. residence, in order to meet the foreign investor or other qualification for an immigrant visa as discussed in Chapter X and to provide a ready occupation for him and his immigrating family. From the U.S. viewpoint, such an acquisition — similarly to an investment in U.S. real estate or a new business establishment — may provide rather strong links between the foreign owner and U.S. economic and/or political policies.

The foreign investor's acquisition of an existing U.S. corporation usually may be accomplished by one of the following techniques: (1) purchase of the U.S. corporation's assets; (2) purchase of the controlling interest in outstanding shares of stock of the corporation from existing shareholders; (3) subscription to a share increase in the corporation itself; or (4) merger of the U.S. corporation into the acquiring corporation, or into a subsidiary corporation formed for the acquisition. Each of these may be accomplished by using as the principal consideration — in addition to commercial, managerial, and/or technical benefits which may be made available by the foreign investor — either cash and/or promissory notes of the acquiring entity or of a subsidiary organized for that purpose, or shares of stock of the foreign corporation or of a foreign or U.S. subsidiary.

Tax and Financing Considerations

Several principal U.S. federal income tax and financing considerations are involved in choosing among these techniques and otherwise structuring the acquisition. In addition — although too varied to summarize here — state and local income taxes, bulk sales and other transfer taxes, and property tax effects such as those referred to in Chapter I must be considered.

Use of Stock

If the potential foreign acquiror is itself a corporation, its stock may be offered to purchase either the assets or the stock of the U.S. corporation, or to subscribe to such stock, or in connection with a merger of the U.S. corporation into the foreign corporation. Such a stock transaction may comply with certain U.S. taxfree reorganization provisions, which will be helpful mainly for the U.S. target corporation or its shareholders who may not wish to be taxed on gain at sale of the assets or of the stock to the foreign corporation. In addition, various favorable tax attributes of the target corporation may be carried over to the surviving corporation, subject to certain limitations.[1]

However, use of such an approach may present certain problems. First, the foreign corporation is prevented from acquiring a stepped-up basis in the target corporation's assets for U.S. depreciation or resale purposes equal to the acquisition price.

Second, such a taxfree reorganization involving transfer of property by a U.S. person to a foreign corporation generally requires a ruling from the U.S. Internal Revenue Service. In theory, the ruling must conclude that the avoidance of U.S. income tax is not a significant purpose of the reorganization. As a practical matter, standards for granting such a ruling were set forth in great detail several years ago, although generally they have not yet been incorporated in new regulations.[2]

If the foreign corporation uses its stock to acquire directly the assets of the U.S. corporation — while that normally would be a taxfree reorganization if a U.S. corporation were the acquiror — here the selling corporation probably will have to pay a so called toll charge or tax on much of its gain on the sale of its inventory, accounts receivable, and certain securities and intangible property in order to obtain taxfree treatment on the balance of its assets. The reason is that, if the foreign corporation later takes such assets out of the United States to sell them in another jurisdiction, the United States may never have the opportunity to tax the gain because it is then a foreign corporation's foreign source income, which usually will not give rise to U.S. tax. This requirement may place the foreign corporate acquiror at a tax disadvantage compared to a potential U.S. corporate acquiror.

An alternative is to offer the foreign corporation's stock to shareholders of the U.S. corporation for their stock. Unless the U.S. shareholders end with more than half of the foreign corporation's stock, the required ruling should be available without a tax burden to the selling shareholders at the time the transaction is consummated.

One method to avoid the ruling requirement is for the foreign investor to capitalize a new or existing U.S. subsidiary and cause it to acquire the target corporation's assets or stock for its own U.S. stock or to merge with the target corporation. No foreign corporation is then involved initially in the taxfree reorganization itself. The contribution of cash or other property by the foreign owner to such a new U.S. subsidiary ordinarily does not require a ruling in order to be taxfree.[3] Alternatively, the consideration paid for such a U.S. merger may even be stock of a foreign parent corporation, if the shareholders of the merged corporation continue to have a substantial equity interest in the surviving U.S. entity — generally equal to at least one-half of the value of their prior interest in the target. In any event, there may be subsequent regulatory or ruling requirements or other tax problems in certain transfers involving the U.S. subsidiary and a foreign parent or subsidiary corporation.

Alternatively, if the acquisition is made by subscription to a capital increase in the target corporation constituting a controlling interest in the target, such a contribution — as in the case of contributions to a new U.S. subsidiary — generally does not require a ruling even if the foreign corporation's stock is the contributed property.

Third, in addition to these tax problems, the use of a foreign or U.S. corporation's stock often requires onerous and time-consuming registration of the stock under applicable securities laws, as noted further below. A U.S. seller is also often reluctant to accept the stock of a foreign corporation if it is not traded on a U.S. securities exchange.

Use of Cash

The foreign investor may simply ignore taxfree treatment because, for example, the seller is eager to sell even if a U.S. tax is payable, or little or no taxable gain is involved. Then the asset purchase, the stock purchase — whether or not followed by merger into an acquiring corporation — or the subscription to a capital increase in the U.S. corporation itself may be effected for cash and/or promissory notes. Each of these involves both tax and — because substantial cash often is required for this approach — financing considerations.

Tax benefits. Alternative acquisition structures may include, *inter alia*, the following:

First, if the target corporation has favorable tax attributes — for example, net operating loss carryovers, tax bases which are higher than fair market value, investment credit carryovers, foreign tax credit carryovers, and the like — then a controlling interest in the stock of the U.S. corporation may be acquired and the corporation kept in existence. However, under certain circumstances the acquisition of the U.S. corporation with such attributes may cause various tax benefits to be denied.[4] In addition, remaining minority shareholders may cause difficulties as noted further below.

Second, if instead a stepped-up tax basis in the target corporation's assets equal to the acquisition price is desired, then the foreign investor may purchase the assets of the U.S. corporation directly. In this case, however, the selling corporation may be taxed on the gain unless it liquidates soon thereafter, triggering tax on any shareholders' gains. In any event, the corporation also will have to pay U.S. ordinary income tax on recapture of any accelerated depreciation, investment tax credits, and the like.[5]

Third, an alternative to obtain such a stepped-up basis is for the investor's corporation to purchase at least 80% of the U.S. corporation's stock and (for an acquisition after August 1982) elect within 75 days thereafter to have the U.S. corporation treated as having sold its assets and liquidated similarly to the second alternative above. The target corporation then is subject to any tax recaptures, and this may reduce its after-tax value to the acquiror and should be considered in negotiating the purchase price. In this connection, the opportunity for the acquiror to purchase separately certain assets of the target for which it desires a stepped-up basis, and yet maintain the target itself with favorable tax attributes or avoid a taxable purchase of other assets which will trigger tax recaptures, has been substantially limited.[6]

Fourth, the foreign acquiror may consider having such a U.S. corporation owned in turn by a foreign corporation organized in a country with which the United States has an income tax treaty, in order to reduce the usual 30% U.S. withholding tax on dividends from the U.S. subsidiary and possibly to accumulate the income outside the acquiror's home country.

Fifth, under a so called cash merger, a new U.S. subsidiary of the acquiror may be capitalized with cash and/or promissory notes and merged into the target corporation in a taxfree reorganization, followed by a taxable exchange by the target corporation's original shareholders of their stock for the contributed property. However, a step-up in basis in the acquired corporation's assets still may require the acquiring corporation to make the election noted in the third alternative above.

Sixth, even where taxfree treatment of the seller is not available, partial tax deferral may be achieved. For example, the taxable gain may be reported on the installment basis, provided the promissory notes given by the acquiror are not payable on demand or readily tradable in an established securities market. Generally, this is true even for shareholders to whom the acquiror's notes are distributed upon liquidation of their corporation after sale of its assets.

Alternatively, upon merger of a U.S. target corporation into the U.S. subsidiary of a foreign corporation partly in exchange for the foreign corporation's stock, a portion of the taxable gain may be deferred by giving the selling shareholders a cash option to receive aggregate cash of not more than one-half of the total price paid, so that the requirement of continuity of interest of the sellers as noted further above for a taxfree reorganization is met upon their receipt of the foreign corporate stock; then only the cash portion generally is taxable to them currently. As a further alternative, instead of foreign corporate stock, the nontaxable portion of the merger consideration to the selling shareholders may even be nonvoting, nonconvertible preferred stock of the U.S. subsidiary redeemable under certain circumstances in the future.[7]

In any event, following the acquisition, the acquiror should consider transfering foreign operations of the acquired corporation to a foreign corporation which is *not* a subsidiary of a U.S. corporation to eliminate or reduce future U.S. taxation and other problems with respect to such foreign operations. A corporate acquiror's election to step up the tax basis of the target's assets generally will not apply to the stock of a foreign subsidiary or a Domestic International Sales Corporation owned by the target, and so should not trigger taxation of such a subsidiary's previously accumulated earnings. Alternatively, the foreign operations may be purchased separately by the acquiror before its acquisition of the target corporation.[8]

It may also be possible to split the acquired assets by having intangible items such as U.S. patents or know-how purchased separately by a foreign entity and licensed to the acquired U.S. corporation for royalties. These will be deductible from the U.S. licensee's operating income, but may be subject to little or no U.S. withholding tax if a tax treaty applies between the United States and the licensor's country.

Because the United States generally requires the expense of searching for an acquisition target to be capitalized for income tax purposes and deducted over at least five years,[9] such search expenses should if possible be incurred by a foreign entity under the laws of a country permitting current deduction of the same, rather than by a U.S. corporation.

Financing arrangements. If the foreign investor intends to acquire at least 80% of the U.S. corporation, generally the most favorable structure to ensure that interest payments on borrowings for the acquisition will reduce U.S. income taxes on the acquired corporation's operating income is to establish a U.S. holding subsidiary to borrow the funds and make the acquisition of shares. Even if the acquired corporation remains in existence, it and the holding corporation may file a consolidated U.S. income tax return under which the interest expense incurred by the holding corporation reduces the taxable income of the acquired corporation.[10] In addition, dividends can flow to the holding corporation free of U.S. tax.[11] If the acquired corporation subsequently is liquidated, the holding corporation will still be able to deduct its interest expense from its own operating income from the assets. Similarly, if the target corporation's assets are to be acquired directly, the establishment of a U.S. subsidiary to make the acquisition with borrowed funds will permit an interest deduction from the operating income of the assets. It may be wise to have whichever U.S. corporation finally holds the assets incur directly a portion of the interest expense so that it can be deducted from operating income more easily for state and local tax purposes.

At least two additional significant U.S. income tax issues are involved in the use of such a U.S. borrowing subsidiary. First, if the U.S. subsidiary is unable to borrow solely on its own credit — because it is newly formed or for other reasons — and must borrow from the foreign investor or obtain the investor's guaranty of its own borrowing, then the U.S. corporation should be adequately capitalized to ensure that the borrowing is treated as debt rather than equity in order that principal repayments and interest deductions will be permitted. Several broad standards for determining whether corporate debt is to be treated as debt or equity are provided by statute. Under pending regulations, where debt to shareholders is substantially proportionate to their respective equity holdings in the corporation, such shareholder loans generally should not exceed three times the shareholders' equity investments and the ratio of total corporate debt to equity should not exceed 10 to one. It seems likely that similar thin capitalization standards will apply to international loans owed to (and possibly from) a foreign person. The interest for each year also usually should be paid not later than two and one-half months after the close of the taxable year of the corporation if it deducts expenses on the accrual basis and is majority owned by one individual or family. The interest rate should be set at an arm's length level equal to that which would be available in a transaction between unrelated parties. In addition, interest deductions for any such acquisition indebtedness are subject to special limitations.[12]

Second, if the U.S. subsidiary borrows from the foreign investor or other foreign lenders, the interest payments will be subject to a 30% U.S. withholding tax which may increase the financing cost — unless an income tax treaty applies to reduce or eliminate the tax. U.S. tax treaties with industrialized countries usually provide for such withholding tax reduction on interest to five percent or even zero and lenders — particularly banks and other financial institutions — often can arrange loans to come under one of such treaties. In addition, the foreign investor may consider establishing a finance subsidiary in a country with which the United States currently has a favorable tax treaty, such as the Netherlands or the Netherlands Antilles.[13]

If the foreign investor intends to acquire less than 80% of the U.S. corporation, it is often difficult to reduce the U.S. tax on the acquired corporation's income by the interest expense of making the acquisition. Accordingly, the foreign parent entity probably should finance the borrowing unless its U.S. acquiring corporation has other income from which to deduct the interest. Alternatively, it may be possible to establish a partnership for U.S. income tax purposes between the target corporation or a subsidiary, and a U.S. or foreign subsidiary of the foreign investor. Then, interest payments by the foreign investor's subsidiary will reduce its U.S. tax on its share of the partnership's income. However, dividends from the subsidiary to its foreign owner may be subject to a U.S. withholding tax of 30%, unless a tax treaty reduces such tax. Alternatively, such a foreign subsidiary may be established in a country with which the United States has a tax treaty that eliminates its withholding tax on dividends from the foreign corporation, even if at least one-half of its gross income is effectively connected with the conduct of a U.S. trade or business.

However, in all tax treaty structuring for the acquisition of a U.S. corporation, the distinction between treaty use and abuse must be considered, particularly because the definition and limitation of such abuse may be of increasing importance for U.S. and other tax authorities.[14]

The value to the foreign investor of maximizing such interest deductions to reduce U.S. income taxes may depend in part on foreign tax laws, either as generally in force or as modified by U.S. tax treaties. For example, in the case of a Dutch or German investor, repatriated income from a U.S. branch or subsidiary may be substantially exempt from local tax. In other countries, such income of the investor may be subject to a local tax rate which still is below that of combined U.S. federal corporate and withholding taxes plus state taxes. Thus, the overall tax objective of such an investor is to reduce U.S. income taxes to a minimum. On the other hand, if the foreign investor may utilize a full foreign tax credit in his own country for U.S. taxes on a branch or first and/or lower tier subsidiary *and* for U.S. withholding taxes, then reduction of U.S. taxes substantially below the effective foreign tax rate may be less important. The value of such interest deductions also may depend on the applicable tax treaty between the United States and the foreign investor's country. For example, the treaty may favor interest payments by the U.S.

subsidiary, rather than dividends, by imposing a lower U.S. withholding tax rate on interest.

The particular source of borrowed funds also will be influenced by factors other than U.S. and foreign taxation. The foreign investor must consider foreign exchange regulations in his country. On the other hand, the reputation of the investor in his home country or another country may make borrowing there easier than in the United States. In addition, the interest rate may be lower if the borrowing is effected in a strong currency. If a foreign bank or other lender takes a pledge of the acquired stock as security for the loan, it should be noted that U.S. securities laws may limit public resale of the shares — even resale under the pledge terms or under foreign laws requiring public auction of collateral.

If U.S. financing sources are desired, these may include institutional lenders, private or public debt placements in the U.S. capital markets, and — as described in Chapter VI regarding new U.S. business establishments — the use of industrial development bonds and/or tax oriented equipment leasing instead of outright purchase. Such financing also may be obtained from the U.S. seller in the form of an installment sale. Alternatively, the timing and/or amount of the purchase price may be made contingent on the subsequent success of the target corporation — for example, by having the target itself pay off from its earnings promissory notes given to selling shareholders, or redeem remaining unacquired stock of the target from such earnings. Particularly in the case of a publicly held target corporation, such purchase price and other acquisition strategy and timing issues often are determined with the assistance of investment bankers. In any event, there are no U.S. legal restrictions on the borrowing of funds in the United States by a foreign investor — whether the purpose is to finance a U.S. acquisition or other investments — except the securities and margin regulations noted immediately below.

Securities Law Considerations

Use of Stock

The offering of stock of a foreign or U.S. corporation owned by the foreign investor to purchase the target corporation's assets, purchase a controlling stock interest in the corporation, merge the corporation into the investor's corporation, or subscribe to a capital increase in the target corporation raises the possible requirement to register the stock offering under U.S. federal and/or state securities laws and the need to review foreign securities laws to assure either their inapplicability or compliance with the same. The necessity of such registration is particularly clear where the offering will be made to a sufficiently large number of persons to constitute a public offering. The principal considerations in determining whether a public offering is involved and in complying with such registration requirements under the federal Securities Act of 1933 (the "1933 Act"), state Blue Sky laws, and other U.S. laws are summarized in Chapter I and should be examined closely in this connection.

It should be noted that, in the case of a *foreign* issuer of securities, special disclosure requirements for new securities offerings under the 1933 Act are few as yet. However, a special Form 20-F applies to registration and periodic reporting under the Securities Exchange Act of 1934 (the "1934 Act") for most foreign nongovernmental issuers whose securities are publicly offered in the United States or are listed on a U.S. national securities exchange. The Securities and Exchange Commission ("SEC") also is adopting a special integrated disclosure system under which large foreign nongovernmental issuers of securities which are required to file periodically under the 1934 Act may substantially shorten their registration statements for *new* securities issues under the 1933 Act by referring investors to those filings. In any event, registration of such securities still may involve difficult translation of foreign financial statements into U.S. currency and accounting practices.[15]

The foreign investor's offering of promissory notes or other debt obligations as part of the acquisition consideration raises similar potential securities law issues. However, the U.S. requirement for profit reporting by geographical and industrial segments also is being reduced for large foreign debt issuers.

In general, the balance of U.S. securities laws apply equally to the use of stock and the use of cash and/or promissory notes for the acquisition; these are described immediately below.

Use of Cash

Privately held target corporation. Except in the case of a purchase of assets only for cash, the broad antifraud provisions of Rule 10b-5 under the 1934 Act apply to purchase or sale of any security or any activity in connection therewith, whether or not a shareholder vote is required *and* whether the securities are privately or publicly held. Under these antifraud rules, a mere showing of nondisclosure of information that a reasonable investor *might* have considered important in making the decision to buy or sell is sufficient to permit suit. On the other hand, an intent to deceive generally is required, rather than mere negligence. Liability applies to all who participate in the transaction — including attorneys, accountants, and the like — who are aware of such deceit. In general, these rules also apply extraterritorially to a foreign person whose conduct causing injury occurs partly within the United States *or* whose conduct abroad has substantial and foreseeable injurious effects in the United States, such as decreasing the value of stock held by U.S. persons. Accordingly, a purchaser often voluntarily complies with the requirements of the 1934 Act governing tender offers for securities of publicly held corporations, as described further below, even when these are not applicable by their terms.[16]

It should also be noted that — whether the target corporation is privately *or* publicly held — shareholders who sell a controlling interest to the foreign investor owe the minority shareholders a fiduciary duty of fairness and, if the purchase of controlling stock is made at a premium, other shareholders who are offered a lower price may bring suit to compel the selling shareholders and the purchaser to pay over a portion of the premium.[17]

Furthermore, if the acquisition requires a favorable vote at a shareholders' meeting under the applicable state law, state proxy requirements may have to be met.

Publicly held target corporation. If the U.S. target corporation is publicly held, any acquisition technique may be complicated by additional provisions of the 1934 Act and related regulations. These apply if either the target corporation's securities are listed on a national securities exchange and registered for public trading, or its assets have a value in excess of $3 million *and* its equity securities are held by at least 500 persons (or 300 after reaching the 500 point). The principal additional federal disclosure, antifraud, and margin requirements generally applicable are:[18]

(1) The target corporation is required by the 1934 Act to file with the SEC quarterly and annual statements of financial and other corporate information on Forms 8-K and 10-K and to report promptly any important events which might affect the market for the corporation's stock. In addition, the corporation is required to send to all shareholders, before each shareholders' meeting, a proxy statement setting forth current financial and other information about the corporation. In the course of preparing the financial statements, the corporation's accountants obtain from legal counsel for the corporation full information about pending or threatened claims, disputes, bad debts, and other adverse factors respecting the corporation. A prospective foreign or other investor may consult these statements and obtain copies from the SEC.

(2) The corporation generally must disclose to the public by way of press releases any serious approach from persons interested in acquiring a substantial interest in it. If the approach is made to a shareholder, he has no duty to disclose same unless he owns a controlling interest in the corporation, in which case he should consider issuing a press release under the same duty of disclosure as the corporation's management. Copies of such releases normally are given to financial newspapers and news services, together with the securities exchanges on which the stock is listed. Often a public announcement is not made until the parties have reached an agreement in principle on the most basic terms and intend to pursue the negotiation of the transaction. However, an announcement usually must be made immediately if discussions become known to a number of persons

or unusual market activity in the target corporation's securities indicates possible investor use of the information.

(3) If an investor plans to acquire a block of the corporation's stock from one or a group of shareholders or to acquire that stock on the open market, he is under no duty to disclose his intention to the public until he owns more than five percent of the corporation's stock. Thereupon he must report to the SEC — principally on Schedule 13D under the 1934 Act — all his purchases and sales, his identity in great detail, and his intentions in making the investment. In addition, ownership of 10% or more of the corporation's stock may trigger treatment of the investor as an insider subject to reporting requirements and corporate recapture of short swing profits if he resells his stock, unless all such stock was acquired at one time or is exchanged upon a merger engineered by a competing acquiror.[19]

(4) If the acquisition requires a favorable vote at a shareholders' meeting under applicable state law, the corporation must provide its shareholders with a proxy statement disclosing all facts relating to the acquisition on which the vote is solicited and file the same with the SEC in advance of its distribution. Under the proxy statement disclosure rules, an omitted fact generally is not material unless a reasonable investor would have considered it important.

(5) If an investor contemplates using borrowed funds for the acquisition, the margin rules of the U.S. Federal Reserve Board limiting credit extension by banks and other lenders in connection with the purchase of stock must be examined. These rules apply principally to credit extensions by U.S. lenders. However, foreign restrictions on investments abroad by U.S. enterprises — for example, in Canada and elsewhere — have prompted discussion of the possible application of the U.S. margin rules even to foreign credit extensions in connection with U.S. stock purchases.

Federal tender offer rules. If the foreign investor intends to make a tender offer to *all* shareholders of such a publicly held U.S. corporation to purchase all or a stated amount of stock for a fixed price during a fixed period of time, then additional special federal tender offer rules are applicable. The principal reason for the popularity of such tender offers in recent years is that an increasing number of large U.S. corporations do not have one controlling shareholder or group of shareholders. This increased use has led in turn to increased regulation under the federal Williams Act, enacted in 1968 and amended in 1970,[20] as well as under various state takeover statutes described further below.

In general, the Williams Act and current SEC rules thereunder require any person seeking to make a tender offer which, if successful, would result in his being the beneficial owner of more than five percent of any class of equity securities in a publicly held target corporation — even if he does *not* yet own more than five percent — to file Schedule 14D-1 and other extensive schedules with the SEC concerning the proposed transaction and parties involved and also to file with the SEC, any securities exchange on which the securities are listed, and the target corporation copies of all solicitation materials to shareholders. Financial statements of the offeror also may have to be filed with the SEC.[21]

A threshold question is whether advance purchases of stock by private negotiations with one or a group of shareholders or on the open market may be considered part of a subsequent tender offer to all shareholders in violation of the advance filing requirements under the Williams Act. If purchase orders for stock are given each day for a specified amount of stock with a specified price limit, such purchases probably do not violate the act. However, the intention to make a tender offer at a later date must not be disclosed to any *arbitrageur* or other person who might accumulate the stock in anticipation of a premium tender offer price to the detriment of sellers who do not possess the same information. In addition, shareholders who sell their stock informally in advance of the tender offer at a price lower than the price offered later may accuse the purchaser of fraud for failure to disclose his ultimate intentions, and the foreign or other investor may have to make an additional payment to those who sold at a lower price just before the tender offer. A similar preliminary problem is that investors acting in concert or as a group — including persons acting for them — generally may not evade the act's requirements by limiting each investor's ownership to five percent or less.[22]

The tender offer must be held open for at least 20 business days, and the tender offeror may not make purchases outside the tender offer while the offer is pending. Furthermore, specific antifraud provisions are applicable to any such tender offer. In the case of an exchange tender offer of stock, because the offeror is required to prepare and file a registration statement and prospectus for its stock offering under the 1933 Act as noted further above, certain additional announcements and solicitations concerning the tender offer may be permitted.[23]

Other federal rules and remedies. It should be noted that, if the investor acquires through a U.S. subsidiary less than half of the stock of such a target corporation and the investment constitutes more than 40% of the subsidiary's own assets, the U.S. subsidiary may then become an investment company subject to the restrictions of the Investment Company Act of 1940.[24]

In addition, since the securities of a publicly held U.S. corporation often are traded in various stock markets, the acquisition may be subject to the rules of one or more securities exchanges. For example, such an exchange may have a policy of refusing to approve the listing of additional stock or of delisting the stock of a corporation which has been acquired by another corporation.

While the SEC is the authority principally responsible for enforcing the federal securities laws, a corporate acquisition may involve risk of a class action in which one shareholder institutes suit for an injunction or monetary damages on behalf of himself and all other shareholders similarly situated whose attorneys, if successful, may collect fees commensurate with the legal effort required and with the total amount of the recovery. A single shareholder also may institute suit on his own behalf. This risk can be substantially reduced by proper disclosure through complete cooperation by the foreign investor and his executives during preparations for the offer. It should be noted that in judicial decisions many facts pertaining to the foreign business of a foreign acquiror have been found to be *immaterial.* However, it may be extremely important under federal securities laws to disclose any relationships among the officers, directors, or shareholders of the foreign acquiror and the target corporation.[25]

Where a tender offer is part of an attempted hostile acquisition in spite of opposition from existing management of the target corporation, because they feel the offer is inadequate or fear loss of their jobs, it may provoke countermeasures from the target itself, including judicial actions to block the transaction. These counteractions may be based on the above federal or state securities law requirements, the enforcement of state takeover statutes described below, or antitrust, corporate law, or foreign investment regulation considerations discussed further below. The offer also may be contested by competing offers from other potential investors. In such event, rapid and full compliance with applicable securities, antitrust, and other laws becomes even more crucial than usual to the potential foreign acquiror.

State takeover statutes. If the foreign investor intends to acquire equity securities of the target corporation, state regulation in the tender offer area — commonly referred to as takeover statutes — must be considered. In certain states, such tender offers also have been interpreted to be subject to state securities law antifraud provisions.[26]

Under the takeover statutes, a takeover generally is defined as an offer to acquire any equity security of a target corporation if, after the acquisition, the offeror would be directly or indirectly the beneficial owner of a specified percentage — varying from five percent to 20%, but commonly 10% — of any class of the outstanding equity securities of the target corporation. Such a statute may apply if the target corporation is incorporated within the state *or* has its principal place of business there *or* has substantial assets there.

These statutes generally provide for a waiting period after filing with state authorities in compliance with disclosure requirements — usually with the Commissioner of Corporations or similar securities authority, the Secretary of State, or the Attorney General. In certain states — for example, Delaware — such formalities are not much more burdensome than federal requirements but, in others, the required material is much more comprehensive than under the federal Williams Act. In addition, in certain states such filing is followed by a hearing before a state government official to determine whether the offer is adequately described or is fair.[27] Apparently very few hostile or contested offers have managed to clear such a state proceeding.

The federal constitutionality of such statutes has been severely questioned. For example, recently the Illinois takeover statute was invalidated as unconstitutional because its application to a target corporation organized outside the state and with substantial out-of-state shareholders interfered with interstate commerce and conflicted with the federal Williams Act which pre-empted the regulation of such tender offers. Other state takeover statutes have been invalidated on similar grounds.[28] Accordingly, the extent of the valid application of such state statutes has been substantially limited, and a potential foreign acquiror should follow further developments in this area.

Antitrust Considerations

The acquisition by a foreign investor of a controlling interest in the assets or stock of a U.S. corporation, whether privately or publicly held, and whether or not effected by merger with an existing or new foreign or U.S. corporation owned by the foreign investor or by another foreign entity, also must involve consideration of U.S. federal and state — as well as foreign — antitrust laws. In general, U.S. federal antitrust laws apply to persons engaged in U.S. commerce *or* to activities affecting U.S. commerce — including an acquisition between two wholly foreign parties each with a U.S. subsidiary or other U.S. activities. The most important of such laws applicable to a corporate acquisition are Sections 1 and 2 of the Sherman Act (respectively, "Sherman Section 1" and "Sherman Section 2"), Section 7 of the Clayton Act ("Clayton Section 7"), and Section 5 of the Federal Trade Commission Act ("FTC Section 5").[29]

Sherman Section 1 broadly prohibits concerted action which results in actual restraint of trade or commerce, but prohibits a corporate acquisition only if such restraints are unreasonable. Sherman Section 2 broadly prohibits transactions involving a specific intent to monopolize or attempt to monopolize, including a combination or conspiracy with such intent. However, in the case of a foreign investor, such an intent is not likely to exist because the investor generally has a relatively small economic position in the U.S. market. Both provisions carry criminal and civil penalties, and apply to individuals as well as corporations and other entities.

FTC Section 5 broadly prohibits unfair methods of competition in or affecting commerce. Unlike the Sherman Act, this provision has been interpreted to bar acquisitions which merely *threaten* to lessen competition or prevent deconcentration in any industry or market.[30] It also applies to all persons, not merely corporations.

Clayton Section 7 is by far the most important of such provisions in the case of a corporate acquisition, and broadly prohibits any corporation engaged in commerce from acquiring the whole of any part of the stock or assets of another corporation if the effect of the acquisition may be substantially to lessen competition or tend to create a monopoly in any line of commerce in any section of the United States. It does not apply to individuals or partnerships, but has been held to apply to a newly organized joint venture corporation.[31]

Required Notices and Advisory Opinions

Clayton Section 7 and FTC Section 5 are enforced within the U.S. government by the Bureau of Competition of the Federal Trade Commission (the "FTC"). Generally, notice of a proposed acquisition of a U.S. corporation together with certain supporting documents is to be given to the FTC if it involves parties of which one has net sales or total assets of at least $100 million and the other has net sales (if a manufacturing corporation) or total net assets of at least $10 million. However, these requirements currently apply only if after the acquisition the acquiror will hold one of the following: at least 15% and more than $15 million in assets of the target; more than $15 million in voting stock of the target; or voting control of a corporation with net sales, or total assets, of at least $25 million. The notice must be given at least 30 days in advance — or 15 days if the acquisition is by a cash tender offer — within which period the FTC may choose to object to the transaction. This period may be extended by the FTC for an additional 20 days to obtain additional information, or an additional 10 days for a cash tender offer. This may delay the making of such a tender offer for a crucial period; however, the offer itself may provide that payment will be made after expiration of the waiting period and only if not challenged by the agency. Noncompliance may result in a court order requiring compliance and a civil penalty of up to $10,000 for *each day* the violation continues.[32]

The Antitrust Division of the Department of Justice (the "Antitrust Division") shares with the FTC enforcement responsibility under Clayton Section 7, and has sole enforcement responsibility within the U.S. government under Sherman Section 1 and Sherman Section 2. In the former connection, notice of a proposed corporate acquisition must be given to the Antitrust Division in the same manner as to the FTC noted above, and it may choose to object to the transaction within the same 15-or 30-day period and require the same extension of such period. These notification requirements and other requests for information which may be made on any proposed or ongoing acquisition frequently are complicated for a foreign investor by the necessity to translate foreign language documents into English and foreign financial statements into U.S. measurements, currency, and accounting practices in order to avoid misunderstanding by government officials. It should be noted that even correspondence and intracompany memoranda may be so obtained by such officials. Accordingly, the investor should try to limit requested information to its activities affecting U.S. commerce and to lines of products of the parties which may be affected by the proposed acquisition.

Even if notice of the proposed acquisition as described above is not required, a potential acquiror also should investigate whether the target corporation itself has been involved in antitrust litigation and is subject to a judicial consent decree or other decision, because clearance from the court or a federal or state government agency may be required before the acquisition can proceed.

Whether or not notice or permission for a proposed acquisition is required, the FTC may be requested to issue an advisory opinion or advance ruling. This opinion may be reversed later by the FTC, however. The FTC has estimated that approximately 60% of such requests have received favorable opinions, approximately 30% no opinions due to inadequate information, and approximately 10% negative opinions. However, the opinions may require from two weeks to three months to be issued.

Similarly, the Antitrust Division provides an informal unofficial business review procedure for, *inter alia,* proposed corporate acquisitions. The Division has estimated that approximately 50% of such requests have received favorable responses, 25% no responses either because the requests were withdrawn or because the Division decided not to respond, and approximately 20% unfavorable responses. This procedure reduces the chance of unexpected government opposition. However, a favorable response states only the enforcement intention at the time and does not prohibit future challenges to the transaction. The review may require up to six weeks, and often may not be instituted until the acquisition is close to consummation. Finally, the request and the response, together with supporting documentation, generally are made available to the public unless a detrimental effect on business operations by such disclosure is demonstrated.[33]

Standards for Compliance

Whether or not a notice or similar requirement or an advisory opinion is involved, the foreign investor's acquisition must be considered in light of the antitrust standards developed by U.S. judicial and administrative decisions. In particular, in the case of a corporate acquisition by another corporation, the standards under Clayton Section 7 are the most broadly applicable and most frequently applied. Under this statute, as mentioned previously, the acquisition is illegal if its effect may be substantially to lessen competition or tend to create a monopoly in any line of commerce in any section of the country.

Horizontal acquisition. The standards by which the prohibited effects are determined vary with the type of acquisition involved. In the first type, a horizontal acquisition in which the two corporations are in competition with each other, the single most important factor in determining the reduction of competition is the respective share of the relevant U.S. market held by each corporation. The market within which the effects must be considered is, first, the line of commerce or product market and, second, the section of the country or geographic market.

As to the relevant product market, the size of the market is determined principally by whether the products are sufficiently similar so that, if the price of one rises, users will readily switch to another. In addition, however, smaller submarkets may exist for antitrust purposes if three or four of the following elements are present: (1) public or industry recognition of the submarket, (2) peculiar characteristics or uses of the products involved, (3) unique production facilities for the products, (4) distinct customers, (5) distinct prices, (6) sensitivity to price changes, or (7) specialized sellers of the products.[34] As to the relevant geographic market, the size of the market generally is determined by whether a user can readily turn to an alternative geographic source of supply. For example, a geographic market for a product which is perishable or costly to transport will be small. A larger market definition may favor the acquisition by demonstrating a smaller fractional effect on the market due to product or geographic interchangeability. However, this approach also may permit a challenge to the acquisition because the law seeks to prevent reduction of *potential* as well as actual competition and a large market definition may emphasize, for example, the variety of potential competition between the parties to the acquisition.

In connection with horizontal acquisitions, the Antitrust Division uses certain guidelines in determining whether to challenge the acquisition under Clayton Section 7 or Sherman Section 1.[35] These guidelines reflect enforcement policy, even if they do not prevent the Division from challenging an acquisition for other reasons. However, the FTC — which shares enforcement responsibility under Clayton Section 7 — did not fully endorse recent revisions to the Division's guidelines. In particular, the recently revised guidelines list various factors and procedures the Division will use in defining the relevant product and geographic market, the firms included in the market, and their respective market shares. The guidelines then divide acquisitions into three categories based upon the so called Herfindahl-Hirshman index, under which the relevant market concentration is derived by squaring the percentage of the market held by each firm included in the market and adding those numbers; for example, a market split equally among 10 firms has an index of 1,000, and one split equally among 5 firms an index of 2,000. In a highly concentrated market, defined as that in which the index after a proposed acquisition would be at least 1,800, the Division is likely to challenge the transaction if it produces an increase in the index of 100 or more; it may also challenge an acquisition increasing the index by as little as 50. In a moderately concentrated market with a post-acquisition index of 1,000-1,800, an acquisition increasing the index by more than 100 may be challenged. These index increase figures may seem surprisingly small to a foreign investor. In cases where the Division may or may not challenge an acquisition, the guidelines emphasize other factors, including a trend toward noncompetitive performance in the market in recent years and the difficulty of entry by other competitors into the market. However, in a market split among so many firms that the post-acquisition index still will be less than 1,000, *no* horizontal acquisition generally will be challenged.

Even an acquisition not between competitors may be challenged due to the reduction of *potential* horizontal competition. For example, the foreign corporation's experience, technology, and/or knowledge of the U.S. market through previous export trade may make the corporation a potential entrant into the United States as an additional competitor by starting a new business or making a so called toehold acquisition of a small business, or may make it a perceived potential entrant whose threat restrains the pricing or anticompetitive policies of existing U.S. businesses. Such competitive benefits may be eliminated by the acquisition of a substantial existing U.S. corporation. The importance of this factor is diminished if the foreign acquiror could enter the U.S. market itself only with great economic and/or technical difficulty. While the theory has been clearly recognized in U.S. judicial decisions, the showing of simply a reasonable probability that the foreign acquiror will eventually enter the U.S. market by internal expansion has not been sufficient to bar an acquisition.[36] The Antitrust Division's guidelines state that an acquisition by one of the most likely entrants is unlikely to be challenged if, *inter alia,* the concentration index in the acquired firm's market is less than 1,800. The FTC also has stated that, where the top four firms have at least approximately 60% of the market, acquisition of a corporation with less than a 10% market share usually will be presumed a toehold acquisition rather than elimination of a potential competitor.[37]

This factor is not yet clearly defined in judicial decisions — for example, the U.S. Supreme Court has expressly reserved the question whether proof that a corporation is simply an actual potential entrant, without proof of the disciplinary effects on existing businesses, is sufficient to bar an acquisition.[38] However, a potential foreign acquiror must be aware of this factor and follow further developments in the area.

Vertical acquisition. In a vertical acquisition in which the foreign corporation acquires a former supplier or customer, the principal anticompetitive effect is the foreclosure of the acquired supplier's competitors from part of their sales market or of the acquired customer's competitors from part of their sources of supply. Thus, once again market concentration is crucial.

The guidelines triggering enforcement interest of the Antitrust Division are unlikely to result in a challenge to an acquisition of a supplier or a customer if, *inter alia,* the concentration index in the acquired firm's market is less than 1,800. Above that figure, similarly to a horizontal acquisition, additional factors include the trend toward noncompetitive performance in the acquired firm's market, the difficulty of entry by other competitors into that market without the acquiror's availability as an independent customer or supplier, and the loss of potential competition if the acquiror were to expand vertically into the market as a supplier or customer. However, because of the probability of a smaller market share of a distant foreign corporation as a purchaser from or supplier to the U.S. market, a vertical acquisition by a foreign investor may involve less risk of such challenge than such an acquisition between two U.S. corporations.

Conglomerate acquisition. Where the foreign investor uses a foreign or domestic corporation to acquire a U.S. corporation with which no relationships exist as competitor, supplier, or customer, a conglomerate acquisition is involved. Here the potential anticompetitive effects include either reciprocal dealing practices or the entrenchment of a dominant market position. First, the acquisition may permit the acquiror to use the buying power of the acquired corporation in order to force other products of the acquiror on third parties. If there is a probability that that power will be used — even if the probability is demonstrated only much later by actual reciprocal dealings — and substantially anticompetitive results will follow, then the acquisition may be found to violate Clayton Section 7.[39]

In the second situation, a large acquiror may be able to use its substantial funds from other operations to improve the acquired corporation's position in the market at the expense of other competitors, thereby entrenching that corporation in a dominant position, or at least may reduce potential entrants into the market by the threat of such action.[40]

Because the challenge to conglomerate acquisitions has emerged only in recent years — except where the acquiror is a potential entrant into the acquired firm's market as described generally above — neither the Antitrust Division nor other administrative or judicial authorities have currently developed clear guidelines in this area. However, such acquisitions do not now appear to be the subject of special attention by the Division.

Defenses

Even if compliance with the foregoing standards is not possible, one defense to an antitrust action challenging the acquisition is that Clayton Section 7 is inapplicable by its terms when the stock is purchased solely for investment purposes and voting power is not used to bring about any substantial reduction in competition. For example, the acquiring corporation may be a holding company and no actual or potential anticompetitive effects may be present.[41]

Second, under narrowly worded judicial decisions and administrative guidelines, an acquisition otherwise violating Clayton Section 7 may proceed when the acquired corporation is in failing condition. However, generally the corporation must be insolvent or in imminent danger of financial failure and have no reasonable alternatives as demonstrated by futile attempts to seek other offers of purchase.[42]

On the other hand, economic or social benefits alleged to follow from the acquisition do *not* constitute defense to a Clayton Section 7 action. Otherwise, for example, favorable competitive effects in one market could be used to offset anticompetitive effects in another, so that a corporation might embark on a series of acquisitions to make it competitive with the industry leader.[43] Similarly, an acquisition generally may not be defended on the basis of increased economies of scale after the acquisition, because enforcement authorities feel that such economies usually are not substantial in corporations below the threshold standards for prohibited market effects under Clayton Section 7 or, in larger corporations, may be available through internal expansion rather than acquisition.

Enforcement Measures

If the foregoing antitrust standards are violated — whether or not a notice or similar requirement or advisory opinion is involved — suit may be brought by the FTC or the Antitrust Division, as appropriate, to obtain a preliminary injunction barring the acquisition or requiring that the acquired corporation be maintained as a separate organization, as well as a permanent injunction against all or part of the acquisition or against specified subsequent activities with anticompetitive effects. Generally, this will require a demonstration to the court by the government authority of either probable success on the merits of the dispute, or at least serious questions concerning those merits, *and* the likelihood of irreparable harm if relief is not granted.[44]

In addition — especially in legal action under Clayton Section 7 — forced divestiture after the acquisition is available in spite of the interests of innocent parties such as other shareholders, if it is the only effective remedy; so also is reconstitution of the acquired corporation as a going concern in order to restore competition.[45] Government authorities may seek monetary damages, but only to the extent of actual injury to the government's property. The Antitrust Division also may seek criminal sanctions including fines and imprisonment for violations of Clayton Section 7 — although this is quite unlikely — or of Sherman Section 1 or Sherman Section 2.

In the event of suit by federal authorities, it is often possible to agree to dispose of the particular product line or facility responsible for the challenge by entering into a consent decree — *i.e.,* a court decision taken with the investor's consent. However, the investor — including any corporate officers — should understand that subsequent noncompliance with the decree will constitute contempt of court for which fines and/or imprisonment may be imposed.

In addition, the Attorney General of any state may bring a civil suit in the name of his state on behalf of residents who have sustained an injury as the result of a violation of Sherman Section 1 or Sherman Section 2,[46] although as yet this remains unlikely in the case of a corporate acquisition.

Finally, private suit may be brought under Clayton Section 7, Sherman Section 1, or Sherman Section 2. This is particularly likely where the hostile management of a target corporation wishes to halt a tender offer, or a disgruntled shareholder is dissatisfied with the terms of a proposed acquisition. A competitor who fears the result of an acquisition also may bring such a suit. Such a private suit may seek injunctive relief similar to that which may be sought by government authorities. In addition, the private party may seek *triple* monetary damages for alleged damage to its business or property as a result of the antitrust violation.[47] Even an approximation of lost profits may be recovered under certain circumstances.

It should be noted that very few corporate acquisitions involving foreign investors have been challenged under U.S. antitrust prohibitions. Government authorities have estimated that, of approximately 2,000 acquisitions involving foreign business enterprises over 10 years, only a dozen were challenged by the FTC or the Antitrust Division, including cases in which a U.S. enterprise attempted to acquire the foreign enterprise. In addition, judicial decisions generally have not supported antitrust challenges by private parties and, in particular, have thus far prohibited very few acquisitions by foreign investors.[48]

However, once a foreign investor has acquired a U.S. corporation, any subsequent *foreign* acquisition or other foreign transaction also may well affect U.S. commerce and be subject to more extensive U.S. antitrust scrutiny, as discussed in Chapter VIII respecting foreign operations.

Corporate Law, Contract Terms, and Related Considerations

The tax, financing, securities law, and antitrust considerations described above often determine whether a proposed acquisition will be attempted, as well as the basic structure for the acquisition. However, effecting the acquisition and, in the usual case of a negotiated rather than a hostile transaction, the acquisition contract negotiations may involve U.S. corporate law considerations and contract terms which differ from those abroad. Certain of these considerations also vary with the particular acquisition technique employed.

Letter of Intent

The principal terms of a proposed negotiated transaction often are set forth in a letter of intent between the parties. For example, the parties there state the basic structure and form of the transaction, the percentage stock interest or assets to be acquired, the amount and form of the purchase price, any other commercial or technical benefits which the acquiror intends to contribute to the target corporation, possible commitments to existing management, and a proposed timetable. In addition, the parties typically undertake to keep confidential the information obtained about each other during the negotiations.

A letter of intent usually creates only an obligation to undertake *bona fide* negotiations for a detailed acquisition agreement, and to keep information confidential as noted above. A more detailed or formal commitment prior to execution of the final acquisition agreement probably has little value in creating an enforceable U.S. legal obligation, because independent consent by the board of directors and/or shareholders of the target corporation usually is necessary to effect the acquisition.

Investigation of the Target Corporation

During preparation of the full acquisition agreement and closing arrangements — or during the acquiror's preparation for a proposed hostile acquisition — several matters should be investigated and, if possible, made subject to the acquiror's approval:

First, all financial statements of the target corporation — particularly those publicly available from any prior federal securities law filings of the target — should be reviewed by the acquiror's accountants. In a negotiated transaction, the acquiror's representatives also should fully familiarize themselves with the target's files, books, and records.

Seconu, statutes of the state of incorporation of the target corporation, of each of its subsidiaries, and of each state where the target does business should be reviewed with particular attention to the formal requirements for a corporate acquisition or bulk sale of assets. The target corporation's own corporate documents and capital structure must be reviewed for unusual voting or other provisions, or for possible defensive measures in the case of a hostile acquisition, such as staggered directors' terms or the existence of authorized and previously unissued stock which might be issued for a defensive acquisition.

Third, prior federal and state securities law filings and tax returns of the target corporation should be reviewed by the acquiror and its accountants for omissions or errors which could give rise to future corporate liability. As noted further above, the acquiror also should determine whether the target corporation is subject to any antitrust or trade regulation judgment and whether there may be problems with the proposed acquisition under federal or state antitrust laws, particularly if a hostile acquisition is contemplated and the target's management could invoke such legal prohibitions. Copies of any other pending litigation papers or outstanding legal judgments against the target corporation should be obtained. If the assets or stock are being purchased out of a bankruptcy proceeding, compliance with applicable bankruptcy procedures will be necessary.[49]

Fourth, employment contracts, benefit plans, and deferred compensation liabilities — including possible unfunded multiemployer[50] or other pension liabilities — of the target corporation under federal and other laws must be examined. The acquiror should review the target's previous and current union and other labor contracts and any outstanding labor problems, including severance pay liabilities. Plans should be made to replace stock option and stock bonus plans — particularly for senior management — with incentive compensation from the new foreign owner.

Fifth, the acquiror should examine every additional material contract of the target corporation to determine the acquiror's own liability upon assumption of the contract and its right to assume the same directly or through a new subsidiary. Contracts with parties related to the target's shareholders, directors, or officers should be particularly closely examined for termination rights. All patents, copyrights, trademarks, trade names and similar intangible assets of the target corporation should be properly registered and the duration of their validity confirmed.

Sixth, the current insurance policies of the target corporation should be reviewed. Product liability, property damage insurance, and title insurance on real estate assets are particularly important. The acquiror should investigate the cost of long-term residual product liability insurance covering preacquisition activities of the target. Updated title reports or abstracts and possibly new title insurance for real estate assets are a wise precaution. In the case of workers' compensation insurance, the target's own favorable experience credits for reduced insurance premiums may disappear upon an ownership change.

Investment Regulation

In the course of the foreign acquiror's detailed examination of the target corporation, special regulatory problems for foreign investors, particularly in the applicable industry, should be investigated. A few examples may be helpful:

(1) In the case of a target corporation in the banking, insurance, communications, or similarly highly regulated industry, extensive federal and/or state permits may be required in connection with the acquisition. These are described in Chapter VI in connection with new investments generally in restricted industries. Such regulation may suggest, for example, the use of a stock purchase rather than an asset purchase or statutory merger, because in certain cases foreign stock ownership alone may not trigger investment prohibitions or permits. Moreover, in such a regulated industry, even restrictions not related to foreign ownership may be relevant to the foreign acquiror. For example, in the drug industry U.S. government approval for marketing of a foreign drug manufacturer's own new products by the newly acquired U.S. operation may require several years.

(2) As noted in Chapter VI, the target corporation may be involved in government contracts or licenses that are not permitted to a business enterprise controlled by foreign investors. Accordingly, it may be necessary to separate the target's facilities requiring, for example, a security clearance and place them in trust with management rights limited to U.S. citizens, or to sell off or terminate such operations.

(3) Acquisition of a corporation with U.S. natural resource interests may cause difficulties under special federal or state restrictions on foreign investment, as noted in Chapter III covering such interests.

(4) A major acquisition may involve review by the interagency Committee on Foreign Investment, although its primary concern is foreign government investment.[51] If the target owns subsidiaries or other assets outside the United States, permission also may be required from the foreign country to permit a change in their ownership. On occasion, as noted generally in Chapter I, a potential acquiror may further wish to consider the use of trusts or other methods to ensure the transfer of acquired assets or stock to neutral persons in case of hostilities between the United States and the foreign investor's country.

Where a hostile rather than negotiated acquisition is contemplated, such regulatory problems also may be invoked by the management or dissident shareholders of the target corporation to try to block the transaction.

Acquisition Agreement

In the case of a negotiated transaction, from the acquiror's viewpoint the full U.S. acquisition agreement will provide for a number of matters in addition to the basic terms set forth in the letter of intent, including the following:

First, the target corporation, and/or its shareholders if they are parties to the agreement, typically will represent and warrant to the acquiror several matters, including: the due organization and good standing of the corporation and its subsidiaries; the number and validity of its outstanding shares of stock; the accuracy and completeness of the corporation's financial statements; the absence of undisclosed material corporate liabilities or adverse litigation, of material adverse changes in the corporation, and/or of any knowledge of facts materially adverse to the future business of the corporation; the corporation's title to corporate assets; its compliance with outstanding contracts; the good condition of its machinery and inventory; the collectibility of its accounts receivable; the maintenance of the corporation's insurance coverage; compliance by the corporation with securities and tax laws; compliance with other material applicable federal and state laws, including environmental and occupational health and safety regulations; and the absence of undisclosed finder's and broker's fees.

Second, the target corporation and/or its shareholders should undertake to hold all required directors' and shareholders' meetings; to use their best efforts to secure all required consents of government authorities and third parties for the acquisition, including any specified tax, securities and other government rulings; to discharge all liabilities not to be assumed by the acquiror; and to obtain from the target's employees such employment agreements and agreements not to compete as may be required by the acquiror.

Third, the target corporation and/or its shareholders generally will covenant not to amend corporate documents, declare dividends or alter the capital structure of the target, incur new indebtedness of the target or conduct the corporation's business other than in the normal course, or fail to comply with applicable tax and other laws prior to closing the acquisition.

In connection with the foregoing, personal guaranties by shareholders or other individuals of representations and warranties in the acquisition agreement may be required. It is also common to require a written opinion from legal counsel for the target corporation that the acquisition is duly authorized, that the acquisition agreement will accomplish the transactions which it purports to accomplish, and perhaps that the seller's representations and warranties are true to the best of such counsel's knowledge.

Fourth, the acquiror's obligation to close the acquisition should be subject to various conditions, including: the continued satisfactory condition of the target's business; certificates of specific facts from the target's officers and/or specific legal opinions from its counsel; completion of all necessary corporate actions, including the resignation of officers or directors and election of their replacements, and any required alterations to the target's corporate documents and/or capital structure; and obtaining of all required third party consents, including collateral agreements such as key employees' employment and noncompetition contracts. The agreement may provide that, in the event of a reduction in the target's net worth prior to the closing, a specified reduction in the purchase price will be made.

Fifth, the acquiror usually will require survival of the seller's representations and warranties after the closing. Accordingly, a portion of the purchase consideration may be held in escrow or otherwise deferred for an agreed period following the closing, as a guaranty for the accuracy of such representations and warranties and as a protection against undisclosed liabilities. This provision often is subject to an exclusion for such liabilities up to a stated minimum amount, with the escrowed sum subject only to amounts beyond that limit.

Sixth, the agreement should allocate any known finder's or broker's fees; attorneys' and accountants' fees of the respective parties; appraisal and engineering costs; accrued and unpaid property taxes, and any sales and transfer taxes; and expenses of any shareholders' proxy solicitation, if required, and of obtaining consents from third parties for the acquisition.

Additional Specific Issues

Purchase of assets. With regard specifically to a purchase of assets of the U.S. target corporation, certain additional considerations and terms may be relevant. Each asset — even the target's name — must be conveyed separately and the technique of conveyance will vary with the nature of the asset and its location. Valuable assets such as licenses or contracts may be nontransferable by their terms, and accordingly should be particularly carefully examined.

One tax related item frequently involved in a purchase of assets is a covenant by the seller not to compete with the acquired business. If this is considered part of the general business goodwill acquired, the acquiror cannot deduct the same for tax purposes by amortizing its cost, but the seller may treat the gain as capital gain. If instead this is a valuable service which is specifically allocated an appropriate portion of the purchase price in the acquisition agreement, its cost can be amortized over the covenant's term, but the seller's gain is taxed as ordinary income. Such a covenant also may be involved in acquisitions other than by a direct purchase of assets.

Under applicable state laws, the board of directors of the target corporation generally must authorize a substantial asset sale; often the shareholders must also consent. Many states permit dissenting shareholders of the target to have their shares appraised and paid for, if shareholder approval is required. It is also advisable to require shareholder agreement for the sale of a subsidiary, if the subsidiary constitutes the target's principal asset.

It should be noted that the transferee of substantial corporate assets often is liable to third parties for corporate debts, even though such liability is not assumed under the asset acquisition agreement.

Purchase of controlling stock interest. It may be particularly prudent in the case of a stock acquisition to place part of the purchase consideration in escrow for an agreed period as security against unknown or undisclosed corporate liabilities, because such debts or legal claims may substantially reduce the stock's worth.

The target corporate documents also should be examined for the percentage of shareholder approval required for various future corporate actions because, unless the acquiror obtains sufficient shares, it may be faced with potentially troublesome minority shareholders. In addition, restrictions on the target corporation by its lenders may require their consent to a change of stock control.

If the target corporation is to be liquidated or merged after the acquisition for tax or other reasons, then restrictions on asset transfers also must be examined as in the case of a purchase of assets.

Subscription to share increase. The principal advantage of this technique is that the acquisition price remains in the target corporation, rather than being paid out to selling shareholders. However, the target's corporate documents should be examined to confirm that existing shareholders do not have pre-emptive rights to subscribe to the newly issued stock.

Where the investor wishes to obtain further subscription rights in excess of the initial issuance, it should be noted that — in contrast to many foreign countries — most states do not permit a new shareholder to pay partly for currently issued stock subject to a future call for the balance. However, the investor may be granted an option to purchase the additional stock later. In certain states, a properly secured promissory note payable later also may be treated as sufficient value for a larger current stock issuance. A further alternative to initial payment for control may be the negotiation of a management contract to assure representation on the target's board of directors. This contract may be made with the corporation itself, with the controlling shareholders, or with both.

If the foreign investor intends to add nonmonetary assets to the target corporation, existing creditors' security interests in corporate assets should be investigated and/or negotiated, since these may reach property acquired later by the corporation.

Merger. Statutory merger of the U.S. corporation into the acquiring foreign corporation, or more likely into a U.S. or foreign subsidiary of the foreign acquiror, under applicable state corporate law accomplishes in one event a substitution of the new corporation for the old, and may provide a taxfree reorganization for the target's shareholders.

However, such a merger generally requires at least a favorable majority vote of the target corporation's shareholders. Dissenting shareholders usually have the right to have their stock appraised and paid for at the appraised value if the merger is consummated.

It should be noted that in a merger even unknown or contingent liabilities of the nonsurviving corporation become obligations of the surviving corporation, and so should be permitted under the parties' agreement to be offset against a deferred portion of the purchase price.

Restrictions on transfer of the target's assets often apply to a merger. Accordingly, a new corporation formed by the foreign investor may instead consider merging into the corporation being acquired, in order not to disturb valuable assets in the target.

Closing and Reporting the Acquisition

Prior to the closing of a negotiated transaction, it is common for legal counsel for the respective parties to conduct a mock closing at which all documents are assembled and examined in order to avoid delays later.

At the closing, the required persons and items usually include, for example, the signatories, a notary public, a cashier's or certified check for any cash consideration, corporate seals, certificates of corporate good standing, tax and other government clearances, documentary stamps and title insurance commitments, and bank certifications of any share endorsements. However, part or all of the closing often can take place simultaneously in the United States and abroad through a telephone conference with a representative of each party at the other's office to verify the execution and accept delivery of duplicate closing documents.

Following the acquisition, applicable reporting requirements of the U.S. Department of Commerce respecting a U.S. corporation or branch owned at least 10% by foreign persons, and of the federal tax authorities respecting transactions of a U.S. corporation controlled by a foreign person, must be satisfied. If the target corporation owns U.S. agricultural property, at least 200 acres of U.S. real estate, or other U.S. natural resources, additional reporting may be required. All of these are discussed in greater detail in Chapter XII regarding reporting of U.S. investments from abroad.

In summary, a foreign investor contemplating acquisition of a controlling interest in an existing U.S. corporation should determine the appropriate acquisition technique at least partly in view of U.S. and other tax and financing considerations. Potential securities and antitrust law issues then must be analyzed. Finally, corporate law, investment regulation, contract terms, and related considerations — including those appropriate to the specific acquisition technique — must be included in the investigation and documentation for the acquisition.

Footnotes to Chapter VII

1. *See generally* I.R.C. §§269, 354-368, 381-383.

2. *See* I.R.C. §367(a); Temp. Treas. Reg. §7.367(a)-1; Rev. Proc. 68-23, 1968-1 C.B. 821; Rev. Proc. 76-20, 1976-1 C.B. 560; Rev. Proc. 77-5, 1977-1 C.B. 536.

3. I.R.C. §351.

4. I.R.C. §§269, 382, 383. More stringent limitations on the use of the target's net operating losses and other tax benefits following an acquisition are not effective until 1984.

5. *See* I.R.C. §§337, 46-50, 1245, 1250.

6. I.R.C. 338; *see* I.R.C. §§311(d)(2), (e), 331, 334(b), 346. Prior law permitted such a step-up under I.R.C. §334(b)(2) upon liquidation of the target by an acquiring corporation within two years after the stock purchase.

7. *See* I.R.C. §§453, 368(a).

8. *See* I.R.C. §§338(e)(2)(D), (h)(6)(B); Chapter VIII *infra.*

9. I.R.C. §195.

10. I.R.C. §§163, 1501-1564.

11. I.R.C. §243.

12. *See* I.R.C. §§267, 279, 385, 482; Treas. Reg. §§1.385-0 *et seq.*; Chapter II *supra.*

13. I.R.C. §§871(a)(1), 881(a); *see, e.g.,* United States-Netherlands Income Tax Treaty of 1948, as amended and presently in force between the United States and the Netherlands Antilles ("U.S.-Netherlands Antilles Treaty"), Art. VIII(1).

14. I.R.C. §§861(a)(2)(B), 875; *see, e.g.,* U.S.-Netherlands Antilles Treaty, Art. XII; Chapter II *supra.*

15. *See* Securities Exchange Act of 1934, S.E.C. Release No. 16371, 44 Fed. Reg. 70132 (1979); Securities Act of 1933, S.E.C. Releases No. 6360, 6361, 6362, 46 Fed. Reg. 58511, 58505, 58507 (1981), No. 6437 (1982). Foreign issuers whose securities are traded in the United States but are *not* publicly offered or listed here are considered not to have voluntarily entered the United States and do not have to comply with registration or reporting requirements under the 1934 Act if they furnish to the SEC certain information distributed to shareholders or otherwise disclosed under foreign law. *See* Securities Exchange Act of 1934, S.E.C. Rule 12g-2(b).

Further discussion of many of the considerations in the remainder of this chapter may be found in portions of L. LeLievre, *Foreign Investment in the U.S.: A Guide for Executives and Counsel* (1977).

16. *See generally* Chapter I *supra;* B. Thomas, "Extraterritorial Application of the United States Securities Laws: the Need for a Balanced Policy," 2 Int'l Financial L. Rev. 545 (1981); *cf.* Schoenbaum v. Firstbrook, 405 F.2d 200, *rev'd in part and remanded,* 405 F.2d 215 (2d Cir. 1968), *cert. denied*, Manley v. Schoenbaum, 395 U.S. 906 (1969); Leasco Data Processing Equip. Corp. v. Maxwell, 468 F.2d 1326 (2d Cir. 1972); Bersch v. Drexel Firêstone, Inc., 519 F.2d 974 (2d Cir. 1975), *cert. denied,* 423 U.S. 1018 (1975); IIT v. Vencap, Ltd., 519 F.2d 1001 (2d Cir. 1975); S.E.C. v. Kasser, 548 F.2d 109 (3d Cir. 1977), *cert. denied,* 431 U.S. 938 (1977); Continental Grain (Australia) Pty. Ltd. v. Pacific Oilseeds, Inc., 592 F.2d 409 (8th Cir. 1979); IIT v. Cornfeld, 619 F.2d 909 (2d Cir. 1980); *see also* Affiliated Ute Citizens v. United States, 406 U.S. 128 (1972); Ernst & Ernst v. Hochfelder, 425 U.S. 185 (1976); Chapter IX *infra.*

17. *See* Perlman v. Feldmann, 219 F.2d 173 (2d Cir. 1954), *cert. denied,* 349 U.S. 952(1955).

18. *See generally* 15 U.S.C. §§78m, 78n; Chapter I *supra.*

19. *See* Foremost McKesson, Inc. v. Provident Sec. Co., 423 U.S. 232 (1976); Kern County Land Co. v. Occidental Petroleum Corp., 411 U.S. 582 (1973).

20. 15 U.S.C. §§78m(d)-(e), 78n(d)-(f).

21. *Cf.* Corenco Corp. v. Schiavone & Sons, Inc., 362 F. Supp. 939 (S.D.N.Y. 1973). The extent to which these must be modified to conform to U.S. accounting practice may vary with the foreign investor's financial strength; *see, e.g.,* Copperweld Corp. v. Imetal, 403 F. Supp. 579 (W.D. Pa. 1975).

22. *See, e.g.,* Order of Attachment in S.E.C. v. American Institute Counsellors Inc. (D.D.C. 1976); *cf.* GAF Corp. v. Milstein, 453 F. 2d 709 (2d Cir. 1971), *cert. denied,* 406 U.S. 910 (1972); Bath Industries, Inc. v. Blot, 427 F. 2d 97 (7th Cir. 1970). If an investor acquires five percent or more of a target corporation's stock and then buys additional stock from a registered investment company which owns at least five percent of the stock, Section 17 of the Investment Company Act of 1940 is violated. *See* 15 U.S.C. §80a-17; Chapter I *supra.*

23. *See* Securities Exchange Act of 1934, S.E.C. Rules 134, 135.

24. 15 U.S.C. §80a; *see also* Chapter I *supra.*

25. *Cf.* Texasgulf, Inc. v. Canadian Development Corp., 366 F. Supp. 374 (S.D. Tex. 1973); Copperweld Corp. v. Imetal, 403 F. Supp. 579 (W.D. Pa. 1975); TSC Indus. v. Northway, 512 F. 2d 324 (7th Cir. 1975), *rev'd and remanded,* 426 U.S. 438 (1976).

26. The former have included, for example, Alaska, Colorado, Connecticut, Delaware, Hawaii, Idaho, Illinois, Indiana, Kansas, Kentucky, Louisiana, Maryland, Massachusetts, Michigan, Minnesota, Nevada, New Jersey, New York, Ohio, Oklahoma, Pennsylvania, South Carolina, South Dakota, Tennessee, Utah, Virginia, and Wisconsin. The latter have included, for example, Mississippi, Montana, and New Mexico.

27. These have included, for example, Illinois, Indiana, Ohio, Pennsylvania, and Wisconsin.

28. Edgar v. Mite Corp., CCH Federal Securities Law Reports ("CCH") §98728 (U.S. Sup. Ct. 1982), *aff'g* 633 F.2d 486 (7th Cir. 1980); *see* Great Western United Corp. v. Kidwell, 439 F. Supp. 420 (N.D. Tex. 1977), *aff'd,* 577 F. 2d 1256 (5th Cir. 1978), *rev'd on other grounds,* 443 U.S. 173 (1979) (Idaho statute); Dart Industries, Inc. v. Conrad, 462 F. Supp. 1 (S.D. Ind. 1978) (Delaware statute); Hi-Shear Industries, Inc. v. Campbell, CCH §97804 (D. So. Carolina 1980) (South Carolina statute); Natomas Co. v. Bryan, 512 F. Supp. 191 (D. Nev. 1981) (Nevada statute); Joseph E. Seagram & Sons, Inc. v. Marley, CCH §98246 (W. D. Okla. 1981) (Oklahoma statute). *But see* AMCA Int'l Corp. v. Krouse, 482 F. Supp. 929 (S.D. Ohio 1979) (Ohio statute held constitutional and not wholly pre-empted by Williams Act).

29. 15 U.S.C. §§1, 2, 18, 45(a); *see also* Chapter I *supra.*

30. *See* Dean Foods Co., 70 F.T.C. 1146 (1966).

31. *See* United States v. Penn-Olin Chemical Co., 378 U.S. 158 (1964).

32. 15 U.S.C. §18a; 16 C.F.R. Parts 801-803; U.S. Dep't of Justice (Antitrust Division), Notification and Report Form for Certain Mergers and Acquisitions (C4). The size criteria apply to the entire corporate structure of each party, rather than to the size of, for example, a subsidiary formed to make the acquisition. These reporting requirements also apply to a proposed acquisition of a U.S. division or other unincorporated business enterprise, if the acquiror itself is a corporation. On the other hand, several specific types of transactions are exempted from the requirements.

33. Further details on these advisory opinion and business review procedures may be obtained from the Office of the General Counsel of the FTC and from the Assistant Attorney General of the Antitrust Division in Washington, D.C.

34. *See* Brown Shoe Co. v. United States, 370 U.S. 294 (1962); United States v. E.I. du Pont de Nemours & Co., 351 U.S. 377 (1956).

35. U.S. Dep't of Justice, *Merger Guidelines* (1982). For guidelines in the analogous situation of a U.S. corporation's sale or acquisition of a foreign corporation, see U.S. Dep't of Justice, *Antitrust Guide for International Operations* (1977).

36. *See, e.g.,* United States v. Falstaff Brewing Corp., 410 U.S. 526 (1973); BOC Int'l, Ltd. v. F.T.C., 577 F. 2d 24 (2d Cir. 1977).

37. *See* The Budd Co., 86 F.T.C. 518 (1975).

38. *See* United States v. Marine Bancorporation, Inc., 418 U.S. 602 (1974).

39. *See, e.g.,* F.T.C. v. Consolidated Foods Corp., 380 U.S. 592 (1965); United States v. E.I. du Pont de Nemours & Co., 353 U.S. 586 (1957).

40. *See, e.g.,* F.T.C. v. Proctor & Gamble Co., 386 U.S. 568 (1967); United States v. Aluminum Co. of America, 233 F. Supp. 718 (E.D.Mo. 1964).

41. *See, e.g.,* Texasgulf, Inc. v. Canada Development Corp., 366 F. Supp. 374 (S.D. Tex. 1973).

42. *See, e.g.,* Citizen Publishing Co. v. United States, 394 U.S. 131 (1969); Int'l Shoe Co. v. F.T.C., 280 U.S. 291 (1930).

43. *See, e.g.,* United States v. Philadelphia Nat'l Bank, 374 U.S. 321 (1963). However, in the case of bank mergers, special legislation permits the convenience and needs of the community to be weighed. Bank Merger Act of 1976, 12 U.S.C. §1828(c).

44. *See, e.g.,* Copperweld Corp. v. Imetal, 403 F. Supp. 579 (W.D. Pa. 1975).

45. *See, e.g.,* United States v. E.I. du Pont de Nemours & Co., 366 U.S. 316 (1961); Maryland & Virginia Milk Producers Ass'n, Inc. v. United States, 362 U.S. 458 (1960).

46. 15 U.S.C. §15c.

47. 15 U.S.C. §15.

48. *E.g.,* the successful Imetal-Copperweld, BOC International-Airco, and Matsushita-Motorola acquisitions described in L. LeLievre, *supra* note 15.

49. *See* 11 U.S.C. §§101 *et seq.*; Chapter VI *supra.*

50. *See* 29 U.S.C. §§1001 *et seq.*; 29 C.F.R. Parts 2670, 2672.

51. *See* Chapter I *supra.* However, this committee does not have authority to prohibit an acquisition or other investment, as indicated by its unsuccessful opposition to acquisition of Texasgulf, Inc. interests in 1981 by a French government controlled oil company.

Chapter VIII

The United States as a Base for Foreign Operations

Under various circumstances, foreign investors may wish or be required to use the United States as a base for new or continuing foreign operations. For example, a foreign business enterprise or its U.S. or foreign subsidiary corporation may wish to export goods manufactured within or imported into the United States to additional Western Hemisphere or other foreign countries. Alternatively, a nonresident alien individual who becomes a U.S. resident or citizen may continue to own all or a portion of his non-U.S. business enterprises or portfolio investments. The details of U.S. planning for foreign operations by a domestic investor cannot readily be summarized in a single chapter; this chapter describes briefly, however, certain key U.S. regulatory and tax considerations involved in export activities and foreign investments from the United States with emphasis on matters which may be of particular concern to foreign investors or somewhat unique to the United States.

Export Activities

Export Restrictions

U.S. export controls are administered, first, by the U.S. Department of Commerce, under whose regulations *all* exports of U.S. goods or technology require licenses. These are the general responsibility of the Office of Export Administration within the Department's International Trade Administration. However, export of technical data in patent applications is governed by the U.S. Patent and Trademark Office. Since 1979, the U.S. Department of Defense also has participated in the identification of critical technologies whose export should be so restricted for national military security. Any item not on the commodity control list under the regulations may be exported under a general license, which is not requested from the Department of Commerce but simply is filled out by the private freight forwarder or other exporter. However, intentional misstatements respecting these or related matters may result in fines or imprisonment.[1]

Export of any item on the commodity control list requires a validated license, principally in order to prevent strategic materials from being obtained by hostile foreign countries, to enforce embargoes in accordance with U.S. foreign policy, and to prevent export of items in short supply in the United States. A validated license may be granted to any person under U.S. jurisdiction either for a continuing export business or for a particular time period or country. Such a license also restricts re-exporting from the original country abroad. For example, an item used by a related enterprise in the original country cannot be re-exported to a third country, unless the item could have been exported directly to that country without such a license. Failure to comply with these requirements may result in the exporting enterprise being prevented from exporting for a period of time or otherwise put on a blacklist. An enterprise abroad which fails to comply with such requirements also may be placed on a blacklist, which has the effect of preventing exports to that enterprise.

Second, under the general Foreign Assets Control Regulations pursuant to the Trading with the Enemy Act, all U.S. export and other transactions with persons of listed countries require licenses from the U.S. Department of the Treasury.[2]

Third, a separate license from the Department of State is required for export of war materiel or related technology. Similarly, the export of nuclear materials, equipment, or technology requires licenses from various U.S. agencies. The Department of the Treasury also administers the Transaction Control Regulations, whose principal aim is to limit the movement of strategic materials by persons within the United States from *foreign* countries to communist controlled countries. Such items include certain particularly sensitive materials on the Department of Commerce's commodity control list. Again, re-export of such items by a related enterprise abroad to a prohibited country generally is contrary to regulations.[3]

Any U.S. individual on the board of directors of a foreign corporation or in a similar position must be aware of these prohibitions. On the other hand, in light of different laws in the country of the foreign enterprise, it may be wise to assure that no U.S. individual serves on such a board.[4] For example, the attempt in 1982 to extend U.S. restrictions on exports to the U.S.S.R. of natural gas pipeline equipment to cover *foreign* based enterprises making goods under U.S. licenses provoked contrary foreign governmental orders to local enterprises.

Notification of export from the United States of certain potentially harmful items — for example, a product which fails to meet standard federal consumer product safety regulations — no longer must be provided to the foreign destination government. However, extensive regulations do apply generally to U.S. shipments of hazardous materials.[5]

Customs Duties

If exported items manufactured within the United States will include components or raw materials previously imported subject to U.S. customs duty, two techniques are available to recover all or most of such duty. First, parts or materials may be imported without duty by posting of temporary importation bonds. Second, the importer may apply for drawback — *i.e.,* refund of 99% of the duty paid upon importation — by asking for a drawback rate from U.S. customs officials prior to export. Alternatively, imported items may be used in manufacturing, packaged, or otherwise manipulated within a foreign trade zone and subsequently shipped abroad without the necessity of paying duty.

In addition, items manufactured within the United States may be exported for sorting or packaging, repairs or alterations, or further processing or assembly abroad — for example, within a Mexican border zone qualifying for special local incentives. If these items then are returned to the United States, U.S. customs duty may be limited to that on the value of such processing abroad or, under certain circumstances, may be eliminated.

These and related matters are discussed further in Chapter V dealing generally with import activities.

Furthermore, government related assistance for exports — such as Commodity Credit Corporation, Export-Import Bank, and Foreign Credit Insurance Association financing programs for export sales — generally is available based on the U.S. situs of production even where the U.S. enterprise is owned by foreign persons.

Income Tax Considerations

Several considerations in connection with U.S. income taxation of export profits should be noted by foreign investors.

Taxation of foreign activities of a U.S. office. Foreign investors who establish a U.S. office or other fixed place of business for U.S. activities or investments may wish to use that office for activities related to foreign sales, licensing, or other foreign investments. Usually, foreign investors are taxed by the United States only on U.S. source income as described in Chapter II. However, certain foreign income attributable to such an office will be taxed under federal law as effectively connected with the conduct of a U.S. trade or business.[6] These include sales profits from inventory and other personal property; royalties and rents from intangible property such as patents and technology licenses; and banking, financing, and securities trading income. Items of such foreign income may be attributed to the office if the office is a material factor in producing the income and the income producing activity is regularly carried on by the office. For example, sales against orders received by the U.S. office may be considered to be made through that office if the orders are accepted or regularly filled there.

However, even such foreign sales income will not be taxable if an office or other fixed place of business outside the United States participates materially in the sale — for example, by soliciting the order, negotiating the contract, or performing significant services incident to the sale. In addition, if the foreign owner of the office is located in a country with which the United States has an income tax treaty, foreign income of such a U.S. permanent establishment usually is not subject to federal taxation.

If foreign income is attributed to such an office, expenses connected with that income — whether incurred in the United States or abroad — may be used to reduce the federal taxable income. In addition, the foreign enterprise generally may credit against its federal income tax the taxes paid or accrued to a foreign country or U.S. possession with respect to such foreign income.[7]

State and local unitary, inventory, and other taxes also should be investigated prior to such export sales from a U.S. office or other U.S. enterprise. A few states extend property and inventory tax exemptions even to *local* goods while they are stored awaiting shipment to a destination outside the state.[8]

Sales to related foreign enterprise. If exported goods are sold to a foreign enterprise, the foreign resale profits of that enterprise ordinarily are not subject to U.S. income taxes. However, such a foreign enterprise generally should not be controlled by a U.S. subsidiary or other U.S. owners, as discussed in greater detail below respecting foreign investments, but may be owned by the foreign investors or one of their foreign subsidiaries. The foreign purchaser also should not itself maintain a U.S. office or other fixed place of business to which its purchases or resales abroad are attributable, as noted above.

More significantly, such export sales between controlled parties must be made at arm's length prices and other terms. Federal tax authorities may reallocate total income among such enterprises, either to prevent evasion of taxes or clearly to reflect income, and applicable regulations interpret this to require controlled taxpayers to deal with each other on such an arm's length basis.[9] These regulations are quite detailed and cover, for example, sales of property, use of tangible and intangible property, provision of services, and loans or advances between related parties. In addition, if a foreign income tax has been paid by the foreign enterprise, a subsequent reallocation of the income to the U.S. enterprise usually results in double taxation of the same income, subject to limited relief under certain U.S. administrative procedures and income tax treaties.[10]

Domestic International Sales Corporation. The Domestic International Sales Corporation ("DISC") federal tax provisions[11] are designed primarily to encourage a U.S. manufacturing enterprise to form a DISC as a wholly owned domestic subsidiary to purchase U.S. products from its parent and resell them for export, or to act as a sales commission agent for its parent on export sales. However, the DISC need not be owned by such a U.S. manufacturing enterprise. Indeed, up to one-half of the cost of the exported goods may be attributable to foreign components.

The DISC itself need not have employees: the employees of a related manufacturer may handle all negotiations, shipping, billing, and collections in its name. The principal requirements for qualification are that at least 95% of the DISC's gross receipts consist of certain export receipts and that at least 95% of the adjusted basis of its assets at the end of the taxable year consist of certain export assets. In addition, the DISC must have only one class of stock, of which the par value of the outstanding shares must be at least $2,500 on each day of the taxable year; must elect to be treated as a DISC with the consent of all of its shareholders; must maintain a separate bank account and books and records; and should have a written agreement with any related manufacturer or supplier to act as a principal or commission agent in export sales.

The DISC is not subject to federal income tax. In addition, it may increase its income by purchasing export goods from a related supplier at less than an arm's length price, including splitting equally the combined taxable income of itself and its related supplier from total export receipts on the sale.

However, the DISC's shareholders are taxed as if they had received at the end of its taxable year a dividend of at least one-half (57½% after 1982 in the case of most corporate shareholders) of the DISC's taxable income (or more to the extent that additional sums actually are distributed or disposition of the DISC's stock is made). This taxable dividend also is not less than a certain fraction of the DISC's income which is determined by the increase in export receipts in comparison to such receipts for a previous base period. The fraction is the ratio between approximately two-thirds of the DISC's average annual export gross receipts for the four years ending four years previously, and its export gross receipts for the current year. Thus, steady increases in such receipts eventually are required for maximum tax deferral. Even if the DISC is owned directly by the foreign investors or by a foreign corporation owned by them, and even if a U.S. income tax treaty is applicable, these deemed dividends, and other dividends and gain on disposition of the DISC's stock, generally will be subject to federal tax at the rates payable by U.S. persons.[12]

In order to utilize the share of the DISC's taxable income which is not currently taxed to either the DISC or its shareholders, the DISC may make producer's loans of up to its accumulated income to a person engaged in the production of export property in the United States. However, these may be difficult for foreign investors to utilize because, if during the DISC's taxable year there is either actual foreign investment or a net increase in foreign assets within the controlled group of corporations of which the DISC is a member, then a corresponding amount of any producer's loan by the DISC generally is taxed currently to the DISC's shareholders as a dividend.

It should be noted that certain state income tax laws — for example, those of Delaware and New York — include tax deferral similar to the federal DISC provisions. However, certain states — such as California — deny or limit such benefits.

The DISC provisions have been challenged by certain other countries as a violation of the General Agreement on Tariffs and Trade — to which the United States is a party — and especially of its prohibition on most so called export subsidies. Accordingly, further developments in this area — and the development of alternative export trading entities such as the export trading company referred to at the end of this chapter — should be followed.

Additional preferential treatment. The special Western Hemisphere Trade Corporation federal tax deduction was eliminated beginning in 1980.[13] However, use of a Possessions Corporation — discussed further below — may be advantageous in connection with manufacturing for export sales. Special regulatory standards for arm's length pricing between a U.S. enterprise and a related corporation organized in Puerto Rico also may permit that corporation a larger share of total income without U.S. federal taxation.[14]

Foreign Investments from the United States

Where foreign investors may wish or be required to use the United States as a base for foreign investments beyond simply export sales, they should be aware of certain further U.S. tax and regulatory considerations.

Taxation of Foreign Investments

First, as noted above in connection with export sales, use of a U.S. office by foreign investors for activities related to foreign sales, licensing, or other foreign investments generally should be avoided because this may result in current U.S. taxation of certain foreign income attributable to that U.S. office.

As a second alternative, the ownership of a foreign branch or of other foreign investments directly by a U.S. corporation, resident individual, or other U.S. person will result in federal taxation of its or his worldwide income on a current basis. However, certain tax planning alternatives may be considered in this latter situation.

Use of foreign subsidiary. If a foreign subsidiary of a U.S. corporation, resident individual, or other U.S. person is used to carry on the foreign operations, the United States generally will tax only U.S. source income of the foreign corporation as described in Chapter II.

However, a foreign subsidiary generally cannot pay dividends to its domestic parent corporation subject to the 85% or 100% dividends received deduction. In addition, a foreign corporation ordinarily may not file a consolidated federal income tax return with its parent or other corporations. Accordingly, in order to consolidate and derive immediate federal tax advantage from foreign start-up and operating losses, the operations usually must be conducted through a foreign branch rather than through a foreign corporation, subject to the foreign loss recapture described below. Even then, deductible accelerated cost recovery allowances for foreign real property and most equipment used predominantly outside the United States are substantially reduced, and the investment tax credit usually is not available for such equipment. Any such foreign branch *or* subsidiary may have to maintain extra books and records at locations and with translations convenient for the U.S. Internal Revenue Service, and penalties for failure to produce foreign based documents may apply.[15]

The organization of a foreign corporation or acquisition of five percent or more in value of the stock of a foreign corporation (or of an interest in a foreign partnership) by a U.S. person requires the filing of information returns with federal tax authorities. Annual information returns also often are required from U.S. officers, directors, and/or substantial shareholders of a foreign corporation (and from a foreign partnership with a U.S. partner). In connection with the transfer of patents, trademarks, inventory, equipment, and other appreciated property — even foreign currency — by a U.S. corporation or other U.S. person to such a foreign subsidiary — for example, by transformation of a foreign branch into a foreign subsidiary — special regulatory and ruling requirements, including possible taxation of certain such appreciation as a toll charge, generally must be met in order to avoid taxation of the entire appreciation on a current basis at capital gain or ordinary income tax rates. In addition, the spin-off or other reorganization of such a subsidiary by the U.S. person may be fully taxable by the United States unless similar regulatory and toll charge requirements are met.[16]

As a means to relieve international double taxation of income, foreign income taxes, excess profit taxes, and taxes in lieu thereof paid directly by a U.S. person generally may be credited at the taxpayer's election against federal income tax, rather than deducted from gross income. In the case of a resident alien, under certain circumstances, the credit may be denied unless his country of citizenship allows a similar credit to U.S. citizens; however, this requirement generally has not been invoked. In addition, a U.S. *corporation* is treated as having paid qualifying taxes paid by certain of its foreign corporate subsidiaries. These can then be credited by the U.S. corporation upon its receipt of dividends taxable at ordinary income rates out of the foreign corporations' accumulated net profits on or with respect to which the foreign taxes were paid.

However, the definition of a foreign tax which qualifies for the credit often is a matter of dispute. In addition, the amount of the foreign tax credit generally is limited to the same fraction of the taxpayer's total federal income tax which taxable foreign source income comprises of the taxpayer's worldwide taxable income. Thus, a loss by the U.S. person in one or more foreign countries limits the credit by reducing taxable foreign income, but usually does not result in a corresponding reduction in the aggregate foreign tax burden. In addition, a prior overall foreign loss of the U.S. person — which may have reduced U.S. income taxes — must be recaptured against later taxable foreign income before that income can be included in calculating the foreign tax credit limitation, so that foreign taxes on that amount of income may not be creditable. The allocation of U.S. expenses to foreign income also may reduce the credit by reducing such foreign income, yet the expenses may not be deductible abroad to reduce the foreign tax burden. Certain special limitations and rules apply to foreign taxes on mineral income, certain interest income, foreign oil and gas income, and dividends from a DISC. However, excess uncreditable taxes may be carried back two years and forward five years under most circumstances.[17]

Where a foreign subsidiary is used, the controlled foreign corporation ("CFC") provisions[18] may impose federal tax on a U.S. parent corporation or other substantial U.S. shareholders by treating certain tainted income of the CFC as a dividend, even if it is not distributed to them. This income consists primarily of the following: (1) foreign personal holding company income, including most dividends, interest, rents, royalties, and the like; (2) income from sales of inventory and other tangible personal property by the CFC for use outside its country of incorporation, where the CFC either buys the property from or sells it to a related U.S. or other person outside its country of incorporation; and (3) income from services performed by the CFC outside its country of incorporation for a related U.S. or other person. These provisions also tax the U.S. shareholders on certain investments by the CFC in the United States, and on income earned by a foreign captive insurance company from the insurance of U.S. risks. It should be noted that, if a CFC is involved in a corporate reorganization and taxfree treatment is not obtained, even the gain from the reorganization may be treated as such tainted income and taxed currently as ordinary income of the U.S. shareholders. These provisions also encompass, for example, a significant portion of the heavy construction business conducted outside the United States by U.S. persons through a CFC, unless the CFC itself is a substantial operating entity.

However, a number of exceptions permit deferral or elimination of current taxation of the CFC's U.S. shareholders. In addition, current taxation of the CFC's undistributed income is accompanied by an indirect foreign tax credit similar to that in the case of a dividend from a foreign subsidary. An individual U.S. shareholder of a CFC also may elect treatment as if he were a U.S. corporation, including the benefit of this indirect credit.

Any gain on the ultimate sale or exchange of CFC stock — or a taxable liquidation of the CFC — usually will be treated as a dividend and taxed as ordinary income to the U.S. shareholders to the extent of *all* of the CFC's earnings and profits accumulated while it was a CFC, even if they include no tainted income. Again, to the extent of such dividend taxation, an indirect foreign tax credit applies.

The somewhat similar foreign personal holding company provisions apply only where more than one-half in value of the outstanding stock of the foreign subsidiary is owned by five or fewer U.S. citizens or resident aliens, and at least 60% of its gross income for the taxable year is certain passive income (or at least 50% for each subsequent taxable year after qualification, until three consecutive nonqualifying years).[19] In addition, a foreign *or* U.S. corporation may be a personal holding company — whose undistributed income is subject to a federal tax of 50% (70% prior to 1982) — if at least one-half in value of its outstanding stock is owned by five or fewer U.S. *or* foreign individuals, and at least 60% of its gross income is certain passive income. However, a foreign corporation owned 90% or more by nonresident aliens is subject to very limited taxation under these latter provisions.[20]

Use of other related foreign enterprises. In order to avoid the difficulties in using a foreign subsidiary of a U.S. corporation or other U.S. person, for example, under the CFC provisions, a foreign parent enterprise may cause foreign sales, licensing, or other foreign investments to be conducted by foreign enterprises owned directly by it or one of its other foreign enterprises, rather than by a U.S. subsidiary or other U.S. owners.[21] However, as noted above in connection with export sales, transactions between a U.S. subsidiary or other U.S. enterprise and such a related foreign enterprise still must be made at arm's length prices and other terms. For example, a license of tangible property such as a patent or other technology by the U.S. enterprise for use abroad by a related foreign enterprise must include an arm's length royalty payable to the U.S. licensor. If not, a subsequent reallocation of the income to the U.S. enterprise may result in double taxation of the same income if a foreign income tax has been paid by the foreign enterprise.

U.S. tax reduction provisions. First, income from U.S. possessions — for example, American Samoa, Guam, Midway and Wake Islands, Puerto Rico, or the U.S. Virgin Islands — often is entitled to favorable federal taxation. A U.S. corporation at least 80% of whose gross income for the three most recent full taxable years is derived from U.S. possession sources and at least 65% (50-60% for 1982-1984) of whose gross income for that period is derived from the active conduct of a trade or business in possessions ("Possessions Corporation") may elect to receive a full credit against the federal tax on foreign income from that active business and from certain possessions investment income. This may be particularly valuable in the case of Puerto Rico, which has its own extensive local tax holiday and incentive program for foreign investments in manufacturing and certain service industries. In addition, dividends and liquidating distributions from such a domestic Possessions Corporation may be received free of U.S. and most Puerto Rico tax by a U.S. parent corporation *or* foreign shareholder. However, after 1982 the shareholders are subject — or, in the case of foreign shareholders, the Possessions Corporation itself is subject — to tax on income from any patents or other intangible property licensed to the corporation, unless the corporation elects to pay for its share of product research of its affiliated group or to limit its income to one-half of the combined income of its affiliated group (other than foreign affiliates) from possessions products or services.[22]

This credit does not apply to operations in the U.S. Virgin Islands. Such operations of a U.S. corporation or other U.S. person generally are subject to U.S. income taxation with a foreign tax credit for V.I. taxes. However, income of a U.S. corporation managed and controlled in the Virgin Islands, and dividends and liquidating distributions from the corporation, may be received free of U.S. and usually V.I. tax under conditions and limitations very similar to those for a Possessions Corporation.[23]

As to individuals involved in U.S. possessions, a *bona fide* resident of Puerto Rico for the entire taxable year is taxable only by Puerto Rico on most local source income. However, this exemption is *not* available to an alien resident of Puerto Rico, who remains subject to worldwide U.S. income taxation just as any resident alien of the United States.

In the case of operations in U.S. possessions other than Puerto Rico and the U.S. Virgin Islands, a U.S. citizen is exempted from federal taxation of *all* foreign source gross income not received in the United States if at least 80% of his gross income for the three most recent full taxable years is derived from such a U.S. possession and at least one-half of his gross income for that period is derived from the active conduct of a trade or business in such a possession. Correspondingly, he is not entitled to the federal foreign tax credit. In addition, any citizen of a U.S. possession other than Puerto Rico and the U.S. Virgin Islands, who is not also a U.S. resident or citizen, simply is taxed by the United States as a nonresident alien. In the case of an individual resident of Guam, he must generally file his income tax returns with Guam rather than the United States.[24]

In connection with increasing U.S. interest in Caribbean countries generally, new U.S. accelerated depreciation, investment tax credit, and other incentives for investments there also have been considered.

Second, in addition to these provisions, a U.S. citizen working abroad who is either a *bona fide* resident for an entire taxable year or physically present for 330 full days in any 12-month period in one or more foreign countries (or a U.S. resident alien meeting the latter foreign presence test) may: (1) elect to exclude each taxable year up to $95,000 ($75,000-90,000 per year for 1982-1985) of foreign earned income; and/or (2) elect to exclude each taxable year any foreign housing cost amount exceeding 16% of the salary of a U.S. federal government employee at grade GS-14 (and to deduct such amount from any taxable foreign earned income to the extent paid by him and not reimbursed by his employer); and (3) exclude any meals and lodging furnished to him in a foreign camp maintained by or for his employer. An individual also may deduct more moving expenses in connection with commencing work abroad than for such a move within the United States.[25]

It should be noted that compensation paid to *nonresident alien* employees of a U.S. corporation or other enterprise or its foreign subsidiary for services abroad generally is not subject to U.S. income tax withholding or reporting by the employer. However, the accrued obligations of a U.S. corporation or foreign subsidiary under a pension plan maintained primarily for nonresident alien employees may be deducted by the employer for U.S. federal income tax purposes similarly to those under a plan for U.S. employees.[26]

Third, as noted generally in Chapter II, dividends and even deductible interest payments from any U.S. corporation may be made to a foreign shareholder free of federal withholding tax — even in the absence of a tax treaty — if less than 20% of the subsidiary's gross income for the three most recent full taxable years is derived from U.S. sources. Thus, even where special U.S. tax elimination or reduction provisions as noted above are not applicable, foreign investors who wish to use the United States as a base for foreign operations should consider establishing a separate U.S. subsidiary to derive most of such foreign source income.

It should be noted that tax treaties generally do not limit or modify U.S. taxation of the foreign income of *U.S.* citizens, resident aliens, corporations, and other U.S. persons.[27]

As in the case of export sales from the United States, state and local unitary and other taxes also should be investigated prior to establishing foreign investments from a U.S. office, subsidiary, or other U.S. enterprise.

Government related nontax assistance for investments abroad — such as the Overseas Private Investment Corporation which helps insure such investments against certain economic and political risks — often is rather limited for foreign investors.

Foreign Currency Transactions

The United States imposes no restrictions on the movement of funds into or out of the United States or on the exchange of U.S. dollars for other currencies. However, as noted in Chapter VI in connection with establishing a new U.S. business enterprise and in Chapter XII in connection with U.S. reporting requirements, commercial banking facilities, broker-dealers in securities, and certain other financial institutions in the United States are required to maintain records and/or report regularly to the federal government respecting any single transfer of funds in excess of $10,000 including those into or out of the United States, and individual travelers to and from the United States are required to report any currency or monetary instruments which they carry in excess of $5,000.

U.S. federal income taxation of foreign currency gains and losses not only is complex but, in many situations, is unclear.[28] However, several basic aspects of such taxation may be summarized as follows:

A person engaged in occasional — *i.e.,* sporadic — transactions in foreign currency for import or export transactions generally uses the transaction method to include foreign currency gains and losses in U.S. taxable income. Under this method, the foreign currency paid, received, or accrued for tax purposes is translated into U.S. dollars at the exchange rate prevailing at the time of each payment, receipt, or accrual. For example, the gain or loss in U.S. dollar value due to exchange rate fluctuations between the date a foreign currency receivable is entered in the accounts, and the date the payment is actually received, is taken into income on the date of receipt based on the rate at that date. Similarly — although the law is somewhat less clear — the actual payment of an obligation in foreign currency generally is a taxable event for recognizing gain or loss due to exchange rate fluctuations following the incurring of the obligation. The character of such transactional foreign currency gain or loss — as either capital or ordinary — usually follows the character of the transaction involved. For example, a gain or loss on a forward currency contract to hedge against possible exchange rate fluctuations for an anticipated receipt or payment in the ordinary course of business is ordinary gain or loss; a gain or loss on a hedge against fluctuations in the value of an equity investment in a foreign subsidiary should be capital gain or loss. It may be possible to sell a forward currency contract to an unrelated bank or other party for capital gain prior to its maturity, even if a gain on closing out the contract shortly thereafter would be ordinary; this will be long-term capital gain if the contract was held more than one year. On the other hand, additional U.S. dollars required because of exchange rate fluctuations to repay a foreign currency loan — at least one obtained to purchase business assets — may be considered an ordinary rather than a capital expense.[29]

Recent commodity futures tax revisions, *inter alia,* (1) require most futures traded on a regulated exchange to be treated as sold at fair market value on the last business day of the taxable year, (2) tax any such gain or loss at a maximum rate of 32% for individuals and approximately 35% for corporations, and (3) deny loss deductions to the extent offset by unrealized gains on a commodity straddle (whether effected on or off a regulated exchange). However, these do *not* apply to a hedging transaction such as a forward currency contract in the ordinary course of business, including a hedge to reduce currency fluctuations with respect to borrowings to be repaid, *if* the gain or loss therefrom will be ordinary. If gain or loss on the hedging contract will be capital gain or loss as described above, then the application of these rules — especially (1) and (2) above — should be considered.[30]

In the case of a foreign branch of a U.S. corporation or other enterprise, the transaction method may be employed. However, generally one of two other methods is used: (a) Under the profit and loss method, so much of the net profit in foreign currency as is actually remitted from the branch is translated for federal income tax purposes at the exchange rate actually used to convert the remittance, and the remainder of the branch's net profit is translated at the exchange rate at the end of the enterprise's taxable year. (b) Under the net worth method, branch remittances are valued at the exchange rate used in their conversion, while all current assets, receivables, and liabilities on the branch's balance sheet at year end are translated at the exchange rate at year end, and the fixed assets on the balance sheet are translated at the exchange rate for the date the assets were acquired; taxable branch income is the sum of these remittances, plus the difference between total assets at year end and the total at the beginning of the year. Accordingly, the net worth method takes into account for U.S. tax purposes certain asset gains and losses which are unrealized under other methods, and thereby increases the branch taxable gain or loss from foreign exchange fluctuations.

The use of the net worth method to calculate ordinary income of a foreign branch in U.S. dollars may include certain gains in connection with capital transactions. Accordingly, the transaction method noted further above should be considered if substantial capital gains are involved. In practice, a modification of the net worth method usually has been used for a branch: this includes translation of only so called monetary assets of the branch at the current year end exchange rate. However, it should be noted that for *financial* reporting after 1982 most gains and losses from translating assets abroad at current exchange rates are not to be reflected in earnings, but are to be placed directly in shareholders' equity on a corporation's balance sheet.[31]

In the case of a foreign subsidiary owned by a U.S. corporation or other U.S. persons, earnings and profits distributed in the form of a foreign currency dividend to U.S. shareholders is translated for U.S. income tax purposes at the exchange rate on the date of the dividend. However, in the case of tainted income of a CFC which is taxed currently even without distribution to the U.S. shareholders, a combination method is required which recognizes certain gains and losses from foreign exchange rate fluctuations with respect to capital as well.[32]

If foreign exchange rules abroad make it difficult or impossible to convert foreign assets to U.S. dollars, that income may be deferred for U.S. tax purposes until it becomes either usable for foreign business needs or convertible. It should also be noted that the foreign exchange rate in official channels — if available — generally must be used. However, where exchange control authorities abroad do not succeed in enforcing exchange regulations, the exchange rate required to be used in calculating income or loss for U.S. tax purposes may be the rate prevailing in the unregulated market.

As to the amount of foreign tax credit in U.S. dollars for foreign creditable taxes paid in foreign currency, under the transaction and the net worth branch methods, the exchange rate on the date the foreign tax is paid usually is used. Under the profit and loss branch method, the exchange rate usually is the rate in effect on the date of an actual remittance with respect to which the foreign tax was paid, and the rate in effect at the end of the taxable year as to foreign taxes on unremitted profits. For the credit for taxes paid by a foreign subsidiary when a U.S. corporation receives a dividend from its subsidiary, the taxes generally are translated at the same rate as the dividend.

Foreign Direct Investment and Transaction Reports

Under Department of Commerce regulations,[33] confidential reports are required from a *U.S.* person having a direct investment in a *foreign* business enterprise, defined as direct or indirect ownership of 10% or more of the voting securities of an incorporated foreign enterprise or an equivalent interest in an unincorporated foreign enterprise, including a foreign branch. Quarterly reports and industry classification questionnaires are required for each such foreign affiliate (including banking affiliate) whose total assets, net sales or gross operating revenues, or net income (or loss) after taxes exceeds $10 million. However, a report is not required for direct transactions with an indirectly owned foreign affiliate if the intercompany balance and royalties for the quarter do not exceed $1 million. In addition, a benchmark survey covering lesser investments was conducted for 1977, and is expected to be conducted again in 1982, 1989, and every five years thereafter.

Reports of license and similar payments to unaffiliated foreign persons, and of other international financial and commercial dealings, are required from U.S. enterprises. Voluntary reports of foreign contract operations may be requested from U.S. construction, engineering, and other technical service enterprises. In addition, the U.S. Federal Reserve Board, Comptroller of the Currency, and Federal Deposit Insurance Corporation require quarterly and other reports — including the sum of credits and commitments to each foreign country — from U.S. banks with branches overseas.[34]

Foreign investors generally may minimize these reporting requirements by owning their foreign operations directly rather than through a U.S. enterprise or resident. However, their ownership of a U.S. enterprise itself still will be subject to reporting requirements for foreign direct investments in the United States as described in Chapter XII and elsewhere in this volume.

Additional Special Rules Affecting Foreign Operations

Several sets of special U.S. rules can have extraterritorial impact on foreign operations which may be of particular concern to foreign investors. Certain aspects of these are summarized briefly here, although a detailed explanation of them is beyond the scope of this chapter.

International Boycotts

Any individual, corporation, or other person participating in or cooperating with an international boycott is denied a federal foreign tax credit for foreign income taxes treated as incurred on income from such participation, and is precluded from using a DISC or a CFC to defer federal taxation of such income. These provisions apply broadly where the person agrees — in writing or otherwise — to participate in or cooperate with a foreign government in an international boycott based on race, nationality, or religion. However, they do not apply to compliance with a boycotting country's direct prohibitions on exports from or imports to a boycotted country — a so called primary boycott — but to secondary and other boycotts prohibiting more indirect dealings with others. The foreign tax credit is reduced by a fraction — referred to as the international boycott factor — the numerator of which reflects the operations in boycotting countries and the denominator of which reflects the worldwide foreign operations of the participant. However, this factor does not apply if the amount of disallowed foreign taxes which are allocable to boycott operations can be specifically identified. Furthermore, taxes so disallowed for credit purposes still may be deducted in computing U.S. taxable income.

In the case of a DISC, a fraction of its income which would otherwise not be currently taxed to its shareholders — proportionate to the international boycott factor — is treated as distributed to them and so is taxable. Similarly, a fraction of the foreign income (and U.S. source non-business income) of a CFC which would otherwise be deferred from U.S. taxation as to its U.S. shareholders — proportionate to the international boycott factor — is treated as additional tainted income taxable to them on a current basis. However, in both cases the amount of income specifically allocable to boycott operations may be substituted for that determined by the boycott factor if such income can be specifically identified.

Finally, a report of operations in any country listed by the Department of the Treasury as a boycotting country, or any other country which should reasonably be known to be engaged in such boycotting, is required from any person if that person *or* a member of a controlled group including that person has operations there.[35]

In the case of foreign investors, certain considerations in connection with these tax provisions should be emphasized. First, they apply to any U.S. subsidiary or other U.S. enterprise with operations in foreign countries whether owned directly or through foreign subsidiaries of the U.S. enterprise, even if the U.S. enterprise is owned or controlled by foreign persons. Accordingly, the use of a U.S. enterprise to carry on operations in boycotting countries should be undertaken only with great caution. Even where merely a U.S. office or other fixed place of business of the foreign investor participates in such a boycott, the foreign tax credit allowed with respect to income effectively connected with the conduct of a U.S. trade or business by that office apparently may be subject to reduction by the international boycott factor.[36]

Second, with respect to the required reporting on the activities of a *foreign* corporation, a report is required from a U.S. shareholder of 10% or more of the voting stock of the foreign corporation. The activities of a *foreign parent or sister corporation* need not be reported by a U.S. subsidiary if the U.S. subsidiary has no CFC deferred income, DISC, or foreign tax credit benefits, of if it forfeits the benefits of those provisions, or if it is demonstrated that the U.S. corporation itself does not participate in a boycott and maintains its activities separately from those of the foreign corporations.[37]

In addition to these federal tax requirements, a foreign government or other request regarding participation in an international boycott involving U.S. exports, imports, or other commerce must be reported by the recipient to the Department of Commerce. The Export Administration Amendments Act of 1977[38] administered by the Department of Commerce also directly forbids participation by any U.S. person in an international boycott. This applies even to resident aliens, to a U.S. permanent establishment of a foreign enterprise registered to do business in any state, and to a foreign branch or subsidiary controlled by a U.S. person. Even the inclusion of U.S. origin spare parts with a foreign subsidiary's manufactured goods may trigger the act's application. However, there are significant exceptions in this act which are not found in the tax provisions. For example, *bona fide* residents of boycotting countries — including local subsidiaries — are not so prohibited as to import and other activities carried on exclusively there. On the other hand, serious civil penalties of up to $10,000 per violation, and criminal penalties of up to $50,000 and five years' imprisonment per violation, do apply. In addition, the export privileges of an offender can be suspended.

Participation in an international boycott also may run afoul of U.S. federal or state antitrust or even civil rights laws.

Bribes and Illegal Payments

The Foreign Corrupt Practices Act of 1977[39] (the "FCPA") sets fines and penalties for any U.S. corporation or other enterprise with its principal place of business in the United States (and its officers, directors, and other representatives) found to be engaged in foreign governmental or political bribery. It also amends the Securities Exchange Act of 1934 to require all publicly held corporations to maintain accurate records and adequate systems of internal controls, whether or not they are involved in international trade. A corporation directly or indirectly making such bribes may be fined up to $1 million, and any individual acting on its behalf may be subject to a $10,000 fine and five years' imprisonment. The statute does not excuse minor or immaterial violations. However, it does appear to require a corrupt intent to affect the recipient's discretionary official acts (as opposed to merely expediting matters to which the payor is entitled) and to assist in obtaining or retaining business. The U.S. Securities and Exchange Commission also may require corporate management to establish employee conduct codes, enhanced internal audit mechanisms, and other measures to foster compliance with these provisions — although disclosure of such illegal conduct currently may be required by the Commission only where a large share of a widely held corporation's business may be affected by potential penalties. Any U.S. enterprise engaged in foreign operations — even if owned or controlled by foreign investors — must be particularly cautious in this area. This is especially true in the case of past operations of a U.S. subsidiary which was publicly held prior to foreign ownership, and all operations of a U.S. subsidiary which remains publicly held even with substantial foreign ownership. However, changes to narrow somewhat the application of the FCPA's provisions have been considered.

For federal tax purposes, no deduction from taxable income generally is allowed for a bribe or kickback to an official or employee of any government or governmental agency where the payment is unlawful under the FCPA. In addition, no such deduction is permitted for a payment to any person if the payment is a bribe, kickback, or other payment which is illegal under any federal or state (but not foreign) law; this usually is applicable to payments in connection with U.S. operations or persons. The amount of any illegal payment to an official, employee, or agent of any government by or on behalf of a DISC also is treated as an additional distribution by the DISC to its shareholders and taxed to them — and this distribution is not limited to taxable income of the DISC. Finally, in the case of a CFC, the amount of tainted income taxed currently to its U.S. shareholders is increased by the amount of any payments to government officials or agents which would be unlawful under the FCPA if the CFC were a U.S. corporation.[40]

With respect specifically to foreign investors, these provisions usually affect only foreign operations conducted through a U.S. subsidiary or a U.S. office to which foreign income is attributable.

Antitrust Laws

Even the activities of foreign investors abroad, such as agreements among such investors or their foreign enterprises, are subject to U.S. federal and state antitrust laws if they involve an intended and substantial effect on U.S. commerce. In case such activities occur, the U.S. contacts needed under the U.S. Constitution to substantiate local judicial jurisdiction over the parties are minimal — for example, the sending of telexes into the United States, the initiation of an arbitration proceeding there, or a conspiracy with a U.S. person. Service of legal process often can be effected abroad either by mail or as otherwise prescribed under foreign law. Thereafter, service on foreign persons of civil investigative demands in connection with the judicial proceedings usually is authorized under U.S. laws or treaties.

The ownership or control of a U.S. enterprise by foreign investors may increase the likelihood of a substantial effect on U.S. commerce due to actions abroad by the foreign owners or by their foreign affiliated enterprises, if only because foreign activities of a U.S. person may more clearly be restrained. Such a U.S. enterprise also may increase U.S. contacts for obtaining local judicial jurisdiction over such foreign activities. However, certain international legal principles may be invoked to limit the impact of U.S. antitrust laws on such foreign activities — for example, comity or courtesy if a foreign country protests the proceeding, sovereign immunity if a foreign government entity is involved, the act of state doctrine protecting conduct in a foreign country which is the result of the foreign government's act, or possibly the defense of sovereign compulsion for an act required by a foreign government. Difficulties also may arise under foreign laws prohibiting disclosure in the United States or elsewhere of banking or other industry documents abroad.[41]

A foreign investor conducting foreign operations from a U.S. enterprise also should note that the U.S. Department of Justice has issued guidelines for compliance with federal antitrust standards in international operations which include, for example, a foreign acquisition, joint bidding or research or manufacturing, grantback licensing, and the like by a U.S. enterprise.[42]

In the case of export activities from the United States, the Webb-Pomerene Act[43] provides a special exemption from U.S. antitrust laws for private export marketing associations formed by competing enterprises, provided that such an association does not reduce their competition within the U.S. market. Perhaps more significantly, the Export Trading Company Act of 1982[44] provides that the Sherman Act and Section 5 of the Federal Trade Commission Act do not apply to conduct or unfair methods of competition involving export trade or commerce and resulting in no injury to export business in the United States. In addition, a bank holding company (or Edge Act corporation owned by such a company) or other persons may operate a U.S. export trading company to export U.S. goods or services, or to provide export trade services to facilitate such exports by unaffiliated persons. However, federal antitrust exemptions which depend on regulation by state laws — such as that for insurance activities — may not apply to unregulated foreign or domestic activities by the same or affiliated enterprises.[45]

Footnotes to Chapter VIII

1. 15 C.F.R. Parts 370 *et seq.*; 37 C.F.R. Part 5; 50 U.S.C. App. §§2401-2420; 18 U.S.C. §1001. Similarly to the Foreign Assets Control Regulations referred to immediately below, these have been modified for special licensing of exports to the People's Republic of China. However, exports to the U.S.S.R. and Libya, for example, have been further limited.

2. 31 C.F.R. Parts 500, 515, 520, 530, 535; *see* Chapter I *supra.*

3. *See, e.g.,* 22 U.S.C. §§3201 *et seq.*; 42 U.S.C. §§2155-2157; 22 C.F.R. Parts 121 *et seq.*; 31 C.F.R. Part 505.

4. *Cf.* Fruehauf Corp. v. Massardy, Decision of May 22, 1965, 14th Chamber, Cour d'Appel, Paris (France), 1965, II La Gazette du Palais, Paris 89-90, 5 Int'l Legal Materials 476 (1965).

5. *See generally* E.O. 12264, 12290, 3 C.F.R. 86, 127 (1981); 49 C.F.R. Parts 100-199.

6. I.R.C. §864(c)(4); *see generally* Chapter II *supra.*

7. I.R.C. §§873, 882(c), 906.

8. *E.g.,* Arkansas, Louisiana, and Maine.

9. I.R.C. §482; Treas. Reg. §§1.482-1 and -2.

10. Rev. Proc. 65-17, 1965-1 C.B. 833; Rev. Proc. 65-31, 1965-2 C.B. 1024; Rev. Proc. 82-29, 1982-18 I.R.B. 13; Rev. Rul. 72-437, 1972-2 C.B. 660; Rev. Rul. 82-80, 1982-18 I.R.B. 7; *cf.* United States-France Income Tax Treaty of 1967, as amended, Art. 25.

11. I.R.C. §§991-997; *see also* Rev. Rul. 72-166, 1972-1 C.B. 220.

12. I.R.C. §§291(a)(4), 996(g).

13. I.R.C. §§921-922.

14. I.R.C. §936; Rev. Proc. 63-10, 1963-1 C.B. 490; *see also* Rev. Proc. 80-57, 1980-2 C.B. 852.

15. I.R.C. §§243, 245, 1501-1504, 168(f)(2), 48(a)(2), 982; Treas. Reg. §1.964-3; Prop. Treas. Reg. §1.6001-1.

16. *See generally* I.R.C. §§367, 1246(f), 1249, 1491-1494, 6031, 6035, 6038, 6046, 6046A; Temp. Treas. Reg. §§7.367(b)-1 through -12; Rev. Proc. 68-23, 1968-1 C.B. 821; Rev. Proc. 69-1, 1969-1 C.B. 381; Rev. Rul. 78-201, 1978-1 C.B. 91; Rev. Rul. 81-4, 1981-1 C.B. 126. *But see, e.g.,* Dittler Bros., Inc., 72 T.C. 896 (1979), *aff'd*, 642 F.2d 1211 (1981) (Internal Revenue Service's denial of

ruling for taxfree transfer of property to foreign corporation held unreasonable).

17. *See generally* I.R.C. §§901-907; Temp. Treas. Reg. §§4.901-2, 4.903-1; Treas. Reg. §1.861-8; Chapter II *supra.*

18. I.R.C. §§951-971, 1248.

19. I.R.C. §§551-558.

20. I.R.C. §§541-547, especially §§545(a), (d); *see* Chapter II *supra.* Even a foreign corporation majority owned by a large number of U.S. citizens or resident aliens may, if used primarily to invest or trade in securities, fall within the adverse provisions applicable to a foreign investment company. I.R.C. §§1246-1247.

21. *Cf.* I.R.C. §958(b).

22. I.R.C. §§936, 243, 332, 861(a)(2)(A).

23. *See* 48 U.S.C. §1397; I.R.C. §934; Rev. Rul. 80-40, 1980-1 C.B. 175. As to U.S. real estate and natural resource interests held through the U.S. Virgin Islands, however, see Chapter III *supra.*

24. *See generally* I.R.C. §§931-933, 935.

25. I.R.C. §§119, 217(h)-(i), 911-912; *see* I.R.C. §1034(k). Less attractive and more complicated rules apply for years before 1982. For an individual working in a U.S. possession, the possession income provisions described above still may be more advantageous.

26. I.R.C. §404A; *see* Chapter II *supra.*

27. *Cf.* United States-Japan Income Tax Treaty of 1972, Art. 4(3). One proposed exception was a provision in the recently negotiated United States-United Kingdom Income Tax Treaty of 1975 which in effect limited the application of the unitary method of state income taxation to certain U.S. corporations and other enterprises controlled by U.K. residents. However, this provision of the treaty was not accepted by the U.S. Senate.

28. *See generally* D. Ravenscroft, *Currency Revaluation and Devaluation — Tax Effects,* Tax Mgt. Portfolio No. 280 (1973). The Department of the Treasury has released a discussion draft of suggested approaches to tax treatment of foreign currency gains and losses which may provide a focus for future changes and clarifications. Announcement 81-4, 1981-2 I.R.B. 37.

29. *See* Corn Products Refining Co. v. Comm'r, 350 U.S. 46 (1955); International Flavors & Fragrances, 62 T.C. 232 (1974), *rev'd & remanded,* 524 F. 2d 357 (2d Cir. 1975), 36 T.C.M. 260 (1977); Hoover Co., 72 T.C. 206 (1979); Carborundum Co., 74 T.C. 730 (1980); I.R.C. §1234A; Rev. Rul. 78-281, 1978-2 C.B. 204; Rev. Rul. 78-396, 1978-2 C.B. 114; Letter Rul. 7847004.

30. I.R.C. §§1092, 1256.

31. *See, e.g.,* Financial Accounting Standards Board, Statements of Financial Accounting Standards No. 8 (1975), No. 52 (1981).

32. Bon Ami Co., 39 B.T.A. 825 (1939); Treas. Reg. §§1.964-1(d), (e).

33. 15 C.F.R. Part 806; *cf.* U.S. Dep't of Commerce Form BE-577.

34. Certain aspects of U.S. reports of international dealings by U.S. persons which may be particularly relevant to foreign investors in a U.S. business enterprise are discussed in Chapter XII *infra.*

35. *See generally* I.R.C. §§908, 952(a)(3), 995(b)(1)(F)(ii), 999; U.S. Dep't of the Treasury (Internal Revenue Service) Form 5713.

36. I.R.C. §§906, 908. Whether the broad denial of foreign tax credits is contrary to the credit provisions of U.S. tax treaties is uncertain.

37. I.R.C. §999(a)(1); U.S. Dep't of the Treasury Boycott Guidelines, 1978-1 C.B. 521.

38. Pub. L. 95-52 (June 22, 1977), 91 Stat. 235; *see generally* 50 U.S.C. App. §§2401-2413; 15 C.F.R. Part 369. These may apply not only to the Arab boycott of Israel, but to other boycotting countries such as Nigeria or Pakistan, except for boycotts in which the United States participates. 50 U.S.C. App. §2403-1a. Although several states have adopted prohibitions on participation in international boycotts, these have generally been pre-empted by the 1977 federal act.

39. Pub. L. 95-213 (Dec. 19, 1977), 91 Stat. 1494, amending 15 U.S.C. §§78q(b), 78dd, 78ff(a).

40. *See generally* I.R.C. §§162(c), 952(a)(4), 964(a), 995(b)(1)(F)(iii). Such payments have been the subject of the controversial 11 questions form and successor questionnaires to U.S. corporations from the U.S. Internal Revenue Service.

41. *Cf.* Timberlane Lumber Co. v. Bank of America, 549 F. 2d 597 (9th Cir. 1976).

42. U.S. Dep't of Justice, *Antitrust Guide for International Operations* (1977); *see, e.g.,* Timken Roller Bearing Co. v. United States, 341 U.S. 593 (1951).

43. 15 U.S.C. §§61-66.

44. Pub. L. 97-290 (1982); *see* Chapters I, VI *supra.*

45. *Cf.* 15 U.S.C. §§1011-1015; Group Life & Health Ins. Co. v. Royal Drug Co., 440 U.S. 205 (1979); St. Paul Fire & Marine Ins. Co. v. Barry, 438 U.S. 531 (1978).

Chapter IX

Portfolio Investments in Stocks and Debt Securities

This chapter discusses various methods by which nonresident alien individuals, foreign corporations, foreign trusts, and other foreign persons may make portfolio investments — *i.e.*, investments that do not involve significant participation in the operations of the enterprise — in equity stocks and debt securities of privately and publicly held U.S. corporations and other U.S. issuers of securities. These include direct ownership of the securities as well as indirect ownership either through other U.S. issuers or through entities organized under the laws of other countries. This is followed by examination of the considerations that will often determine for the foreign investor which alternative is most suitable. However, it will be assumed that the foreign investor has satisfied himself as to the soundness of his investment from a purely financial point of view, including possible fluctuations in foreign exchange rates of the U.S. dollar.

Alternative Methods of Investment

There are no general restrictions on the number or type of securities of U.S. issuers that may be held by a foreign portfolio investor. However, such an investor, in common with a U.S. person, is subject to statutory duties to render certain reports if, for example, he holds more than five percent of a class of equity securities of an issuer registered with the U.S. Securities and Exchange Commission under Section 12 of the Securities Exchange Act of 1934.[1]

There are also certain restrictions on foreign ownership — such as those described in Chapter I generally and Chapter VI in the context of establishing a new business enterprise — which should be reviewed where even a portfolio investment in an applicable field is contemplated. These include, for example, the restrictions contained in the Federal Communications Act with respect to ownership of securities of entities engaged in the radio or television broadcasting business, and the Civil Aeronautics Act with respect to ownership or securities of entities engaged in U.S. civil aviation.[2] In the case of a major portfolio investment by a foreign government, review by the interagency Committee on Foreign Investment referred to in Chapter I may be involved. As noted generally there, investors also may wish to plan for the transfer of U.S. securities and other portfolio investments to neutral persons in case of hostilities between the United States and other countries.

A foreign investor may own such U.S. securities (1) directly, (2) indirectly through the ownership of securities of other U.S. issuers, (3) through entities organized under foreign law which are essentially private in nature, or (4) through foreign entities which are, by U.S. tests, widely held. Each of these will be examined in turn.

Direct Ownership of Securities of U.S. Issuers

This ownership can fall into one of three broad categories. The owner may hold an interest in a general business corporation or business trust; an obligation of a governmental body, or a body sponsored by or related to a governmental agency; or an interest in an unincorporated venture.

Business corporations or trusts. An equity interest in a business corporation or a business trust may be represented by shares. Where a corporation is concerned, these are shares of capital stock; where business trusts are concerned, they are shares of beneficial interest. Every business corporation must have at least one class of capital stock, which must be voting stock having the right to elect the directors and to vote on those matters reserved by corporate law, the charter, or the by-laws to action of the shareholders. Except where incorporated under the laws of certain states, business corporations also may issue nonvoting stock, and stock which is preferred as to dividends or liquidation or both. Shares of beneficial interest of business trusts have such voting and other rights of participation as the trust instrument establishing the business trust and the particular laws of the applicable state may provide.

Both business corporations and business trusts, subject to limitations imposed on them by their governing instruments and governing law, also can issue debt securities of various types, possibly convertible into stock or shares. The foreign owner has the same standing as the U.S. citizen or resident owner in that he is a preferred, secured, unsecured, or subordinated creditor of the issuing corporation or trust.

A growing class of securities investments in the United States has been that of marketable options. In addition to such trading in the over the counter market, there are a number of exchanges[3] on which options to purchase certain equity securities at a specified date in the future and at a specified price may be bought and sold. These markets are equally available to the foreign investor and the U.S. investor. The cost of such an option is customarily a minor fraction of the price for which the equity security is selling at the time.

Obligations of governmental bodies. The U.S. federal government issues securities which are its own direct debt obligations. They are of varying terms and frequently carry special provisions relating to their principal purposes. Generally, they may be classified as Treasury bonds, which are commonly used for medium- to long-term financing, and Treasury bills, which are short-term financing obligations and which are accordingly frequently rolled over or otherwise refinanced by the federal government. In addition, the federal government has many instrumentalities which themselves issue obligations in accordance with the statutes that govern their operation. Examples of these are Federal National Mortgage Association (FNMA or "Fannie Mae") bonds, and bonds issued by the Tennessee Valley Authority (TVA) and the Farmers Home Administration (FHA). Agencies and instrumentalities of the federal government also guarantee obligations as to payment of both principal and interest, such as the so called modified pass-through obligations of the Government National Mortgage Association (GNMA or "Ginnie Mae") which are backed by mortgages held on real estate owned primarily by private persons. From time to time, the federal government guarantees the payment of principal and interest on obligations issued by certain private corporations incorporated in the United States in cases where enabling legislation has been enacted because of a particular financial problem relating to the private corporation; this has occurred in the past with respect to Lockheed Aircraft Corporation, a prime defense contractor, Chrysler Corporation, and a number of the railroad corporations of the country which have needed additional funds for new equipment, repair, and even bare survival.

In addition, to varying degrees — frequently measured by the real estate tax base or otherwise limited by law — each of the states and many of their subdivisions borrow from the public by issuing a variety of debt obligations. These subdivisions include municipalities such as cities, townships, and counties; subordinate authorities formed for governmental or quasi-governmental purposes such as the General State Authority in Pennsylvania, numerous public power generation and transmission authorities, municipal and regional water and sewer authorities, and the like; and multistate authorities such as the Delaware Port Authority and the Port Authority of New York and New Jersey. These debt obligations range from short-term tax anticipation notes to middle-term and long-term bonds, both secured and unsecured. In addition to bonds which look to the revenues produced by the state, municipal, and multistate authorities for servicing of the debt as to principal and interest, many states and municipalities have the power under special state constitutions or statutes to back bonds issued by private organizations. These look to the revenues generated by those private organizations for the payment of principal and interest, but also to the full faith and credit of the state concerned.

There is no general limitation on ownership of any of these governmental obligations by or on behalf of foreign investors.

Unincorporated ventures. Portfolio investment by foreign persons in U.S. securities also may be made through partnerships and other unincorporated ventures which are not organized as business trusts. Such investments often may not be considered investments in securities by foreign persons, but there is little doubt that such interests constitute securities under U.S. statutes and judicial decisions. Notwithstanding that federal legislation and administrative policies have reduced the U.S. tax attractions of such investments for U.S. persons in recent years, a significant source of U.S. capital accumulation has been the public or private sale of limited partnership interests primarily to persons of significant means for use in one or another type of enterprise. For example, such financings have been used to acquire major items of industrial, commercial, or residential real estate or a combination thereof; to finance motion picture and phonograph record production and distribution; and even to finance racehorses. Participation in the exploration for and exploitation of oil, gas, and mineral deposits has for some time been attractive to investors other than the major national and international natural resource corporations. Such participation frequently is obtained by the sale of limited partnership interests, or by the sale of exploration programs which cannot be categorized as limited partnership interests because of special economic, legal, and tax consequences. This type of investment usually is as fully available to the foreign person as to U.S. persons.[4]

Indirect Ownership Through Ownership of Securities of Other U.S. Issuers

Investment in the equity or debt securities of U.S. enterprises which own or control numerous operating subsidiary corporations essentially is in the same category as direct ownership of the operating entities. However, there are two primary types of U.S. entities that issue their own securities and merely allow the holders of those securities a participation in a portfolio of the securities of U.S. and other issuers held by the entity: investment companies registered under the federal Investment Company Act of 1940[5] and widely held by the public, and personal holding companies which essentially are closely held.[6]

Investment companies registered under the Investment Company Act of 1940. In this highly regulated industry, the most prominent and common type of investment company is the open-end management investment company or mutual fund. This type of entity usually is incorporated, but also may be organized as a business trust. It stands ready at all times to redeem its own shares at the request of the holder for an amount essentially equivalent to the next determined per share net asset value. Most such companies engage in continuous offering of their shares to existing and new investors. These companies have only a single class of securities in the hands of the public — voting common stock, or voting shares of beneficial interest in the case of a trust.

There are also closed-end management investment companies which do not engage in continuous offering of their shares and which do not stand ready to redeem their shares. The majority have only one class of securities — common stock. A few have two classes of equity securities, common and preferred stock, while a few others have a class of debt securities as well as a class of equity securities.

These management companies, both open-end and closed-end, may be diversified or nondiversified in their portfolios, may concentrate in a single classification or a limited number of classifications of industries, or have a policy of not so concentrating, and may stress the achievement of one or two investment goals — such as long-term capital growth, capital growth with growth of income, emphasis on income, and the like — to the exclusion of alternative goals. All of these matters are governed primarily by the Investment Company Act of 1940 and the rules of the U.S. Securities and Exchange Commission promulgated under that act, and secondarily by certain state securities laws — so called Blue Sky laws — discussed in Chapter I and further below.

Another form of registered investment company is the unit investment trust. This currently is used primarily in two ways: to hold open-end management investment company shares as the underlying investments of so called variable annuities, and to hold a portfolio of state or municipal debt obligations or of other governmental debt obligations such as Ginnie Mae modified pass-through mortgage backed obligations. Both of these usually are accomplished without management functions exercised by the unit investment trust.

Finally, a limited type of investment company offers and sells to the public face amount certificates which are geared to earning for the investor a fixed face amount at maturity through investment and reinvestment in a portfolio of conservative investments complying with the limitations imposed on insurance companies by the laws of the District of Columbia. Excess earnings also go to the benefit of the investor, creating hope of realizing a slightly greater sum.

Personal holding companies. A personal holding company in terms of portfolio investments is a closely held corporation which may have substantial assets, but whose voting and other equity securities are held by a relatively limited number of owners. This is less than the minimum of 100 shareholders which triggers registration under the Investment Company Act of 1940[7] if other tests are met under that act, and less than 500 holders of a single class of equity securities which may require registration as a publicly held corporation under the Securities Exchange Act of 1934.[8]

The other context in which the term is used is federal income tax law, under which a 50% (70% prior to 1982) penalty surtax applies to the corporation if it has a high proportion of certain types of investment income, is majority owned directly or indirectly by five or fewer individuals, and has not distributed to its owners a substantial portion of the income earned during the taxable year.[9]

In any case, the objective of a personal holding company usually is to buy, sell, hold, and trade in securities or other investments either of varied or limited types, but without making any public offering of the securities of the corporation itself. Many personal holding companies were at one time themselves operating companies which subsequently either discontinued the operating businesses or disposed of their assets to larger entities and, after receiving money or securities from the acquirors, either continued to hold the securities as investments or to use the cash received upon disposition of such securities to acquire more diversified portfolios of investments. In recent years, many of such corporations have in turn disposed of their investments to investment companies registered under the Investment Company Act of 1940, distributed the shares of such companies to their own shareholders, and then ceased to exist.

Indirect Ownership Through Privately Held Foreign Entities

There are essentially no restrictions on the number or type of securities of U.S. issuers that may be held by a foreign investor — either an individual acting for himself or in a fiduciary capacity, or a legal entity — unless such an entity or its owners fall within very limited areas as to which the United States has a trade embargo under, for example, the Trading with the Enemy Act as described in Chapter I. Accordingly, there are numerous methods by which foreign entities not sufficiently widely owned to be considered publicly held may hold such U.S. securities. A few examples of these privately held entities may be noted here.

Trusts organized in common law countries. In many countries whose legal system is derived from the English common law or from English statutes, investments, including securities of U.S. issuers, may be held by a trust. The concept of a trust — with very limited exceptions — has not been adopted by countries in Europe and elsewhere that adhere to civil law. Under this approach, a *settlor* transfers to a *trustee* certain assets on condition that those assets be held by the trustee and administered for the benefit of designated *beneficiaries* for purposes set forth in the trust instrument. The settlor must be legally capable of transferring assets; the trustee must be capable of acting as a trustee under the laws of the country or subdivision of operation; the assets must be so transferable, such as unrestricted interests in securities; and the purposes and administration of the trust must not be illegal where the trust is to be administered, nor may receipt of the trust benefits be illegal where the beneficiary receives them.

Such trusts may be established in countries that are tax havens such as Bermuda and the Cayman Islands, which are so considered because taxes with respect to the income and other gains generated by the trust or its administration — generally provided that such activities do not involve the conduct of a local business — are minimal or nonexistent. Other common law countries in which trusts for the benefit of foreign persons have been established in apparently increasing numbers — provided that the beneficiaries are not residents of that country — are the New Hebrides in the Pacific, the British Virgin Islands, and Hong Kong.

Trusts may be established in other common law countries and such trusts — subject to foreign exchange controls — may hold securities of U.S. issuers for the benefit of foreign persons. These include the United Kingdom itself, Canada, and a number of others. However, these may not be considered tax havens because of relatively high income taxes.

Private trusts frequently are established under the laws of one of the states of the United States for investments in securities to serve the purposes of a settlor and beneficiaries. However, this alternative probably would not be extensively used by a foreign investor in U.S. securities except in unusual circumstances, because in most cases it would result in additional local administration, possible U.S. taxation, and at least tax reporting and identification that a foreign person often finds undesirable.

Other entities in tax haven countries. Many countries have laws which allow the formation of what would under U.S. concepts be considered closely held corporations and grant them varying degrees of freedom from income, gains, and/or property taxation as well as from exchange controls provided that they do not engage in local business. Frequently, the same countries have laws granting tax and exchange control relief or concessions to partnerships that are not engaged in local business. To varying degrees, the Bahamas, Bermuda, Gibraltar, the New Hebrides, and Liberia are typical examples. By way of more detailed examples, three such situations may be noted here.

The Principality of Liechtenstein, located on the east border of Switzerland adjacent to Austria,. has several entities through which, among other matters, foreign persons may own the securities of U.S. issuers. The best known of these is the *Anstalt*, an establishment which is a separate legal entity having many of the attributes of a U.S. or other corporation and certain attributes of a trust. The *Anstalt* can have broad powers, may be set up by a single founder, and may have a board of directors with as few as one member provided that, in all instances, one member of the board is domiciled in the country. Where it does not carry on economic activities in the country, its local taxes are minimal. The principality also permits the formation of a family foundation, the creation of a trust enterprise which is very close to the concept of a trust under common law, and the incorporation of a limited liability share corporation, all of which result in minimal income taxation where the entity conducts economic activities exclusively outside the country. The selection of the appropriate entity therefore usually is based on other objectives of the foreign investor.

While the Principality of Monaco generally is not considered a tax haven, the large income that it derives from its casinos and related activities, coupled with its small geographical size and residential population, have combined to permit it to avoid the imposition of personal income tax and generally to levy — except where prevented by its treaty with France — low income taxes on business enterprises. Thus, the formation of a privately held Monegasque corporation is worth considering where the objective of the corporation is to hold securities of U.S. issuers and where the purchase and sale of such securities customarily will take place outside the French franc area. Discussions may be held in advance with the Monaco tax authorities to determine a profits tax base that is fair and realistic both to the principality and to the Monegasque corporation.

Hong Kong also should be carefully examined, since the formation there of a private corporation which does not engage in the banking or insurance business but in investment operations outside the colony is relatively simple, free from both administrative and foreign exchange restrictions, and essentially free from income taxation. Partnerships also can be formed in the colony, and the law of Hong Kong relating to them essentially is based on the English Partnership Act of the Victorian era. The limited partnership is recognized under principles similar to U.S. law as described in Chapter I. However, the partnership is taxed as a separate entity, although at a very low rate.

Entities in countries not considered tax havens. Many other countries which recognize the rights of private capital impose relatively heavy tax burdens both at the corporate or other entity level and at the owners' level. In the Federal Republic of Germany, the income tax implications at both the entity and the ownership levels must be carefully considered before, for example, determining whether to hold U.S. securities indirectly through a *Kapitalgesellschaft (KG)* or a *Gesellschaft mit beschränkter Haftung (GmbH)*. These are respectively substantally equivalent to a partnership and a closely held corporation under U.S. laws. Similarly, a Dutch closely held corporation — *Besloten Vennootschap (B.V.)* — holding portfolio U.S. securities investments on behalf of a Dutch person is not subject to severe restrictions by the Netherlands. However, the Dutch tax burden at the corporate level is substantial. On the other hand, exemption from Dutch corporate tax on dividends received *is* available to a Dutch holding corporation which has held at least five per cent of the capital of the dividend paying corporation from the beginning of the accounting year *and* provides an essential service or function for the group to which the holding company belongs. Thus, while this entity may be profitably used by a foreign person to invest in securities of a U.S. issuer, this generally does not include merely passive investments in U.S. securities.

In certain countries, strict foreign exchange controls or outright prohibition of ownership of foreign investments — both securities and other types — may make the use of a local entity to hold securities of U.S. issuers either impractical or illegal. Limitations of this nature in varying degrees may be found in, for example, Colombia, Italy, Norway, and even Japan and, more recently, France. The United Kingdom has suspended such restrictions, but changing economic and political conditions may see their reimposition (which may be accomplished without new legislation). On the other hand, in other countries where such exchange or ownership restrictions do not apply, high tax burdens and the strength of the U.S. dollar against other so called hard currencies may make such investments abroad of limited value to local residents.

Indirect Ownership Through Widely Held Foreign Entities

Investment corporations and trusts. The Scottish are generally given credit for conceiving the widely held investment corporation or investment trust as a pool of funds to provide a broader diversification of investments than otherwise could be achieved individually. The direct descendants of this concept are the widely held investment corporations and the unit trusts organized in the United Kingdom. The former are incorporated entities whose stock is listed on the stock exchange and is not subject to redemption upon a shareholder's demand. A unit trust, on the other hand, is an unincorporated pool of assets which sells interests to the public and redeems shares upon demand of the owners. These are roughly equivalent to, respectively, closed-end investment companies and mutual funds in the United States.

Moreover, there has developed over the last several years in the United Kingdom an active investment vehicle commonly referred to as equity linked life assurance. The benefits payable under these assurance contracts vary with the results of the underlying portfolio of equity securities, rather than being fixed and guaranteed. In the United States, as noted above, there has developed a close approximation: a variable annuity contract which provides annuity benefits to the living, rather than life insurance benefits to the surviving beneficiaries of a deceased contract holder.

Any of these entities may invest directly in both debt and equity securities of U.S. issuers, if the investment policy so permits. However, the now suspended foreign exchange restrictions of the sterling area and the scheduled territories for many years limited the extent to which entities organized and operating in the United Kingdom could purchase or use the proceeds of sales of U.S. securities to acquire additional such securities where payment was to be made in currencies other than sterling. It now remains to be seen how extensively this new freedom will be utilized.

Collective investment entities in Canada have developed more along the lines in the United States than those in the United Kingdom, on the European continent, or elsewhere. There are many mutual funds incorporated in Canada under federal laws or the laws of one of the provinces. The entitlement of Canadians to invest indirectly in the securities of U.S. issuers by virtue of purchasing the publicly offered stock of those mutual funds is unrestricted by any foreign exchange controls.

The same freedom from foreign exchange restrictions exists with respect to investment companies organized and operated in the Federal Republic of Germany or in the Netherlands.[10] Customarily, these collective investment funds have the general attributes of mutual funds in that they usually offer their shares for sale to the public on a continuous basis and stand to redeem their shares upon a holder's demand, with minor exceptions. However, they are usually not incorporated vehicles, but unincorporated pools of funds contributed by investors and held under a custody arrangement to buy, sell, hold, or trade in various types of securities for the benefit of all of the investors. Management of the investments is provided by a separate entity, which is customarily a corporation related to a bank. In both Germany and the Netherlands, shares in these investment vehicles are marketed through the banks which — contrary to the situation in the United States, Canada, and the United Kingdom — function both as commercial banking enterprises and as securities brokers and dealers. These have from time to time invested in securities of U.S. issuers depending on the state of the U.S. securities markets, the foreign exchange situation, the general U.S. economic atmosphere, and their investment objectives.

In most other countries, the widely held investment company is not a particularly important investment vehicle. In certain countries, this reflects the absence of a legal structure to permit collective investments. In others, it reflects the fact that securities markets within the country are of a very limited scope and depth, or that the balance of payments of the country will not permit the export of local currency for investment in foreign securities, including those of United States issuers. In still others, it reflects a lack of private capital available for investment in the hands of the public. An exception has been the development under French law over the past decade of the equivalent of a U.S. mutual fund, the *Société d'Investissements de Capital Variable* or *SICAV*. However, the recent accession in France of a government favoring nationalization of major industries and businesses rather than private ownership may well result in both a major shrinkage of the French securities market and disappearance of the *SICAV*.

Offshore investment companies in tax havens. A number of corporations have been organized in tax havens which impose little or no tax burdens on such corporations or on nonresident alien holders of their stock, to function as investment companies primarily for investments in securities of U.S. issuers. These corporations are organized and operated to permit the continued public offering of their stock and to permit shareholders to redeem their stock for substantially the underlying net asset value per share within a reasonable time after such redemption request has been made. Only a few of them are active currently; this is due primarily to recent conditions in the U.S. portfolio securities market and the previous decline during the 1970's in the foreign exchange value of the U.S. dollar. However, in view of possible changes in such trends, the principal such structures should be summarized briefly.

As a result of the strong banking facilities in Luxembourg, as well as its proximity to the vital financial centers of Europe, a number of such corporations have been organized there under Luxembourg's special holding company laws. Since Luxembourg law prohibits the corporation from redeeming its own stock, the equivalent of share redemption effected by open-end investment companies of other countries is accomplished through the organization of a repurchase subsidiary of the holding corporation. The Luxembourg banking commission also requires the issuance of a relatively detailed explanatory memorandum for each stock offering.

Favorable local taxation together with the income tax treaty between the Netherlands and the United States as extended to the Netherlands Antilles has led to the use of the *Naamloze Vennootschap (N.V.)* organized under the laws of the Antilles. These corporations are intended to be publicly held, and local corporation laws permit the inclusion of virtually all of the features that would customarily be found in a corporation organized in one of the major corporate situs states of the United States. There are no restrictions imposed by the Antilles on the holding of securities of U.S. issuers, and tax benefits may be passed along to foreign shareholders through increased earnings and profits. These corporations also have the advantage of being able directly to redeem their own stock. The geographic and time zone proximity to the United States also may be useful. Treaty revisions limiting or eliminating these benefits may, however, become effective in the foreseeable future. Somewhat similar treaty benefits in the British Virgin Islands were terminated by the United States in mid-1982.

A few corporations specializing in the sale of stock to foreign investors and investment of the proceeds in U.S. securities have been organized in Bermuda. Each such corporation once required a specific act of the Bermuda legislature but organization may be perfected more recently under a general corporation law. Where business is not to be conducted within Bermuda and the shares are not to be sold to Bermuda residents, accounts may be maintained in a foreign currency such as U.S. dollars and investments in securities of U.S. issuers may be freely made. Moreover — in contrast to most companies laws based on the English model — a Bermuda corporation may redeem for substantially net asset value its stock held by a shareholder, provided that its charter allows for such requested redemption.

More recently, entities have been organized in tax havens to sell their equity or debt securities to foreign persons and use the proceeds to invest in subsidiary corporations of such entities which, in turn, use the funds to acquire and lease to major U.S. corporations large items of machinery or other equipment, or lease oil, gas, or mineral rights in connection with projects being exploited by major U.S. natural resource corporations. Because of the high quality of U.S. entities obligated on such leases, it is contemplated that the leases may be guaranteed or insured, or may be used as collateral for the acquisition of additional machinery or equipment, or of additional oil, gas, or mineral rights. The foreign investor also may benefit because the aggregate income and other taxes imposed by the United States and by the tax haven may be lower than if the investment were held directly in the U.S. corporation involved in leasing of machinery or equipment, or in leasing or other participation in oil, gas, or mineral rights: this is both because business essentially is conducted outside the United States and because favorable income tax treaty provisions may apply.[11]

Similarly, one of the several forms of U.S. investment companies registered under the federal Investment Company Act of 1940 is used to hold a selected portfolio of mortgage participations guaranteed by the Government National Mortgage Association and to pass through to the purchasers of its own shares the interest payments received on those mortgages without further imposition of federal income tax at the level of the investment company, as discussed below. A foreign corporation can be organized to do much the same either directly or through the use of its own subsidiaries. Participation in a portfolio of U.S. government bonds, Federal National Mortgage Association bonds, or Government National Mortgage Association bonds or mortgage participations may be provided in such fashion that the portfolio is fully managed at all times, yet the foreign holder receives a greater income than by direct ownership by eliminating in accordance with tax treaty provisions the withholding by the paying agent of U.S. federal income tax.

General U.S. Income Taxation of Securities Investments

In connection with generally available methods of investments in U.S. securities, certain basic aspects of the impact of federal, state, and local income taxation should be summarized briefly. However, it should be noted that exceptions to these rules may be omitted here, for example, because of their limited applicability.

As described generally in Chapter I, a U.S. corporation is subject to federal income taxation of its worldwide net income after deductions at the rate of 15% (16% for 1982)-40% of the first $100,000 of such income and 46% of any excess. The windfall profit excise tax of 15-70% also may apply where crude oil sale is involved. More specifically as to portfolio securities and similar assets, profits of the corporation from the disposition of capital assets held for more than one year usually are taxed at up to 28% (although such profits of individuals are taxed at a maximum federal rate of 20%). In the case of commodity futures, the long-term holding period is only more than six months and, for taxable gains from futures traded on a regulated exchange, the maximum federal tax rate for a corporation generally is approximately 35% (32% for individuals). However, most such futures traded on a regulated exchange must be treated as sold at fair market value on the last business day of the taxable year, and loss deductions are denied to the extent offset by unrealized gains on a commodity straddle (whether effected on or off a regulated exchange).

While the corporation is allowed a deduction for interest paid to creditors, it is *not* currently allowed a deduction with respect to dividends paid to its shareholders in determining income subject to corporation income tax. As noted further above, where the corporation falls into the definition of a personal holding company and a high proportion of its income is passive personal holding company income, a 50% surtax on its undistributed net income applies to the corporation.[12] If it is not so classified, the corporation may accumulate earnings in order to avoid dividends to its shareholders who are subject to a second federal income tax. In the event of an unreasonable accumulation, however, a surtax applies to the unreasonably accumulated surplus.[13]

A U.S. corporation generally is entitled to exclude from taxable income at least 85% of a portfolio or other dividend it receives from another U.S. corporation.[14] Regulations set forth key attributes by which an entity can be determined for federal income tax purposes to be a corporation as distinguished from a partnership or other entity.[15] These tests are applied to business trusts and other unincorporated entities: if they have more corporate attributes than partnership attributes, they are taxed as corporations.

Investment companies which have the attributes of corporations, are registered under the Investment Company Act of 1940 for the entire taxable year, and meet certain tests of diversification may elect special tax benefits so that there is little or no taxation at the corporate level if they distribute at least 90% of their ordinary income each year. They may also avoid capital gain taxation by distributing net realized capital gains or, on the other hand, pay capital gain taxes and distribute *pro rata* to shareholders a credit with respect to such taxes which may be reclaimed by the shareholders upon proper filing of a claim for refund. Somewhat similar provisions apply to real estate investment trusts.[16]

Legal entities which have more partnership tax attributes than corporations are treated for federal income tax purposes as if they were partnerships. As described in Chapter I, the partnership under federal tax law is not a taxpaying entity, but its taxable income flows through *pro rata* in accordance with the partnership agreement to the respective partners, with the result that one level of federal income taxation is avoided.[17]

It should be remembered that, as described in Chapters I and II, individual states and other governmental subdivisions also impose taxes on business enterprises involved within their respective jurisdictions — which may include equity or debt holdings.

Under the U.S. Constitution, the federal government may not impose income tax on states, municipalities, other subordinate authorities or instrumentalities, or multistate authorities. In addition, it does not impose income tax on its own instrumentalities or agencies. Similarly, state and local governments may not impose income and related taxes on the federal government or its agencies or instrumentalities.

For these and related reasons, interest paid by states, municipalities, subordinate authorities, and multistate authorities on their debt obligations generally is not subject to federal income tax *or* state income tax within the states where issued.[18] Likewise, interest paid by the federal government or its agencies or instrumentalities on their debt obligations is not subject to state or local taxation. However, this federal interest remains subject to federal individual and corporate income taxation to the same extent as any other interest income.

Considerations in Determining Which Alternative Is Most Suitable

Selection of the proper method of investment by foreign persons in equity or debt securities of a publicly or privately held U.S. issuer depends on careful analysis of conflicting factors. While tax considerations frequently are a major motivation for selecting one form of international investment over another, tax reduction should not take precedence over investment objectives, investor protection, and other considerations. This section examines several of these considerations.

Investment Objectives of the Foreign Owner

When a foreign investor determines in the light of financial circumstances to invest in the securities of one or more U.S. issuers, only the threshold question has been resolved.

Nature of underlying interest. A wealth of financial information is available with respect to business activities in the United States. The portfolio securities investor — since he will not have operating control of the business — first must determine generally whether his investment should be made in an industrial, mercantile, or service enterprise or, alternatively, in enterprises providing machinery or other equipment to industry, or exploiting real estate or oil, gas, or mineral reserves. Within each of these general categories, attention must be paid to subcategories — for example, heavy or light manufacturing industries; wholesale, retail, or franchised mercantile operations; public utility, transportation, or management services; machinery and equipment leasing or sale; real estate construction, operation, financing, or sale; and integrated or segregated involvement with natural resource enterprises. Another decision is whether to invest in securities of a governmental body, of a government owned enterprise such as an electrical power generating system, or of a type which carry a government guarantee such as industrial revenue bonds.

Goals and values of the investor. The financial goals of the individual or institutional foreign investor will partly determine the investment method. For example, each investor must decide the priority of short- or long-range appreciation in the invested capital. In general, the greater the emphasis placed on capital appreciation, the greater the likelihood of loss in declining securities markets or economic adversity. In addition, diversification among industries or segments of the governmental or private economy, as well as among various issuers operating in a particular segment or industry, is more likely to provide protection against or at least mitigation of losses than is concentration of investments in a more limited range of industries, industry segments, or issuers. Furthermore, the special financial circumstances of a particular investor may require maximization of current income, as opposed to unrealized appreciation of the value of the investment.

It is also possible that an individual investor's religious or cultural values — such as restrictions on charging interest under Islamic principles, or a desire to foster the growth of certain types of businesses — will dictate somewhat the investments and the structures to be used or to be avoided.

Investor Protection Afforded the Foreign Owner

The degree of protection afforded portfolio investors by the laws of the countries in which they reside or in which the issuer of the equity or debt securities is located varies widely, even among those countries generally considered to be advanced in matters of finance and commerce. In certain countries, virtually no such protection is afforded; in other cases, an investor may receive protection from his country of *residence*; and, in a few instances, an investor may receive protection by extraterritorial application of laws of the *issuer's* country relating to issuance and sale of securities. The protection of foreign and other portfolio investors afforded by the highly developed securities laws of the United States and by the corporation laws of those states in which many U.S. corporations are organized, as well as the laws and procedures of such investor protection in certain other countries often considered financial centers, are examined below.

Domestic and extraterritorial applications of U.S. securities laws. As described generally in Chapter I, under the federal Securities Act of 1933[19] a U.S. issuer must, with few exceptions, make full disclosure of the facts necessary to allow an investor to make an informed judgment with respect to investment in securities which are publicly offered. This is normally accomplished by delivery to each offeree of a prospectus which is part of a registration statement filed with the Securities and Exchange Commission (the "SEC"), which in turn contains other data relating to the issuer including important documents and financial information. However, state and municipal governments and agencies and their authorities, multistate authorities, and the federal government and its instrumentalities and agencies are not required to use a prospectus or other disclosure document in connection with public offerings of their securities. Likewise, issues of securities of banks, life insurance companies, and railroad and motor transportation companies that have been approved by their respective regulatory agencies may be effected without compliance with this act. Certain transactions in any securities — such as a private rather than public offering — are exempt under the SEC's so called 140 series of rules and Rule 506, a more liberal private offering exemption rule replacing Rule 146 effective June 30, 1982. For purposes of determining whether an offering is small enough to be private, it may even be possible to exclude sales to nonresident aliens if their securities are subject to conditions preventing resale into the United States.[20]

Notwithstanding such exemptions from the use of a prospectus and the filing of a registration statement under this act, its provisions also absolutely prohibit fraud and misrepresentation in *any* offer or sale of securities made by use of the instrumentalities of interstate or foreign commerce of the United States.

The Securities Exchange Act of 1934[21] provides that information relating to existing publicly held securities and their issuers must be kept current by periodic reports to securities holders and the SEC. It also requires that holders of voting securities be fully informed with respect to the activities of the entity concerned when such holders are called on to vote — for example, by proxies — and that holders of publicly held nonvoting equity securities be provided with equivalent information. The act prohibits fraud and misrepresentation in any offer and sale or purchase of securities where the instrumentalities of U.S. commerce are used. Portions of the act limit the use of credit to purchase securities under so called margin regulations, provide for registration and regulation of brokers and dealers in securities, regulate the operation of stock exchanges and over the counter markets in unlisted U.S. securities, and govern the activities of professional transfer agents and securities depositories. The access of foreign banks and other entities, and of U.S. entities controlled by foreign persons, to membership and benefits of national securities exchanges also is so controlled. Filings made in compliance with either of these acts are open to inspection at the SEC and may be copied upon payment of a reasonable fee.

One of the most detailed U.S. securities laws is the Investment Company Act of 1940.[22] In addition to supporting the disclosure principles first adopted with the Securities Act of 1933, this later act closely regulates the relationship between registered investment companies and entities that provide them with investment advice and management or underwrite their securities. It requires a substantial portion of directors to be independent of the investment company's employees, adviser, and underwriter, and prohibits financial transactions between the investment company and its employees and servicing entities that may operate to the detriment of the shareholders of the investment company. This law also prohibits reciprocal and other circular ownership of investment companies, limits the use of leveraged indebtedness, and encourages independent custody of assets and the use of fidelity bonds to protect against loss or misuse by employees of portfolio securities, cash, and other property of the company.

As also noted briefly in Chapter I, other major federal securities laws protect investors in U.S. securities or those who make use of U.S. securities brokers or investment advisers. The Investment Advisers Act of 1940[23] regulates and requires extensive record keeping by entities engaged in rendering investment advice. The Trust Indenture Act of 1939[24] protects holders of a large issue of debt securities by requiring the presence of an independent corporate trustee to ensure that the provisions of the indenture creating the issue and the relationship with the security holders are carried out, and that holders' rights are enforced if there is a default by the issuer. The Public Utility Holding Company Act of 1935[25] originally was enacted to break up major interrelated gas and electric utility systems. Most of these systems have been dissolved, but a few have been able to comply with the intensive scheme of regulation required by the act and so remain under the supervision of the SEC.

The most recent such federal securities law is the Securities Investor Protection Act of 1970.[26] This statute was enacted following a series of failures of U.S. brokerage firms which left many of their customers with little or nothing of the funds and securities held for them; accordingly, it provides for the orderly liquidation of such entities in financial trouble and affords a substantial measure of financial protection to their customers.

A number of U.S. judicial decisions involve the extraterritorial application of these U.S. securities laws. This area is both complex and rapidly expanding. It is clear that the foreign direct holder of U.S. securities who has been defrauded or otherwise injured by a violation of these laws either committed in the United States or devised in the United States may recover for that injury in U.S. courts. On the other hand, where the wrongful conduct was committed wholly outside the United States or no acts other than mere preparatory functions were conducted in the United States, and the activities do not have a significant effect on securities markets within the United States and the injured parties are foreign persons, U.S. courts have been very reluctant to apply such U.S. securities laws. In addition, where the foreign investor is an indirect holder of the securities of a U.S. issuer through a foreign or other entity, the injured party carries a heavy burden of showing sufficient U.S. activities and contacts in order to obtain such protection. Since the laws of foreign investor protection within the United States seem to be developing with increasing rapidity, this area should be followed carefully for further developments.[27]

As described in Chapter I, most of the states of the United States — as well as the District of Columbia and the Commonwealth of Puerto Rico — govern the activities of brokers and dealers, and in many instances the offering and sale of securities, as well as the offering and sale of investment advisory services within their respective borders. The private rights which they grant to injured parties are as available to foreign investors injured by wrongful conduct within the state as they are to local persons. These so called Blue Sky laws generally are not helpful where wrongful conduct does not occur in the particular state; however, such conduct may well occur in several states in connection with a single investment, so that the investor may have a choice of states in which to pursue legal remedies.

Other U.S. protective laws. State corporation laws provide a substantial measure of protection for both foreign and other investors who directly hold equity securities issued by corporations organized there. For example, the direct holders of voting securities — all general business corporations must have at least one class of such voting securities — have the right to vote on the election of directors and on other important corporate decisions such as amendment of the articles of incorporation, consolidation or merger, generally the sale of substantially all of the corporate assets, and dissolution of the corporation. In addition, creation of a preference or change of rights that would affect one of the classes of the corporation's securities requires a favorable vote of that class even if ordinarily that class has no voting rights. Such business corporation laws generally are explicit with respect to the exclusive sources of funds which may be used for the payment of dividends, the rights of shareholders to inspect or copy the books and records of the corporation, the rights of a portion of them to demand the calling of a shareholders' meeting, and the compensation of shareholders dissenting from a proposed corporate combination or reorganization.

Except for the general rule that payment of dividends may not impair the capital of the corporation, the rights of holders of debt securities of a U.S. corporation are governed, for the most part, not by general corporation laws but by the laws of contracts and creditors' rights.

In addition to the protection afforded by corporation laws, direct holders of securities in a U.S. corporation are also the beneficiaries of general protective legal doctrines developed in this country. The doctrine of *ultra vires* — by which an act of a corporation beyond the scope authorized by its articles or governing statute is invalid — has largely disappeared in recent years. However, under the doctrine of corporate opportunity, a director or officer generally may not seize for himself an opportunity belonging in the first instance to the corporation; the doctrine of corporate waste prohibits directors, officers, and employees from disposing of corporate assets without receiving a fair return; and the doctrine of fraud and deceit prohibits a corporation and its agents from deceiving or committing a fraud on a shareholder. These doctrines can serve both U.S. and foreign shareholders.

Additional protection is afforded holders of securities of U.S. issuers that are listed on the several national securities exchanges — the best known of which are the New York, the American, the Philadelphia, the Midwest, and the Pacific Coast Stock Exchanges — by the rules of those exchanges and the undertakings demanded by the exchanges as a condition of accepting the listing. For example, the New York Stock Exchange requires that listed corporate issuers appoint an audit committee composed of at least three outside directors. Such rules also require that certain important questions be presented to shareholders for their vote, even though such a vote would not otherwise be required by the governing corporation law, corporate articles or by-laws, or any federal regulatory statute.

Laws and procedures of foreign countries. Other countries likewise protect securities investors. Their laws may apply to U.S. and other foreign securities marketed there, *and* to securities of local corporations and other enterprises established there to hold U.S. securities.

In the United Kingdom, the Companies Act which provides for the organization of limited liability corporations also provides substantial rights for stockholders of such a corporation, including protection for minority stockholders. In addition, English law provides for the use in a public offering of a disclosure document that is somewhat different in concept from the U.S. prospectus, but nevertheless often is effective in informing prospective investors and the brokerage community about the issuer and its securities issues. The takeover code of the London Stock Exchange and the rules of that exchange provide further protection for investors in securities issued by U.S. as well as U.K. and other enterprises quoted on the exchange. An investor in a U.K. corporation which in turn has investments in U.S. securities — whether such investor be local or foreign as to the United Kingdom — apparently is entitled to the protection of these laws. Comprehensive regulations also protect holders of shares of unit trusts and equity linked life assurance contracts, although they are not as detailed as those in the United States. These provide a further measure of protection for those who invest indirectly in the securities of U.S. issuers through the use of such U.K. investment vehicles.

Canada's federal and provincial corporation laws provide the same general protection for stockholders, and to a lesser degree for holders of corporate debt, as the corporation laws of the United States and the United Kingdom. In addition, the provinces have enacted securities laws to govern the conduct of brokerage businesses, and the offer and sale of securities within each province. The primary model — with the exception of the province of Quebec with its French civil law influence — is the province of Ontario. In addition to securities law revisions, legislation amending the Business Corporations Act, and a new Commodity Futures Act,[28] similar laws of this and other provinces require full disclosure by prospectus, prohibit insider trading, and regulate investment brokerage businesses.

The Federal Republic of Germany to a degree regulates its securities industry through its controls over banks which conduct business in the country and which, in addition to performing commercial banking business, act as securities brokers and dealers. Germany also has a number of stock exchanges which apply their own rules to securities traded there. Moreover, with particular regard to investment companies, Germany has adopted both a domestic investment company law *and* a foreign investment company law.[29] These laws regulate in great detail the activities of domestic and foreign investment companies, endeavor to minimize their potential conflicts of interest, and require the use of a sales prospectus in connection with the public offering of shares of such companies within the country. These laws provide a measure of protection to the investor purchasing in Germany the shares of U.S. registered investment companies, offshore investment companies designed to invest in U.S. securities, *or* German investment companies which invest in securities of U.S. issuers.

Other major financial centers, particularly in Europe, provide similar protection through statutes or close administrative supervision. For example, the Netherlands has a comprehensive corporation law and an active Amsterdam Stock Exchange exercising supervision of transactions there. Similarly, the Luxembourg banking commissioner has been active with respect to securities offerings of corporations organized there. In France, the *Commission des Opérations de la Bourse* — the so called *COB* — supervises the operations of the Paris Stock Exchange and thus provides a certain measure of protection for investors in securities traded over that exchange.

Developing principles in Western Europe. In order to encourage transnational portfolio investments within the European Economic Community and other industrial countries of Western Europe, certain supranational steps have been taken to protect investors against self-dealing and other such reprehensible conduct by promoters, and to make regulatory burdens more uniform so that criteria applied by one country cannot be used to exclude from that market securities issuers organized under the laws of another country. First, a set of voluntary principles to govern the operations of collective investment funds has been prepared by an international group of investment company and securities experts under the Organization for Economic Cooperation and Development.[30] This group included representatives of the U.S. SEC staff involved in the administration of the U.S. Investment Company Act of 1940. Second, the European Community is considering adoption of a statute requiring that member countries within a prescribed period introduce local legislation containing minimum standards for the conduct of operations and the securities offerings of entities such as investment companies and investment trusts.[31] This may provide additional protection for investors in securities issued by such companies and trusts, and thus make more attractive their use by foreign investors as an indirect means of investing in the securities of U.S. issuers.

However, it should be noted that the United States itself has failed to modify its Investment Company Act of 1940 or to grant many exemptions from its provisions. Thus, it has excluded from U.S. markets the offering and sale of shares by investment companies and trusts organized under foreign laws, although the constraints and investor protection afforded by the foreign country may be quite similar to those afforded under the U.S. act. Moreover, the United States has not made the U.S. tax treatment of shareholders of registered domestic investment companies particularly attractive to foreign investors. This has been a substantial factor in the use, for U.S. portfolio securities investments, of offshore investment companies whose shares are marketed in foreign countries.[32]

Tax and Other Constraints on the Foreign Investor

Anonymity. Continental European, South American, and other civil law countries have a long tradition of corporate and governmental securities issued in bearer form rather than in names registered on the issuer's books. To the contrary, in common law countries such as the United States, Canada, and the United Kingdom, the use of bearer certificates — with the exception of certain bond issues — is virtually unknown. The transfer of investment funds itself — if in excess of $10,000 through a bank, securities broker-dealer, or other financial institution in the United States, or in excess of $5,000 by a traveler to the United States — must be recorded as noted in Chapter VI in connection with establishing a new U.S. business enterprise and Chapter XII in connection with U.S. reporting requirements. Anonymity also is not assured even where U.S. securities are held for the sake of convenience in the name of a U.S. brokerage firm, bank, or other custodian or depository in so called street name. As described in greater detail in Chapter XII, both U.S. issuers of securities and U.S. holders of record may be required to make certain reports of U.S. portfolio investments by foreign persons.

As noted generally in Chapter I, after 1982 any corporate or domestic governmental issues of publicly offered obligations of longer than one year generally must use registered rather than bearer debt instruments to avoid substantial federal tax penalties. However, these may be largely avoided if such obligations are sold *only* to non-U.S. persons; even then, capital gain treatment or the use of losses upon a foreign holder's disposition of the obligations is made unavailable, but this will often not change the general federal taxation of such a foreign holder as discussed further below. Insofar as U.S. entities are concerned, each foreign recipient of dividends, interest, or other periodic investment income also should provide to the payor of the income a U.S. taxpayer identification number if he has a U.S. office or U.S. business income.

A degree of anonymity may be obtained by the foreign investor having his U.S. securities held instead by a foreign trust or nominee — particularly a foreign bank acting outside the United States. A number of foreign countries have bank secrecy laws that stringently preserve the anonymity of customers and depositors. These include Switzerland, the Bahamas, the Cayman Islands, Liechtenstein, and Panama, as well as a number of other countries with laws almost equally strict. Accordingly, the desire for anonymity may not significantly narrow the choice among available alternative methods of investment directly or indirectly in U.S. securities where the securities — whether of U.S. issuers or of foreign issuers which in turn invest in securities of U.S. issuers — can be acquired directly by such a bank on instructions from its customer which will be subject to the bank secrecy laws of the country in which the bank is located. However, a foreign subsidiary of a U.S. bank may be more easily forced to disclose in the United States the identity of beneficial owners.

Limitations on the use of such nominee holders should be noted. First, in those cases where the beneficial owner of the securities would be entitled to a lower U.S. withholding tax rate on investment income due to a tax treaty between the United States and his own country, he may forfeit that tax advantage if he selects a holder that is not itself located in the same treaty country.

Second, as described further above, the federal Securities Exchange Act of 1934 requires disclosure of substantial information by beneficial owners of more than five percent of any class of equity securities of certain publicly held corporations — whether or not acquired in connection with a takeover bid. Furthermore, any person owning 10% or more of any such class of equity securities must file statements with the SEC detailing his ownership, and is prohibited from profiting by purchases and sales of the securities which occur within six months of each other. It seems likely that substantial violations of such U.S. securities (or other) laws from abroad will result in attempts to force a foreign bank or other nominee — even in Switzerland — to disclose the beneficial owners for whom it acts.

Likewise, foreign persons who engage directly (or through a foreign broker) in commodity futures trading on U.S. exchanges are subject to the jurisdiction of the U.S. Commodity Futures Trading Commission and possible reporting requirements, which may be enforced also against intermediaries such as a foreign bank acting as nominee or a futures commission merchant who handles the trading.[33]

Third, even a fairly small portfolio investment (in terms of amount invested or percentage owned) in U.S. real estate or natural resource interests held by a foreign person directly or through a U.S. or foreign corporation or other legal entity may be subject to special reporting as described in Chapter XII.

Foreign exchange regulations. In a number of countries, the local currency is directly convertible into U.S. dollars or other foreign currencies without restriction as to time or amount. Investors resident in such countries — for example, the Federal Republic of Germany, the Netherlands, and Switzerland — are allowed to use their local currencies freely to acquire securities expressed or payable in or to be purchased with U.S. dollars. Furthermore, when such U.S. investments are liquidated by sale, or by payment at maturity date as in the case of a debt obligation, they may freely use the U.S. dollar proceeds to acquire other U.S. dollar investments or for conversion into other currencies. A chief issue even in such circumstances is the wisdom of holding equity or debt securities that represent U.S. dollar investments in view of the decline in the value of the dollar in various such foreign currencies since 1971; however, this may be offset by its subsequent major recovery in value.

On the other hand, the currencies of a number of countries are non-convertible where the purpose of the conversion is to permit investment in securities or other investments of the United States or another foreign country. For example, most of the South American and African countries fall into this category, as do certain European countries. Under such circumstances, the foreign investor desiring to make an investment in U.S. securities must consider possible local or other investment vehicles that will permit indirect investment by use of the local currency. Alternatively, the prospective investor may be able to use unrepatriated U.S. dollars or other freely convertible foreign currencies to make an investment in U.S. securities.

Certain countries have partial restrictions on currency convertibility. For example, investments in U.S. dollar equity or debt securities by persons in the United Kingdom or the scheduled territories until such controls were lifted could be made only by funds accumulated in convertible currency accounts lawfully maintained outside the investor's country *or* by the use of so called premium dollars purchased from the Bank of England at a rate higher than the normal exchange rate together with surrender of a portion of the proceeds of a subsequent sale or other liquidation of the dollar investment to the Bank of England. France permits its residents to use French francs to purchase foreign securities from other residents. However, it has recently extended the exchange controls it imposed in other areas to prohibit the conversion of francs into foreign currencies for purposes of securities portfolio investments. Restrictions of these types make direct investments in U.S. securities, in the absence of specific permission from the currency authorities, an expensive proposition.

Another means by which foreign exchange controls are effected is by a requirement that a portion of each foreign investment made by a resident of the country be invested in securities issued by public or private entities of that country or other investments physically located within that country. This type of control often has been imposed by Italy.

U.S. income and estate taxation. A major consideration in assessing the desirability of available alternative methods of investment in the securities of U.S. issuers is the extent to which U.S. income and estate taxes may be imposed on the foreign investor. The impact of general U.S. income taxation at the level of a U.S. corporation or other entity organized under the laws of the United States was described briefly further above in connection with alternative methods generally available for such portfolio investments. As to considerations in determining which alternative is most suitable for a foreign investor, the impact of federal and state taxes at the *foreign ownership* level also must be considered.

The Foreign Investors Tax Act of 1966[34] changed the structure of federal tax provisions applicable to nonresident aliens, foreign corporations, and other foreign persons as described more fully in Chapter II. It was designed in part to stimulate further foreign investment in the United States to help offset unfavorable U.S. balances of trade. In connection with U.S. portfolio securities investments, dividends, interest, original issue discount on certain bonds with a maturity of more than six months, and other fixed or periodic income received by such foreign persons from U.S. sources are subject to a flat 30% federal withholding tax (reduced by treaty in certain cases, as indicated below) if such income is not effectively connected with the conduct of a trade or business within the United States by the foreign recipient.

Long-term or short-term capital or other gain from the sale of U.S. securities (apparently including options[35]) or of commodities or commodity futures — if it is not so effectively connected with a U.S. trade or business — generally is *taxfree* to a foreign investor. The foreign investor may even give discretionary authority to a U.S. broker or other agent to trade securities or certain commodities for the investor's account and will not thereby be treated as engaged in U.S. trade or business for federal income tax purposes. This taxfree treatment also generally extends even to deductible capital gain distributions from a U.S. regulated investment company to foreign holders.[36] Unless the foreign investor does receive such effectively connected income, he is usually not required to file a U.S. federal income tax return, since the withholding tax obligation of the payor satisfies his federal income tax obligation on most non-effectively connected income.

However, there are several exceptions to this taxfree treatment:

(1) A nonresident alien present in the United States at least 183 days in the taxable year of sale is subject to a 30% tax on such capital gain.

(2) A widely held foreign investment company with its principal office in the United States at any time during the taxable year (including through certain activities of a U.S. investment adviser) may be considered to be engaged in U.S. trade or business. This may be advantageous in order to eliminate the 30% withholding tax and permit the 85% or 100% intercorporate dividends received deduction on dividends paid to the company on its U.S. stock investments connected with the U.S. business.

(3) A foreign partner in a widely held U.S. *or* foreign partnership with its principal office in the United States may be treated as engaged in U.S. trade or business.

(4) As described in greater detail in Chapter III, a foreign investor's gain on disposition of U.S. real estate or natural resource interests (including those held through a real estate investment trust) or of stock of a U.S. corporation owning such interests, or on distribution of such interests by a foreign corporation, usually is subject to federal capital gain or ordinary income tax.[37]

It should be noted that a foreign corporation owned at least one-half by foreign persons also may be owned in part by unrelated *U.S.* persons, without eliminating the taxfree character of its capital gains or subjecting the U.S. investors to taxation on undistributed earnings or other onerous federal tax provisions.[38]

Tax treaties between the United States and other countries for the most part reduce the federal withholding tax rate on U.S. dividends from 30% to between five percent and 15%. The treaty also may eliminate altogether the withholding of federal income tax on payments of interest on debt securities of U.S. issuers. For example, the use of a corporation organized by the foreign investors in the Netherlands Antilles, perhaps with a subsidiary in the Netherlands, to make U.S. portfolio securities investments may permit realization of part or all of such treaty benefits without substantial local taxation. Such treaty benefits also override the general 10% federal withholding tax on dividends and interest payments to an individual (domestic or foreign). In all tax treaty structuring, however, the distinction between treaty use and abuse must be considered.[39]

Federal gift tax does not apply to U.S. securities and other intangible property transferred by a nonresident alien. However, the value of securities of U.S. issuers belonging to a nonresident alien at his death is subject to federal estate taxation. An estate tax tax credit roughly equivalent to a $60,000 exclusion from the taxable estate applies to such a foreign decedent.[40] Again, the United States has entered into several treaties with other countries reducing the imposition of double estate taxes in the United States and the country of the decedent's domicile, as noted in Chapter II. However, such federal estate taxation may remain a factor encouraging investment in U.S. securities indirectly through a foreign corporation or other foreign entity.

In this connection, the issuance of debt obligations by foreign — especially Netherlands Antilles — finance subsidiaries of U.S. issuers to finance U.S. and foreign operations currently not only permits taxfree interest payments by the subsidiary to foreign holders, but avoids possible federal estate tax on the obligations.[41]

In addition to taxfree interest on municipal bonds and similar governmental debt obligations — as described further above in connection with the general U.S. income taxation of securities investments — it should be noted in the case of a foreign investor that such a foreign person may own U.S. bank deposits and certain similar deposits without being subject to federal income tax on the interest or federal gift or estate taxes on their transfer.[42]

If a foreign investment company or other foreign entity — non-U.S. or out-of-state U.S. — conducts business in a U.S. state, it may be subject to local income and other taxes. However, such local business conduct often is inapplicable to portfolio investments.

Furthermore, a donor or decedent who is not domiciled in a state often is not taxed there as to securities or other intangible property unless — as seems unlikely in the case of portfolio investments — they have been used in a business conducted there. However, as noted generally in Chapter II, these laws must be examined to determine whether they attempt to impose such state gift, estate, or inheritance taxes — particularly if the securities are kept in the state or the issuer's principal place or major part of its business is located there.

Foreign tax laws. A further factor affecting the method which a foreign investor may choose for an investment in U.S. securities is taxation in the country of the investor's own tax residence.

Unlike the United States, most countries impose worldwide income tax only on local residents, and exclude even their citizens who may be *bona fide* residents of other countries. For example, a number of U.K. citizens in the highly paid fields of athletics and entertainment have changed residence to other countries with less burdensome income taxes. Similarly, a nonresident alien who has invested directly or indirectly in securities of a U.S. issuer but is a *bona fide* resident of a country other than that of which he is a citizen generally will not be subject to taxation by his home country on the profits on such investment, unless they are paid through an enterprise of his home country and subjected to a withholding tax there.

On the other hand, the country of which he is a resident at the time may, although it is not his country of nationality, impose a tax on such investment income received by him while such a resident from sources outside that country. However, a number of countries tax at a reduced rate or do not tax at all investment and other income received from foreign sources, except possibly where such income is received as a direct result of the conduct of business within the country.

In many countries, tax laws have been deliberately structured to favor portfolio investments considered socially desirable by the local government. This may in turn influence the method which an investor there may select to invest in U.S. securities, or make it impractical to do so at all. For example, Canadian income tax deductions are granted to residents for investments in so called Registered Retirement Savings Plans. This tax incentive apparently has been one reason that Canadian direct investment in the shares of U.S. mutual funds, notwithstanding free currency convertibility, has not been as popular as otherwise might be the case, because such approved investments favor Canadian enterprises.

In the United Kingdom, income tax deductions are available for amounts put aside by individuals for life assurance premiums. No such benefits generally are obtained for mere investment in the shares of domestic investment companies or unit trusts of foreign investment companies, or for investments directly in the securities of other types of issuers. Accordingly, a substantial portion of investments — including in U.S. securities — by individuals resident in the United Kingdom is effected indirectly through the purchase of premiums on equity linked or property linked life assurance contracts.

The foreign investment company law of the Federal Republic of Germany encourages foreign investment companies to qualify public offerings of their shares in Germany by proper registration with local banking authorities, by applying the lowest tax burden to income of a German holder from such qualified shares. The law encourages such foreign companies alternatively to appoint a tax representative in Germany to help assure that income received by German owners of the company's shares is properly reported and subjected to German tax, by applying only a slightly higher tax burden to income from such shares. However, for shares held by German residents in a foreign investment company which has neither qualified for public distribution of its shares under the law, nor appointed such a tax representative and provided German tax authorities with the appropriate tax calculation information, a penalty tax applies to income of the German shareholder.

Footnotes to Chapter IX

1. 15 U.S.C. §78*l*; *see* Chapters I, VII *supra.*

2. 47 U.S.C. §310; 49 U.S.C. §§1401, 1403; *see generally* Chapters I, VI *supra.*.

3. Options in certain listed securities are currently traded on the Chicago Board Options Exchange and the American, Philadelphia, Midwest, and Pacific Coast Stock Exchanges. In addition, warrants to purchase listed stock are in a number of instances separately traded on the various U.S. national stock exchanges. The New York Stock Exchange's application for authority to trade options in certain listed equity securities was pending with the Securities and Exchange Commission as of early 1982; the New York Exchange's authority to proceed with trading of financial options (such as options on debt obligations) also was awaiting resolution of regulatory problems under a recent judicial decision.

4. *See* Chapters I, III, VI *supra.*

5. 15 U.S.C. §§80a-1 through 80a-52. The definitions of an investment company are contained in §80a-3(a), and the exemptions from that section are found in §80a-3(b). The classification and sub-classification of investment companies are spelled out in §§80a-4 and -5, respectively.

6. These corporations are not necessarily small either in aggregate assets or in size of income. The term primarily is applied to a corporation which is held by a limited number of equity shareholders and has as its primary purpose the holding of portfolio securities rather than the direct operation of businesses through the use of subsidiaries.

7. 15 U.S.C. §§80a-3, 80a-8. The definitional provisions are in §3(a), while §7(a) makes it unlawful for a domestic company meeting this definition to engage in business without registration under §8(b) of that act.

8. 15 U.S.C. §78*l*; *see* Chapter I *supra.* Paragraph (2) of §78*l*(g) contains certain exemptions from such registration for domestic corporations, while paragraph (3) sets forth the basic rule allowing the Securities and Exchange Commission to exempt from such registration securities of foreign issuers. It should also be noted that §78*l*(a) requires registration of securities traded on a national securities exchange.

9. I.R.C. §542. In addition to the basic definition contained in §542, the income test set forth in §543 must be met. The rules for determining constructive ownership of the corporation which appear in very detailed form in §544 must be observed. The tax imposed by §541 only operates on undistributed personal holding company income and provision is made in §547 for avoiding such tax by the use of so called deficiency dividends.

10. *Cf. Gesetz über Kapitalanlagegesellschaften (KAGG),* Law Concerning Capital Investment Companies, originally promulgated April 16, 1957, and subsequently amended.

11. *See* Chapters III, VI *supra*; *see also* Chapter II *supra.*

12. *See* note 9 *supra.*

13. I.R.C. §§531-537. It is difficult to sustain the burden of proof that accumulations of taxable income in excess of $250,000 are within reasonable business needs where the corporation is an investment company. The surtax can apply to an investment company registered under the Investment Company Act of 1940 which does not take advantage of the special tax election provided by I.R.C. §§851-855. *Cf.* Rev. Rul. 77-399, 1977-2 C.B. 200; *see* note 16 *infra.*

14. I.R.C. §243. The special rules and restrictions set forth in §§243(c), 244 and 246(c) must be carefully observed, and the provision applicable to certain foreign corporations spelled out in §245 should be taken into account.

15. Treas. Reg. §301.7701-2. This regulation as well as certain of the provisions of Treas. Reg. §§301.7701-3 and -4 should be carefully observed to determine the nature of the enterprise for U.S. federal income tax purposes. In general, federal tax authorities may attempt to redefine for income tax purposes associations, corporations, partnerships, and trusts. With respect to such characterization of foreign entities, see also Chapter II *supra.*

16. I.R.C. §§851-855, 856-860. This has been very helpful in the merchandising of investment company securities, and recently has been extended to include such flow-through tax treatment for investment companies that invest in taxfree state and municipal securities. *See also* note 36 *infra.*

17. I.R.C. §§701-761.

18. *Cf.* I.R.C. §103.

19. 15 U.S.C. §§77a-77aa.

20. 15 U.S.C. §§77c, 77d; *see also* Chapter I *supra.*

21. 15 U.S.C. §§78a-78hh; *see especially* §78j and Rule 10b-5; *see also* §§78f, 78k,78k-1, 78*o*-3, 78*o*-4, 78q-1 relating to securities markets and entities engaged in those markets.

22. *See* note 5 *supra.*

23. 15 U.S.C. §§80b-1 through 80b-21. This brief act has been implemented by a detailed body of regulations issued by the SEC.

24. 15 U.S.C. §§77aaa-77bbbb.

25. 15 U.S.C. §§79 through 79z-6.

26. 15 U.S.C. §§78aaa-78*lll.*

27. *See generally* Comment, "Subject Matter Jurisdiction in Transnational Securities Fraud Cases," B.C. Indus. & Com. L. Rev. 413 (1976); A. S. Young, Jr., "The Rights and Liabilities of Shareholders," 5 Int'l Bus. Lawyer 427 (1977). This latter article deals primarily with rights of shareholders of U.S. corporations. *See also* Chapter VII *supra*, note 16.

28. *See* S.O.C. 47, 48, 49 (1978).

29. *Gesetz über den Vertrieb Ausländischer Investmentanteile und über die Besteuerung der Erträge aus Ausländischen Investmentanteilen (AuslInvestmG),* Law Concerning the Distribution of Foreign Investment Shares and the Taxation of Revenues from Foreign Investment Shares, promulgated July 28, 1969, and subsequently amended. For the domestic investment company law, see note 10 *supra.* An updated translation of the domestic law was published in early 1982 by H. Niebler, Dr. Jur. LL.M. of the Bar of the Federal Republic of Germany, with editorial assistance from this chapter's author, and a supplement updating the foreign investment law translation has been prepared.

30. O.E.C.D., *Standard Rules for the Operations of Institutions for Collective Investment in Securities* (1972).

31. The E.E.C. Commission submitted to the Council in 1976 a document entitled "Proposal for a Council Directive for the coordination of laws, regulations and administrative provisions regarding collective investment undertakings for transferable securities," COM (76) 152 final.

32. It should be noted that in April 1982 an application was pending before the SEC for the registration under the Investment Company Act of 1940 of a German investment company and for the granting of a number of exemptions thereunder.

In 1973, the SEC submitted proposed legislation to the U.S. Congress permitting the incorporation of so called Foreign Portfolio Sales Corporations which would be registered under the Investment Company Act of 1940 and be subject to its detailed regulations, yet would be advantageous from a U.S. tax standpoint for prospective foreign investors. *See* Investment Company Act of 1940, S.E.C. Release No. 7751, 38 Fed. Reg. 8593 (1973). Although this was supported by both the SEC and the U.S. Department of the Treasury, it is not under active consideration by the Congress.

33. *See generally* A. S. Young, Jr., *supra* note 27; Chapters I, VII *supra*; *cf.* S.E.C. v. Banca Della Svizzera Italiana, 92 F.R.D. 111 (S.D.N.Y. 1981); United States v. Vetco Inc., 644 F.2d 1324 (9th Cir. 1981); 7 U.S.C. §§1 *et seq.* and regulations thereunder, *e.g.,* 17 C.F.R. Part 15. The United

States and Switzerland have negotiated an agreement for Swiss disclosure of beneficial owners involved in certain violations of U.S. securities laws.

34. Pub. L. 89-809 (Nov. 13, 1966), 80 Stat. 1539; *see especially* I.R.C. §864(b); Chapter II *supra.* The basic provisions have remained in effect notwithstanding numerous general changes made by the Tax Reform Act of 1976 and other tax revisions, except as to real estate and natural resource investments affected by the Foreign Investment in Real Property Tax Act of 1980, as amended, which is described in Chapter III *supra.*

35. I.R.C. §§1234(b), 1234A.

36. I.R.C. §§851-855. Investment company distributions of taxfree interest on state and municipal securities also are taxfree for foreign persons to the same extent as for U.S. persons. I.R.C. §852(b)(5). For the possible use of a U.S. trust to generate taxfree non-effectively connected capital gain for a foreign beneficiary, see Chapter XI *infra.*

37. I.R.C. §§871(a)(2), 864(b)(2), 243, 882, 897; Treas. Reg. §1.864-2(c)(2)(ii).

38. *See generally* Chapter VIII *supra.* With respect particularly to the possible taxation of U.S. owners of a widely held foreign investment company, *see* I.R.C. §§1246-1247.

38. *See generally* Chapter VIII *supra.* With respect particularly to the possible taxation of U.S. owners of a widely held foreign investment company, *see* I.R.C. §§1246-1247. .

39. *See generally* Chapters I, II *supra*; *cf.* Rev. Rul. 79-251, 1979-2 C.B. 271 (interest received by Netherlands Antilles corporation on GNMA modified pass-through obligations, even though secured by U.S. real property, is taxfree under applicable income tax treaty). Another possibility may be a corporation resident in the U.S. Virgin Islands. *See also* descriptions of these jurisdictions in Chapter III *supra.*

40. I.R.C. §2102(c); *see generally* Chapter II *supra.*

41. *Cf.* United States-Netherlands Income Tax Treaty of 1948, as amended and presently in force between the United States and the Netherlands Antilles, Art. XII. For similar treatment of certain U.S. finance subsidiaries' debt obligations issued before July 1974, see I.R.C. §§861(a)(1)(G)-(H), 2104(c).

42. I.R.C. §§861(c), 2104(c).

Chapter X

Immigration Laws

A nonresident alien individual investor in the United States who seeks entry and/or residence in the United States must consider at least two principal factors which often are interrelated: U.S. immigration and naturalization laws, and tax planning. This chapter examines the former, and the next chapter the latter, together with certain observations respecting their relationship.

U.S. immigration laws[1] are administered principally by the Immigration and Naturalization Service ("INS") within the Department of Justice and by the Department of State through U.S. consulates abroad. These laws classify aliens coming to the United States from abroad either as nonimmigrants or as immigrants. Nonimmigrants are aliens who wish to enter the United States for a temporary purpose but who do not seek permanent residence — although certain employment within the United States may be authorized for such individuals — and, accordingly, remain nonresident aliens for U.S. immigration law purposes. The procedure for obtaining a nonimmigrant visa depends principally on the specific type of visa sought. By contrast, immigrants are aliens with permission to live and work in the United States on a permanent basis and often are referred to as resident aliens or permanent residents of the United States for immigration purposes.

The procedure for obtaining an immigrant visa — referred to as a green card, although the card issued currently is white — often is quite complicated. One advantage of an immigrant visa is that the holder becomes eligible for U.S. citizenship within five years (three years if married to a U.S. citizen). In the meantime, he is free to travel in and out of the United States under the passport of his country of nationality, although generally he must reside in the United States. He also enjoys most of the rights, privileges, and responsibilities of a U.S. citizen, except notably the right to vote and the right to hold certain public offices.

Nonimmigrant Visas

The following list of available nonimmigrant visas includes selected points respecting their particular application to foreign investors. Nonimmigrant visas generally are obtained outside the United States by application to a U.S. consulate, although in certain cases the application process is initiated by filing a visa petition in the United States with INS. Within certain limitations, a nonresident alien in the United States on the basis of one nonimmigrant visa status also may change that status for another nonimmigrant status without the inconvenience of leaving the country.

A Visa

These visas are issued to senior government employees, ambassadors, and ministers and generally are referred to as diplomatic visas. While such visas are not available to the typical foreign investor, the holder of an A visa is not precluded from making investments and many foreign diplomats do indeed hold directly or indirectly beneficial interests in U.S. investments.

B-1 Visa

These generally are referred to as business visitor visas and are issued to nonresident aliens who are compensated abroad and come to the United States for purposes relating to their businesses abroad. The B-1 visa thus can readily function as a foreign investor visa, since its holder may purchase U.S. businesses or properties, seek the counsel of U.S. business and professional advisers, and effect investments for and on behalf of foreign enterprises.

Although these visas are relatively easy to obtain, they do have certain drawbacks. First, although the visa itself may be of unlimited duration, at the point of U.S. entry the INS officer generally will not admit the holder for a period in excess of six months and often will restrict initial entry to 30 or 60 days. Extensions of this initial period must be obtained from INS within the United States and frequently are similarly restricted to short periods of time. INS offices in metropolitan areas typically are overcrowded, making the extension process often very time consuming or, if professional assistance is employed to try to expedite the process, costly.

The second and more perplexing problem for the foreign investor may be that a B-1 visa cannot be utilized if he will be working within the United States. While passive investments generally are not deemed to involve such work, active investments arguably may — particularly if the investor will receive compensation from the U.S. investment.

B-2 Visa

These are tourist visas and can be obtained fairly easily for pleasure trips. However, U.S. border officials generally limit the initial stay under such a visa to 30 days or less, requiring the inconvenience of obtaining frequent extensions from INS. If a business purpose develops during the visitor's stay, it is possible to apply to INS for change of nonimmigrant status to a B-1 or other visa.

C and D Visas

C visas are transit visas, are very restrictive, and usually are not applicable to aliens who seek to invest in the United States.

D visas usually are granted to crew members of visiting vessels, are very restrictive, and likewise are unlikely visas for foreign investors.

E-1 Visa

These are referred to as treaty trader visas. These visas are available only to nationals of certain of those countries with which the United States has concluded a treaty of friendship, commerce, and navigation.[2] In order to obtain this visa, the alien must be involved with an enterprise which conducts substantial trade principally between the United States and the country of his nationality. The definition of substantial trade is unclear, but where the trade merely supports the treaty trader and his family, it may be considered to be substantial where good faith efforts have been made to conduct international trade. The term "principally" is interpreted as requiring in excess of one-half of all trade conducted by the alien's enterprise. The trading enterprise also must be majority owned by nationals of the applicant's country. However, the applicant either may be the principal or sole investor or may be an executive, managerial, or key technical employee of the enterprise meeting these criteria.

The E-1 is a very useful and popular visa, since it permits stays of up to a year and ordinarily can be renewed for successive years as often as desired, as long as the alien's enterprise qualifies.

E-2 Visa

These are referred to as treaty investor visas. Like the treaty trader visas, they are limited to nationals of certain of those countries with which the United States has concluded a treaty of friendship, commerce, and navigation. Since few countries wish to encourage U.S. or other foreign currency to leave the country freely for investments abroad, there are fewer such treaties with the United States which include investment as well as trade.[3] Similarly to the E-1 visa, an alien who seeks to obtain an E-2 visa must be the principal investor or a key employee of an investing enterprise majority owned by nationals of the same country. Where he has a partner, the partner must be of the same nationality. In this connection, it should be noted that resident aliens of the United States are not regarded as foreign nationals for E-1 *or* E-2 purposes.

The investment also must be in a business which is actively conducted. Dormant or inactive operations, such as investments in undeveloped real estate or unworked forest lands, will not qualify. It must be a substantial investment, which excludes investing a small amount of capital in a marginally profitable enterprise solely for the purpose of earning a living. An investment of at least $100,000 usually is recommended. On the other hand, unlike an E-1 visa, an E-2 visa does not require that the alien's enterprise involve importation, exportation, or other types of trade.

F-1 and F-2 Visas

F-1 visas typically are given to students and normally are not considered applicable to foreign investors. However, a student may be an investor as long as he maintains the academic requirements of his university or other school and does not accept unauthorized employment.

The spouse and dependents of an F-1 visa holder are eligible for F-2 visas. While employment is not authorized, an F-2 visa holder is not precluded from making and overseeing investments as long as the same is not deemed to constitute work. Since the F-2 visa holder does not have the burden of meeting educational requirements, it is possible for one spouse to qualify as a student while the other functions as an investor. If the U.S. investments become operational, the alien may apply for a change of status either to a treaty investor, or to a resident alien subject to quota numbers being available as discussed further below.

G Visa

These visas are issued to representatives of foreign governments serving with international organizations — notably the United Nations — their staffs, servants, employees, and members of the immediate families of all such individuals. Like A visas, these are of limited interest to the typical foreign investor, but holders of such visas are not precluded from investing in the United States.

H Visa

H visas — including H-1, H-2, and H-3 — normally are not applicable to foreign investors. They are temporary work or training visas and, since the status of an alien in a work or training program must be maintained for the duration of the visa, there is little mobility or opportunity to perform other functions. However, since professionals may be eligible for H-1 visas to perform professional services, this category may be applicable to an investor in a business in which he will perform such services.

I Visa

These visas are reserved for persons working in the communications media. Such visa holders generally have great mobility as well as time to perform other functions, including seeking out and effecting U.S. investments, as long as this does not constitute additional work.

J-1 and J-2 Visas

J-1 visas are intended for foreign nationals coming to the United States pursuant to an approved program for exchange visitors. Once the J-1 visa holder has completed the educational or other program for which the visa was obtained, he may be required to return to his country of nationality for a minimum of two years before being eligible to apply for a U.S. immigrant visa if the program in which he participated was government financed or if he has job skills designated as essential by his home country.

On the other hand, the spouse and dependents of a J-1 visa holder are eligible for J-2 visas and may work to support themselves or family members other than the J-1 visa holder. A J-2 visa is an excellent investor visa if a stay of no more than two to three years in the United States is required for the investment. Such a visa is not advisable for longer periods, since it is exceedingly difficult to renew or exchange for another visa once it expires.

K Visa

This visa is used strictly for the temporary entry to an alien fiancé(e) of a U.S. citizen or resident alien, and cannot be extended. Therefore, it is not relevant to the needs of the typical foreign investor.

L Visa

L visas are designed to facilitate the transfer of aliens employed abroad by a corporation (or other firm or legal entity) for continued employment in the United States by the same or an affiliated enterprise. Such an individual must (1) serve in a managerial or executive capacity, or (2) possess specialized knowledge which makes his presence in the United States necessary to the U.S. enterprise. He must have been in the employ abroad of the first corporation or other entity continuously for at least one year immediately preceding the date of transfer to the U.S. enterprise. However, there is no requirement that the two enterprises have been related for the one-year period. The entity abroad must transfer him to a U.S. branch office or a subsidiary or affiliated U.S. corporation. A U.S. corporation is considered affiliated with a foreign corporation if a substantial portion of the voting stock of one is owned by the other, or if such a portion of both corporations is owned by a third person.

The L visa is a good mechanism for foreign investment where the investor establishes a U.S. branch, subsidiary, or affiliate of a foreign corporation, particularly one which he owns. After establishing the U.S. enterprise, he can transfer himself to the United States on the L visa or spend as much time as he wishes in the United States and draw compensation for the same. Moreover, even an L visa holder who works for another corporation can be an investor or facilitate foreign investment without violating his visa as long as he maintains his full-time employment status.

The L visa may be initially obtained for periods of up to three years. In addition, the visa often can be converted to an immigrant visa under the sixth preference category because the requirements are quite similar, as described further below.

The possession of an L visa also ensures L visas for the alien's spouse and children, but they cannot work in the United States unless they independently qualify for a visa status which permits gainful employment. However, the spouse of an L visa holder is not prohibited from undertaking U.S. investments. The spouse continues to qualify for an L visa as long as the principal L visa holder maintains qualifying status.

Grounds for Exclusion

A nonresident alien applying for a nonimmigrant visa under the requirements of one of the above categories may be denied such a visa if he is excludable on one of several grounds specified in the immigration laws.[4] Among the excludable categories are individuals who are retarded or insane, who suffer from contagious diseases, who have committed criminal offenses or acts involving moral turpitude, who are likely to become public charges in the United States, who have engaged in fraud in attempting to obtain a U.S. visa, or who are anarchists or members of the Communist party. These grounds for exclusion are the same for nonimmigrant *and* immigrant visas as discussed further below; however, waivers of all grounds of excludability are available for nonimmigrant entry.

Immigrant Visas

Quotas and Preferences

Nonresident aliens applying for U.S. immigrant visas generally are subject to quotas restricting the number of such individuals who may immigrate to the United States during each calendar year. Under current quotas, generally no more than 270,000 nonresident aliens may immigrate annually to the United States from all countries. Moreover, the annual quota is 20,000 immigrants for any one country including 600 from each colony, commonwealth, or other dependency of that country.[5]

However, it should be noted that so called illegal aliens unlawfully migrating to the United States have drawn attention to such issues as employment competition with U.S. citizens and lawful residents.

increased U.S. social services costs, and the exploitation of such aliens by employers. These may lead to substantial modifications in U.S. immigration laws, including penalties on U.S. employers who knowingly hire illegal aliens, an increased annual quota for immigrants, and possibly an amnesty for certain illegal aliens present for at least five years in the country.

Certain categories of individuals are exempt from the quota system. These include particularly immediate relatives constituting the spouse, unmarried minor children, and parents of a U.S. citizen (except that, in the case of a foreign parent, the U.S. citizen must be at least 21 years of age).

Applicants subject to immigration numerical limitations are further divided into categories and each category is allocated a certain percentage of the available quota numbers according to a system of preferences.[6] The preference categories are as follows:

(1) The unmarried sons and daughters (adults or minors) of U.S. citizens are allocated the first 20% of the annual quota.

(2) The spouses and unmarried sons and daughters (adults or minors) of lawful U.S. resident aliens are allocated the next 26% of the quota.

(3) The succeeding 10% of the quota is allocated to professionals, scientists, and artists considered to have exceptional abilities.

(4) Married sons and daughters of U.S. citizens are allocated the next 10% of the quota.

(5) Brothers and sisters of U.S. citizens are allocated the next 24% of the quota. However, this preference category is applicable only where the U.S. citizen is at least 21 years of age.

(6) The next 10% of the quota is allocated to individuals capable of performing specified skilled or unskilled labor for which a shortage of employable and willing persons exists in the United States, as determined by the labor certification process described further below.

(7) Separate annual quotas are allocated to refugees — from, for example, communist controlled countries or countries within the Middle East — who are likely to encounter political, religious, or racial persecution if returned to their countries of nationality and whose admission is justified by humanitarian concerns.

(8) The final category — generally referred to as nonpreference — consists of various other groups, including individuals sufficiently financially secure so as not to be required to work in the United States and individuals who have invested substantial sums in U.S. business enterprises in which they will act as principal managers.This may be expanded as noted further below.

Additional Restrictions

Obtaining a quota number does not necessarily assure the right to immigrate to the United States. First, as described earlier in connection with nonimmigrant visas, the nonresident alien must not be excludable on one of several specified grounds. On acceptance of an immigration application, a security check is made to determine whether the applicant is excludable on any of such grounds. The investigation may be relatively time consuming, since a police clearance certificate will be required from authorities in every city and country where the applicant has resided from the age of 16. If the applicant anticipates opposition from his government, or feels that his record may be questionable in any respect, appropriate investigation and preparation should be made before the application is filed in order to determine the precise facts. An individual whose criminal, medical, political, or other problems may be sufficiently severe to preclude U.S. admission may be able to obtain a waiver on a nonimmigrant basis, but not if he seeks to enter as an immigrant; in the event this is a possibility, it may be wise to consider seeking a nonimmigrant visa. However, certain grounds for excludability may be waived in the case of a refugee.

Second, even if quota number eligibility is established and even if the individual is not excludable, he will not be assured immediate entry into the United States under an immigrant visa unless quota numbers are available for the country of his nationality *and* for the preference category for which he qualifies. If quota numbers are not available, the applicant will be placed on a waiting list and will obtain his visa only at such time as a quota number becomes available. This waiting may be substantial, spanning several months or even years. Before commencing proceedings for an immigrant visa, it is prudent to determine whether quota numbers are reasonably current in the category most clearly applicable to the particular individual and, if not, whether he can qualify for another more current category or whether a nonimmigrant visa may be preferable.

It should also be noted that, after an appointment has been scheduled for a final interview at which an immigrant visa is made available, the individual must apply for the visa within one year or his immigrant visa registration will be terminated, unless by the end of the second year he establishes that his failure to do so was due to circumstances beyond his control.

Familial and Other Narrow Preferences

The specific procedure for obtaining a quota number varies depending on the category of exemption or preference involved. Where there is a familial relationship for the immediate relative category or for the first, second, fourth, or fifth preference, the procedure requires principally the filing by the U.S. relative of a petition on Form I-130 with the INS in the United States or abroad, depending on the place of residence of the petitioner. Alternatively, where both parties are physically present there, authority to adjudicate such petitions has been delegated to U.S. consulates abroad. Upon approval of the petition, preference is established and the nonresident alien immediately becomes eligible for an immigrant visa provided that a quota number is available for the preference. In the case of a spouse or minor children of a U.S. citizen who are exempt from the quota system, once the I-130 petition is approved they need not await quota numbers to obtain visas.

Although this procedure is fairly straightforward, it is often not available to the typical foreign investor. However, whenever a nonresident alien contemplates immigration to the United States, the first possibility to be considered is the existence of an appropriate familial relationship: many of the difficult, time consuming, and expensive procedures discussed in the balance of this chapter thus can be avoided.

The third preference for professionals, scientists, and artists of exceptional abilities often is not available because the standards for exceptionality are quite high. However, this may be applicable where an investor expects to serve in a professional capacity.

For individuals who are subject to likely persecution in the country of nationality and are members of groups designated each year by the President as of special humanitarian concern, the separate quotas for refugees may apply if they have not been offered permanent resettlement by any third country that they have entered in flight from persecution. They are admitted conditionally for one year, whereupon an examination is made to determine continued qualification as a refugee.[7]

Sixth Preference

In order to qualify for the sixth preference, a nonresident alien must have (1) a job offer from an employer in the United States, and (2) a certification from the U.S. Department of Labor that no qualified and willing U.S. resident can be found to fill that position. This latter requirement is referred to as a labor certification.

The first step in seeking a sixth preference qualification and related labor certification is to determine the nature and quality of the skills of the prospective immigrant and secure him an offer of such employment from a *bona fide* U.S. employer. If the individual possesses more than one skill, it is wise to select that skill which is most specialized, unusual, or in short supply in the area of the United States where he seeks to reside and the application for labor certification will be filed.[8] The offer must be *bona fide,* provide compensation within the prevailing rate of pay, and be for a fairly long period of time such as two or three years. For an investor, it should be noted that both the labor certification and the sixth preference petition may be applied for by his own U.S. corporation, since the corporation is considered a separate legal entity.

After making the offer, the U.S. employer and the alien must complete the labor certification application to the Department of Labor on Form ETA 750, and file the same with the employment office of the *state* where the employment is to take place. The employer must show that he has made a *bona fide* effort to hire U.S. citizens and/or resident aliens for the position — generally including placement of newspaper advertisements — which effort was not fruitful. The employer must then consider any applicants for the position who are referred by the state employment office and, if these individuals are not hired, convincing explanations for the same must be given.

The state employment office will thereafter forward the application to the appropriate regional office of the U.S. Department of Labor with its findings. The Department may or may not supplement the findings of the state employment office, but generally will approve the application if it is convinced that the employment offer is *bona fide* and that no U.S. individuals have been found to fill the position despite a *bona fide* effort by the employer.

Processing the labor certification application may require from one to six months for the state employment office and another one to three months for the Department of Labor. Fortunately, these labor certification delays may be avoided in certain cases because the Department of Labor provides automatic labor certifications to certain groups listed in what is referred to as Schedule A, which are changed from time to time in response to labor conditions.[9] Schedule A is divided into four groups, Group I of which lists specific occupations deemed to be in short supply. Group II consists of individuals of exceptional abilities in the arts or sciences, including college and university professors. Group III consists of individuals who come to the United States to engage in religious occupations such as the preaching or teaching of religion. Group IV probably is the most interesting to potential foreign investors and may be described as follows:

(a) Aliens who have been admitted to the United States in order to work and who are currently working in executive or managerial positions with the same international corporations or organizations with which they were continuously employed for at least one year before they were admitted; and

(b) Aliens who will be engaged in the United States in executive or managerial positions with the same international corporations or organizations with which they have been continuously employed for the immediately prior year.

Accordingly, a nonresident alien who qualifies for the L non-immigrant visa described further above often also qualifies for the sixth preference under Schedule A. However, there are certain differences between the two sets of requirements — notably (1) the availability of L status to individuals possessing specialized knowledge, whereas the automatic labor certification is available only to those filling executive or managerial positions; (2) the availability of L status to an individual employed by any U.S. affiliate of the foreign entity for which he was employed before U.S. admission, even a foreign subsidiary substantially owned by the same third person owning the U.S. entity, whereas the automatic labor certification is limited to employment by the same international corporation or organization, which generally is interpreted to require employment by a U.S. branch or subsidiary of the prior foreign employer itself; and (3) the availability of L status even where the U.S. affiliate is newly created, whereas the automatic labor certification requires that the U.S. subsidiary or branch have been in existence for at least one year before the transfer (or before the application for adjustment of status from that of nonimmigrant). Where the sixth preference is oversubscribed for the applicant's country of origin, the alien frequently obtains an L visa and later applies for adjustment of status based on a sixth preference petition. However, a possible question exists as to whether an alien desiring to enter the United States permanently is entitled to such temporary visa status.

The Department of Labor also publishes what is referred to as Schedule B, a list of occupations and professions as to which no shortages exist in the Unites States.[10] A nonresident alien seeking labor certification for a profession listed on Schedule B must obtain a waiver from the Department by showing that labor conditions where he has received an offer of employment are different from those elsewhere in the United States.

If the labor certification is granted, it is forwarded by the Department of Labor to the employer. This labor certification may be used not only for petition in the sixth preference but for petition in the third preference — where the applicant is, for example, a professional — or in the non-preference category as noted further below. Accordingly, where quota numbers are likely to be available for the nonpreference category, for example, that approach should be pursued to avoid delays in the further adjudication of a sixth preference petition.

In the case of a sixth preference petition, when the labor certification is received the employer files a petition for sixth preference classification on Form I-140 with INS. INS has the responsibility to determine *bona fide* compliance with the foregoing requirements and the qualifications of the alien for the position. If the employer is located in a large city, an additional six months may be required for this processing by INS. However, at the time the Form I-140 is filed, if the sixth preference category is open to him and he is already in the United States, the alien may file his own application for adjustment of status from nonimmigrant to immigrant on Form I-485 and receive permission at that time to work.

Until this application is filed, the employee may not work in the United States and the penalty for doing so is denial by INS of the application for adjustment of status, which requires the alien to obtain his immigrant visa from an appropriate U.S. consulate abroad. Accordingly, the employer must keep the position unfilled prior to the grant of a labor certification, or support the expense and inconvenience of the employee's round trip to obtain his immigrant visa abroad.

Nonpreference

Whatever portion of the annual quota is not used for the first through seventh preferences is available to qualified nonpreference applicants. In order to qualify, a nonresident alien must either (1) obtain a labor certification to perform skilled or unskilled labor as described above; *or* (2) show by documentary evidence that either (a) his assets and income are sufficient to permit him not to perform work in the United States, referred to as the self-supporting qualification, or (b) he has invested, or is actively in the process of investing, substantial capital in a business enterprise in the United States of which he will be a principal manager, referred to as the investor qualification.

These latter two alternatives have been of particular relevance to many foreign investors. In order to meet the self-supporting qualification, a nonresident alien must bring into the United States assets sufficient to provide him an adequate income and/or must make other showing of such an assured income, for example, as beneficiary of a trust.[11] Each case is determined according to its own facts and circumstances including, for example, the applicant's age, family size, financial requirements, and liquidity. Each consular or INS officer makes his own case by case determination as to the appropriate sums, and in the case of application abroad it is usually possible and advisable to obtain an informal opinion from the appropriate U.S. consulate prior to filing an application.

The investor qualification technically requires a comparatively small investment — at this time a minimum of $40,000 — but a larger amount may be required in any case by the consular or INS officer, and the actual investment must be made or in process prior to filing the visa application.[12] This usually necessitates one or more advance trips to the United States. The U.S. business enterprise must employ one or more U.S. citizens or resident aliens, excluding the applicant and members of his family, and the applicant must act as a principal manager. There is no limitation on the type of investment, but the investment must be such as to provide full time managerial employment for the investor. Real estate investments may qualify provided they are of an active type — for example, significant commercial or multiple residential projects. Here also, since the consular or INS officer makes his own decision, in the case of application abroad an advance informal opinion is advisable.

However, it appears that few quota numbers will be available for the investor category in the immediate future, even for those who can qualify. In this connection, legislation to establish a separate preference category for individuals, for example, each investing at least $250,000 and employing at least four unrelated U.S. individuals has been considered.

Any such nonpreference applicant is permitted to include his spouse and unmarried children in the application and these family members will be entitled to the same quota number as the applicant.

The Choice of Where to Apply

Application for an immigrant visa — unlike that for the usual non-immigrant visa — may be made to a U.S. consulate outside the United States or to INS in the United States. Applications filed outside the United States usually are accepted in the U.S. consulate in the country of the immigrant's last residence, although a consulate elsewhere — for example, in the country of nationality — may be willing to assume jurisdiction. The necessary documentation may even be prepared in the United States by an attorney or other individual and filed abroad on behalf of the applicant. However, various factors may influence the decision whether to apply from outside or within the United States, such as the following:

(1) If the application is filed outside the United States and the applicant already has a multiple entry nonimmigrant visa, then entry into and exit from the United States will not be restricted during the pendency of the application. However, once the application is filed, a *new* non-immigrant visa — particularly a tourist visa — may be difficult or impossible to obtain. Accordingly, it is advisable for an applicant to obtain the longest term nonimmigrant visa possible prior to filing the application.

(2) If the applicant already is in the United States on the basis of a nonimmigrant visa, he may apply to the appropriate INS office for an adjustment of status to that of an immigrant on Form I-485, mentioned above in connection with petition in the sixth preference. The appropriate INS office is located in the district, for example: (a) where the immigrant's relative resides, if the petition is based on a familial relationship; (b) where the employer has his place of business, if the application is based on an offer of employment; (c) where the immigrant has his U.S. residence, if the application is based on the nonpreference self-supporting qualification; or (d) where the immigrant has his business, if the application is based on the nonpreference investor qualification.

There are several principal drawbacks to filing the application in the United States rather than abroad. The first is that an application for adjustment of status will not be accepted at all by INS unless a quota number is available for the applicant's country of origin and for the preference category for which he seeks to qualify. It is not possible to come to the United States on a nonimmigrant visa, file application for adjustment of status and have the same approved in the United States, and thereafter wait in the United States for a quota number to become available.

The second drawback to filing in the United States is that generally no exit can be made from the United States during the pendency of the application without permission from INS, which is usually granted only for family emergencies or necessary business travel. Such exit will invalidate the application and render impossible any future application for adjustment of status, or require the applicant to remain outside the United States until the visa is granted abroad.

The third and perhaps greatest drawback to filing in the United States is the lengthy delay which may result, although this situation may improve. Since INS offices in many metropolitan areas are flooded with applications of various kinds and must spend a substantial fraction of their efforts on the enforcement of other immigration laws, several months may be required for approval of an application even where it is obviously meritorious. In addition, not infrequently, applications are mislaid by INS resulting in further delay and frustration. By contrast, an application filed with a U.S. consulate abroad may be accorded more consideration. For the same reason, an application filed inside the United States usually is more difficult to withdraw or to modify if an exigency arises than one filed in a consulate, where informal response is more likely prior to a final determination.

A further drawback to filing in the United States is the possibility that the applicant will be considered a U.S. resident and/or domiciliary for federal or other income, gift, and/or estate tax purposes even prior to granting of the immigrant visa if he resides in the United States and files an application for adjustment of status. Consequently, it is necessary to implement any required tax planning prior to filing the application, without assurance that the application will be approved.[13] In addition, the U.S. Internal Revenue Service still may assert that residence for tax purposes commenced at an earlier date before such planning was implemented. An application filed outside the United States, on the other hand, does not generally of itself have the same effect for tax purposes and therefore usually permits delay in tax planning until after the application is approved — but before the alien moves to the United States.

Filing in the United States also may have advantages. First, if the potential immigrant already is in the United States, such filing avoids a costly trip to the appropriate U.S. consulate abroad. In addition, where the immigrant files his application abroad but a supporting application must be filed by a U.S. person on the immigrant's behalf — such as Form I-130 in the case of relatives, or Form I-140 in the case of employers — while this supporting application may be filed in the United States, it must be filed abroad by that person bringing it to the U.S. consulate in person, at possible substantial cost and inconvenience, to avoid the normal INS delay in processing within the United States.

Second, generally it may be worthwhile to file the application within the United States if the applicant does not wish or expect to leave the United States while the application for adjustment of status is pending, and/or if the appropriate INS office is one which is not particularly crowded and thus can act on the application expeditiously.

Third, if any legal hurdle or factual or documentary problem is encountered, the applicant is not stranded abroad during resolution of the problem. In addition, appellate review of any such resolution within the United States generally is far more extensive than the available review of consular decisions.

General Immigration Approaches for a Foreign Investor

Although factual peculiarities exist in each case, a nonresident alien investor who seeks permanent residence in the United States should consider the following general approaches in meeting U.S. immigration requirements:

(1) In lieu of or before initiating the immigrant visa application, the investor should ascertain whether a nonimmigrant visa is desirable to come to the United States to make one or more initial investments. If so, an E, L, or B-1 visa may be particularly useful.

(2) If nonpreference quota numbers are available, the basis of the application for an immigrant visa should be either the self-supporting qualification or the investor qualification as described above, because these permit maximum freedom of activity and are least time-consuming to obtain. The decision *between* these two categories will depend principally on whether: (a) the investor wishes to disclose and/or submit to U.S. tax substantial assets and income which may not have been disclosed previously to his country of origin, and he does not contemplate working in the United States, so as to meet the self-supporting test; or (b) he prefers to make the required investment in an active U.S. business enterprise requiring full time managerial employment, so as to meet the investor qualification.

(3) If nonpreference numbers are not readily available, the investor should consider applying for immigrant status through sixth preference. If he incorporates his U.S. business, the corporation can serve as the employer. Where it is related to a going business abroad by which the investor has been employed for at least one year, labor certification under Schedule A generally can be obtained.

(4) If the investor is in the United States, he should explore whether applying for adjustment to immigrant status through the local INS district

office or immigrant visa processing through the appropriate U.S. consulate abroad is faster, particularly taking into account as well the difficulty of traveling abroad during processing in the United States.

Footnotes to Chapter X

1. *See generally* 8 U.S.C. §§1151 *et seq.*

2. These countries include Argentina, Austria, Belgium, Bolivia, China (both People's Republic and Taiwan), Colombia, Costa Rica, Denmark, Estonia, Ethiopia, Finland, France, Federal Republic of Germany, Greece, Honduras, Iran, Ireland, Israel, Italy, Japan, Korea, Latvia, Liberia, Luxembourg, Muscat & Oman, the Netherlands, Nicaragua, Norway, Pakistan, Paraguay, the Philippines, Spain, Switzerland, Thailand, Togo, Turkey, United Kingdom, Vietnam, and Yugoslavia. *See* C. Gordon & H. Rosenfield, 1 *Immigration Law & Procedure* 2-76 (1978).

3. These countries include Argentina, Austria, Belgium, Brunei (Borneo), China (both People's Republic and Taiwan), Colombia, Costa Rica, Ethiopia, France, Honduras, Federal Republic of Germany, Iran, Italy, Japan, Korea, Liberia, Luxembourg, Muscat & Oman, the Netherlands, Nicaragua, Norway, Pakistan, Paraguay, the Philippines, Spain, Switzerland, Thailand, Togo, United Kingdom, Vietnam, and Yugoslavia. *Id.*

Although the President of the United States announced that effective January 1, 1979, the United States recognized the People's Republic of China as the sole legal government of China, existing international agreements and arrangements between the United States and Taiwan generally continue in force. *See* Memorandum of Dec. 30, 1978, 44 Fed. Reg. 1075; Pub. L. 96-8 (April 10, 1979), 93 Stat. 14.

4. 8 U.S.C. § 1182. Restrictions on entry and stay of Iranian nationals which were imposed in 1980 in response to the taking of American hostages in Tehran in 1979 have been substantially removed. *See* 46 Fed. Reg. 25597, 37239, 55513 (1981).

5. 8 U.S.C. §§1151(a), 1152(a)-(c).

6. 8 U.S.C. §§1152(e), 1153(a). Any unused visas in one category generally are allocated first to the next lower category.

7. 8 U.S.C. §§1101(a)(42), 1157, 1159; 8 C.F.R. Parts 207, 209. The refugee provisions were revised in 1980.

8. An exception to this procedure applies to labor certification as a physician, for which the applicant must have obtained medical education from a school approved by the U.S. Commissioner of Education or have passed the Visa Qualifying Exam prepared by the U.S. Department of Health and Human Services for admission as a physician.

9. 20 C.F.R. §656.10.

10. 20 C.F.R. §656.11.

11. 8 C.F.R. §212.8(a); 22 C.F.R. §42.91(a)(14)(ii).

12. 8 C.F.R. §212.8(b).

13. *See generally* Chapter II *supra,* Chapter XI *infra.*

Chapter XI

Tax Planning for Individual Investors

This chapter first summarizes various basic U.S. federal income, gift, and estate tax planning techniques available to nonresident alien individuals, including reference to certain principles and approaches described earlier in this volume.

In addition, an investment in U.S. real estate or other assets or operations by a nonresident alien often begins solely as a business proposition and is followed by a desire for U.S. residence. Indeed, frequently the first step for a nonresident alien seeking permanent residence in the United States is to establish a U.S. business enterprise. Accordingly, this chapter also examines certain federal income, gift, and estate tax issues and techniques applicable to nonresident aliens who wish to obtain U.S. residence.

Income Tax Planning for Nonresident Aliens

Proper federal income tax planning for a nonresident alien who is not contemplating or influenced by U.S. residence considerations consists principally of identifying and utilizing income tax benefits and avoiding tax pitfalls under the Foreign Investors Tax Act of 1966 and the Foreign Investment in Real Property Tax Act of 1980,[1] other provisions of the U.S. Internal Revenue Code, and U.S. income tax treaties. Tax planning for such a nonresident alien also should consider relevant aspects of state and local income, gift, and inheritance or similar taxation, such as those noted in Chapter II. The detailed discussion below, however, will focus on federal tax planning considerations.

Code Benefits

The Internal Revenue Code's tax benefits for nonresident alien investors are, for the most part, not tax loopholes but intentional incentives to encourage foreign investment in the United States. Chapter II outlines the principal tax measures themselves; the following description indicates briefly certain ways in which these provisions are utilized:

Capital gains. Gains, profits, and income from the sale or exchange of personal property sold or exchanged within the United States are defined as U.S. source income.[2] However, if the nonresident alien seller is present in the United States for less than 183 days in the taxable year of sale of such capital assets[3] *and* the gains are not effectively connected with the conduct of any U.S. trade or business,[4] such gains are *not* subject to U.S. income tax. Thus, by planning a transaction to occur in a year in which the alien can satisfy these requirements, U.S. income tax can be avoided. Installment basis reporting also may be considered, if the alien cannot qualify for taxfree treatment in the year of sale.

Trading in securities or commodities. A nonresident alien generally is exempt from U.S. income tax on gains from securities and commodities trading through resident agents — including brokers, commission agents, custodians, other independent agents, and employees, even those with discretionary authority.[5] In addition, nonresident alien investors arguably may deal with wholly owned corporations under the shelter of these same provisions. These provisions also may add support to the taxfree sale of stock of an otherwise collapsible corporation by a nonresident alien.

Real property gains. Gain from the sale or exchange of a U.S. real property interest (including real property located in the United States or shares of a U.S. real property holding corporation) is defined as income effectively connected with the conduct of a U.S. trade or business. Certain tax treaty and deferral devices may be available, and planning should include use of tax shelter generated by longer term real property holdings.[6]

Net taxation of real property income. As described in Chapter III, an election is available to a nonresident alien to report U.S. real property income as if it were effectively connected with the conduct of a U.S. trade or business. Thus, where allowable deductions — including depreciation on improvements — offset real estate income, there will be less or no taxable income. The principal disadvantage of the election in the past, *i.e.*, the taxation of most otherwise nontaxable capital gain upon disposition, has become largely irrelevant in light of the Foreign Investment in Real Property Tax Act.

Personal service loan-outs. Compensation for personal services in the United States by a nonresident alien present in the United States not more than 90 days during his taxable year, if performed for a nonresident alien, foreign corporation, or foreign partnership not engaged in business in the United States, or for a non-U.S. office of a U.S. person, is defined as income from outside the United States and not taxed unless it exceeds $3,000.[7] More importantly, it may be possible for an alien temporarily performing such services in the United States — for example, a performer on tour — to act under contract to a foreign entity in a tax treaty jurisdiction and, by treaty, to avoid or reduce withholding and other U.S.

tax on all or a major portion of his compensation up to a much larger amount.

It should be noted that most nonresident *and* resident aliens departing from the United States or any U.S. possession may be required to obtain a certificate of compliance (or so called sailing permit) from the local District Director of the Internal Revenue Service.

Treaty Benefits

Chapter II lists and notes certain effects of the income tax treaties maintained by the United States — usually with other high tax jurisdictions — to reduce double tax burdens and for other purposes. The use of these treaties by a nonresident alien in planning an investment in the United States is appropriate for various types of income such as the following:

Interest. Except for taxfree interest on bank deposits, most other U.S. source interest payments to a nonresident alien are subject to a 30% withholding tax unless reduced by treaty. Treaties may reduce this withholding to 5-15% or even eliminate it entirely. Certain treaties distinguish between interest on secured and unsecured obligations.[8] Incorporation of the payor in a tax treaty jurisdiction may avoid withholding on interest paid; for example, interest paid on shareholder loans by a U.S. corporation *or* a Cayman Islands corporation may be subject to U.S. withholding; locating the payor in the Netherlands Antilles may eliminate the U.S. withholding.

Dividends. The treatment of dividends is much like that accorded interest: treaty reductions are available, and locating the payor in a treaty jurisdiction may serve to eliminate U.S. withholding.

As noted in Chapter II, the exemption of bank deposit interest, and any treaty reductions in U.S. withholding taxes on other interest and dividends, override the general 10% federal withholding tax on such payments to an individual (domestic of foreign).

Rents and royalties. Treaty rate reductions on rents from tangible and intangible properties provide substantial planning opportunities. One-, two-, and further-tiered structures may be utilized to receive rental and royalty income free of U.S. withholding taxes and at reduced rates of tax in the foreign jurisdictions of initial and later receipt. For example, U.S. film rents paid to a Netherlands Antilles corporation can be paid from there to a Dutch parent entity without withholding in the United States or the Antilles or any substantial tax in the Netherlands, subject to suitable tax rulings there.[9]

Capital gains and industrial and commercial profits. Treaty benefits accorded such profits may shift the tax burden from the United States to a jurisdiction in which additional deductions are available or the tax rate is lower than the United States would impose. Planning for such benefits requires careful control of the form and manner in which business is conducted in the United States because the absence of a U.S. permanent establishment, as noted in Chapter II, usually is determinative.

Real property income. Taxation of income from U.S. real property often can be reduced by use of tax treaties. For example, as noted in Chapter III, certain tax treaties provide an election to be taxed on net income, as does the Internal Revenue Code, but under a yearly election. Under current law this distinction is perhaps less important than it was formerly. In addition, under the Foreign Investment in Real Property Tax Act, existing tax treaty disposition provisions generally will not be overruled until 1985. Planning opportunities for real estate gains continue in the meanwhile. For example, shares of a U.S. real property holding corporation may be able to be sold by a Netherlands corporation with no U.S. tax.[10]

Use of U.S. trust. A domestic trust may collect U.S. bank deposit interest, or possibly non-effectively connected capital gain, and distribute it taxfree to a nonresident alien beneficiary even without benefit of a treaty.[11] Such a U.S. trust may even be able to accumulate *foreign* income with little or no foreign country tax, due to a tax treaty between the United States and the source country, but receive a refund of U.S. tax paid on the income when it is distributed to such a foreign beneficiary.

In all such treaty planning for individuals, the distinction between treaty use and abuse must be considered, particularly because the definition and limitation of such abuse may be of increasing importance for U.S. and other tax authorities.[12]

Gifts by or to Nonresident Aliens

As described in Chapter II, federal gift tax applies to gifts by nonresident aliens of certain types of property situated in the United States.[13] In general, gift tax planning is designed to convert tangible property situated in the United States to non-U.S. situs or intangible property so that taxfree transfers may be accomplished more readily.

Real Property

A gift of U.S. real property is subject to gift tax. However, if the real estate is acquired by a U.S. or foreign corporation or is contributed to an existing corporation and later a gift is made of the stock — whether to a U.S. *or* a foreign person — no U.S. gift tax is imposed. No income tax ruling generally is required for such a contribution of property by a nonresident alien to a domestic corporation. The fairly limited circumstances under which a possible U.S. income tax on the donor may be involved in such a gift of stock are noted in Chapter III.

Such a corporation also may be used to take advantage of the income tax structures described in Chapter III. However, the Foreign Investment in Real Property Tax Act imposes income tax on a contribution of *appreciated* property either to a foreign corporation — since its shares of stock generally may be sold by a foreign owner free of U.S. tax, unless it elects to be treated as a domestic corporation under the act — or even to a domestic corporation *if* it is owned by a resident of a country with a U.S. tax treaty that may exempt a stock sale from U.S. income tax. Also, if U.S. resident donees will own more than one-half of the corporation, they may receive little or no U.S. income tax advantage from such a foreign corporation.

Tangible Personal Property

Similarly to real estate, U.S. tangible personal property can be used to capitalize a corporation and a gift made of the shares, or a gift of cash and sale of property may be considered. An alternative in the case of such moveable property is to transport the property outside the United States prior to the transfer. However, U.S. tax authorities may attempt to tax the transaction as if the two steps were not discrete.[14]

Intangible Property

Not only corporate stock, but all other U.S. *or* foreign intangible property — for example, contract rights, patents, and the like — generally may be transferred by a nonresident alien by gift without U.S. gift tax.

General Gift Tax and Treaty Considerations

Any U.S. gift tax planning for a nonresident alien also must take account of certain general considerations of such planning applicable even to U.S. domiciliaries. In particular, in order to be effective, a transfer by gift must be complete. Cessation of control by the donor is necessary and, if power to control enjoyment of the property remains with the donor, the gift will *not* be deemed complete or may be complete only to a limited extent. For example, a gift of real property subject to revocation after five years will be a gift for U.S. tax purposes of the use of the property for five years. If, at the end of the five years, the gift is not in fact revoked and by its terms cannot be revoked thereafter, an additional gift — subject to U.S. gift tax, if applicable to the transfer — is made of the real property at its value five years hence.

On the other hand, a nonresident alien contemplating a gift to a U.S. person of intangible or otherwise nontaxable property may wish to consider an incomplete gift in trust or otherwise. For example, instead of making an immediate completed gift of non-U.S. real property, or of a stock portfolio, the nonresident alien may place such property in a foreign trust for the U.S. donee under the terms of which the gift is incomplete. A later completed gift of such property with substantial appreciation — or of its intangible sale proceeds — will still be free of U.S. gift tax *and* will have avoided U.S. income tax on the appreciation which the *donee* otherwise would have paid. However, if the property includes, for example, U.S. corporate stock or other property subject to U.S. estate tax as described further below, the death of the foreign donor before the gift is completed may result in inclusion of the property in the donor's taxable U.S. estate. Accordingly, such U.S. assets probably should be placed in a foreign corporation owned by the trust.

It should be remembered that in the case of nonresident aliens higher rates (and no tax credit) apply to federal gift as opposed to estate taxes, as described in Chapter II generally, unlike the unified rates and credit for U.S. domiciliaries. Thus, at least for U.S. tangible property which is equally subject to U.S. gift and estate taxation, a nonresident alien's gift may result in higher U.S. tax than a testamentary disposition later.

Finally, as noted in Chapter II, the United States maintains certain gift tax treaties. These principally provide relief from double gift taxation rather than furnishing unusual tax planning opportunities. If the donor or donee is a resident of such a treaty country, however, the effect of these treaties should be investigated.

Estate Planning for Nonresident Aliens

Many of the approaches described above for gift tax planning also are effective in federal estate planning in the case of the death of a nonresident alien. However, such planning varies due to categories of property peculiarly includible in the U.S. taxable estate of a nonresident alien and other rules noted in Chapter II.[15]

Real Property

Since U.S. real property owned directly by a nonresident alien is subject to U.S. estate tax, such an owner often is well advised to hold property instead through a foreign corporation as described in Chapter III. This remains true despite the denial of many of the income tax benefits previously available in such foreign corporate ownership.

Tangible Personal Property

If such property is to be used permanently in the United States, it may be owned through a foreign corporation to minimize U.S. estate tax .

Intangible Property

While a nonresident alien generally is not taxed on gifts of intangible property, he is subject to estate tax on certain of such intangibles, as follows:

Domestic corporate stock. Such property is taxable in the U.S. estate of a foreign decedent. Accordingly, either the corporate assets or the U.S. corporate stock itself may be held by a foreign corporation or perhaps a foreign trust. Additionally, use of such an entity in a tax treaty juridiction may reduce the U.S. withholding tax on corporate dividends, as noted further above.

U.S. debt obligations. These also may be held through a foreign corporation or perhaps a trust. Again, as noted further above, organization of such a holding entity in a tax treaty jurisdiction may reduce U.S. income taxation.

However, as noted in Chapter II, state inheritance tax may attempt to reach even such stock or securities of a foreign corporation if its principal place or the major part of its business is in the state, or the stock or securities are kept there.

Powers of Appointment

A power of appointment by a nonresident alien over property deemed situated in the United States for U.S. estate tax purposes will cause inclusion of such property in the U.S. estate of the nonresident alien. To the extent that transfer of such property would not incur gift tax if made during the donor's lifetime — for example, as to stock in U.S. corporations — the power should be so exercised prior to death. If transfer of the property subject to the power would be a taxable gift upon exercise of the power, steps such as those described further above should be taken to transform the property into non-U.S. situs or intangible property not subject to gift tax, or into similar property not subject to estate tax.

General Estate Tax and Treaty Considerations

Certain general estate planning considerations applicable even to U.S. domiciliaries may be appropriate to planning for nonresident aliens. One example is the divided ownership of an asset taxable in a U.S. estate in the event that foreign corporate ownership cannot be employed. If a husband and wife own equal interests in U.S. real property — a vacation residence, for instance — each estate can utilize lower graduated tax rates and available estate tax credits.

On the other hand, since the general marital deduction is not available to a nonresident alien decedent, a transfer to his heirs other than the spouse should be used more often than in the case of a U.S.

domiciliary, in order to avoid inclusion of the decedent's share in the estate of the surviving spouse.

Where estate tax planning is based on gifts made during the donor's lifetime, it is important to note that a gift of less than a complete interest will result in inclusion of the property in the donor's estate at its value as of the date of death (or alternate later valuation date) rather than at its value at the date of the uncompleted gift. If a nonresident alien has transferred by gift to a trust property includible in his U.S. estate, the terms of the trust must be examined to ensure, for example, that the nonresident alien has not retained a life estate in the trust property, that enjoyment of the property does not depend on the beneficiary's surviving the donor, that the transfer is not revocable, and so forth.[16]

Furthermore, U.S. tax provisions on generation-skipping trusts are currently effective for newly created transfers after June 11, 1976. In light of these provisions, a trust established with U.S. situs property for the benefit of a foreign decedent's grandchildren should *not* also include his children as trust beneficiaries, even for their lifetimes, because this will cause inclusion of the U.S. property in each child's estate. As noted generally above, however, one alternative is to transform such U.S. situs property into non-U.S. property by, for example, having it held through a foreign corporation.

A further planning consideration for a nonresident alien is to exclude his *non*-U.S. situs estate from heirs who are or might become U.S. residents and/or domiciliaries subject to subsequent U.S. worldwide income and/or estate taxes themselves. For example, a nonresident alien might, in his will, establish a foreign trust with non-U.S. property for the benefit of his grandchildren, if his children were U.S. residents. In view of U.S. tax provisions on generation-skipping trusts, the decedent's U.S. resident children should not be included as beneficiaries of the trust even for their lifetimes, because this can cause inclusion of foreign property of the foreign decedent in each child's estate.[17]

Finally, it should be noted that the United States maintains estate tax treaties with several countries, as listed in Chapter II. These treaties are designed not so much to provide planning opportunities as to reduce double estate taxation. Many of such treaties have been liberalized particularly to provide local tax relief to long-term alien residents.

Pre-and Post Residence Planning

General U.S. Tax Regime for Resident Aliens

As noted in Chapter II, a resident alien is subject to federal income taxation on his worldwide income in much the same way as a U.S. citizen.

Furthermore, if domiciled in the United States, he is subject to the unified federal gift and estate tax on his property wherever situated. Other principal potential U.S. federal tax consequences of residence include the following:[18]

(1) Treatment of a wholly or partly owned foreign corporation as a controlled foreign corporation, a foreign personal holding company, a personal holding company with respect to additional types of income, and/or a foreign investment company;

(2) Liability for filing information returns on an interest in a foreign corporation or foreign partnership, or in foreign bank accounts;

(3) Tax ruling requirements and/or imposition of U.S. excise tax for certain capital transfers abroad;

(4) Liability for filing information returns on a transfer to a foreign trust and on such trust's income, and/or possible taxation as the owner or beneficiary of such a trust;

(5) Subjection of a foreign trust or estate of which the resident is a fiduciary to U.S. taxation;

(6) Liability under U.S. international boycott and illegal payment rules and prohibitions;

(7) Taxation of U.S. bank deposit and other interest payments and dividends — which are free of U.S. tax generally or may be subject to reduced tax under a treaty for a nonresident alien — including application of the general 10% federal withholding tax on such payments to an individual;

(8) Eligibility for use of a Subchapter S corporation, for income averaging and head of household tax rates, and for filing a joint income tax return where both spouses are residents at the end of the year.

The resident alien also may be subject to more extensive state and local taxation: income, gift, estate or inheritance, property, sales or use, and miscellaneous other taxes as noted in Chapter I. On the other hand, foreign taxes on the alien may be reduced when he becomes a U.S. resident. The detailed discussion below, however, will focus on U.S. federal tax planning considerations.

Definitions of Residence

Definitions of alien residence for U.S. immigration law purposes and for federal income, gift, and estate tax purposes differ in important respects, but the former may influence the latter. These issues may be summarized briefly as follows:

Immigration. Under U.S. immigration laws, an alien becomes a permanent resident entitled to an immigrant visa by satisfying certain objective criteria as described in Chapter X.

In addition, the Immigration and Naturalization Service and the Internal Revenue Service regard the claiming of tax benefits as a nonresident alien to be inconsistent with permanent resident status under the immigration laws.[19] However, such a permanent resident may file abroad for an immigrant visa, may defer applying for his visa to enter the United States for up to one year (or two years under certain circumstances) after it is available, and may repeatedly use his immigrant visa to return to the United States after stays abroad of up to one year each. Thus, he may not immediately become a resident under the criteria for tax purposes simply upon becoming entitled to an immigrant visa.

Income tax. The Internal Revenue Code contains no objective definition of a resident for income tax purposes, but regulations generally define a resident alien as "an alien actually present in the United States who is not a mere transient or sojourner" and specify that such transiency is determined subjectively by the alien's "intention with regard to the length and nature of his stay" in the United States.[20] While nonimmigrant status under the immigration laws provides a presumption of nonresident income tax status, this may be rebutted by other facts even without an immigrant visa. For example, a U.S. stay of one year or more may raise a presumption of such residence. U.S. presence following the filing of an application for an immigrant visa from within the United States may be particularly compelling — even before the visa is granted. Judicial decisions examine the facts and circumstances in each instance to determine the subjective intent required, often relying on domestic legal, economic, family, and social connections as opposed to ties remaining abroad, together with physical presence within the United States.[21]

Gift and estate tax. Determination of domicile for imposition of worldwide federal gift and estate tax generally requires both stronger subjective intent and greater U.S. presence than for income tax residence — particularly in the case of estate tax. As a general rule, an individual may have only one domicile although he may have more than one residence. While the precise definition of domicile may vary with local law in a particular national or state jurisdiction, U.S. domicile usually is acquired by living in the United States with evident intention to remain permanently.[22]

Coordination with Immigration Planning

All planning for potential U.S. residence should coordinate the requirements of intended immigration status with tax considerations. For example, qualification of the alien individual for self-supporting status, or by investment in a U.S. business enterprise providing employment to U.S. persons, or for an intercompany transfer may require certain tax planning techniques or prohibit others. These and other U.S. immigrant categories are described in Chapter X and should be examined simultaneously with the U.S. tax planning steps and examples set forth below.

Asset Plan

The initial step in U.S. tax planning for possible U.S. residence is the preparation of a detailed asset and income requirement summary. This should include:

(1) Foreign corporate, partnership, and proprietorship assets;
(2) Foreign portfolio investments;
(3) Foreign real property;
(4) U.S. corporate, partnership, and proprietorship assets;
(5) U.S. portfolio investments;
(6) U.S. real property.

Income Tax Planning Before Residence

Once the asset and income requirement summary is completed, U.S. income tax planning for residence can begin. Many of the techniques employed for U.S. citizens may be used, particularly to protect the new resident from falling within such onerous federal tax provisions as the controlled foreign corporation, foreign personal holding company, personal holding company, and similar sections referred to further above. The most critical issue is advanced planning and timing. Examples of such tax planning include the following:

Acceleration of income. For the new resident this is the recognition of foreign (and taxfree U.S.) income in the last taxable year of nonresidence, provided foreign taxing authorities will impose a lesser tax burden on the income than possible later U.S. taxes. Such acceleration may be accomplished by, *inter alia*: (1) sale of appreciated assets — either outright, or in installments but without installment basis U.S. reporting (which generally requires the seller to elect out of such reporting), or for a private or commercial annuity causing recognition of any gain on the assets in the year of transfer; (2) acceptance of prepayments of sums otherwise due later; and (3) exercise of options which otherwise may generate taxable income later. Without such acceleration, for example, royalties and other payments for a work completed before the alien becomes a resident may be subject to U.S. income and even self employment social security-type taxes.

A corollary to this procedure is the deferral of expenses which may be deductible later by the new resident.

Conversion to capital gain. This generally may be accomplished by sale of assets expected to generate future ordinary income in order to recognize capital gain based on a multiple of such earnings, rather than taxation on those earnings as received later.

However, if U.S. capital gains are involved, the nonresident alien may wish to avoid being present in the United States for 183 days or more during the taxable year of sale because, as noted further above and in Chapter II generally, U.S. capital gains which might otherwise be taxfree may then be subject to a 30% U.S. tax. For the purpose of this calculation, a nonresident alien who is not engaged in U.S. trade or business and has not previously established a federal taxable year generally is treated as having a calendar taxable year.

Where continuing involvement by the alien individual is desired, an alternative is transfer of assets into a foreign holding corporation or trust. However, this requires careful review of the onerous sections referred to above which may apply following U.S. residence. For example, a foreign corporation owned at least one-half by another nonresident alien — even a member of the family of the new resident — or by several unrelated parties may be a decontrolled corporation permitting later conversion of the resident alien's share of further appreciation in value to capital gain.[23]

Income splitting. Income producing foreign property (and most U.S. non-real property) may be distributed among various family members prior to residence — generally free of U.S. gift tax, as discussed below—in order to take advantage of lower progressive income tax rates applicable to each individual. Establishment and funding of U.S. trusts should be considered for the same purpose.

Use of foreign trust. Prior to residence, one or more foreign trusts may be established with existing cash or other foreign property (and most U.S. non-real property) without U.S. reporting, excise taxes on appreciation, or gift taxes on the transfers. Distributions of income from such a trust to a U.S. beneficiary will be taxed to that beneficiary as received.[24] Where trust income of several years is distributed later, the tax is based on a complicated throwback calculation to attempt to tax the income as if it had been distributed in the year earned. In addition, even capital gains are taxed as ordinary income upon distribution. Finally, a nondeductible interest charge of six percent is added to the tax attributable to income earned in prior years, for each year that the income was accumulated by the trust. Nonetheless, it is possible that future generations may give up (or perhaps never acquire) U.S. residence prior to distribution and avoid the U.S. tax. In the meantime, current U.S. income taxes may be minimized and distributions may be organized to reduce or eliminate income subject to such throwback or interest charges.

Timing of arrival benefits and requirements. The timing of commencement of U.S. tax residence may be accelerated or deferred in certain cases. Where sale of a foreign principal dwelling residence and purchase of such a U.S. residence is contemplated, this may even be postponed until after moving to the United States because gain on the foreign residence generally may be reinvested taxfree in the U.S. residence.[25] For individuals contemplating U.S. residence because of political or similar problems abroad which may result in expropriation of local assets there, the acceleration of residence for federal tax purposes may permit substantial foreign expropriation losses to be deducted and carried forward for up to 10 years to reduce U.S. income taxes, subject to adjustments if recovery of all or part of the loss is obtained.[26]

In addition, as noted above, resident alien spouses may file a joint income tax return for the entire taxable year in order to take advantage of lower tax rates, and resident aliens may be entitled to other federal income tax benefits. An election to be treated as a resident for the entire taxable year may be made by any alien whose spouse is a U.S. resident (or citizen) at the close of the taxable year; in fact, each spouse who is then such a resident may be the basis of the other's election for that year. However, such an election also gives retroactive year-long effect to worldwide U.S. taxation and many U.S. reporting requirements such as foreign trust reporting. Thus, any acceleration, incorporation, or other planning techniques must be coordinated with this election.[27]

In this connection, fiscal year and accrual method reporting also may be considered. For example, a new resident may be able to elect a taxable year other than the calendar year — unless that year is inconsistent with his prior U.S. business record keeping and federal tax returns, if any. Then he may have a short initial taxable year after taking up residence in the United States, and will be resident for the entire second taxable year for joint return or other purposes without needing a retroactive residence election. Such a noncalendar taxable year also may be useful in deferring taxation of portions of post-residence income from calendar year partnerships and other enterprises.[28]

Income Tax Planning After Residence

While new alien residents generally are subject to the same regime of U.S. taxes as citizens, their continuing foreign contacts may facilitate U.S. income tax planning after residence.

Decontrolled foreign corporation. Under the controlled foreign corporation and similar provisions referred to above, certain foreign income of a foreign corporation may be taxed currently by the United States even if not distributed to its U.S. shareholders. This is true, for example, of a foreign personal holding company, which is a foreign corporation of which five or fewer U.S. citizens and/or resident aliens own more than one-half of the value and whose income is comprised at least 60% of dividends, interest, royalties, annuities, gains from the sale or exchange of stock, securities and futures in commodities, fees from personal service contracts, and certain rents. However, if such a foreign corporation is owned at least one-half by foreign persons unrelated to the resident alien owners (or, in the case of the controlled foreign corporation provisions, even foreign relatives of the residents are acceptable), then its income generally will not be taxed to the U.S. residents until distributed.

It should be noted that, for a resident alien to be entitled to the general U.S. foreign tax credit on foreign source income, the country of his nationality may have to grant a similar credit to U.S. citizens residing there. However, this has normally not been invoked.[29]

Use of foreign trust. If a foreign trust is established by a foreign relative or other foreign person before the intending resident alien assumes U.S. residence, high profit investments or those to be held for long-term appreciation may be made by such a trust so that current income and/or long-term gain may be accumulated for future generations. However, the generation-skipping taxation noted further above must be considered in any such long-term planning.

The foreign trust also may be used for split investing — *i.e.*, to participate in future investments with the resident alien by acquiring the appreciating portion of the investment and giving the resident higher investment leverage and increased tax shelter. For example, the trust may enter into a long-term ground lease of real property to the resident alien who owns and depreciates buildings on the property.

Furthermore, the trust may permit better timing of future income distributions to the resident.

Gift and Estate Tax Planning Before Residence

By transferring U.S. or foreign intangible property, foreign tangible personal property, and foreign real property before acquiring U.S. domicile, the intending resident alien may avoid later U.S. gift tax on the transfers and remove the property from his U.S. taxable estate. It should be noted that the general U.S. rules relating to retention of controls by the donor as noted further above still may cause inclusion in the taxable estate of the donor of certain property disposed of by such gift.

Conversion of tangible property to intangible prior to gift. As described above in connection with gifts generally by nonresident aliens, even property which otherwise will be subject to U.S. gift tax upon transfer often may be transformed into nontaxable form well before the gift — for example, by contribution of U.S. real property to a U.S. corporation as capital or an addition to capital, and a later gift of part or all of the shares without gift tax.

Alternatively, gifts of such property may be postponed until after residence in order to utilize the unified gift and estate tax credit not available for gifts by nonresidents.

Use of trust. Although the disposition of property to family members prior to residence can be used to reduce the overall U.S. gift and estate tax burden, the new resident may not be willing so to transfer all control of the property to the spouse or children. In such a case, the trust described above for income tax planning can do double service: foreign property and/or non-income producing property generally may be transferred to a foreign trust to be insulated from U.S. estate tax; certain U.S. property and/or income producing property generally may be transferred to a U.S. trust to avoid the onerous throwback and interest charges on foreign trust distributions.

Gift and Estate Tax Planning After Residence

After U.S. domicile, the unified U.S. gift and estate tax will apply to the new resident. In addition to gift and estate tax planning common to U.S. citizens — such as use of the unlimited deduction for property transferred to a spouse for at least the spouse's lifetime benefit — the resident alien may wish to forgo gifts and/or inheritances from nonresident aliens or other persons and suggest that such property be transferred instead to his children or other heirs directly or in trust, to avoid U.S. gift and estate taxes which could be imposed if he were to receive the property and later retransfer it.

For a resident alien to be entitled to the estate tax credit for foreign death taxes on foreign property, the country of his nationality may have to grant a similar credit to U.S. citizens residing there.[30] There is no U.S. gift tax credit for foreign gift taxes, even for a U.S. citizen or resident.

The new resident also should note that, although contributions to foreign charities generally are not deductible for U.S. federal income tax purposes, they are for a resident alien (or citizen) free of gift tax and deductible from the resident's taxable estate.[31]

Planning for the Departing Resident Alien

It is often difficult to abandon U.S. residence or domicile for tax purposes.[32] If this is contemplated, however, income deferral available to U.S. citizens and residents is particularly attractive to the departing resident alien because such deferral may be the first step to tax elimination. Such deferral techniques may include, *inter alia,* the following:

Installment sale. Except in the case of sale of a U.S. real property interest, an installment sale may permit taxfree receipt of part or all of the capital or other gain in a subsequent taxable year during which the new nonresident alien is present in the United States for less than 183 days (in the case of capital gain) and is not engaged in a U.S. trade or business with which the gain is connected.[33]

Deferred compensation. If ordinary income is received under qualified deferred compensation plans or other delayed payments in a later taxable year in which the new nonresident is not engaged in a U.S. trade or business with which the income is connected, it may be subject to a flat 30% U.S. withholding tax (or lesser treaty rate) instead of higher progressive rates. Income for services performed abroad then may escape U.S. tax altogether.[34]

Taxfree sale or exchange. The taxfree exchange of like kind property may provide an opportunity for the resident alien (although this taxfree treatment might be denied to a nonresident alien) to exchange appreciated U.S. real estate or other property for foreign or other property, the future sale of which will not generate U.S. source income for the new nonresident. Similarly, the sale of a U.S. dwelling residence and purchase of a foreign residence may, with the proper election, defer tax on the gain on the U.S. residence until disposition of the foreign residence, at which time the new nonresident may not be subject to U.S. tax.[35]

Gift to spouse. U.S. situs real or tangible personal property — which cannot be transferred by a nonresident alien donor to his spouse free of gift tax — may be transferred by a resident alien to his spouse free of such tax under the unlimited marital deduction before he becomes a nonresident.[36]

Planning for the Departing Citizen

If a resident alien becomes a U.S. citizen, he should note that the United States claims the right to tax its citizens and, in certain cases, former citizens without regard to residence. More particularly, when one principal purpose of relinquishing U.S. citizenship is the avoidance of U.S. federal income, gift, or estate tax, special tax provisions apply to the expatriate — even if he becomes a nonresident — as follows.[37]

Income tax. For 10 years after the loss of U.S. citizenship, the U.S. source income of such a tax expatriate — whether or not effectively connected with the conduct of a U.S. trade or business — is taxed at the greater of (1) what he would pay as a nonresident alien and (2) what he would pay as a U.S. resident. In addition, contrary to the usual source of income rules for nonresident aliens, all gains from sales of real property located in the United States and of stock of U.S. corporations and domestic debt obligations is considered such U.S. source income.

To mitigate the impact of this taxation, the expatriating citizen may, for example: (a) defer foreign source personal service income until after expatriation; (b) enter into a taxfree exchange of U.S. property for foreign real property such as noted above, to permit later taxfree sale after expatriation; or (c) enter into an installment sale of U.S. property, which may yield untaxed foreign source income from interest if the sale is to a foreign buyer. It should also be noted that sale of stock of one or more foreign corporations — controlled or not controlled — to a foreign buyer after expatriation may not be taxable.

Gift tax. For 10 years after the loss of U.S. citizenship, such a tax expatriate will be subject to U.S. gift tax on transfer of real and tangible personal property situated in the United States *and* intangible property deemed situated there. Again, unlike the case of a nonresident alien, such U.S. intangible property includes stock of U.S. corporations and debt obligations of U.S. persons.

Estate tax. The estate of such a tax expatriate will for 10 years after the loss of U.S. citizenship be taxed according to the rate schedule applied to U.S. citizens and residents, but with a maximum unified tax credit of only $13,000. In addition, the property subject to tax is determined as if the expatriate were a nonresident alien, *but* includes his proportionate share of U.S. property owned by any foreign corporation which would have been a controlled foreign corporation if he were a U.S. resident and in which he is at least a 10% owner directly or indirectly.

Tax treaties. Certain U.S. income, gift, and estate tax treaties override these provisions in the case of such a tax expatriate who becomes a resident of the treaty country. However, the newer U.S. treaties typically deny these benefits.[38]

Footnotes to Chapter XI

1. Pub. L. 89-809 (Nov. 13, 1966), 80 Stat. 1541; Pub. L. 96-499 (Dec. 5, 1980), 94 Stat. 2599.
2. I.R.C. §§861(a)(5), (6).
3. I.R.C. §871(a)(2).
4. I.R.C. §871(b).
5. I.R.C. §864(b)(2).
6. I.R.C. §897; *see* Chapter III *supra*.
7. I.R.C. §§861(a)(3), 864(b)(1).
8. For example, the United States-Netherlands Income Tax Treaty of 1948, as amended ("U.S.-Netherlands Treaty"), Art. VIII, includes mortgage interest, while the treaty as amended and presently in force between the United States and the Netherlands Antilles ("U.S.-Netherlands Antilles Treaty"), Art. VIII, does not.
9. U.S.-Netherlands Antilles Treaty, Arts. IX, XII.
10. *Cf.* U.S.-Netherlands Treaty, Arts. X, XI.
11. I.R.C. §861(c), 871(a). *Compare* Isidro Martin-Montis Trust, 75 T.C. 381 (1980); Otto H. Wittschenm, 5 T.C. 10 (1945); Rev. Rul. 81-244, 1981-42 I.R.B. 13; Rev. Rul. 70-599, 1970-2 C.B. 172; *with* Rev. Rul. 59-245, 1959-2 C.B. 172.
12. *See* Chapter II *supra*.
13. I.R.C. §§2501(a)(2), 2511; *see* Treas. Reg. §25.2511-3(b).
14. *Cf.* Geoffrey C. Davies, 40 T.C. 525 (1963); De Goldschmidt-Rothschild v. Comm'r, 168 F.2d 975 (2d Cir. 1948).
15. *See* I.R.C. §§2101-2108.
16. *See* I.R.C. §§2036-2038.
17. I.R.C. §§2601-2622; *see especially* I.R.C. §§2612(a), 2614(b).
18. With regard to these items, see respectively: *(1)* I.R.C. §§542(a), 552(a), 951(a), 1246; *(2)* I.R.C. §§6031, 6035, 6038, 6046, 6046A, 1246(f); Treas. Reg. §1.6046-1(c)(2); U.S. Dep't of the Treasury (Internal Revenue Service) Forms 957, 958, 959, 2952, 3646; *(3)* I.R.C. §§367, 1491-1494; *(4)* I.R.C. §§665-668, 679, 6048; Treas. Reg. §301.6048-1; Temp. Treas. Reg. §§16.3-1, 404.6048-1; U.S. Dep't of the Treasury (Internal Revenue Service) Forms 3520, 3520-A; *(5)* Treas. Reg. §§1.871-2(a), 301.7701-5; B. W. Jones Trust, 46 B.T.A. 531 (1942), *aff'd,* 132 F.2d 914 (4th Cir. 1943); Rev. Rul. 60-181, 1960-1 C.B. 257; *(6)* I.R.C. §§162(c), 952(a)(4), 995(b)(1)(F)(iii), 999; Prop. Treas. Reg. §1.999-1; U.S. Dep't of the Treasury Boycott Guidelines, 1978-1 C.B. 521; U.S. Dep't of the Treasury (Internal Revenue Service) Form 5713; *(7)* I.R.C. §§3541 *et seq*; *(8)* I.R.C. §§2(b), 1303(b), 1371(a), 6013(a); Rev. Rul. 79-23, 1979-1 C.B. 3. *See also* Chapters II, VI, VIII *supra.*

A resident alien has since 1978 been entitled — like a U.S. citizen — to the automatic two-month extension to file his federal income tax return if he is abroad on the return's due date, which is usually April 15. *Compare* Treas. Reg. §1.6081-2 *with* Letter Rul. 7930023.

19. *See* Internal Revenue Service Pub. No. 519. *But see* Saxbe v. Bustos, 419 U.S. 65 (1974); Rev. Rul. 76-82, 1976-1 C.B. 1972 (Mexican and Canadian aliens who commute to work in the United States on seasonal basis permitted to obtain immigrant visas, under immigration programs no longer in force, but treated as nonresident aliens for income tax purposes).

20. Treas. Reg. §1.871-2(b).

21. *See* Treas. Reg. §1.871-4; Tongsun Park, 79 T.C. No. 17 (1982); Ian W. MacLean, 73 T.C. 1045 (1980); Robert M. Brittingham, 66 T.C. 373 (1976); Rudolph Jellinek, 36 T.C. 826 (1961); Joyce de la Begassiere, 31 T.C. 1031 (1959), *aff'd per curiam,* 272 F.2d 709 (5th Cir. 1959); David O. Tilburn, T.C. Memo 1955-256, 14 T.C.M. 950; Rev. Rul. 81-70, 1981-1 C.B. 389; Rev. Rul. 72-297, 1972-1 C.B. 212; Rev. Rul. 72-140, 1972-1 C.B. 211; Rev. Rul. 69-611, 1969-2 C.B. 150; *see also* Chapter X *supra.* For a more extensive description of the determinative factors for federal income tax purposes, see B. Packman & M. Rosenberg, "How Foreigners (Unintentionally) Become U.S. Residents," 57 Taxes 85 (1979). However, advance rulings on federal tax residence generally are not issued by the Internal Revenue Service on the basis of proposed (as opposed to completed) events. Rev. Proc. 80-38, 1980-1 C.B. 771.

22. *See* Treas. Reg. §20.0-1(b); Elkins v. Moreno, 435 U.S. 647 (1978) (nonimmigrant aliens in the employ of international organizations may become U.S. domiciliaries); Jan W. Nienhuys, 17 T.C. 1149 (1952); Rev. Rul. 80-209, 1980-2 C.B. 248; Rev. Rul. 74-364, 1974-2 C.B. 321.

23. *See* I.R.C. §§871(a)(2), 958, 1248.

24. I.R.C. §§641 *et seq.*; *see especially* I.R.C. §§643(a)(6)(C), 665-668.

25. I.R.C. §1034; *see* I.R.C. §121.

26. I.R.C. §§80, 165(g), 166, 172(b)(1)(D), (b)(3), (d)(2), (h), 1212(a), 1231, 1351, 6167, 6503(e).

27. I.R.C. §§6013(g), (h). This election may prevent the alien from claiming U.S. income tax treaty benefits as a resident of a treaty country, even if he remains a citizen of that country. Prop. Treas. Reg. §1.6013-6. With respect to continued tax segregation of each spouse's income where one spouse remains a nonresident alien, see I.R.C. §879. With respect to Subchapter S election difficulties in the absence of the election, see, *e.g.*, Ward v. Comm'r, 661 F.2d 226 (Ct. Cl. 1981).

28. *See* I.R.C. §§441, 446. *Compare* Rev. Rul. 80-352, 1980-2 C.B. 160; *with* I.R.C. §441(g); Jose E. More, 66 T.C. 27 (1976), *aff'd,* 562 F.2d 38 (2d Cir. 1977); Severino R. Nico, Jr., 67 T.C. 647 (1977), *rev'd in part,* 565 F.2d 1234 (2d Cir. 1977); Ian W. MacLean, 73 T.C. 1045 (1980); Letter Rul. 7844042.

29. I.R.C. §901(c).

30. I.R.C. §2014(h). If the foreign country's tax is imposed not on the estate's full net value but, for example, on the appreciation in value of the decedent's property, the tax also may not qualify as an estate tax for the U.S. credit; however, it may be deductible from the taxable estate as a claim thereon. *Compare* I.R.C. §2053(a) *with* I.R.C. §2053(d); *cf.* Letter Rul. 8203135 (Canadian tax).

31. I.R.C. §§170, 642(c), 2055, 2106(a)(2), 2522.

32. *See* Treas. Reg. §1.871-5; Sutton v. United States, 43 Am. Fed. Tax Rep. 2d 79-1033 (E.D. Tenn. 1979), *aff'd,* 642 F.2d 453 (6th Cir. 1980); Kazuko S. Marsh, 68 T.C. 68 (1977); William N. Dillin, 56 T.C. 228 (1971); Rev. Rul. 70-461, 1970-2 C.B. 149.

33. *See* I.R.C. §§453, 871, 897; Chapters II, III *supra.*

34. *See* I.R.C. §§871(a), (f). However, U.S. social security monthly benefit payments to the alien may have to terminate after he has been outside the United States for six consecutive calendar months. 42 U.S.C. §402(t)(1).

35. I.R.C. §§1031, 1034; *see* I.R.C. §121.

36. *See* Chapters I, II *supra.*

37. *See* I.R.C. §§877, 2107, 2501(a)(3), 2511.

38. *Cf.* United States-Jamaica Income Tax Treaty of 1981, Art. 1 (3); proposed Model U.S. Income Tax Treaty of 1981, Art. 1.3; Model U.S. Estate and Gift Tax Treaty of 1980, Art. 1.3. U.S. tax authorities may question whether even an older treaty overrides the statutory expatriation provisions. *Cf.* Rev. Rul. 79-152, 1979-1 C.B. 237.

Chapter XII

Reporting of U.S. Investments from Abroad

While the United States does not extensively regulate investments from abroad,[1] recent years have witnessed the rapid growth of reporting requirements to various U.S. federal and state authorities in connection with such foreign investment. Generally, reports are required from individuals or entities which reside in or are subject to the jurisdiction of the United States and have dealings with or are owned by foreign individuals or entities. This chapter principally deals with reports to the federal government arising out of the following U.S. investments by foreign persons: (1) the establishment of a new U.S. business enterprise or the acquisition of an existing U.S. business enterprise other than real estate, (2) the ownership of U.S. real estate or other natural resources either directly or through another entity, and (3) portfolio investments.

The new establishment and acquisition types of investments, if they involve ownership of at least 10% of the U.S. enterprise, are considered to be *direct investments* and generally are reported to the Bureau of Economic Analysis (the "BEA") of the U.S. Department of Commerce and, in certain cases, to the U.S. Department of the Treasury (the "DOT"). *Portfolio investments* generally are all non-direct investments and usually are reported to the DOT or the Federal Reserve Bank of New York.[2]

A foreign person's interest in U.S. real estate or other natural resources may be either a direct investment or — especially in the case of a limited partner's interest — a portfolio investment. Additional reporting of such an interest may be required under the terms of the Foreign Investment in Real Property Tax Act of 1980[3] and, if the land is agricultural, under the Agricultural Foreign Investment Disclosure Act of 1978.[4]

Selected aspects of other reporting requirements, including those arising out of banking activities, are described in later sections of the chapter. Examples of reports to the various states are discussed at the end of the chapter.

Foreign Direct Investments

The concept of foreign direct investment is the centerpiece of the federal reporting scheme set up by the International Investment Survey Act of 1976,[5] which applies to both direct and portfolio investments from abroad. Foreign direct investment includes "the ownership or control, directly or indirectly, by one foreign person of ten per centum or more of the voting securities of an incorporated U.S. business enterprise or an equivalent interest in an unincorporated U.S. business enterprise, including a branch."[6] A foreign person may be an individual or an entity;[7] a business enterprise is a venture organized for profitmaking purposes or otherwise to secure economic advantage, and includes joint ventures and often the mere ownership of real estate.[8]

Foreign direct investment generally must be reported to the BEA. Here the initial and/or periodic filings usually are made by the U.S. affiliate — the U.S. business enterprise in which a foreign person has a 10% or greater interest in ownership or control.[9]

A chain of foreign ownership may exist — for example, a U.S. business enterprise may be wholly owned directly by a Netherlands corporation, which is in turn wholly owned by a Netherlands Antilles corporation, which is owned 50% by each of two foreign individuals. Then the foreign entity which is the first person in the chain located outside the United States (in this example, the Netherlands corporation) is referred to as the foreign parent. However, even indirect foreign owners may have a direct investment: in the above example, each foreign individual has only an indirect ownership interest in the U.S. affiliate, yet for reporting purposes each individual has a direct investment in the U.S. affiliate, because each of their individual voting interests is 50% (which is greater than the 10% direct investment triggering level). Indirect ownership percentages may be calculated by multiplying the individual's percentage of direct interest in the highest tier business enterprise (here 50% of the Netherlands Antilles corporation) by the enterprise's percentage ownership of the next lower tier business (here 100% of the Netherlands corporation) and so on down to the U.S. affiliate in question. Even for a wholly U.S. chain of ownership with U.S. subsidiaries and sub-subsidiaries, tracing rules govern whether the triggering 10% level of foreign direct investment has been reached and, therefore, which of the U.S. enterprises are U.S. affiliates of the foreign parent.

Certain foreign investments are not required to be reported to the BEA. Exemptions from the reports fall into two general categories: those arising out of the nature of the investment and those resulting from the size of the investment. As discussed further below, for example, real estate held exclusively for personal use and not for profitmaking purposes is exempt from reporting to the BEA. Also exempt are airline, shipping, and similar facilities providing services only to their own operations. In addition, limited partners usually are not considered to have a direct investment in the partnership because they do not have general voting rights, although they are considered to have a portfolio investment. The size of the investment also is crucial: as discussed below, direct investment in a U.S. affiliate with limited U.S. real estate or other assets may be exempt from BEA reporting. Many individual BEA forms have additional exemptions, as discussed further below. Prior to 1980, any person claiming any exemption from filing with the BEA was required to furnish the BEA with a certification letter regarding the basis of such claim. Revised regulations have added supplements to many of the forms themselves, to be completed and filed by persons claiming exemptions.[10] Unless an exemption is otherwise available and filed for, reports are required even if the affiliate is sold or inactivated during the reporting period.

The potential penalties for failure to report on the requisite BEA forms are stringent: in the case of failure to report, civil fines of up to $10,000 and/or an injunction requiring reporting; for intentional failure to report, up to $10,000 in fines and/or for individuals, including any officer, director, employee or agent of a corporation who knowingly participates in any such violation, up to one year's imprisonment. These have generally not been invoked to date but, in light of growing interest in the monitoring of foreign investment in the United States, increased enforcement is quite possible.[11]

Every such BEA and DOT survey form bears a legend that the information reported is confidential and may be used only for analytical and statistical purposes. In an analogous situation, reports of foreign boycott requests were revealed by the Department of Commerce under court order in a suit based on the Freedom of Information Act of 1966.[12] However, the International Investment Survey Act specifically prohibits Freedom of Information Act requests concerning the BEA and DOT reports referred to above, and the relevant agencies apparently have denied requests on the basis of that prohibition as well as refused requests by other government agencies for the reported information.

In addition to the investment survey forms referred to above and described in greater detail immediately below, general federal and state taxation of foreign persons may require annual or more frequent tax returns. In particular, any U.S. corporation — or foreign corporation engaged in U.S. trade or business through, for example, an unincorporated U.S. branch — which is owned directly or indirectly at least one-half in voting power or value by a foreign person is required after 1982 to file with the federal tax authorities information (1) identifying any other corporations which are similarly controlled by the same persons and with which it has any transactions during its taxable year and (2) describing its relationship to and transactions with each of such corporations.[13] Regulations are to specify further the forms — expected to be available in 1983 — and details required. These filings should be accorded the same strict confidentiality given to other U.S. federal tax returns. However, the United States has various income tax treaties which promote the sharing of tax information between countries, and such sharing pursuant to a treaty may reduce the value of confidentiality afforded in the United States.

Establishment of a New U.S. Business Enterprise

Both initial and periodic BEA reports may be required due to foreign direct investment in a newly created U.S. corporation, general partnership (or general partnership interest in a limited partnership), joint venture, branch or other U.S. business enterprise. The reporting forms themselves have been altered periodically, particularly during the BEA's annual review. However, the most recent forms are discussed below.

Initial investment reports. The first BEA reporting form required from most foreign investors is *Form BE-13.* This single form was consolidated in 1982 from the previous BE-13 Report consisting of Forms BE-13A — filed by the U.S. affiliate — and BE-13B — filed by the foreign parent, or by the surviving U.S. affiliate in an acquisition or merger. Form BE-13 and its predecessors apply to direct investment transactions which occur after 1978 and must be filed no later than 45 days after the direct investment transaction occurs — for the creation of the new U.S. business enterprise, 45 days after the shares or other indicia of ownership are issued. The newer version of Form BE-13 is used for transactions occurring after 1981. Initial filing — whether timely or late — concerning transactions before 1982 (but after 1978) is to be completed on the predecessor Forms BE-13A and BE-13B which applied to the transaction period.[14]

If a variety of transactions involving a U.S. affiliate occur within the 45 days, the BEA staff has allowed a single Form BE-13 to be used to aggregate the information from all of the related transactions. For example, if a U.S. affiliate created on January 1 purchases another U.S. corporation on January 10, both the creation of the first affiliate and the acquisition of the second can be reported on a consolidated basis on one Form BE-13. Beginning in 1981, if a U.S. holding company is established with $5 million or less of initial capital for the purpose of subsequently establishing or acquiring a U.S. business enterprise within 180 days after the holding company's formation, then filing concerning such formation may be deferred and consolidated into a later report when the second business enterprise is established or acquired within such 180-day period. If the establishment of the holding company *and* the secondary investment do not both take place within the 180 days, Form BE-13 regarding the holding company must be filed within 45 days after such 180-day period.

Form BE-13 (like the BE-13A portion of earlier versions) is filed by the newly created U.S. business enterprise which is established and operated by a foreign parent either directly or through an existing U.S. affiliate (if there is no merger of the two U.S. business enterprises). If the newly created business enterprise is merged into an existing U.S. affiliate, that surviving affiliate files the form. If a U.S. intermediary comprising "any agent, nominee, manager, custodian, trust or any person acting in a similar capacity"[15] holds or manages the newly created U.S. affiliate, the intermediary also is responsible for reporting for the affiliate on Form BE-13 (or, for transactions before 1982, on Form BE-13A), unless it instructs the affiliate to report, provides the affiliate with relevant information possessed by the intermediary, and informs the BEA of the instructions given to the affiliate.

For direct investment in a new establishment made after 1980,[16] an exemption from reporting on Form BE-13 is available if the new U.S. affiliate has no more than $1 million in total assets and owns less than 200 acres of U.S. land immediately after being established. If so, the new U.S. affiliate still must file an exemption claim on *Supplement C* to Form BE-13 which requires identification of the affiliate and information substantiating the exemption.

The 1982 version of Form BE-13 requires reporting of: (1) the type of transaction and date of completion; (2) the identity and ownership structure of the new U.S. affiliate; (3) the identity of the U.S. business enterprise, or business segment or operating unit of a U.S. business enterprise, that has been acquired by and merged into an existing U.S. affiliate; (4) selected financial and operating data; (5) investment incentives and services provided by state or local governments (including quasi-governmental entities); (6) the identity of the foreign parent and ultimate beneficial owner (referred to below); and (7) the cost of the investment. The third item does not apply to the establishment of a new U.S. business enterprise. If the new U.S. affiliate has corporate subsidiaries with which it can consolidate financial and operating data, the Form BE-13 should be filed on a consolidated basis; investments which cannot be consolidated with the affiliate must be reported on separate Forms BE-13.

The newer version of Form BE-13 calls for significantly less information than that required by the form's predecessors, Forms BE-13A and BE-13B. However, Form BE-13 still requires identifying information concerning the ultimate beneficial owner (the "UBO") of the U.S. affiliate. For BEA reporting, the UBO is that individual or entity at the end of a chain of ownership which is owned not more than 50% by another person. While this suggests certain planning opportunities, an arrangement created with the purpose of divesting a UBO of an interest as part of a plan to avoid reporting is ignored. If the UBO is an individual, residence must be disclosed. The 1982 Form BE-13 also requires the date the transaction was completed, the cost of the investment, and an indication if a foreign government (including a government owned or quasi-governmental business enterprise or government run pension fund) has a five percent or greater direct or indirect interest in the U.S. affiliate. The 1982 version eliminates, *inter alia,* reporting of the sources of financing for the transaction, which section's inclusion in the previous Form BE-13B had been particularly criticized.

Form BE-607, an industry classification questionnaire, is filed by the newly established U.S. affiliate concurrently with Form BE-13. Unlike the BE-13 Form, a new Form BE-607 must be filed whenever there is a change in the U.S. affiliate's industry code, *i.e.,* a change in the type of business conducted. Since filing for an incorporated entity must be on a consolidated basis, if a subsidiary of a U.S. affiliate subsequently becomes involved in a different industry segment, a new Form BE-607 must be filed by the consolidated group.

Finally, if the newly created enterprise is a joint venture, the U.S. venturer may have to report on *Form BE-14* unless Form BE-13 has been filed for the transaction, as also discussed further below in connection with the acquisition of an existing U.S. enterprise. The venture is exempt if its capital (including loans from the joint venturers) is $1 million or less and it owns less than 200 acres of U.S. land, both measured as at the date of establishment. Like all direct investments, joint ventures should be reported only if at least 10% of ownership or control is exercised by a foreign person.

It should be noted that Forms BE-13 and BE-14 define an associated group of persons acting together to influence a business enterprise's management as a single person for determining reporting obligations.

Periodic investment reports. In addition to those initial reports described above, a new U.S. business enterprise created as a direct investment of a foreign person requires periodic reports to the BEA. U.S. affiliates classified as banks frequently report separately to the BEA, as discussed under special federal reporting further below; this discussion, therefore, concerns only nonbank enterprises.

Quarterly reports are filed on *Form BE-605*[17] covering transactions of a U.S. affiliate with its foreign parent. No reporting under Form BE-605 is required from a U.S. affiliate if each of the following items is between negative $5 million and positive $5 million during the entire year: (1) its total assets, (2) its actual or expected annual sales[18] or gross operating revenues excluding sales taxes (not gross margins), and (3) its actual or expected annual net income after provision for U.S. income taxes. Filing on Form BE-605 is on a fully consolidated basis, so the U.S. affiliate combines its data for exemption purposes with all U.S. affiliates in which it owns more than one-half of the voting stock.[19] If the U.S. affiliate is indirectly owned by a foreign person through another U.S. enterprise, however, and has no direct transactions or positions with a foreign parent (or any foreign affiliate thereof owned more than one-half by the same foreign persons as the parent) at any time during the year, the U.S. affiliate is exempt from filing a Form BE-605. Unlike the BE-13 report and the Form BE-12 discussed below, where a printed supplement to the form is used to claim an exemption, a certification of exemption in letter form giving the levels of the three exemption categories substantiates exemption from Form BE-605.

Reporting on Form BE-605 is required beginning in the quarter in which any of the trigger levels is exceeded; in such case, reports for prior quarters of that year also may be required retroactively. Once the exemption level has been surpassed, it is also deemed to be exceeded in the following year. Filing is required within 30 days after the end of each calendar or fiscal quarter, except the final quarter of the calendar or fiscal year, when reports may be filed within 45 days after year end.

Form BE-605 principally is concerned with transactions between the reporting U.S. affiliate and its foreign parent, including the direct payment of interest, rentals, and various fees. A variety of general information also is required, principally showing the debt and equity positions of the foreign parent in the U.S. affiliate during the quarter. Thus, the parent's net realized and unrealized share of the U.S. affiliate's capital gains or losses for the quarter, as well as any distributions (such as in liquidation or as dividends) are reported. Similar information is reported concerning the U.S. affiliate's transactions and accounts with each of the foreign parent's foreign affiliates — *i.e.*, any member of the affiliated foreign group owned more than one-half by the same foreign persons as the foreign parent.[20]

Annual reports are made on *Form BE-15*, except that this is replaced by the Form BE-12 every five years for a so called benchmark investment survey. If a BE-15 is required in one year, it is deemed to be required in the following year. The exemptions from, for example, Form BE-15 for 1979 applied the $5 million levels used for Form BE-605 to consolidated figures for the calendar year, and further required that the U.S. affiliate own less than 200 acres of U.S. land during the year. In 1981, the BEA changed its regulations to allow future BE-15 reports to be based on the U.S. affiliate's fiscal rather than calendar year. Furthermore, the maximum land ownership for exemption was increased to less than 1,000 acres (if the $5 million levels are not exceeded) for 1981 and subsequent annual reports.[21]

Reports for the five-year benchmark surveys of foreign direct investment in the United States are to be filed on *Form BE-12*. The completed form (or the exemption form) is due from every U.S. affiliate in which a foreign person had a direct investment at any time during the calendar year. For exemption purposes, the assets, sales, and income tests and the U.S. land ownership test of Form BE-15 also apply to the Form BE-12, but the maximum levels for exemption currently are only $1 million and less than 200 acres for the BE-12 (rather than $5 million and less than 1,000 acres). An exemption form (printed as the last page of the Form BE-12) must be filed to substantiate the claim for exemption.

The last current Form BE-12 was for 1980 and was due by August 15, 1981. It required lengthy identifying, financial, and operating data, as well as reporting of investments and transactions between the U.S. affiliate and foreign parent, all data being provided as at the end of the U.S. affiliate's 1980 fiscal year. Comparisons with data as at the close of the 1979 fiscal year also were required for certain items, and the identity of the ultimate beneficial owner or UBO was required to be disclosed. The next benchmark survey has been postponed to 1987, to coincide with other U.S. economic surveys. The benchmark surveys are scheduled to continue every fifth year thereafter.[22]

New one-time foreign investment survey forms also are issued occasionally by the BEA, such as the previous questionnaire covering the fish processing industry.[23]

Periodic reports of international financial and commercial dealings. The new U.S. enterprise may have business relations with affiliated or unaffiliated foreign persons, whether financial — such as with lenders or borrowers — or commercial — such as with trade creditors or customers. It may also maintain positions in foreign currencies, or keep U.S. dollar deposits abroad. Further, it may enter into agreements with unaffiliated foreign persons to buy, sell, or use intangible assets or other proprietary rights — such as license, royalty, rental, or management agreements — or to perform construction and related services. Each of these may require periodic reporting to the Federal Reserve Bank of New York, the DOT, or the BEA. This reporting generally is not limited to enterprises owned by foreign persons, but such enterprises may be particularly likely to be involved in these reportable dealings.

DOT *Form FC-3* is a monthly report denominated in specified foreign currencies which indicates gross assets, gross liabilities, and forward currency positions. Form FC-3 is required for any nonbank business concern or nonprofit institution located in the United States which employs 100 or more persons. The outstanding amounts of liquid assets, short-term trade receivables, other assets, short-term trade payables, other liabilities, forward currency contracts bought and sold, and net overall positions in the currencies specified — all as at the close of business on the last day of the calendar month — are reported on the form. An exemption is available if the dollar equivalent of each of the above items to be reported for any specified foreign currency is less than $3 million. If any reportable item for any foreign currency exceeds that trigger level, the form must be completed for each foreign currency in question and for each item to be reported. The form is to be filed with the Federal Reserve Bank of New York not later than one month following the last calendar day of the month reported. Estimates may be submitted to the extent that final data are not available. If estimated data are submitted for the month which coincides with the end of a calendar quarter, final data based on accounting records as at the end of such quarter are to be reported on a revised report not later than 45 days following the last day of the quarter. Extensions must be specifically requested from and authorized by the DOT.

U.S. affiliates may also be required to file one or more of the DOT's Treasury International Capital (the "TIC") nonbank forms. These forms are required from all U.S. persons — other than banks, bank holding companies and their subsidiaries, securities brokers and dealers, and the U.S. federal government and its agencies, corporations, and other instrumentalities — which for their own account or the account of other U.S. persons have liabilities to or claims on unaffiliated foreigners, unless the amounts of these liabilities and claims fall below the exemption levels as specified on each form. These reports may be particularly required of exporters, importers, industrial and commercial concerns, and nonbank financial institutions such as insurance companies and savings and loan associations. They include the following:

Form CM is a very brief monthly report of U.S. dollar deposit and certificate of deposit claims on banks abroad and must be filed with the Federal Reserve Bank of New York not later than 30 days following the last day of the calendar month covered in the report. No report is required if the total of all such U.S. dollar claims on banks abroad amounts to less than $10 million at the end of the month.

Forms CQ-1 and 1(A) are quarterly reports filed by U.S. persons detailing their *financial* liabilities to and claims on unaffiliated foreigners. Affiliation is defined by the same percentage as under the BEA reports — 10% or greater direct or indirect common ownership or control. Initial reporting on Form CQ-1 or 1(A) is required for the first quarter in which the reporting person's financial liabilities to *or* financial claims on unaffiliated foreigners equal at least $2 million; reporting is also mandatory for the following quarter. After that period, reporting of financial liabilities is necessary only if the aggregate of those liabilities equal at least $2 million for that quarter; financial claims are likewise reportable only if in the aggregate they alone equal at least $2 million for the quarter. The forms are due not later than 30 days following the last day of the calendar quarter to which the report applies. Certain liabilities to foreigners are not reported on Forms CQ-1 and 1(A), particularly including liabilities resulting from foreign ownership of the reporter's capital stock or long-term bonds or debentures (reported as foreign portfolio investments discussed further below), direct investments of foreigners in the reporting person or affiliated entities (reported to the BEA as described above), forward currency contracts, and loans from U.S. offices of foreign banks. Certain financial claims by the reporting person against foreigners also are not contained in the report, particularly including long-term bonds or debentures and direct investments. In the event that no more than 20 foreign countries are involved, reporting may be made on the shorter Form CQ-1(A), which otherwise requires the same information as Form CQ-1.

Forms CQ-2 and CQ-2(A) are quarterly reports by U.S. persons of their *commercial* liabilities to and claims on unaffiliated foreigners. The exemption levels (and number of countries for the appropriate choice of form) for Forms CQ-2 and CQ-2(A) are identical to those described above for Forms CQ-1 and 1(A). The form is due not later than 45 days following the close of the calendar quarter reported. These commercial liabilities and claims include, for example, foreign trade payables, prepayments by foreigners for goods and services, foreign trade receivables, advance payments made to foreigners for future goods or services, accrued royalties, and the value of goods abroad owned by the reporting person (but not by its foreign affiliates). Excluded from reporting are, for example, direct investments (both inbound and outbound), forward currency contracts, acceptances made for foreigners under letters of credit granted by banks in the United States, and credit advices issued by banks in the United States under letters of credit issued by foreign banks for U.S. exports.

The TIC Forms CM, CQ-1 or 1(A), and CQ-2 or 2(A) differ in a number of respects from Form FC-3 described further above. Form FC-3 requires the reporting of all financial assets and liabilities denominated in specified currencies, even those liabilities to and claims on U.S. persons, while the TIC forms are limited to liabilities to and claims on foreigners. Additionally, Form FC-3 includes affiliates' claims and liabilities, which are excluded from the TIC forms. Form FC-3 includes assets and liabilities held for collection by banks in the United States; these amounts are not included in the TIC forms. Form FC-3 lists spot and forward purchases and sales of foreign currency, while the TIC forms include the net amount of spot purchases and sales only. Furthermore, Form FC-3 classifies assets and liabilities by currency rather than country, while amounts reportable on the TIC forms are classified by country of domicile of the foreign person.

Failure to report on any of the above described DOT forms can result in a civil penalty of up to $10,000. Intentional failure to report may result in criminal prosecution and, upon conviction, a fine of up to $10,000 and/or in the case of an individual, imprisonment for up to 10 years. These penalties extend to any officer, director, or agent of any corporation who knowingly participates in such a violation.

The new U.S. affiliate's business relations with foreign persons also may require it to report on BEA *Form BE-93,* which is required from U.S. persons who have entered into agreements with unaffiliated foreign persons to buy, sell, or use intangible assets or other proprietary rights. The form includes most license, royalty, rental, management, and other fees, but does not include oil and other natural resource royalties. Form BE-93 is unrelated to the International Investment Survey Act, the statutory authority for the previously described BEA investment reporting forms, but is instead required by the Bretton Woods Agreement Act of 1945.[24] However, lack of affiliation here also depends on less than 10% direct or indirect common ownership or control. Reporting pursuant to Form BE-93 is required if the combined foreign receipts and payments covered by the form equal at least $25,000 in the aggregate for the calendar or fiscal year, and the report is due within 90 days after the close of each calendar or fiscal quarter. The principal items reported on Form BE-93 are license, royalty, management, and administrative fees. Only capital movements into and out of the United States are reported; these include even receipts from and payments to an unaffiliated U.S. enterprise if made for the account of its own foreign parent or foreign affiliates. No reporting is called for when no capital changes hands, as is the case when reciprocal exchanges of tangible assets are made. Form BE-93 also does not include receipts from or payments to unaffiliated foreigners for the rental or lease of tangible assets, or the sale of commodities, or contracts to perform services abroad unless connected with the transfer of intangible assets or rights.

Form BE-47 is a voluntary form to be filed by a U.S. enterprise furnishing construction, engineering, consulting, or other technical services to unaffiliated persons in any of certain situations: (1) in a project abroad; (2) as part of a technical assistance program for a foreign country, even in a U.S. project; or (3) in connection with a contract with an unaffiliated foreign person, again even in a U.S. project.[25] Form BE-47 is due annually, unless the reporter elects instead to file at the conclusion of a multiyear contract.

In addition, as noted further above generally with regard to foreign direct investments, after 1982 a U.S. corporation, or foreign corporation engaged in U.S. trade or business, which is owned at least one-half by a foreign person is required to file a return with federal tax authorities covering its transactions during each taxable year with other corporations in the same controlled group.

Acquisition of an Existing U.S. Business Enterprise

Often the foreign investor will prefer to acquire all or part of an existing U.S. corporation or other business enterprise rather than establish a new enterprise. Although the forms required to report an acquisition include all of the BEA forms described in the preceding section of this chapter, certain special issues may arise in the same reports and certain additional forms may be required. The entire U.S. enterprise does not need to be acquired for direct investment reporting to be triggered — a 10% or greater interest is considered to be a reportable direct investment.

Initial reports. Acquisition of any of the following three types of U.S. enterprises requires filing of *Form BE-13* (or, for pre-1982 acquisitions after 1978, the predecessor Forms BE-13A and BE-13B): (1) an already operating U.S. enterprise in which a foreign person or its existing U.S. affiliate acquires the requisite voting interest and which continues to be operated as a separate legal entity, whether or not incorporated; (2) a business segment or operating unit of an existing U.S. enterprise which a foreign person or its existing U.S. affiliate acquires and organizes into a new separate legal entity, whether or not incorporated; and (3) a business segment or operating unit of an existing U.S. enterprise, or the entire enterprise, which is acquired by and merged into an existing U.S. affiliate of a foreign person.

In the first two types of acquisitions — where the acquired enterprise survives as a separate legal entity — the acquisition will be totally exempt from reporting on Form BE-13 if at the time of acquisition or immediately thereafter the new U.S. affiliate has total assets (on a consolidated basis, but excluding the foreign parent's and existing U.S. affiliate's share) of $1 million or less and it owns less than 200 acres of U.S. land. Where the acquired enterprise is merged into an existing U.S. affiliate, the same exemption level applies to the total cost of the acquisition, rather than to the total assets acquired; the land ownership test is applied to the number of acres included in the acquisition.[26] Supplement C to Form BE-13 must be filed by the U.S. affiliate to claim exemption from reporting.

It should be noted that for acquisitions after 1980 the BEA staff has indicated that *no* BE-13 reporting currently will be required if an existing reporting U.S. affiliate is acquired — for example, shares of a U.S. corporation are acquired by one foreign corporation from another.

Unusual situations may arise in the acquisition context which make completing the Form BE-13 difficult. A potential reporter may consult the BEA for guidance in these circumstances, but the forms do clarify one potential problem area. In a so called creeping direct investment, where the initial investment by the foreign person (either directly or indirectly through an intervening U.S. affiliate) is less than 10% but subsequent acquisitions bring the ownership to the trigger level, the entire investment must be reported at the time the investment level reaches at least 10%; however, only the last transaction's data are reported.

Direct investment by acquisition also may give rise to reporting on

Form BE-14, a short informational form. While Form BE-13 generally is filed by the U.S. affiliate, Form BE-14 is filed by unaffiliated U.S. persons. These include any U.S. person — including but not limited to a real estate broker, business broker, accountant, or attorney — who assists or intervenes as an intermediary in a foreign direct investment acquisition. (It should be remembered that, in the establishment of a new U.S. business enterprise, certain U.S. intermediaries may have to file instead Form BE-13, and Form BE-14 may have to be filed by a U.S. person who enters into a joint venture with a foreign person to establish a new U.S. business enterprise, as noted in the previous section). The intermediary should have reason to believe that the acquiror is foreign before the reporting requirements arise, but in that case default may occur 45 days after the transaction regardless of the intermediary's actual knowledge. Although there are stringent penalties for failure to file, these generally have not been invoked to date.

The principal exemption from filing Form BE-14 is identical to the exemption for acquisitions under Form BE-13: the acquired enterprise's total assets must be $1 million[27] or less and it must own less than 200 acres of U.S. land. Additionally, however, an intermediary is exempt from filing Form BE-14 if it has filed Form BE-13 concerning the acquisition.[28]

Form BE-14 presents several definitional difficulties.[29] Particularly troubling is the lack of clarity of the concept of intermediary, which could be extended to impose reporting requirements on even incidental participants in an acquisition — such as engineers or lenders — who may assist in the transaction. Furthermore, requiring an attorney to disclose information regarding the activities of his client usually is contrary to the principles of attorney-client privileged communication.[30] The alternative of having the direct participants file Form BE-13, and the general flexibility of BEA enforcement to date, have so far reduced concern on this issue.

As in the case of a newly established U.S. business enterprise, if an intermediary takes an active role in an acquired U.S. enterprise — for example, by holding or managing the enterprise for the foreign parent — then the intermediary also will have responsibility for Form BE-13 filing, unless the intermediary follows the procedures outlined in the first section above.

Additionally, as described further above with regard to establishing a new U.S. business enterprise, *Form BE-607* must be filed with the U.S. affiliate's initial report.

Antitrust and securities notices. Advance notices of certain large acquisitions to the U.S. Federal Trade Commission and the Department of Justice on *Notification Form C4* are required as described in Chapter VII. Compliance with federal tender offer and other securities law filing requirements also may be necessary.

Periodic reports. The newly acquired U.S. affiliate may incur reporting obligations under *Form BE-605* (except in the case of a bank branch or agency) and *Forms BE-15* and/or *BE-12.* Its international activities may also lead to reporting under DOT *Forms FC-3, CM, CQ-1 or 1(A)* and *CQ-2 or 2(A),* as well as BEA *Forms BE-93* and *BE-47*, all as described above in connection with a new U.S. business enterprise.

In addition, as noted further above generally with regard to foreign direct investments, a newly acquired U.S. corporation, or a foreign corporation engaged in a newly acquired U.S. trade or business, which is owned at least one-half by a foreign person must after 1982 file a return with federal tax authorities covering its transactions during each taxable year with other corporations in the same controlled group.

Foreign Investments in Real Estate and Other Natural Resources

Perhaps more than any other area of foreign investment, U.S. real estate and other natural resource investments from abroad — either directly or through an intervening entity — have given rise to an increasing number of federal reporting requirements. Several separate and often overlapping reporting schemes operate in this area: (1) the reporting of general direct investment to the BEA and, in certain cases, to the DOT, similarly to the non-real estate transactions described in previous sections of this chapter, and of portfolio investments to the DOT or the Federal Reserve Bank of New York as discussed further below; (2) the reporting of foreign interests in agricultural land to the Agricultural Stabilization and Conservation Service (the "ASCS") of the U.S. Department of Agriculture under the Agricutural Foreign Investment Disclosure Act ("AFIDA"); and (3) the reporting to the DOT under the Foreign Investment in Real Property Tax Act ("FIRPTA") by a U.S. real property holding corporation, by a foreign corporation and a domestic or foreign trust or estate with a substantial foreign investor, and by certain substantial foreign investors themselves.[31]

Direct and Portfolio Investment Reporting

A foreign person's investment in U.S. real estate or other natural resources may be a direct investment in a U.S. business enterprise reportable to the BEA on the initial and periodic reports described in the first section of this chapter.

However, any of several exceptions or limitations on such reporting may apply. First, in order to constitute a business enterprise, the property must be acquired or held for profit; thus, purchase for personal use is not reportable. A primary residence which is leased by an owner while he is outside the United States, but which he intends eventually to reoccupy, is considered to be held for personal use. If the foreign owners of a corporation hold real estate intended for their personal use in the name of their otherwise inactive corporation, the real estate is also deemed to be held for personal use.[32] Second, the BEA only monitors direct investments, so only 10% or greater interests[33] are reported to the BEA. Third, all limited partnership interests are reported to the DOT or the Federal Reserve Bank of New York. Finally, as discussed in the previous sections, each BEA report has its own triggering levels, generally based on the dollar amount and acreage of the investment.

Although the general aspects of these forms have been described previously, the ownership of real estate or other natural resources raises certain additional issues for BEA reporting. Perhaps the greatest practical difficulty results from the apparent inapplicability of many of the reporting items on the BEA forms to the direct foreign ownership of such property. However, in the 1982 *Form BE-13* (and the 1981 version of Form BE-13A) the direct acquisition of real estate is specifically included within the first part of the form. The property itself is considered to be the U.S. affiliate of the foreign owner, but the BEA reports are filed by the direct foreign owner (or a manager or other intermediary). For the name and address of the U.S. affiliate, the direct foreign owner's name and an indication that the affiliate is real estate or another natural resource are used — for example, "XY Real Estate S.A., real estate investments" — and an address for correspondence is given, often in care of a U.S. intermediary; the address of the property itself is now not needed. Many items on the forms that may not be applicable to direct foreign ownership of property, such as an employer identification number for the property, often must be left blank. Other items should be adapted to the property context; the date of acquisition, for example, will generally be the closing or settlement date of the property acquisition.

The forms also may be difficult to work with if the real estate or natural resource investment is held through a joint venture. A foreign joint venturer currently is to report on *Form BE-14* the entire venture as its U.S affiliate, including all financial and operating data, and the joint venturer's percentage of the U.S. business enterprise.

Applying the various BEA forms' exemption limits to real estate or natural resource investments also differs slightly from applying the exemptions to other direct investments.[34] Under current regulations, all of a foreign person's direct investments in U.S. real estate are aggregated for purposes of applying the dollar and acreage exemption level tests for periodic reports such as *Forms BE-605*, *BE-15* (after 1980), and *BE-12*. Such investments apparently must be aggregated even if a U.S.

corporation is inserted between the foreign person and the U.S. real estate, unless the U.S. corporation is actively engaged in business unrelated to the real property itself; it is not clear what percentage of the U.S. corporate affiliate's activities must be non-real estate to remove it from aggregation. Aggregation also occurs at the level of the ultimate beneficial owner or UBO, not merely of the foreign parent or another intervening foreign entity. If the aggregate of such holdings exceeds $1 million or equals at least 200 acres (or $5 million or 1,000 acres for annual Form BE-15), the holdings must be reported even if individually they would have been exempt. For purposes of the exemption levels, the real estate is valued at its cost (including debt incurred for its acquisition), unless it is carried directly on the books of the reporter (in which case the book value is used). Although multiple real estate investments may be aggregated for purposes of the exemption levels, and although the BEA apparently encourages consolidated reporting, each investment may still be reported separately if desired.

Because Form BE-13 is a transactional report covering each investment when made, separate real estate investments are not aggregated. However, as noted generally further above, certain multiple transactions, otherwise separately reportable, may be combined into one Form BE-13 if all events occur within a 45-day period. Thus, if a foreign person forms a U.S. corporation which immediately purchases U.S. real estate, one Form BE-13 may be filed, triggered by the establishment of the corporate affiliate, but including in its assets the real estate purchased. Beginning in 1981, if a U.S. holding company is established with $5 million or less of initial capital for the purpose of subsequently acquiring within 180 days after its formation, *inter alia,* U.S. real estate, then filing of Form BE-13 — and the accompanying *Form BE-607* industry classification questionnaire described earlier in this chapter — may be deferred and consolidated into a later report when the real estate is subsequently purchased within such 180-day period. If the establishment of the holding company and the real estate purchase do not take place within the 180 days, the BE-13 regarding the holding company must be filed within 45 days after such 180-day period. Since Form BE-13 may be difficult to work with for such aggregate reporting, the foreign investor may prefer to file separate forms for each reportable transaction, but in complicated structures separate reporting can become onerous.

Where a real estate or other natural resource investment is not a direct investment because the interest is a limited partnership interest, it is a *portfolio investment* and, as discussed further below, reporting is made to the DOT and the Federal Reserve Bank of New York, while the requisite exemption form or letter is filed with the BEA. If a foreign general partner's interest in a limited partnership or in a general partnership meets the 10% threshold, it should be reported as a direct investment on Form BE-13.

It should be noted that a variety of real estate investments that are exempt from reporting to the BEA are also exempt from portfolio investment reporting. Portfolio investments generally only involve ownership of U.S. securities, so a direct purchase of land should not be a portfolio investment. The direct acquisition by a foreign person of a nine percent undivided or general partner interest in U.S. real estate, for example, is neither a direct nor a portfolio investment.

Agricultural Land Reporting

AFIDA was enacted in 1978 largely to require reporting of foreign acquisition of farm property which was perceived as increasing prices of such property beyond the reach of American farm families; the law as enacted, however, covers property in urban areas and types of real estate not commonly considered to be agricultural. The law calls for less reporting than does the International Investment Survey Act which is the basis of general direct and portfolio investment reporting, but the penalties for noncompliance with AFIDA are greater. In general, AFIDA and the regulations of the Department of Agriculture require any foreign person who acquires or disposes of an interest in U.S. agricultural land to report such transactions within 90 days after the transaction date to the ASCS.[35] *Form ASCS-153,* which is available at local offices of the ASCS and from the Department of Agriculture in Washington, D.C., requires certain information regarding the agricultural land involved, the foreign person, and the transaction itself.

The term "foreign person" under AFIDA is more encompassing than similar terms in many other federal foreign investor reporting statutes. This includes an individual who is not a citizen or permanent resident of the United States or certain U.S. possessions, and a corporation or other legal entity organized *or* with its principal place of business outside the United States. However, a foreign person also includes a U.S. corporation or other entity in which a foreign person or combination of foreign persons holds directly or indirectly a significant interest or substantial control. When an interest in agricultural land is held by a U.S. entity deemed to be a foreign person, reporting is initially required with respect to such U.S. entity, rather than its foreign owner.

A significant interest or substantial control comprises a five percent or greater interest in the entity in question; this has been interpreted to be limited to equity interests. The five percent trigger figure is an aggregate of all foreign investment in the property in question — even if the foreign persons are unrelated and acting independently. The term "combination" has been proposed to be restricted to a group of foreign persons or governments who act in concert and, for unrelated foreign persons each with less than a five percent interest and all acting independently, the aggregate triggering level for a significant interest or substantial control would be raised to 20%.[36] When a chain of ownership is used, the five percent test is calculated through the chain, with indirect ownership interests being computed by multiplying the foreign person's percentage of direct interest in the highest tier enterprise by that enterprise's percentage ownership of the next lower tier business and so on down to the property, in the same manner as for direct investments under the BEA reports. Although layers of entities will not obviate the necessity for reporting, the identity of the ultimate beneficial owner or UBO may be protected as discussed below.

A U.S. corporation or other legal entity which owns agricultural land is required to exercise due diligence to determine whether there is sufficient foreign ownership to require reporting. In general, the entity should at least review its ownership records to determine whether there is sufficient foreign ownership to require reporting. If a U.S. corporation has more than 100,000 shares of voting stock outstanding and its share register shows that an aggregate of more than five percent of those shares are held by foreign addressees and U.S. investment institutions, the corporation is required to ask each investment institution of record which of the shares it manages are held for foreign persons. Apparently, however, many investment institutions will not reveal this information. AFIDA's coverage of U.S. entities which own agricultural land and in which foreign persons hold a significant interest or substantial control also means that a U.S. corporation may find itself with AFIDA reporting requirements after five percent or more of its stock is purchased by foreigners (or groups of foreigners) even if the purchase was in a takeover attempt successfully opposed by the company.

AFIDA covers foreign interests only in agricultural land, which is defined generally by the current use of the property or, if the land is currently idle, its last use within the past five years. Uses covered by the act are agricultural (including even livestock and poultry raising), forestry, and timber production. The usage test is not met even if the land has been used for agricultural purposes for years prior to its sale to the foreign person, if its use at the time of sale is nonagricultural. Furthermore, it is possible that having agricultural land rezoned for a nonagricultural use will be sufficient to convert productive or idle agricultural land to nonagricultural land for reporting purposes.[37] Even if the use test is met, the land is not agricultural for AFIDA purposes if (1) it is less than one acre (proposed to be increased to 10 acres) in the aggregate *and* either (2) the annual gross sales of agricultural, forestry, or timber products from it are less than $1,000 or (3) all such products are produced for the personal or household use of individuals holding an interest in the land.

Because agricultural land under AFIDA can include small, currently idle plots, real estate not generally considered agricultural may be reportable, such as a one acre vacant parcel last used to grow Christmas trees four years previously. In a foreign person's acquisition of vacant land, it may therefore be wise to include in the acquisition agreement a representation by the seller that the land has not been used in the past five years for agricultural purposes as defined in AFIDA. Such a provision should help protect the foreign acquiror from liability for wilful failure to file and, if tied to an indemnification provision, could protect the acquiror from financial loss if fines are later assessed.

AFIDA covers any interest of the foreign person in the agricultural land except a security interest, which is defined as a mortgage or other debt security instrument. Regulations further exclude from reporting (a) leaseholds of less than 10 years, (b) contingent future interests, (c) noncontingent future interests which do not become possessory upon termination of the present possessory interest, and (d) surface or subsurface easements and rights of way used for a purpose unrelated to agricultural production. Furthermore, an interest in mineral rights generally is not equivalent to an interest in agricultural land.

Certain investments fall into unclear areas under AFIDA. It is unclear, for example, whether land purchase options are reportable under the statute, although Form ASCS-153 includes options and purchase contracts as reportable items. If so, the 90-day reporting period should commence when the contract is signed, not when the deed transferring the property is recorded. Likewise, although security interests are not agricultural interests, it is uncertain whether a shared appreciation mortgage in which the lender has a right to a portion of the appreciation of the asset is a reportable interest.

Reports of a foreign person's agricultural interests are filed on Form ASCS-153 with the Department of Agriculture's ASCS office covering the county in which the property is located or administered. For property stretching across more than one county, separate offices usually exist and filings must be submitted for each county covered. Separate forms are also to be filed for each type of interest held in a given county — for example, one form for owned and one for leased lands — and for each acquisition, even if the properties separately acquired are contiguous.

Unlike other U.S. foreign investor reports, completed Forms ASCS-153 are expressly made available for public inspection at the Department of Agriculture in Washington, D.C., shortly after receipt of a copy from the ASCS by the Secretary of Agriculture. Additionally, every six months the Secretary is required to send the completed forms submitted from a given state to that state's appropriate authorities.

Information required on Form ASCS-153 includes identification of the land, the foreign owner, the type of interest held, the method of acquisition or transfer, the value of the land, its use and usually its intended use, and the relationship of the foreign owner to the reporter.[38] However, items requesting the estimated current value of the land and the unpaid balance of the purchase price may call for highly speculative responses or generally confidential information.

In transactions where the reporting person at the direct ownership tier is a U.S. corporation or other legal entity owned five percent or more by foreign persons on an aggregate basis, the name and address of each substantial foreign investor at the next higher tier is to be disclosed on the form. The first tier entity may also be requested to disclose information regarding holders of less than five percent interests. Each second tier foreign person so reported may then be requested to report, if it is also a legal entity with the requisite foreign ownership; generally, this occurs only when the second tier is a U.S. entity defined as foreign because of direct or indirect foreign ownership of the entity. At the second tier, information on owners of less than five percent interests — foreign or U.S. — also may be requested. Reporting of ownership appears to be limited to this third tier.

Penalties under AFIDA are substantial and enforcement is not uncommon. If the requisite report is not filed, penalties accrue at a weekly rate of .01% of the fair market value of the property up to 25% of the fair market value. That maximum penalty is also imposed for failure to report at all or for the submission of a report which is known by the reporter to be incomplete or to contain false or misleading information. Four factors may be considered which may reduce a given penalty: (1) total time for which the violation existed — *i.e.,* the ASCS may be willing not to assess penalties if the filing is not substantially tardy; (2) method of discovery of the violation; (3) extenuating circumstances concerning the violation; and (4) nature of the information misstated or not reported. A procedure for penalty assessment, review, and collection has been established.[39]

Real Property and Other Tax Act Reporting

As described generally in Chapter III, FIRPTA has greatly affected the U.S. federal income taxation of foreign investors who dispose of interests in U.S. real estate and other natural resources. The central definitions under FIRPTA are discussed in greater detail in Chapter III and reference should be made to that chapter prior to evaluating the reporting scheme discussed here.

FIRPTA adds a new Section 6039C to the U.S. Internal Revenue Code which requires annual reports to be filed with the Internal Revenue Service with respect to a U.S. real property interest ("U.S. RPI") held on or after June 19, 1980. Three principal categories of individuals or entities are required to report under Section 6039C: (1) certain non-publicly held corporations; (2) certain foreign corporations and foreign or domestic partnerships, trusts, or estates; and (3) certain other foreign investors.

First, any non-publicly held U.S. corporation which at any time is during the calendar year, or was during the four preceding years, a U.S.

real property holding corporation due to at least 50% of the fair market value of its assets being comprised of U.S. RPI, and which during the current year has one or more foreign shareholders, is required to file a return for that year on Form 6659 listing the names and addresses, if known, of shareholders known to the corporation to be foreign and such other information, including stock transfers to or from each such foreign person, as the Secretary of the Treasury may require. If the foreign shareholder does not furnish the requisite information to the U.S. corporation to allow it to complete the report and the foreign owner's shares are held by a nominee, the nominee is required to furnish the information.

Second, any foreign corporation (whether or not its stock is publicly traded) and any foreign or domestic partnership, trust, or estate which at any time during the calendar year includes a substantial investor in U.S. real property must file a return for that year on Form 6660 with information concerning the entity itself and the interests held in it by the substantial investor. For a foreign corporation, such a substantial investor is any person, domestic or foreign, whose *pro rata* share of the fair market value of the foreign corporation's U.S. RPI exceeds $50,000 at any time during the year. For other foreign or domestic entities, only a foreign person may be a substantial investor and again such person must have a *pro rata* share of the fair market value of the entity's U.S. RPI greater than $50,000. In either case, insertion of any corporation between the reporter and the U.S. RPI will not eliminate the filing responsibility. Attribution rules also apply to aggregate holdings by an individual's spouse and minor children. In addition to filing its own return concerning its substantial investors' interests, each entity required to report under this provision must furnish to each substantial investor the name and address of the reporting entity, the substantial investor's *pro rata* share of the U.S. RPI held by the reporting entity, and such other information as may be required by the Secretary of the Treasury.

These attribution rules through foreign corporations and among family members apparently require the reporting of information for every tier in an ownership chain up to the ultimate beneficial owner or UBO, like certain information in the BEA reports (and unlike reports under AFIDA). However, it is important to note that this second filing requirement may be waived if the foreign corporation or other entity furnishes security adequate to ensure payment of any potential FIRPTA and other U.S. federal income tax liabilities with respect to any U.S. RPI held by such entity. Indeed, as referred to in Chapter III, regulations extend this exemption to all three types of FIRPTA reports. As a practical matter, the Internal Revenue Service will be unable to evaluate the adequacy of security without having information on the entity and its investment; the furnishing of security, therefore, will mainly prevent the disclosure of the foreign corporation's (or other entity's) substantial investors abroad. The regulations describe the details of furnishing (and renewing annually) such security, including the following types referred to in the legislative reports accompanying the statute: (1) a recorded security interest in a tract of U.S. land held by the foreign (or domestic) entity; (2) a guaranty by a person from whom the Service can reasonably expect to collect any unpaid tax; or (3) an undertaking to pay any tax assessed, by a foreign corporate or other owner with substantial U.S. business assets against which the Service can levy a claim for taxes.

Third, any foreign person not engaged in U.S. trade or business during the calendar year, but whose U.S. RPI equals or exceeds $50,000 in value at any time during the year and who is not otherwise required to file the second type of report above, must file a return for that year on Form 6661 listing (among other information) his or its name and address and a description of any U.S. RPI. Attribution rules apply to aggregate interests held by partnerships, trusts, estates, and family members. However, interests held indirectly through U.S. or foreign corporations apparently are not included here because they are to be covered by the other reports.

Regulations provide further details and forms — expected to be available by early 1983 — for these returns. For example, the determination whether an investor's *pro rata* share of he fair market value of a foreign corporation or other entity's RPI exceeds $50,000, thereby triggering reporting requirements described above, is based on his share of the gross asset values, rather than net values after subtracting debt against each asset.

Failure to file any of the above returns (or furnish the above statement to a substantial investor) may be punished by a fine of $25 for each day that such failure continues. The maximum possible fine imposed on any one person for failure to file any one type of return under Section 6039C is $25,000 per calendar year, and the fine imposed on a foreign person for failure to file the third type of return noted above also cannot exceed five percent of the fair market value of all U.S. RPI owned by that person during the year. These information returns under Section 6039C must be filed — generally by May 15 for the preceding calendar year — even if no tax is due and if no transaction takes place during the year, and even if no U.S. income tax return must be filed.

In addition, as noted further above generally with regard to foreign direct investments, a U.S. corporation, or a foreign corporation engaged in U.S. trade or business, which is owned at least one-half by a foreign person is required after 1982 to file a return under Section 6038A of the Internal Revenue Code covering its transactions during each taxable year with other corporations in the same controlled group.

Filings under Sections 6039C and 6038A should be accorded the same strict confidentiality given to other U.S. federal tax returns. However, as noted further above, various U.S. income tax treaties which promote the sharing of tax information between countries may reduce the value of confidentiality afforded in the United States.

Foreign Portfolio Investments

If a foreign person's U.S. investment does not qualify as a direct investment, but does constitute a security, it may be a portfolio investment required to be reported to the DOT or the Federal Reserve Bank of New York on a monthly and/or quinquennial basis. Under the applicable forms, such a security is interpreted generally to include long-term — having no maturity or a maturity longer than one year from the date of issuance — marketable public or private issues of debt or equity. Stocks, bonds, and debentures are the most typical such portfolio investments. However, limited partnership interests, stock rights and warrants, and a wide variety of other instruments are also included.

In general, reports on monthly *Form S* are required from all banks, banking institutions (including bank holding companies), brokers, dealers, or other persons in the United States who on their own behalf or for their customers engage in purchase or sale transactions of long-term securities with foreign persons. The U.S. individual acting directly by order of the foreign purchaser or seller files the form; if the foreign person acts directly, the U.S. person on the other side of the purchase or sale must file. If an exemption is not available, the Form S is due within 15 days following the month to which the report applies. Banks or banking institutions file reports with the local Federal Reserve Bank; brokers, dealers, and other persons file with the Federal Reserve Bank of New York.

A general exemption from filing Form S is available to persons otherwise required to report whose aggregate purchases and sales of long-term securities, whether as principal or agent, in transactions with foreign persons are less than $500,000 during the calendar month. Two general concepts underlie the further special exclusions from reporting under Form S: the DOT is interested only in charting capital movements into and out of the United States, and with this particular form is interested only in monitoring long-term investments. Accordingly, initial offerings of new foreign issues that can only be offered for sale to persons who are not U.S. residents are not to be reported on the form. Likewise, if the securities are subject to repurchase or resale agreements, the transactions are not reported. Further excluded are transactions in securities having a contractual maturity of one year or less, such as U.S. treasury bills and certificates of indebtedness. However, certain of these excluded items may have to be reported by nonbanks on the TIC series of forms described in the first section of this chapter, or by banks on the DOT forms referred to further below. Finally, transactions and participations in loans with various U.S. and international governmental and quasi-governmental banks are excluded.[40]

The current Form S format is a chart matching securities by type with the country of the purchasing or selling foreign person. The amount debited or credited is entered — *i.e.,* the cost of purchase plus commissions and other costs, or the proceeds of sale less commissions, tax, and other costs. Specific instructions are provided for particular types of transactions, including redemption of securities, transactions in foreign arbitrage accounts, trust accounts, and foreign currencies, and exchange of long-term securities or conversion of debt obligations into domestic equity shares. Penalties for failure to report and intentional failure to report are identical to those under the BEA reports discussed further above.

The International Investment Survey Act also requires that a survey of foreign portfolio investments in the United States be conducted by the DOT at least once every five years.[41] The latest such survey evaluated foreign portfolio investments as at December 31, 1978, and the next scheduled quinquennial survey will evaluate such investments as at December 31, 1983. While it is not yet clear what forms for reporting will then be required, the 1978 survey may be instructive. Two types of forms were required: Form TD F 90-19.1 from U.S. issuers of securities held by foreign persons, and Form TD F 90-19.2 from U.S. holders of record, generally referred to as Form FPI-1 and Form FPI-2, respectively.

Reporting on *Form FPI-1* was required from every U.S. issuer irrespective of whether it had evidence of foreign investment in its securities, if at the last available closing date of its accounting records in 1978 it had consolidated assets of more than $50 million if a nonbank business enterprise, or more than $100 million if a banking enterprise. Smaller issuers were also required to report if they had knowledge of foreign ownership of their securities or were informed by the DOT that there was such foreign ownership. A total exemption from reporting was available for issuers with consolidated assets of less than $2 million.

Form FPI-2 was required from any U.S. person who acted on behalf of a foreign person as a holder of record of any security of a U.S. issuer. Where multiple affiliated nominees, trustees, or holders of record were used, a consolidated report was required. A total exemption from Form FPI-2 was accorded to those U.S. persons whose aggregate holdings on behalf of foreign persons were $50,000 or less based on fair market value as at December 31, 1978; again, affiliated holders had their holdings aggregated for purposes of the exemption.

A special *Form FPI-3* was required to be filed to substantiate any exemption. The reports (or the exemption forms) were to have been filed with the DOT no later than March 31, 1979.

After 1981, annual surveys of foreign portfolio investments are to be made by the DOT in years that the quinquennial survey is not used. Forms for this survey currently are still being developed.

Special Investments and Activities

A foreign investor or his U.S. agent may face a variety of U.S. federal reporting requirements which result from the special industries or activities involved, including those discussed below.

Banking, Insurance and Financial Activities

As described in Chapter VI, banks and banking institutions are substantially regulated in the United States and both federal and state laws should be carefully investigated before an investment in this industry is made. For purposes of this chapter, however, only federal reporting requirements which arise in connection with foreign based banking operations are discussed.

First, direct and portfolio investment reports to the BEA and DOT may be required because of foreign direct and portfolio investments in U.S. banks and banking institutions, under criteria substantially identical to those applicable to investments in other industries as described in the first sections of this chapter. In addition, transactions of an unincorporated U.S. bank branch or agency with its foreign parent are reported on quarterly *Form BE-606B* rather than Form BE-605. Exemption levels, deadlines, and definitions are identical to the Form BE-605, but Form BE-606B has fewer line items. Additionally, bank reports for the last current five-year benchmark survey — for 1980 — were made on special *Form BE-12 BANK* with exemption levels, filing instructions, and deadlines identical to its nonbank counterpart, but with fewer line items.

Two forms also are required by the U.S. Federal Reserve Board beginning in 1981 from foreign organizations that conduct banking business in the United States, to assist in its supervisory activities under the Bank Holding Company Act of 1956 and the International Banking Act of 1978.[42] The Annual Report of Foreign Banking Organizations on *Form F.R. Y-7* contains information open to public inspection, while information on the Foreign Banking Organization Confidential Report of Operations on *Form F.R. 2068* is to be held confidential. All foreign banking organizations are required after June 1981 to file the reports within 120 days after the end of each fiscal year: Form F.R. Y-7 is filed with the Federal Reserve Bank of the district in which the foreign banking organization's largest U.S. banking business is conducted, and Form F.R. 2068 is filed directly with the Federal Reserve Board's Division of Banking Supervision and Regulation.

Form F.R. Y-7 requires financial information to the extent and in the manner disclosed in the home country. Other information concerning organizational structure, capital structure and control, shareholders, and nonbanking business conducted in the United States also is required.

Form F.R. 2068 is considered by the Federal Reserve Board to require information that is exempt from disclosure under the Freedom of Information Act, although the Board will share the information with other banking regulatory authorities at the federal and state levels. The form requires a detailed chart of affiliated enterprises and a disclosure of revenue and expenses as calculated in accordance with local accounting practices, which practices must be explained. Also required are disclosures concerning loan loss experience, gains and losses on securities, hidden reserves, and financial data on foreign subsidiary corporations.

A third report on *Form F.R. Y-8f,* which is also confidential, monitors the effects of intercompany transactions and is to be filed quarterly. It requires disclosure of asset transfer and other intercompany transactions and balances between a U.S. bank subsidiary (and its own subsidiaries) and the U.S. bank's foreign parent and its majority owned subsidiaries. The Federal Reserve Board also reserves the right to require the filing of additional statements of information to carry out its responsibilities referred to above.

A nonbank foreign investor also should be cognizant that reports to the DOT or appropriate Federal Reserve Bank by a bank or banking institution in the United States (whether or not the bank itself is a branch or subsidiary of a foreign bank) may be required merely because of the bank's dealings with any foreign person. U.S. securities brokers or dealers which borrow from foreign persons by selling them securities with repurchase agreements or which have custody liabilities to foreign persons also must report. However, disclosures made on any of these forms are aggregate reports of dealings with all foreigners and no details of specific transactions with any one customer are released. The forms are required on a monthly, quarterly, annual, or quinquennial basis.[44]

With respect to U.S. insurance activities by foreign persons, it should be noted that BEA *Form BE-13* and DOT *Form CQ-1* — both of which forms are described further above in connection with foreign direct investments in the United States — do clearly require reporting of such activities.

Other Specialized Investments

Annual reporting to the BEA on *Form BE-29* (vessel operations) or *BE-36* (aircraft operations) may be required regarding revenues for carrying imports to, and expenditures in, the United States by shipping and air transport operators of foreign nationality.[43]

Special additional federal reporting may be involved for foreign investments in U.S. minerals or other natural resources (discussed in Chapter III) or certain restricted industries (Chapter VI).

In addition, federal customs declarations, or bank or securities broker-dealer records, are required for movements of U.S. or foreign currency or monetary instruments in excess of $5,000 ($10,000 in the case of bank or broker-dealer records) into or out of the United States, as noted in Chapters VI and VIII. Special reporting also may be required — without regard to foreign ownership — in connection with investments abroad from the United States (Chapter VIII), or with investments generally in U.S. stocks and debt securities (Chapters I and IX).

Foreign Agents Registration Act

Under the Foreign Agents Registration Act of 1938[45] (the "Agents Act"), any person engaging in certain described activities in the United States as an agent of a foreign principal must file *Form OBD-63* with the U.S. Department of Justice. The Agents Act also regulates the activities of such agents in the United States, but its first aim is to compel the disclosure of influence within the United States of foreign principals by its reporting requirements. It defines person in a broad sense to include individuals, partnerships, corporations, or any other combination of individuals. Foreign principals include foreign governments and political parties, individuals who are not citizens of and not domiciled within the United States, and legal entities which are not organized under the laws of the United States (or elsewhere under its jurisdiction) and do not have their respective principal places of business there.

Whether a person is required to register as an agent of a foreign principal is determined by examining both the relationship of the person to the foreign principal and the activity of the person in the United States. First, the person must act as "an agent, representative, employee, or servant, or . . . in any other capacity at the order, request, or under the direction or control, of a foreign principal or of a person any of whose activities are directly or indirectly supervised, directed, controlled, financed, or subsidized in whole or in major part by a foreign principal."[46] Second, the foreign agent, acting in the United States for or in the interest of his foreign principal, must directly or through another person: (1) engage in political activity; (2) act as a public relations counsel, publicity agent, information service employee, or political consultant; (3) solicit, collect, disburse, or dispense contributions, loans, money, or things of value; or (4) represent the interest of such foreign principal before any agency or official of the government of the United States. Any person who agrees or purports to act as an agent as defined above is also a foreign agent.

However, registered news or press associations or newspapers, magazines, or periodicals which are owned and controlled by U.S. persons are not considered to be agents of a foriegn principal. Furthermore, there are eight primary exemptions from the reporting requirements of the Agents Act, which are based on the status of the agent and/or his activity. Generally, exemptions are available for: (a) members of the diplomatic corps engaged purely in diplomatic activities; (b) staff members and employees of duly accredited diplomatic missions; (c) consular officers whose names, status and character of duties are of public record with the U.S. Department of State; (d) persons engaged only in private, nonpolitical activities in furtherance of the trade or commerce of a foreign principal (or, under certain circumstances, of a domestic person, which activities also result in benefit to a foreign person) or in other activities which do not serve predominately a foreign interest; (e) relief and human aid assistance; (f) religious, scholastic, academic, or fine arts activities; (g) actions for a foreign government the defense of which the U.S. President deems vital to the defense of the United States (no country has been so certified since 1946); and (h) legal representation on behalf of a disclosed foreign principal before any court of law or agency of the United States, provided such representation does not include attempts to "influence or persuade agency personnel or officials other than in the course of established agency proceedings, whether formal or informal."[47] Under a number of these exemptions, the agent's identity and relationship with the foreign principal still must be disclosed.

Form OBD-63 provides information on the registrant, the foreign principal, the activities to be conducted, the financial relationship between the parties, and information regarding the planned dissemination (if any) of political propaganda. Exhibits to the form set forth information concerning each foreign principal, and the agreement or understanding between the registrant and the foreign principal. Each partner, officer, director, associate, employee, and agent of a registrant is required to file *Form OBD-66* unless such person engages in no activity in furtherance of the interest of the registrant's foreign principal or unless the services rendered are of a secretarial, clerical, or similar capacity.

The Agents Act also requires periodic reporting on supplemental *Form OBD-64,* which is filed at six-month intervals while the agency relationship continues. This form must also be filed within 30 days after termination of the registrant's obligation to register.

State Reporting

Special state reporting requirements directed to investments from abroad (as opposed to any out-of-state U.S. or foreign investor) are relatively rare. These are likely to arise — even in major commercial states such as California, Illinois, and New York — only for an investment in which non-U.S. ownership is restricted by the state. As described in previous chapters, an investor's U.S. activities are regulated by various state and local authorities in any area not reserved exclusively to the federal government. The areas of such state and local regulation previously covered include principally the following: organization of business enterprises, securities regulation, and taxation (discussed in Chapters I and II); inheritance restrictions (Chapter I); real estate and other natural resources (Chapter III); banking and other restricted industries (Chapter VI); qualification of an out-of-state corporation to do business in the state (Chapter VI); state takeover statutes and corporate acquisition requirements (Chapter VII); and general shareholder protection (Chapter IX). Of these, only the inheritance restrictions, the real estate regulations, and the controls over certain restricted industries appear to differentiate broadly between U.S. and non-U.S. persons.

In the case of inheritance restrictions, disclosure of foreign heirs to the state probate or other court which deals with inheritance transfers of local assets will be involved. In the case of investments in restricted industries, usually extensive reporting to the state agency which regulates the industry will be required.

In connection with real estate and other natural resource investments, it may be useful to describe examples of certain types of state real property reporting requirements for foreign investors. It should be noted, however, that definitions in connection with such state reports — for example, that for agricultural land — often differ from federal definitions and from state to state.[48]

(1) Many states require reporting without regard to the federal real estate reporting by foreign investors. For example, in Arkansas, foreign parties acquiring any interest in agricultural land must register the purchase with the Circuit Clerk of the circuit where the land is located within 60 days after acquisition.[49] A foreign party includes a U.S. entity in which a significant interest or not insubstantial control is directly or indirectly held by a foreign party. If agricultural land is acquired for nonfarming purposes, the foreign owner still must file within 60 days after the date of purchase with the Arkansas Secretary of State and, if this intended use does not occur within five years, the foreign owner must register with the Circuit Clerk as noted above. Failure to report may lead to a state action for an order of divestiture within two years and a penalty, in the case of intentional failure to file, of up to 25% of the value of the property.

Florida requires that any alien corporation owning or leasing land or holding a mortgage on land there establish a registered office and agent prior to the acquisition of its interest (if made after August 1981) and file an annual report with the Florida Department of State.[50] Failure to comply apparently may result in lack of legal title to the interest acquired.

Iowa requires any interest in land beneficially owned by nonresident aliens, foreign governments, entities created under the laws of foreign countries, and entities majority owned by nonresident aliens to be registered with the Iowa Secretary of State. Reports also must be made with the Secretary each year regarding agricultural land acquired by such foreign parties. Agricultural land holdings of nonresident aliens acquired after 1979 are limited to 320 acres acquired for an immediate or pending use other than farming and actually converted to such use within five years after the date of purchase. Annual reports are also required from corporations and limited partnerships owning or leasing agricultural land or engaging in farming; these reports include, *inter alia,* the identity of any nonresident alien partner or owner of five percent or more of any class of corporate stock.[51]

Minnesota imposed restrictions on foreign ownership of agricultural land effective in 1977, including ownership through any corporation directly or indirectly owned more than 20% by nonresident aliens. Foreign ownership of such land previously acquired is permitted provided the owner files annual reports with the state Commissioner of Agriculture.[52]

In Missouri, foreign persons (defined broadly, as in AFIDA, to include certain U.S. corporations) must report to that state's Director of Agriculture concerning any interest held by them in Missouri agricultural land. Similar reports must be filed for every acquisition or transfer of such land by foreign persons, with limited exceptions.[53]

In Nebraska, any corporation holding agricultural land must file a report which discloses, *inter alia,* the percentage of alien members of the board of directors and the name and address of each alien owning 10% or more of the corporation's voting stock.[54]

In North Dakota, foreign persons may own agricultural land only if acquired prior to July 1, 1979, and if the foreign owner reports annually to the state Commissioner of Agriculture.[55]

Under Ohio law,[56] a nonresident alien acquiring any interest in Ohio property in excess of three acres or with a market value exceeding $100,000, or any interest in mining or minerals, must file a report with the Ohio Secretary of State within 30 days after the acquisition. Sales of these interests must also be reported and the reports are available for public inspection. Similar reports, with similar triggering levels, are required from a corporation or other business entity in which any one nonresident alien owns a 10% or greater interest or in which more than 40% of the ownership, in the aggregate, is owned by nonresident aliens. Noncompliance is punishable by a fine of at least $5,000 and up to 25% of the market value of the property.

Oregon requires from each corporation an annual report which discloses, *inter alia*, the name of each foreign country (if any) in which the reporting corporation conducts farming or owns or leases farm land.[57]

(2) The states of Kentucky, North Carolina, Pennsylvania, and South Dakota provide for varying degrees of state review of reports by aliens to the federal government, particularly the AFIDA reports described further above in connection with federal reporting of agricultural land investments from abroad.[58] In this connection, Kentucky law provides that real estate owned by a nonresident alien for more than eight years escheats to the state, and the other three states impose various restrictions on real estate ownership or inheritance by foreign persons.[59]

Similarly, Illinois and Virginia require reports of foreign ownership of agricultural land in those states, which requirements may be satisfied by complying with AFIDA. While AFIDA requires reports concerning leaseholds of 10 years or more, however, the Illinois statute[60] covers leaseholds of greater than five years. In Virginia, no filing is required if an exemption from AFIDA reporting exists.[61]

In summary, a foreign investor — and any U.S. agent or joint venturer involved with such an investor — must be cognizant of increasing federal and state reporting requirements applicable to foreign direct and portfolio investments in the United States.

Footnotes to Chapter XII

1. *See generally* Chapters I, III, VI *supra.*

2. *See* E.O. 11961, 3 C.F.R. 86 (1978), as amended by E.O. 12013, 3 C.F.R. 147 (1978); E.O. 10033, 3 C.F.R. 226 (1949-1953 compilation).

3. *See generally* Chapter III *supra.*

4. 7 U.S.C. §§3501 *et seq.*; *see also* 7 C.F.R. §§781 *et seq.*

5. 22 U.S.C. §§3101-3108.

6. 15 C.F.R. §806.15(a)(1).

7. 15 C.F.R. §§806.7(c), (e).

8. 15 C.F.R. §806.7(f).

9. 15 C.F.R. §§806.15(a)(2), (g)(3)(i) and (ii), (g)(4).

10. *See* 15 C.F.R. Part 806; 46 Fed. Reg. 7214, 23225, 30336 (1981).

11. 15 C.F.R. §806.6. All BEA forms currently are filed with the U.S. Department of Commerce, Bureau of Economic Analysis, BE-50(IN), Washington, D.C. 20230. The BEA generally will answer questions regarding the forms by telephone.

12. Green v. Dep't of Commerce, 489 F. Supp. 977 (D.D.C. 1980); *see* 5 U.S.C. §§552 *et seq.*; Chapter VIII *supra.*

13. I.R.C. §6038A; Chapter II *supra.*

14. The first version of Forms BE-13A and BE-13B covered transactions occurring in calendar years 1979 and 1980. In mid-1981, the BEA amended both Forms BE-13A and BE-13B; the new versions were to be used for transactions in 1981.

15. 15 C.F.R. §806.7(n).

16. For pre-1981 (non-real estate) new business establishments, only a partial exemption from Form BE-13A was available and the trigger level was over $500,000 in assets. Under those rules, a partial exemption under Form BE-13A resulted in a total exemption under Form BE-13B.

17. Prior to 1981, quarterly report Form BE-606 was used by unincorporated nonbank enterprises and Form BE-605 was used only by corporations.

18. Beginning in 1981, the BEA dropped the term "net" in describing sales and apparently has interpreted the exemption to apply to sales less returns and allowances.

19. Form BE-606 referred to in note 17 *supra* had no similar consolidation requirements. The General Instructions to the current Form BE-605 state that separate reports may be filed if the U.S. affiliates are "not normally consolidated due to unrelated operations or lack of control, provided written permission has been requested from and granted by" the BEA.

20. If the U.S. affiliate has multiple independent foreign parents (as distinct from foreign affiliates), a separate report must be filed reflecting the U.S. affiliate's transactions with each foreign parent. In the case of a foreign parent which indirectly owns the U.S. affiliate through another U.S. enterprise, the BEA staff has allowed an exemption from quarterly filings upon application to the BEA.

21. 46 Fed. Reg. 23225 (1981); 47 Fed. Reg. 23705 (1982).

22. 22 U.S.C. §§3103 *et seq.*

23. *See* Form BE-21P; 46 Fed. Reg. 60191 (1981).

24. 44 U.S.C. §3508.

25. *Id.*; E.O. 10033, 3 C.F.R. 226 (1949).

26. Prior to 1981, the exemption level was $500,000. The requirement of less than 200 acres was first made explicit in the 1981 BE-13 Report, which also for the first time specifically indicated that the test should be applied only to the land acquired.

27. Prior to 1981, the exemption level was $500,000.

28. The BEA staff apparently has extended this exemption to situations where the intermediary knows that a Form BE-13 has been filed, even if the intermediary played no part in the filing.

29. *See, e.g.,* P. Trooboff & E. Falender, "Foreign Investment in U.S. Real Property — Federal Reporting Requirements," in *Foreign Investment in the United States* (D.C. Bar Ass'n 1980).

30. *See, e.g.,* American Bar Association *Code of Professional Responsibility,* Disciplinary Rules 4-101, 5-101, 5-102.

31. *See* notes 3, 4 *supra.* These and other terms under FIRPTA are discussed more fully in Chapter III *supra.*

32. This corporate ownership exemption was first permitted in 1981. The general exemption from reporting for real estate acquisitions for personal use is substantiated by an entry to be filed on Supplement C, the exemption claim for Form BE-13.

33. For interests in oil and gas rights, the 10% test is applied to the foreign person's interest in the business enterprise's profits.

34. Any exemption from full reporting generally still must be substantiated by filing the requisite exemption form or exemption certification letter.

35. Reports concerning all agricultural land holdings previously acquired and still held were to have been filed on or before August 1, 1979. Reporting of new acquisitions and transfers became required effective February 2, 1979. For holdings of nonagricultural land which subsequently becomes agricultural, or by U.S. persons who subsequently become foreign, reports are required within 90 days after such change of status.

36. 45 Fed. Reg. 6115 (1980).

37. *See* R. Zedalis, "Disclosure of Foreign Investment in U.S. Agricultural Land," 31 Mercer L. Rev. 711 (1980).

38. The section of the form concerning the representative of the foreign investor should indicate the individual to be reached regarding the report; usually this is the officer of the reporting entity who completes it — even if he is not an agent of the foreign investor.

39. 7 C.F.R §§781.4, 781.5.

40. Included are the U.S. Export-Import Bank, the International Bank for Reconstruction and Development, the Inter-American Development Bank, the Asian Development Bank, and other similar institutions.

41. *See generally* 22 U.S.C. §3103; 31 C.F.R. Part 129.

42. *See generally* Chapter VI *supra.*

43. 15 C.F.R. Part 802.

44. *See, e.g.,* 31 C.F.R. Part 128; U.S. Dep't of the Treasury Forms BC, BL-1, BL-2, BQ-1, BQ-2, FC-1, FC-2, FC-4. For descriptions of several similar forms required from *nonbank* business enterprises located in the United States, see the discussion in the first section of this chapter covering a new U.S. business establishment's periodic reports of international financial and commercial dealings.

45. 22 U.S.C. §§611-621.
46. 22 U.S.C. §611(c)(1).
47. 22 U.S.C. §613(g). *See* Att'y Gen. of the United States v. Covington & Burling, 411 F. Supp. 371 (D.D.C. 1976), 430 F. Supp. 1117 (D.D.C. 1977).
48. *See generally* U.S. Dep't of Agriculture, *Report to the Congress on State Controls and Reporting Requirements for Foreign-Owned Real Estate in the United States* (1980); R. Waldmann, *Direct Investment and Development in the U.S.; A Guide to Incentive Programs, Laws and Restrictions* (1980); H. Brodkey, "Foreign Investment in U.S. Real Estate: Update," in *Lawyer's Supplement to the Guarantor* (Chicago Title Ins. Co. 1979).
49. Ark. Stat. Ann. §§77-2201 *et seq.*
50. Fla. Stat. §692.05.
51. Iowa Code Ch. 567, §§172 C.5,.6.
52. Minn. Ann. Code §500.221.
53. Mo. Rev. Stat. §442.592.
54. Neb. Rev. Stat. §76-1503.
55. N.D. Cent. Code §§47-10.1 *et seq.* However, this does not apply to Canadian citizens.
56. Ohio Rev. Code §§5301.254, 5301.99.
57. Ore. Rev. Stat. §57.757.
58. Ken. Rev. Stat. §264.105(1); N.C. Gen. Stat. §64-1.1; Penn. Stat. Ann., Title 68, §§41-47; S. D. Comp. L. Ch. 43-2A.
59. Ken. Rev. Stat. §381.300;N.C. Gen. Stat §29-11; note 58 *supra.*
60. 5 Ill. Ann. Stat.§§601 *et seq.*
61. Code of Va. §§3.1-22.22 *et seq.* (Supp. 1982).

Glossary of Citation Terms

Listed below are many of the principal standard abbreviations and reference terms for the citations in the footnotes to this volume. References are to U.S. federal entities unless otherwise noted. In this connection, it should also be noted that the volume's citation forms generally follow current U.S. rules, but have been modified somewhat for use as well by persons abroad.

Abbreviation	**Reference Term**
aff'd	affirmed
aff'd per curiam	affirmed in a concise judicial decision
aff'g in part	affirming in part
B.T.A.	Board of Tax Appeals Reports
C.B.	Cumulative Bulletin of the Department of the Treasury
C.C.P.A.	Court of Customs and Patent Appeals (superseded after September 1982 by the Court of Appeals for the Federal Circuit)
cert. denied	certiorari to a higher court denied
cert. dismissed	certiorari to a higher court dismissed
cf.	cited authority supports a statement of law analogous to that in the text
C.F.R.	Code of Federal Regulations
Cir. (1st-10th, Fed.)	Circuit Court of Appeals for one of ten geographical circuits or (after September 1982) the Federal Circuit
Comm'r Pat.	Commissioner of Patents
Ct. Cl.	Court of Claims (superseded after September 1982 by the Court of Appeals for the Federal Circuit and the Claims Court)
Cust. Bull.	Customs Bulletin
D.C. (*e.g.*, S.D.N.Y., D.D.C.)	District Court for geographical districts, *e.g.*, Southern District of New York, District of the District of Columbia
e.g.	for example
et seq.	and those that follow
E.O.	Executive Order
F.2d	Federal Reporter, Second Series
Fed. Cas.	Federal Cases
Fed. Reg.	Federal Register
F.R.D.	Federal Rules Decisions

F. Supp.	Federal Supplement
F.T.C.	Federal Trade Commission Cases
id.	citation to the same authority as that in the immediately preceding citation in the same footnote, or in the immediately preceding footnote
infra	reference to groups of authorities or textual materials set forth below
I.R.B.	Internal Revenue Bulletin
I.R.C.	Internal Revenue Code of 1954, as amended
Letter Rul.	private ruling of the Department of the Treasury
L.J. or L.Rev.	law journal or law review, a regularly issucd journal of a law school or professional society containing learned articles on legal topics
N.W.2d	Northwestern Reporter, Second Series of state court decisions
overruled by	judicial decision overruled by a subsequent ruling in a different judicial decision, usually not involving the same parties
P.2d	Pacific Reporter, Second Series of state court decisions
Pub. L.	Public Law
Prop. Treas. Reg.	Proposed Regulation of the Department of the Treasury
rev'd and remanded	reversed and remanded to lower court for further proceedings consistent with the higher court's decision
Rev. Proc.	Revenue Procedure of the Department of the Treasury
Rev. Rul.	Revenue Ruling of the Department of the Treasury intended to be of general application
Stat.	United States Statutes at Large
supra	reference to groups of authorities or textual materials previously set forth
T.C.	Tax Court of the United States Reports
T.C.M.	Tax Court Memorandum Decision concisely stating disposition of matter
T.D.	Decision of the Department of the Treasury
Treas. Dec.	Department of the Treasury Decision Reports
Treas. Reg.	Department of the Treasury Regulation
T.S.U.S.	Tariff Schedules of the United States
T.T.A.B.	Trademark Trial and Appeal Board within the Patent and Trademark Office
U.S.	United States Supreme Court Reports
U.S.C.	United States Code

U.S.C. App.	United States Code Appendix
U.S.C.I.T.	United States Court of International Trade
U.S.L.W.	United States Law Week reporting recent Supreme Court and other federal court decisions
U.S.P.Q.	United States Patent Quarterly

Index

References are to page numbers except as otherwise indicated. All terms refer to the United States unless otherwise noted.